SEARCH FOR CONSENSUS
The Story of the Democratic Party

SEARCH FOR CONSENSUS

The Story of the Democratic Party

WITHDRAWN

Ralph M. Goldman

TEMPLE UNIVERSITY PRESS
Philadelphia

Temple University Press, Philadelphia 19122
© 1979 by Temple University. All rights reserved
Published 1979
Printed in the United States of America

Library of Congress Cataloging in Publication Data

Goldman, Ralph Morris, 1920–
  Search for consensus.

  Includes bibliographical references and index.
  1. Democratic Party—History.   I. Title.
JK2316.G62   329.3'009   79-1207
ISBN 0-87722-152-9

For Joan
and the happy outcomes of
our own search for consensus

Contents

Tables

x

Acknowledgments

This book has been in the writing for almost as long as the history of the Democratic Party, or so it seems. Hence, my collegial and intellectual debts have, in some instances, been longstanding. Avery Leiserson of Vanderbilt University was there at the conception. Bertram M. Gross of City University of New York gave encouragement at an important stage of gestation. Nelson Polsby of the University of California at Berkeley helped with the delivery (of an earlier version). To them, my apologies for the metaphor and my thanks for their support.

An early draft of this book was read by Austin Ranney of the American Enterprise Institute for Public Policy, Jeff Fishel of American University, and John S. Saloma, my colleague at San Francisco State University. Their advice was invariably sound, for which I am particularly grateful. The book has since had a substantial revision and expansion. The Temple University Press staff, and especially editor-in-chief Kenneth Arnold, has been unusually able and helpful, affording me perhaps the most pleasant publishing experience I have had thus far.

Everett C. Ladd, Jr., and Diane L. Reed of the Social Science Data Center at the University of Connecticut went out of their way to help with data sources on voter ideological orientations. For devoted clerical effort I owe thanks to my daughter, Meg, and Janet Bowlin, formerly of The George Meany Center for Labor Studies.

The errors, shortcomings, and misinterpretations are, of course, all mine.

SEARCH FOR CONSENSUS
The Story of the Democratic Party

.

1

Some Preliminary Theory and Early History

THE Democratic party of the United States is one of the oldest surviving human organizations. In its perennial search for a national consensus and for the perfection of its own representativeness, the party's successes and failures have been a critical element in the development and integration of the nation. In many respects, the Democratic party has served as the political balance wheel of the Republic.

This account of the party's history over nearly two centuries gives particular attention to the organizations and reorganizations carried on by Democrats in response to the aspirations of their leaders, the demands of interests comprising successive Democratic coalitions, and the party's efforts to be representative of the changing political community at large. Often referred to as "the majority party," Democrats have learned to what extent their majority consists of disparate, unruly, and sometimes adamant minorities. When the Democratic party has succeeded in giving accurate measure to the national consensus, the nation has rewarded it as the party most fit to govern. But building coalitions and being representative are not achieved by magic; they are the achievements of a human and humane politics carried forward by skillful politicians.

Political Parties and Community Decisions

In the last century-and-a-half, with the rise of the concept of popular sovereignty and the growth of mass electorates, political parties have become significant informal organizers of governments

3

and political communities. The Democratic party has been one of the first and most significant of these. As the American party system evolved and became more formally organized, particularly after the Civil War, intraparty factions arose as significant informal political organizations. This history will be concerned to a large degree with the factional struggles within the Democratic party.

Both formal and informal organizations have leaders who are usually the most visible contestants over position and policy. How and what the community or organization decides are matters of major concern to these leaders. The "how" involves one of three fundamental methods of collective choice: violent, verbal, or numerical. Each method is a way in which a group, organization, political party, or other collectivity may manifest agreement or disagreement about an issue.

The *method of violence* achieves a collective decision by subjecting some part of the collectivity to bodily pain, damage, or other deprivation. The property or resources of dissidents may be damaged or destroyed in order to weaken their influence over the collective choice. Extreme violence may remove opponents entirely from the collective decision process, as in revolutions, civil wars, purges, and genocide. The forms of political violence come under many names: international war, mob violence, civil disorder, *coup d'ètat*, assassination, and so forth. The method of violence is still the most primitive of the approaches to collective choice. It has nonetheless been institutionalized in various forms: international war; capital punishment; and, in communities that have succeeded in becoming politically integrated, the public monopoly over the principal instruments of violence by the central government.[1]

The *method of words* arises from, in Aristotle's phrase, man's unique faculty of language. When "reasonable" men discuss political differences in order to arrive at logical and rational decisions, they tend to use words. Bentham observed that the liberty of a people is proportional to the opportunity for free criticism of government and free association in opposition to it. Barker offers the traditional description of free political discussion:

So far as the society exists by dynamic process, it exists for and by the mutual interchange of conceptions and conviction about the good to be attained in human life and the methods of its attainment. It thus exists for and by a system of social discussion, under which each is free to give and receive, and all can freely join in determining the content or substance of social thought—the good to be sought, and the way of life in which it

4

issues. Now, such discussion is also, as we have seen, the essence of democracy.[2]

Words that may influence collective choice may be found in philosophies, ideologies, dogmas, doctrines, propaganda, political slogans, debates, constitutions, laws, campaign literature, directives, etc. Words describe realities that group members are urged to notice and act upon, provide guides for members' attitudes and conduct, tell what is to be valued and what opposed, offer evidence and argument, give occasion for political ritual, and influence choice. Whoever has listened to a typical American political campaign knows that he or she is in the presence of the method of words. The verbal method is meaningless where there is no free speech or freedom of association.

The *method of numbers* assumes that conflict and cooperation are inherent in human association. "Just as the universe needs 'love and hate,' that is, attractive and repulsive forces, in order to have any form at all, so society, too, in order to attain a determinate shape, needs some quantitative ratio of harmony and disharmony."[3] The "ratio" of consent to dissent, when given an explicitly quantitative character, as in voting, best exemplifies the method of numbers. Organizations such as legislatures and political parties that parcel out regular units of decision power and allow these units to be brought together in any combination their possessors wish are in effect creating a system of representation and making feasible the discovery of a decision-making ratio, whether by majority rule or some other numerical standard.

The numerical method of collective choice is the most recent in political usage and the most pertinent to a study of a democratic party system. Ballots, in the form of wooden balls, were known in Rome during the century before the Christian era and in India about 300 B.C. However, doctrinal justification for the method of numbers was not developed until the time of the medieval Roman Catholic Church, the secret ballot being adopted for papal elections in 1562.

In the four centuries since, the method of numbers has become complex and well institutionalized in political communities eager to permit the maximum political disagreement short of violence and chaos. The allocation of units of prerogative in collective decisions has become the subject of apportionment theories and practices. The evolution of popular suffrage and civil liberties has been spurred by the question "who shall vote." It has been possible to

5

adjust the decisive ratio—plurality, majority, special majority, etc.—to particular consensual needs of political communities at different times. The variety of issues up for community choice, largely the selection of public officers and the adoption of public policies, has increased.

The method of numbers has been a major stimulus to the rise of political parties over the last two centuries. As Clokie concludes, the distinctive characteristic of the modern political order is the governing status of political parties, the widening of political participation, and "the growing tendency to appeal to numbers."[4] The political parties have been the principal collectors of a winning consensus on the one hand and the managers of vigorous dissent on the other.

The method of numbers is also associated with another human invention for dispersing and sharing power, namely, the representative assembly. The ancient world had few arrangements for representation. Not until the Middle Ages were the first theories of representation systematically put forth, again in response to the needs of the church. The medieval church was "both the initiator and the carrier of political innovations in representative government."[5]

It was in such representative assemblies as the English Parliament, the colonial legislatures, and the United States Congress that cliques evolved into political parties dedicated to the mobilization of winning legislative and electoral majorities. Most importantly and most pervasively, however, were the arrival of the mass electorate and the full implementation of the concept of popular sovereignty. In England and elsewhere, this development called forth the best efforts of party leaders, whether in a single, two-, or multiparty system. Today, more than 500 political parties function in the more than 150 nations of the world, and few political leaders, whether democrat or dictator, would think of operating without one.

Theorists today speculate a great deal about the distinguishing attributes of the political party as a form of social organization. A political party, some say, is any organized group that manages the operations of governmental bodies. Others believe that parties serve as brokers and mediators in reconciling the competing interests of groups in a community, mobilize the electorate through intensive communication efforts called "campaigns," and educate the populace on public policy issues. Still another point of view suggests that the distinctive activity of political parties is deciding upon nominations for public office.

6

Another theoretical approach views party politics as a special area of human activity in which particular kinds of exchanges or transactions are consummated. In economic life, material goods and services are exchanged for each other or for a variety of currencies. The best "deal" is that in which all transactors believe that they have come off with a trade that is quite satisfactory to themselves. Similarly, in the political life of the community, "deals" are also made with the help or participation of political brokers called "party politicians." Unfortunately, political deals have not yet gained the legitimacy ascribed to economic transactions. As expressed by Edmund Burke, this brokerage function is of some significance: "All government, indeed every human benefit and enjoyment, every virtue, and every prudent act, is founded on compromise and barter. We balance inconveniences; we give and take; we remit some rights, that we may enjoy others."[6] Sir Henry Maine was even more to the point: "The process of cutting up political power into petty fragments has in him [the political leader] its most remarkable product. The morsels of power are so small that men, if left to themselves, would not care to employ them."[7]

Political parties, however defined, were hardly what the authors of the Declaration of Independence had in mind in 1776 when they asserted that "to secure these [inalienable] rights, Governments are instituted among Men, deriving their just powers from the consent of the governed." Popular sovereignty was a novel political concept at that time. Political parties were little more than ephemeral parliamentary cliques in England and in the colonial legislatures. Parties were not yet mass mobilizers of the popular sovereigns in the electorate or measurers of the consent of the governed. Whatever party-like groups existed were known as "electioneering" clubs or caucuses. The committees of correspondence that organized the American Revolution were also party-like in many features.

Popular sovereignty was slow in taking hold. Even as late as 1828 only about 1.2 million votes were cast for president in a total population of more than 12 million, that is, only about 10 percent of the population. But this was nearly three times the number who voted four years earlier when only 400,000 voted. Even in England, the other laboratory of popular sovereignty, the great Reform Bill of 1832 brought out only a half million voters, that is, about 3 percent of a population of 16 million.[8]

For nearly two centuries, the Democrats and their predecessors have been particularly devoted to the problem of defining and giving practical effect to the concepts of popular sovereignty and national consensus. Measuring and representing "the consent of the governed" have been the special organizational challenge for Democrats during most of its history. The party's successes have led to extensions of the suffrage, popular participation, and administrations supported by a strong consensus. The party's failures on the other hand, have led to civil war and racial strife.

The Democratic preoccupation with their party as a representative institution in pursuit of a civic consensus was in large measure anticipated by the Madisonian argument for a "well-constructed" republic. That argument addressed itself to the fundamental purpose of any system of representation, namely, the incorporation of an ever-broadening number and variety of citizens into the system of governance. "Factional" (group) struggle is an inevitable feature of human affairs, according to Madison. Hence, the key to successful self-governance is an inclusive system of representation, that is, one that brings together as many interests and groups as possible whether they get along well with each other or not. This has been the thrust of the Democratic party in its coalition-building and its recurrent efforts to modify its system of representation. What excluded interests should be included? What process of factional struggle may best lead to the broadest party consensus and the most representative reflection of the national civic consensus? These concerns have produced an organizational "personality" characterized by openness, inclusiveness, and vigorous factional contention, and periodic high levels of intraparty consensus that often signaled new stages in the political maturation and integration of the American political community.

A recent demonstration of the hazards of the Democratic search for representativeness occurred in connection with the rules of the 1972 national convention. New rules developed by the McGovern Commission on Delegate Selection had resulted in a dramatic increase in the number of women, blacks, and youth—hitherto under-represented at Democratic national conventions—among the 1972 convention delegates. The numerical proportion of persons with these characteristics was, in other words, brought much closer to their proportions in the general population of the United States. However, despite its greater "representativeness" with respect to certain social and demographic characteristics of its delegates, the convention as a whole proved to be seriously out of attitudinal touch with the Democratic party voting rank-and-file ("party-identifiers," as they are called by political scientists) on such salient policy issues at the time as public welfare, inflation, school busing, crime, aid to Southeast Asia, abortion, women's liberation, and others. When the policy attitudes of a national sample of Democratic party-identifiers was compared with those of a sample of the delegates to the 1972 Democratic national convention, the differences were significantly greater than normal despite the demographic representativeness of the delegates. Democratic delegates and Democratic party-identifiers were in fact found on opposite sides of the issues, with the latter closer to the views of delegates to the 1972 *Republican* national convention.[9]

Such a startling discrepancy between Democratic leadership and rank-and-file views on the issues raises the question whether demographic characteristics are an accurate criterion for achieving policy and other kinds of representativeness. A representative institution such as the national nominating convention must reflect the leadership, policy, and related attitudes of the party's rank-and-file and of the voters generally if it is to serve its institutional purposes. Today, as in the Democratic party's past, the challenge continues to be one of designing rules and procedures that effectively accomplish this representational function. That the party has in the past faced up to the dilemmas of representativeness successfully is perhaps best evidenced by its longevity and its record as the principal political incorporator of the nation.

These theoretical speculations are simply reminders that the Democratic party has served as an important manager of the method of numbers in arriving at community decisions, has helped convert the concept of popular sovereignty into a working system, and has struggled incessantly with the difficult task of giving practical effect to the idea of representativeness.

Precursors of the Party

The story of the party ostensibly begins in Baltimore, Maryland, during the second week of May 1840, when several hundred politicians decided henceforth to call their organization the "Democratic party." Officially, the meeting was the third national nominating convention of the Democratic-Republican party. The rechristening marked the beginning, in name at least, of the modern national Democratic party. Organizationally speaking, however, the

9

party, as a formal national entity, was already eight years old, born in the same city in May 1832.

The precise birth-date of the Democratic party will undoubtedly remain a moot question among party historians. Some point to June 1791, when Thomas Jefferson and James Madison concluded a "botanizing expedition" up the Hudson Valley in New York. Out of this trip came the first national political coalition between South and North, the latter represented by Governor George Clinton of New York, with an assist from Tammany Hall's Aaron Burr. The "expedition" was typical of the coalition-building that eventually came to be a hallmark of the Democratic party's search for consensus.

Others cite April 2, 1796, when the first Democratic-Republican congressional caucus met to bring discipline to the adoption of national policies and to presidential selections. Those who look for indications of formal organization will prefer May 21, 1832, when Jacksonians from across the nation came together for their first formal national nominating convention. This convention established an enduring national party with direct organizational links to the present. The name change at the convention of 1840 was a relatively casual event. On May 6, 1840, the platform resolutions were adopted simply as "principles of the Democratic Party of the Union" and so reported in the convention proceedings.

Historically, the Democratic party's antecedents reach back into colonial life. This was a political organization that helped conduct a great revolution, shared in the inauguration of a new nation, functioned as its first loyal opposition, safeguarded the nation's democratic institutions even when it held a one-party monopoly (1804–1824), and, under Jackson, modernized the political system by making the presidency the single most representative office in the land.

The formative years in the English political experience and in the colonies were important. They set patterns of political procedure and habit that persist to this day and continue to influence the Democratic party style.

Some of England's most far-reaching constitutional developments were recent history for the leaders of colonial America around 1760. A few decades earlier Whig and Tory voting alignments had emerged in Parliament. Robert Walpole had introduced during the period 1721–1742 an innovation called "cabinet government" wherein all the king's ministers at any one time were chosen from the same parliamentary party. Remaining parties became "the opposition." These developments led Lord Bolingbroke to warn against the baneful effects of partisan strife in words that were echoed in President Washington's Farewell Address a half century later.

> The Heat and Animosity, which perpetual Contests and frequent Turns of Party raise, have cary'd many . . . to do what in any other Situation, or Temper of Mind, they could carefully avoid; . . . the just Man hath been, on such occasions, sometimes unjust; the good-natur'd Man ill-natur'd; and the friendly Man unfriendly. [10]

Bolingbroke was alluding to parties in a representative assembly, not to any party-in-the-electorate. The English electorate was minuscule. Even at the turn of the century, some fifty years after Bolingbroke wrote, only about one percent of the population voted. [11] In America, however, the situation was significantly different. Americans were equally concerned with electoral parties. The party-in-the-electorate was the innovative American emphasis. Colonists, accustomed to sharing the privations of a common struggle against nature, found it easy to gather into informal organizations called "electioneering caucuses" or "factions." These were the bases not only for colonial legislative alliances but also for the party-like groupings that mobilized voters to support specific leaders for public office. The method of numbers spread early and rapidly in colonial electoral practice.

Each of the colonies, with the exception of Pennsylvania, had a bicameral legislature. Members of the upper houses were usually appointed by the king, the royal proprieter, or the legislature with consent of the colonial governor. Members of the lower houses were by the 1750s, without exception, elected by the qualified voters. Suffrage requirements, however, were restrictive.

Imitating their forebears in Parliament, colonial assemblymen constantly engaged their governors in battles over control of public moneys, and, in time, the assemblies of Massachusetts, Connecticut, Rhode Island, and Maryland came to be centers of substantial political power. To sustain and reinforce that power, members of the assemblies and their constituency friends came together from time to time to agree upon candidates for office behind whom they could unite and to take steps to promote the electoral fortunes of these candidates.

The conduct of elections differed from colony to colony. Three general patterns have, however, been identified. [12] In communities under Puritan influence, mainly in New England, paper ballots early replaced the *viva voce* method. This was a departure from English voting practice and reflected and stimulated both organized electoral competition and independent voting. This was accompanied by the development of proxy voting which made it unnecessary for voting freeholders to appear in person at the colonial seat of government in order to elect colonial officers. Proxy voting also led to the practice of counting votes according to electoral districts, which in turn facilitated constituency efforts to compose slates of congenial candidates and promote their election. The second pattern, mainly in the royal colonies, followed English *viva voce* practice. The third pattern, found in the proprietary colonies, used the paper ballot and experimented with a variety of election methods. It has been estimated that the overall colonial electorate in the 1770s just prior to the Revolution numbered slightly less than 3 percent of the total population, a level of electoral participation that, as we have seen earlier, the English did not reach until after the passage of the Reform Bills of 1832.[13] In sum, parties-in-the-electorate were distinctively an American innovation that soon became a model for the French revolutionaries and the English reformers.

Thus, even before the reign of George III began in 1760, American colonists were committed to "the method of numbers" and divided among themselves into cliques, caucuses, and electioneering committees for the purpose of mobilizing votes for the election of public officers and the adoption of public policies in their town meetings and legislative assemblies. In the colony of Massachusetts, for example, this division saw the rise of a "Court party" friendly to the royal governor and a "Country party" comprising the same kinds of small shopkeepers, craftsmen, and laboring people that were then being attracted to the Whig party in England.

One of the first urban political machines, the Caucus Club of Boston, under the leadership of Deacon Samuel Adams and his son Sam, became a major component of the Country party. The Caucus Club in fact became the prototype of similar electioneering organizations elsewhere in the colonies. A primary objective of these clubs, soon to be known as "patriotic societies," was to capture seats in the colonial legislatures, there to make felt their opposition to royal economic measures. The colonial complaint was not so much about the amount of British taxes; it was about the lack of political participation in the decisions creating these taxes: "no taxation without representation."

Perhaps the most significant reaction to the British Stamp Act of 1765 was the capture of majority control of the Massachusetts House of Representatives by the Country party, putting Sam Adams in the position of clerk of that body. For a decade Sam Adams used this clerkship as the base from which to encourage the organization of local patriotic societies in other colonies.[14]

As local caucuses spread and gained control of legislatures, they found themselves also in command of legislative committees of correspondence, standing committees responsible for reporting official activities to sister assemblies throughout the colonies. Here was the skeleton for a "party of the Revolution."

The committee of correspondence first became an informal and extralegal instrument of revolution on November 2, 1772, when Sam Adams successfully pushed through a petition to form one outside the legislature at the town meeting of the city of Boston. Within two years this Boston Committee of Correspondence was in touch with more than three hundred towns in Massachusetts and with similar committees as far south as Charleston, South Carolina. These extralegal committees soon joined hands with those in the colonial legislatures. In 1774, when the royal governors of North Carolina and New Hampshire dissolved their colonial assemblies, the members were reconvened on the initiative of their respective committees of correspondence. Similarly, when a shipment of tea arriving in Boston Harbor on December 16, 1773, was destroyed, the Boston Committee of Correspondence was able to project that minor local skirmish into a continental outrage. The New York committee was the one that initiated a recommendation on May 23, 1774, that committees of correspondence everywhere take steps to convene a continental congress.

Many activities of the committees of correspondence were similar to those of modern parties. They held regular meetings in many localities, consulted with similar committees in their vicinity, prepared political matter for use in the press and in pamphlets, coordinated the development of local and continental policy proposals, promoted committee organizational efforts in surrounding localities, and solicited local citizen support for the continental cause. The committees of correspondence were the precinct organization of the Revolution.

In the very first Continental Congress it became evident that the colonists were not entirely agreed upon their objectives. There were in fact three factions: loyalists, conservatives, and radicals.[15] The conservative group, led by Joseph Galloway, Speaker of the

13

Pennsylvania Assembly, believed that some solution could be worked out within the framework of the British constitutional system. The radicals were headed by Sam Adams, whose negotiating talents proved to be unbeatable. Solidly supported by the representatives of the New England committees of correspondence which he had done so much to organize, Adams was also able to win support from the Southerners. He did this by proposing a continental army to be commanded by an eminent Virginian, George Washington. Adams's leadership also produced the Declaration of Independence and the Articles of Confederation.

The Continental Congress came to rely heavily upon local committees of correspondence as the sinews of the Revolution, particularly since many of the colonial governments were either opposed to or divided on the issue of seeking independence. Had it been a stationary war, it is doubtful that Washington could have accomplished the military mission. The Continental Army, sometimes running away from and sometimes bypassing the British, kept constantly on the move, refreshing its resources with the help of friendly committees of correspondence at each new locality, exciting the more lethargic local citizens by putting them in direct contact with the great revolutionary effort and moving on before their welcome had worn thin. Washington's was a beggar army, engaged in a political as well as a military campaign, "passing the hat" on a continental scale.

With victory and independence came problems of self-government. In the absence of a national executive, management of the new government was lost in the complex factional struggles of Congress. The "nationalists"—the conservatives of the early continental congresses—grew in numbers and became the prime-movers in calling and conducting the Constitutional Convention. When a Constitution was proposed, the nation became embroiled in what amounted to a constitutional referendum. Hamilton, Madison, and Jay combined forces to prepare a campaign handbook called *The Federalist.* Only about 5 percent of the total population became involved in selecting delegates to the state ratifying conventions.[16] Given the limited suffrage of that day, this was a substantial turnout.

As the prospect of defeating the nationalist plan for a centralized government faded, the Antifederalists, many of whom had been the radicals of the Continental Congress, negotiated a set of constraints on all governments, state and national: the Bill of

Rights. These first ten amendments to the Constitution guaranteed specific freedoms. Such constraints upon the national government's prerogatives in certain areas of political action assured the citizenry nonviolent opportunities for dissent under the new system of measuring the "ratio of consensus."

With adoption of the Constitution, the Federalists moved into control of the new national government they had done so much to create. Antifederalism subsided, giving the first Washington administration a chance to organize itself and the nation. But the call for new partisan effort was not long in coming. The policy and personal disagreements between Hamilton and Jefferson in the cabinet and the division of congressional forces into "Hamiltonians" and "Madisonians" soon led to the reactivation of old political organizations, stimulated the organization of new ones, and led to a coalition called the Democratic-Republican party.

The Jeffersonian Caucus

In the earliest stages of their development, political parties find their most natural habitat in representative assemblies. The numerous membership of such bodies, particularly when chosen from distinct and independent constituencies, could hardly function as decision-making organizations without the alliances and coalitions that are a major preoccupation of party politicians. Political parties tend first to emerge as alliances among members of the legislature, then as coalitions for winning the chief executive offices of the government. Often, particularly in parliamentary systems, the chief executive officer is a member of the legislative assembly, as in the case of the British prime minister.

Article I of the Constitution provided an initial distribution of sixty-five seats in the House of Representatives. The Senate consisted of twenty-six members. According to the population census in 1788, the largest number of House seats went to Virginia. As the most eminent representative from the largest state, James Madison held a "natural" seniority from the outset. Madison, as it turned out, also became the leader of the first loyal opposition in the American system.

Most members of Washington's administration conducted themselves as though they were participants in a parliamentary system. Washington himself assumed the style of a "Whig king." Alexander Hamilton, following Prime Minister William Pitt's example, took for himself responsibility for formulating and promoting the budget and most legislative programs. It had been Pitt's view that one of the ministers should hold the principal place in the confidence of the king and also be "the person at the head of the finances." Hamilton adopted this approach and tried to convert the office of Secretary of the Treasury into a prime ministry.

The Federalists held all twenty-six seats in the Senate and fifty-three of the sixty-five seats in the House during the First Congress. In the Second Congress there were ostensibly seventeen Federalists among the thirty senators and fifty-five Federalists among the sixty-nine congressmen. Actually, partisan patterns of voting hardly existed during the first three sessions of Congress. With the Fourth Congress (1795–1797), however, came a hardening of party lines and the development of the party caucus. About 65 percent of the Federalists and 74 percent of the Democratic-Republicans voted with their fellow-partisans consistently. By the Seventh Congress (1801–1803) some 80 percent of the Federalists and 94 percent of the Democratic-Republicans exhibited partisan voting patterns.[17]

The party caucus became the major instrument for achieving cohesion. The first congressional caucus took place on April 2, 1796, when Democratic-Republicans gathered to discuss the controversial issue of appropriating funds for the implementation of the Jay Treaty with England. Popular opinion on the treaty coincided with pro-treaty Federalist predispositions toward England and anti-treaty Democratic-Republican sympathies for France. The treaty had passed the Senate by the minimum constitutional two-thirds margin, 20–10. On the appropriations question, the Democratic-Republicans, with an apparent 57–49 majority in the House, decided to organize in caucus for the ensuing floor debate. After a month-long debate in the House meeting as a Committee of the Whole, a vote resulted in a 49–49 tie, broken in favor of the treaty by the chairman of the Committee of the Whole, a Democratic-Republican whose political career ended shortly thereafter. Madisonians, in a round of letters to their constituents, castigated their congressional colleagues who had deserted under pressure. Party loyalty in congressional politics was for the first time demanded and the caucus would presumably serve as the arena for its arrangement and protection.

Congress was physically and politically the most convenient place for consultation among national politicians. Very soon, preferences for president and vice president became grist for caucus discussion. In 1796, the Democratic-Republican caucus tightened lines in support of Jefferson for president. As we shall see, Jefferson instead became vice president in that year. Elected president in 1800, Jefferson gave great attention to working through the Democratic-Republican caucus to advance his legislative program and to assure that the presidential succession would pass to Madison. It was an era in which presidents acknowledged the supremacy of Congress among the branches of the national government. Jefferson, Madison, and Monroe deferred accordingly.

The Jeffersonian Party-in-the-Electorate

The Hamilton-Jefferson split in President Washington's cabinet and the accelerating partisan alignments in Congress, particularly in the House of Representatives under Madison's guiding hand, set the pace for party divisions in the electorate. This fit in with colonial, revolutionary, and Confederation experience, and many hands were familiar with electioneering. Jefferson and other national Democratic-Republicans provided much of the stimulus for reactivating many old local party organizations and creating new ones.[18] The Jeffersonians recognized that the people would need to be organized if the incumbent Federalists were to be overtaken.

The press was symptomatic of Jefferson's problem. A study of 512 of the newspapers published during the period from 1790 to 1800 revealed that 139 were strongly Federalist and another 121 moderately so. On the Democratic-Republican side, only 72 were strong supporters and 57 moderately so. The remaining 123 were of doubtful leanings.[19] Most Federalist papers took their cues from John Fenno's *Gazette of the United States* while Democratic-Republicans looked to Philip Freneau's *National Gazette*. In general, newspaper partisanship was blatant and often offensive.

In the period from 1789 to 1792 local party organization was uneven in the nation. In some places there were committees of correspondence capable of nominating slates and campaigning for them, for example, New York and Pennsylvania. In other places the absence of electioneering organizations led to multiple candidacies for particular offices. For example, in 1792 there were eleven major candidates for four congressional seats in New Hampshire. In Boston, twenty-seven candidates ran for five positions as presidential elector. The system of local ticket-making was not often effective; candidates entered races despite being eliminated from tickets by their party leaders.

17

A major local stimulus to the organization of the Democratic-Republican party was the numerous patriotic societies established between 1793 and 1800. At first not interested in nominating tickets and managing election campaigns, these societies were primarily concerned with issues that divided the nation and with expressing their opposition to the policies of the Federalist administrations.

The first society to appear was organized by German-Americans in Philadelphia: the German Republican Society. On April 13, 1793, the *National Gazette* announced the society's formation and published its first circular, a document with a modern ring which in part read:

In a Republican government it is the duty incumbent on every citizen to afford his assistance, either by taking part in its immediate administration, or by his advice and watchfulness, that its principles may remain uncorrupt; for the spirit of liberty, like every virtue of the mind, is to be kept alive only by constant action. It unfortunately happens that the objects of general concern seldom meet with the individual attention which they merit and that individual exertion seldom produces a general effect; it is, therefore, of essential moment that political societies should be established in a free government, that a joint operation may be produced, which shall give that attention and exertion so necessary for the preservation of civil liberty.[20]

Late in May a Norfolk and Portsmouth Republican Society appeared in Virginia. A third society proved to be quite influential. Organized in Philadelphia, it had important national leaders among its members, was at the seat of the national government, and was aggressive in urging the formation of similar societies in every section of the nation. The constitution of the Democratic Society of Pennsylvania was adopted on July 3, 1793. About forty-one such popular groups were subsequently organized; eleven others in 1793, twenty-four in 1794, three in 1795, and others later; from one to five in each of the thirteen states. Tammany societies, primarily veterans groups, were also scattered throughout the states, in Virginia, Rhode Island, North Carolina, Pennsylvania, New York, and probably elsewhere. About 1794–95, the New York Tammany Society began to debate important current issues and give greater attention to the electoral process.

Certain characteristics of these post-Revolution popular organizations were clearly indigenous, traceable to the Sons of Liberty, the Associators, and the committees of correspondence. These included the simple practice of associating together for public action, the use of committee systems and correspondence, and the system of visitation. It was charged that the democratic societies of 1793 were modeled after the French Jacobin clubs. Actually, English democrats during the 1780s, impressed with the effectiveness of the American committees of correspondence, began to organize their own. The French revolutionaries followed the English example. All through the 1780s and 1790s there was much interaction among these popular movements on both sides of the Atlantic.[21]

In general, these societies were county political associations holding monthly meetings in county courthouses. In some places they were city associations with a somewhat different organizational structure. The societies in some areas replaced mass meetings as nominating agencies. All democratic societies had active committees of correspondence, as in revolutionary days. The corresponding committee of the Pennsylvania Democratic Society, somewhat analogous to the old Boston Caucus, served as clearinghouse for societies in other states.

The democratic societies of Philadelphia were the first to claim that partisan alignments were legitimate and legal. Parties, they claimed, were an essential instrument of balance in the turbulent sea of liberty. Their main efforts were directed to local and congressional objectives. In 1793, they helped return the first Democratic-Republican majority to the House of Representatives.

Some Federalists tried to launch counter-societies to offset the influence of democratic societies. Federalist political organization, however, had a somewhat different emphasis and was mainly a collaboration among groups already established: merchants through their chambers of commerce, manufacturers, bankers, various professional groups, wealthier agrarians, the Congregationalist and Episcopalian churches, the aristocratic Society of Cincinnati. Federalist antipathy to partisan organization prevented effective action. The efforts of the Federalist press, on the other hand, were prodigious. This press in some instances went so far as to avoid all mention of the democratic societies and, on occasion, falsely reported that particular societies had disbanded.

When Washington denounced the democratic societies, the societies suffered some losses in membership. In his message to the Third Congress on November 19, 1794, the president specifically condemned the activities of "certain self-created societies" and implied that they had been responsible for the Pennsylvania Whiskey Insurrection. The matter might have rested with Washington's statement, but it was followed in Congress with a Federalist resolution strongly supporting Washington's denunciation. Unable to have the resolution defeated, Madison worked for a watered-down version. With Speaker of the House Muhlenberg breaking a tie, the compromise resolution was substituted.[22] In the scuffle, however, President Washington himself was tarnished with some of the developing partisanship of the day.

The presidential campaign of 1800 brought significant progress in the development of party organization in the electorate. Democratic-Republicans in New York and Pennsylvania had perfected a considerable organization. Virginia and New Jersey Democratic-Republicans began to refine theirs. The growth of party was noticeable in varying degrees in other states. Organization in many places acquired modern characteristics. Aaron Burr and Tammany introduced the device that came to symbolize modern organizing proficiency: the card-index of voters' names. Modern procedure of campaign management is described in the correspondence of Alexander Wolcott, a Democratic-Republican state manager for Connecticut and collector of the port of Middletown. Wolcott, giving detailed instructions, urged his correspondent to have each county leader appoint a manager for each town in his county, and then have each town manager appoint district managers. District managers were to report which voters were "republicans, federalists, or doubtful."[23] Wrote a Federalist leader in Congress to the Federalist minister to Portugal and Spain:

The opposition to the government is not less ardent and determined than when you left us; but on the contrary its various parts are more combined, and the systems which it pursues better organized. The great object which it is now pursuing is to secure the Presidency for the Leader of it.[24]

Working politicians were also becoming aware of the problem of "pivotal states" in presidential elections. In the election of 1796, a change of less than 100 popular votes in Pennsylvania would have elected Pinckney instead of Jefferson.[25] In 1800, a shift of 214 votes in New York City could have turned the election for the presidency against Jefferson.[26]

Thus it was that the Jeffersonian Democratic-Republicans built the congressional caucus into a nominating and election system and the patriotic and democratic societies into mobilizers of the party-in-the-electorate. Noting that Jefferson wanted to be remembered most for the Declaration of Independence, the Virginia Statute on

Religious Liberty, and the founding of the University of Virginia, Richard Hofstadter expresses surprise at the omission of Jefferson's achievements in political party development.

Surely this democrat and libertarian might have taken justifiable pride in his part in creating the first truly popular party in the history of the Western world, and in his leading role in the first popular election of modern times in which the reins of government were peacefully surrendered by a governing party to an opposition. . . . He was . . . a central figure in developing responsible constitutional opposition, an accomplishment which alone would grace any man's tombstone.[27]

2

Democratic Transformation of the Presidency

WHEN the Founding Fathers created the office of President, many of them, particularly Washington and Hamilton, thought they had invented a constitutional monarchy such as their political cousins in England were striving to develop. The electoral college was designed to bring representative wise men from across the nation into consultation about the most distinguished citizen to be chosen for this office. If any of the Founding Fathers had thoughts about political parties and popular participation as part of this presidential system, they were usually negative or privately held thoughts. None foresaw that political parties would some day convert the electoral college into a vehicle for popular rather than elite control of the choice of presidents. None imagined that presidents would someday be party leaders rather than constitutional monarchs. Nor did any anticipate that a political party like Andrew Jackson's Democrats would, within two generations, transform the very character of the presidency.

Today, it is relatively easy to locate presidential party leaders. There is the president who, to paraphrase Woodrow Wilson, cannot escape being leader of his party. There are also the president's most recently defeated opponent who sometimes actively undertakes to lead the "loyal opposition," the White House staff, the cabinet, the party national committee and its chairperson, the vice-presidency, those "presidential politicians" in the states and communities who become active in presidential election years, the national convention, and sometimes the leadership of organized interest groups whose responsibility it is to maintain access to prospective presidents. In general, this is the core within which presidential party leadership is found in recent times.

In the early days of the Republic, however, there was little organization or clarity about either presidential or national party leadership. The presidency was an experimental office with almost no staff. Party organization was congressional or local: Democratic-Republicans, Federalists, patriotic societies, caucuses, and committees of correspondence. Presidential politicians were few: Jefferson, Hamilton, Adams, the Clintons, Burr, etc. Out of these circumstances, Jefferson marshaled the first opposition party to win the presidency, helped create "King Caucus" as an informal coalition-building forum for selecting presidents and promoting legislative programs, and paved the way for an "era of good feeling" in which his party dominated national politics. These were the political conditions that confronted Andrew Jackson and his colleagues when they embarked upon their campaign to win the presidency in the early 1820s.

Crises in College and Caucus

The electoral college system for electing presidents and vice presidents operated for the first three elections as originally conceived. Each state in the Union was apportioned a number of electoral votes equal to the size of its delegation in the Senate and the House of Representatives together. Each elector was to vote for two persons for president. An absolute majority of the total number of electors was needed to elect the president. The runner-up, necessarily with fewer votes than a majority, became vice president. If there were no majority or a tie for president, the election would be made from the top five names by the House of Representatives, each state's delegation casting only a single vote. A tie for the vice-presidential second place, if one occurred, was to be decided in the Senate. Simple as it seemed, most of the authors of the Constitution lived to see this "method of numbers" generate intense competition for the presidency, stimulate the development of national political parties, and, within a dozen years, lead to a constitutional crisis that was solved only with passage of the Twelfth Amendment.

There were apportionments of 81 electors in the first presidential election (Rhode Island and North Carolina had not yet ratified the Constitution and did not participate) and 135 electors in the second. As the most populous states with the largest congressional

23

delegations, Virginia, Massachusetts, Pennsylvania, and New York, in that order, possessed most of the votes in the electoral college, and their presidential preferences carried greatest weight. The Founding Fathers numbered about one hundred, and, of these, according to Padover, only about twenty were of more than average ability and stature.[1] Virginia had George Washington, Thomas Jefferson, James Madison, and Patrick Henry. Massachusetts offered such names as John Adams and John Hancock. George Clinton, Alexander Hamilton (not native born, hence not eligible), and John Jay came from New York, Benjamin Franklin and Albert Gallatin from Pennsylvania. The potential candidates were not many, and the hero of the Revolution, as the most distinguished citizen of Virginia, was clearly the front-runner to become first president of the new nation. The vice-presidency was the real issue of choice in 1788 and 1792.

The first partisan coordinators of voting in the electoral college were Hamilton and Jefferson. Their correspondence with colleagues in the thirteen states—an onerous procedure in an era of quill and stagecoach—was the extent of their informal presidential party organizations. The election of Washington was unanimous; sixty-nine votes, with twelve absent. The principle of regional representation and Massachusetts' status as second largest state gave it claim to the vice-presidency, its two prospects being Adams and Hancock. Hamilton, reluctant to support Adams, but on the other hand fearful that he might defect from the Federalist cause, urged his electoral colleagues to throw away some of their second votes on candidates other than Adams. Adams received thirty-four votes, and thirty-five others went to men like Jay, Hancock, Clinton, and others.

The reelection of Washington and Adams in 1792 followed a similar course: 132 for Washington, 77 for Adams, 50 for Clinton, and 5 for others. The Adams-Clinton division, however, reflected a tightening of partisan lines. The Jeffersonians had concentrated their support behind Clinton, after giving strong consideration to Aaron Burr. This election also witnessed the beginning of the winner-take-all principle of awarding all of a state's electoral votes to the dominant party in that state. Nine of the fifteen participating states in 1792 cast straight-ticket votes for Washington-Adams and four for Washington-Clinton. The effects of coalition-building and presidential party coordination were already evident in this alignment.

What constituencies did the presidential electors represent?

They varied. Between 1788 and 1800, approximately 50–60 percent of the electors were chosen by state legislatures, another 20 percent by popular vote on statewide tickets, and 20–30 percent by popular vote in single-member, usually congressional, districts. Hamilton corresponded mainly with state legislative leaders about selection of and instructions to Federalist electors. Jefferson, on the other hand, coordinated the efforts of those who nominated and supported popularly elected statewide and district candidates for elector. Their difference in approach was highly significant. The Jeffersonians were building a party-in-the-electorate which in turn eventually radically altered the functioning of the electoral college. As a consequence, when the Jeffersonians came to power in 1800, they pressed for election procedures in the states that raised the proportion of popularly chosen presidential electors from 40–50 percent in 1788–1800 to 55–70 percent in 1804–1820. Between 1824 and 1828, the Jacksonians further succeeded in raising the proportion to 95 percent, thereby completing changes in the "method of numbers" that would thereafter make presidents beholden to the popular presidential electorate rather than to state or congressional legislators. The Jacksonian changes also reestablished the separation of powers and reinforced presidential independence from Congress.

Long before these changes in procedure for choosing presidential electors took place, the electoral college experienced substantial partisan and arithmetical stress. Washington's expected retirement spurred ticket-building for 1796. The Federalists by now had distinguishable factions: Adams's "Half Federalists" and Hamilton's "High Federalists." Reluctantly, Hamilton acquiesced to Washington's wish that his vice president, Adams, be his successor. Hamilton then concentrated his attention on the vice-presidential choice and agreed with suggestions that Thomas Pinckney of South Carolina could provide southern balance to an Adams ticket. He urged his Federalist colleagues in the North to vote a straight Adams-Pinckney slate. It hardly disturbed Hamilton that some southern Democratic-Republicans were thinking of joining the southern Federalists in favor of Pinckney, raising the possibility of edging out Adams for the presidency.

For their part, the Democratic-Republicans, fresh from their election gains in the congressional races of 1794 and grateful to the democratic societies for their work in that campaign, were looking optimistically toward 1796. Jefferson was expressing the hope that his colleague Madison would soon be promoted "to a more efficacious post," and Madison was telling Jefferson to be "preparing" himself.[2]

Shortly after their first congressional caucus on the Jay Treaty appropriation on April 2, 1796, Democratic-Republicans in the House of Representatives, with Jefferson as their overwhelming choice for president, met again in caucus to consider candidates for vice-president.[3] This was the first such congressional nominating caucus. Among those most prominently mentioned were Aaron Burr, John Langdon, Pierce Butler, and Robert R. Livingston, with Burr the favorite.

The efforts of Hamilton on the one hand and the Democratic-Republican congressional caucus on the other could be seen in the electoral college results of 1796. With 138 electors casting two votes each, the winning majority for president was 70 votes. The tally was: Adams, 71; Jefferson, 68; Pinckney, 59; Burr, 30; others, 48. Five states voted the Adams-Pinckney slate. Four voted for Jefferson-Burr. The others scattered their votes. Thus, the leaders of opposing parties won the nation's two highest offices.

Even closer partisan collaboration would be necessary in 1800, and steps were early undertaken to achieve this. As vice-president, Jefferson was in an excellent position to manage the preparation for 1800. He conciliated Burr, who had been offended by Virginia's failure to vote for him in 1796. He reestablished the Virginia "triumvirate" of earlier years—Madison, Monroe, and himself—as a working team which would become the "Virginia Dynasty" in later years. Democratic-Republican party-line voting tightened in the Fifth and Sixth Congresses. Under the leadership of Albert Gallatin, the principal Democratic-Republican in the House of Representatives at this time, New York colleagues were invited to express their preference for a vice-presidential candidate to be supported along with Jefferson, and Burr was named. Then, at a secret meeting of most of the Democratic-Republicans in Congress at the party's unofficial headquarters in Philadelphia, Marache's boarding house, a Jefferson-Burr slate was agreed upon.

The decision was implemented too well. Every presidential elector who voted for Jefferson also voted for Burr, leading to a 73–73 tie between the two in the electoral college, with Adams and Pinckney trailing behind. The choice went to the House of Representatives where each of the sixteen states in the Union had one vote, and a majority of nine was needed to be elected. As it turned out, the otherwise happy situation was a crisis.

On the first House ballot, Jefferson received eight votes (one short of a majority), Burr six, and two state delegations remained tied between the two. The House of Representatives was itself a lame duck body, with the Federalists holding a 63–43 majority. Seven state delegations were controlled by the Federalists, six by Democratic-Republicans, and three were divided. As ballot after ballot was taken, Hamilton was regularly consulted by his congressional friends. Burr remained silent, unwilling to defer to Jefferson's seniority. Finally, Hamilton's Federalist colleagues, whose votes for Burr were sustaining the stalemate, abstained from casting their pro-Burr votes on the thirty-sixth ballot. The final vote was ten states for Jefferson, four for Burr, and two not voting. Burr became Jefferson's vice president but remained an outcast in Jefferson's first administration and was not on the ticket for his second.

The electoral college crises of 1796 (when leaders of opposite parties were elected to the two highest offices in the nation) and 1800 (when leaders of the same party stalemated each other) caused the Jeffersonians to reexamine the Constitution's procedure and to propose the Twelfth Amendment to the states in January 1804. The new procedure simply required the electors to make separate lists for president and vice president and to vote separately for each. Further, an absolute majority was needed for election to both offices. Thus, the Jeffersonians protected the presidency from a major source of uncertainty created by the emergence of presidential parties and party tickets for the two national offices. The great national prize was henceforth clearly the presidency. Not until the Twenty-second Amendment, which limited the presidential terms to two and, in practice, made the vice president an important contender for the succession during the lame duck term of a president, did the vice-presidency recover from the demotion of 1804.

In addition to the constitutional amendment, other important changes were taking place in the political environment of the presidency as a consequence of party developments. The relative electoral college strength of the states was changing, with New York forging ahead of Virginia and Massachusetts and with the new states of Ohio, Tennessee, Mississippi, and Kentucky experiencing rapid population growth that would soon be reflected in the electoral college and in Congress, for example, Henry Clay of Kentucky as Speaker of the House in 1812. As noted earlier, Jeffersonians in the state legislatures were putting through changes in state election laws giving the party-in-the electorate a greater role in the selection

27

of presidential electors. Despite the change in statutes, however, voter participation declined between 1804 and 1824 because of the decline in party competition; the Federalists were disappearing from the congressional ranks and most politicians referred to themselves as Jeffersonians or Republicans. Perhaps the most important change was the ascendancy of "King Caucus" as the real, albeit unofficial, presidential nominating and electing body.

That presidential and congressional politics were thoroughly dominated by the Jeffersonian Republicans is amply demonstrated by Table 1. Most members of Congress were Republicans from 1804 to 1824, most attended the presidential nominating caucuses between 1804 and 1816, and most of the votes in the electoral college went to their choices.

Table 1 also summarizes the presidential politics of the era. With Burr displaced by Clinton as his vice-presidential associate, Jefferson, fully endorsed by the Republican caucus, captured nearly all the votes in the electoral college in 1804. A caucus minority resisted Madison for the succession in 1808 and persisted in 1812 when caucus attendance began to decline and the selection of a vice-presidential candidate was troublesome. As Madison's second term drew to a close in 1816, James Monroe was serving as secretary of state, the position normally held by the heir apparent. A substantial element in Congress, however, favored Secretary of the Treasury William H. Crawford, former president *pro tempore* of the Senate. Monroe, the third of the Virginia Dynasty, was given a close contest by Crawford, 65–54. The now traditional second term was conceded to Monroe in 1820; he carried all but one vote in the electoral college. Disenchantment with the caucus procedure, however, had by now grown to the point that it was no longer held— not even for a courtesy endorsement of the incumbent president.

By 1824 the Union had grown to twenty-four states, the Senate to 48 members, the House of Representatives to 213, and the electoral college to 261. The oversized Republican party was really a collection of personal factions: Clay men, Crawford men, Adams men, Webster men, Calhoun men, etc. Presidential aspirants rested their claims on the support of their colleagues in Congress, well-organized parties in their constituencies, regional coalitions and similar power bases outside the caucus structure. Between 1818 and 1824 King Caucus was roundly denounced by most presidential politicians. In February 1824 a special Republican committee of twenty-four members of Congress conducted a survey of the 231

Republican Congressional Caucus Nominating and Electoral College Votes, 1804–1824

Date of Caucus	Republicans in Congress		Republicans		Presidential	Vice-Presidential	Republican Electoral College Majorities
	House (Total)	Senate (Total)	Attending Caucus	Abstentions			
Feb. 25, 1804	102 (142)	25 (34)	110	15–20 Burr men	Jefferson, acclamation	Clinton, 67; Breckenridge, 20; others, 21	162–14
Jan. 23, 1808	118 (142)	28 (34)	94	50–55 "anti-caucus" congressmen	Madison, 83; Clinton, 3; Monroe, 3	Clinton, 79; Langdon, 5; others, 4	122–47
May 12, May 18, June 8, 1812	108 (186)	30 (36)	About 83	50–55 Clinton men	Madison, 82	Langdon, 64; Gerry, 16; others, 2; Langdon declined; Gerry, 74; others, 3	128–89
March 16–17, 1816	117 (186)	25 (38)	About 119	About 23	Monroe, 65; Crawford, 54	Tompkins, 85; Snyder, 30	183–34
1820	156 (186)	35 (46)	No caucus held; no formal action	—	Monroe	Tompkins	231–1
Feb. 14, 1824	187 (213)	44 (48)	68	Over 160	Crawford, 64; others, 4	Gallatin, 57; others, 9; Gallatin declined	Jackson, 99; Adams, 84; Crawford, 41; Clay, 37; (vice president: Calhoun, 182; others, 79)

Sources: Louis C. Hatch, *History of the Vice-Presidency* (Westport, Conn., reprint of 1934 ed.: Greenwood Press, 1970), pp. 13–43, 149, 162–66; Edward Stanwood, *A History of the Presidency*, (Boston: Houghton, Mifflin, 1928), vol. 1, pp. 90–91, 99, 109–10; *National Intelligencer* (February 16, 1824).

party members in both houses and found that 78 percent deemed it "inexpedient" to hold the usual nominating caucus. Ironically even as the caucus breathed its last, another crisis developed in the electoral college that denied the presidency to the candidate with the greatest number of popular votes and turned the entire House of Representatives into a caucus-like conspiracy. At least, this was the charge made by Andrew Jackson and his supporters.

Jacksonian Mobilization of the Electorate

The Jacksonian Revolution was in large part based upon the success with which the Jackson men brought the era of congressional selection of presidents to an end. A lawyer and plantation owner active in the economic, political, and military life of frontier Tennessee in the early years of its statehood, General Jackson's national fame came in his late forties. His victory against the British at New Orleans, although it came *after* the signing of the peace treaty in 1815, did much to bolster the young nation's self-respect. It had been a humiliating war, climaxed by the burning of the capital city. The legend of his victory against the British established Jackson as the principal national hero of the period and a major presidential candidate. His status as an outsider to Washington politics, however, placed hurdles in the way of that candidacy. In surmounting them, the Jacksonians transformed the presidential selection process, the national electorate, and the presidency itself.

The Panic of 1819 had pauperized farmers and workingmen everywhere in the country. Severe popular discontent was aggravated by widespread land purchase frauds. The times seemed ripe for the rise of a popular hero.[4] Furthermore, throughout the nation in the early 1820s, particularly along its frontiers, restrictive suffrage requirements were being removed, and tens of thousands of newly enfranchised citizens stood ready to join the electorate.

In January 1822, the *Nashville Gazette* proposed Jackson for the presidency. The state's general assembly formalized the nomination the following August. The move struck a responsive chord throughout the Southwest, Illinois, and Indiana. The Tennessee legislature next elected Jackson to the United States Senate. In December 1823 he took his seat in Washington, where he could be seen by the nation and its principal president-makers.

Resistance to the congressional caucus left the Republican party with no national organ through which the various competing factions could decide upon a single candidate. There were, however, several other methods for placing candidates before the country. Jackson, as we have seen, was put in nomination by a state legislature. Three months later, a caucus of Kentucky state legislators nominated Clay. The Georgia state legislature nominated Crawford and passed a resolution declaring that only the congressional caucus could legitimately make presidential nominations. In 1823, John Quincy Adams was nominated by a mixed convention, that is, a conference of state legislators and party leaders from districts without party representation in the Massachusetts legislature. Nominations and endorsements were also being made by mass meetings. Delegate conventions, to which party members chose special representatives according to some system of apportionment, were also known at this time, but used only in state and local politics. All four men were, of course, running as Democratic-Republicans.

Crawford, in ill health at this time, was considered the choice of the Virginia Dynasty. In the North, he had the support of the political wizard Martin Van Buren, senator from New York and leader of an influential state machine, the "Albany Regency." Van Buren considered Crawford "the best man," in the Jeffersonian tradition, and tried to work in his behalf through the congressional caucus. When the caucus met on February 14, 1824, however, only about one-fourth of the eligible Republican congressmen appeared to place the ailing Georgian in nomination.[5] In the customary heir-apparent position at the State Department sat John Quincy Adams. Henry Clay's reputation was being cemented by his work on the Missouri Compromise and his achievements as three-time Speaker of the House. Still another possibility was Monroe's secretary of war, John C. Calhoun of South Carolina.

Jackson's distinguished adversaries proved to be excellent foils. John Quincy Adams bore the marks of his father's federalism and disdained the "vulgar" requirements of partisan strife. Henry Clay was a master of the legislative not the electoral arena. John C. Calhoun was inconsistent: a nationalist under Monroe and Adams, a states' righter later under Jackson. Daniel Webster, the "stentorian voice" of Boston aristocracy, openly served the interest of the National Bank. Against each of these men Jackson seemed to carry the old Jeffersonian battles: against federalism, against the political ascendancy of New England, against the economic ambitions of the moneyed interests.

Although Jackson's campaign took eight years to carry him to presidential victory, in the process, the men around him perfected a national party organization that facilitated systematic contact with the people. Jackson might have remained a local favorite son had it not been for the political and organizing skill of a small group of devoted Tennessee politicians. These men converted Jackson's military fame into political alliances across the nation, established party organs where none had been before, and everywhere paved the way for popular acceptance of the hero. The voters responded by giving Jackson a plurality of the popular vote, but the electoral college count was short of the necessary absolute majority. (See Table 2.) Another presidential election crisis ensued as the choice was referred to the House of Representatives.

The House of Representatives had remained, from the 1790s through the 1820s, the principal center of national politics. In 1811, Henry Clay became its Speaker and held that position almost continuously through 1825. His influence was climaxed in 1824 when he withdrew his name and transformed Adams's popular minority of 31.9 percent into a House majority of 54.2 percent.

TABLE 2
Presidential Election of 1824, in Percentages

Candidate	Popular Vote*	Electoral College	House Vote
Jackson	42.2	37.9	29.2
Adams	31.9	32.2	54.2
Clay	13.0	14.2	—
Crawford	12.9	15.7	16.6

*The total popular vote for presidential electors was 362,744.
Source: Compiled by author.

Ironically, the presidential election crisis came at a time when all congressional caucus actions had become anathema. Yet, in choosing Adams, the House of Representatives had become a caucus-of-the-whole. Jackson and his managers made the most of it. Jackson returned directly to Tennessee from Washington declaring at every stop that Clay had purchased a cabinet position (secretary of state) by making a president. Jackson subsequently resigned from the Senate.

The Jacksonians' most notable achievement was their success in forming a coalition with Martin Van Buren, leader of New York's Albany Regency. Van Buren's genius for political organization was well established. The "Little Magician" had a reputation for pulling victories out of very deep political hats. Born to extreme poverty, he never lost his personal or political identification with working people. With Jackson's name as the catalyst, Van Buren was able to weld together a coalition of the Albany Regency, the Richmond Junto, and the hardy group of Tennessee politicians associated with Jackson. The Jacksonians continued as Democratic-Republicans. Adams supporters began to refer to themselves as National Republicans.

In Congress, Van Buren carefully developed issues and tactics that gave heart and muscle to the new Jacksonian alliance. He worked diligently, for example, to alter state procedures for popular selection of presidential electors. By 1828, only Delaware and South Carolina continued to choose presidential electors in their state legislatures. (See Table 3.) In New York, when state legislative selection of electors was replaced by popular election in 1828, this added over a quarter of a million new voters to the million previously able

TABLE 3
Percentage of Electoral College Strength Chosen by Different Methods, 1788–1828

| Year | By Legislature | By Popular Vote | | |
		General State Ticket	District	Total by Popular Vote
1788	49*	22	29	51
1792	59†	23	18	41
1796	52‡	21	27	48
1800	63	18	19	37
1804	30	38	32	70
1808	41	38	21	59
1812	44	32	24	56
1816	44	42	14	56
1820	31	45	24	69
1824	27	53	20	73
1828	5	69	26	95

*Massachusetts legislature chose eight of its electors from the sixteen elected by popular vote. New Hampshire chose by legislature all those unable to win a majority of the popular vote.

†Massachusetts chose eleven by legislature and five by the popular-legislative procedure; all counted as legislative here.

‡Massachusetts chose nine by legislature and seven by the popular-legislative procedure; all counted as legislative here. New Hampshire chose by legislature all those unable to win a majority of the popular vote.

Source: Bureau of the Census, *Historical Statistics of the United States, 1789–1945* (1949), p. 288.

to vote. Van Buren also was instrumental in transforming the *United States Telegraph* into the leading national Jackson newspaper.

Extension of the suffrage and intensification of presidential politics were accompanied by party organizational activity at the local level. Ward and county committees in the cities and school-district and township committees in the rural areas met frequently, developed political information, endorsed local candidates, and campaigned with increasing intensity and skill during this period. State committees concerned themselves more and more with the standard activities of political parties: political rallies, distribution of literature, selection of representatives to political conventions, collection of funds, prevention of fraudulent voting, printing of ballots, preparation of lists of eligible voters, and measurement of voter preference. The Jackson managers in Tennessee concentrated their prime attention upon the mobilization of a new party-in-the-electorate.

In hope of achieving a stronger alignment with the Richmond Junto and a "substantial reorganization of the old Republican Party," Van Buren suggested, on January 13, 1827, that a national nominating convention be called to name a candidate to oppose Adams in the forthcoming election.[6] Although unimplemented until 1832, Van Buren's national convention proposal was intended to make it difficult for Congress to intervene in the 1828 presidential election process. Van Buren was also keenly aware that a party institution such as the national convention could also be an instrument of constraint, particularly in the case of a man of such military fame as General Jackson. For Jackson to be elected on account of his military reputation was one thing, he wrote; quite another if "the result of a combined and concerted effort of a political party. . . . "[7]

The electoral tide for Jackson was strong by 1828. The general outran Adams by a popular margin of 140,000 votes and an electoral college victory of 178 to 83. The increase in popular voting was dramatic. In New Hampshire, Missouri, New Jersey, Pennsylvania, and Illinois, the numbers more than tripled between 1824 and 1828. Voting participation more than doubled in Kentucky, Maine, Ohio, Virginia, Indiana, and Tennessee. There was a 225 percent increase over 1824 in total national turnout.

The four-candidate contest of 1824 was reduced to a two-man, two-party (Democratic-Republicans versus National Republicans) race by 1828. If the 1824 Jackson-Crawford and Adams-Clay popular votes are combined for each state, a comparison with the Jackson-Adams contest of 1828 shows substantial similarity between the two elections despite the reduction in number of presidential candidates. By 1828, with only 5 percent of the strength of the electoral college being decided by state legislatures, nearly 43 percent of the electoral votes was contested in two-party, competitive states. The remaining half of the electoral college, however, remained, as in 1824, at the disposition of one-party states. Together, though, the elections of 1824 and 1828 fixed the long-run shape of the presidential election process: a basically competitive system, with varying degrees of monopolistic tendency in one-party states.

Some theories of voter behavior suggest that voters in a mass electorate almost always tend to divide evenly between parties in a two-party system. This implies that voters act as mere flips of a coin producing a normal distribution in the aggregate outcome. The 1824–1828 presidential patterns suggest, however, another explanation of evenly divided electorates, namely, that the majoritarian rules of the game compel leaders to accomplish alliances in order to reduce the voter's alternatives to two. Yet another explanation is organizational, that is, parties will work, with varying success, to pull voters in one of two directions after the alternatives have been reduced to two. In later years, the national nominating conventions were essentially alternative-reducing mechanisms for each of the parties.

Van Buren and Incorporation of the Jacksonians

President Jackson was the first to retain a personal political staff, popularly referred to as the "Kitchen Cabinet." This group helped the president to consider the partisan implications of his acts and, perhaps more importantly, maintain communication lines with his allies in Congress and in the state organizations. While the composition of the Kitchen Cabinet changed over the years, the general characteristics of its members tended to be the same: they were primarily men who understood how to evaluate and influence the voting behavior of legislators and the electorate. Senator Van Buren was constantly in touch with the members of this staff, which included such persons as the Jacksonian managers in Congress, the president's private secretary, the editor of the administration's official newspaper, the leader of the Jacksonian party in New Hampshire, and others. While the Kitchen Cabinet proposed strategies and tactics in the political battles undertaken by the president, it was nonetheless Jackson who chose the battlegrounds. Its "chief of staff" over the years was always Van Buren.

The coalition over which Jackson presided as party leader was at all times an uneasy one. Northeastern Jacksonians tended to support the protective tariff and oppose western demands for large expenditures on internal improvements. States' rights southerners stood for tariff reduction and the principle that any state in the Union could nullify any federal law—at this time, the tariff—with which it was in basic disagreement. Western frontier Jacksonians wanted cheap land, usually at the expense of the Indians, transportation and other internal improvements, and low-interest loans.

The mantle of opposition leadership fell to Henry Clay after 1828. A master legislative strategist, Clay never conquered the requirements of electoral organization. In 1824 he reluctantly supported Adams against Jackson because Jackson's popularity was the greater threat to himself. Despite a resolution from the Kentucky legislature urging him to support Jackson, Clay thought his own chances for the presidency would be enhanced if he took the traditional route through the office of Secretary of State. In supporting Adams, however, Clay forfeited much of his own popular influence in the frontier states. Four years later Jackson swept to victory in Kentucky, Ohio, and Missouri, all formerly "Clay states." Upon his departure from the Cabinet in 1829, Clay was generally recognized as the leader of the anti-Jackson forces, yet in his own bid for reelection to the Senate in 1831, he won by only a slim majority in the Kentucky legislature.

Clay set about building common ground for the scattered anti-Jacksonians under the "National Republican" banner. His best starting place was the Senate itself where there was a Jacksonian majority of only four votes in 1831 (reduced to a 20–20 tie by 1833). The House, on the other hand, maintained overwhelming Jacksonian majorities until 1837. The state electorates presented the most difficult problem of all. About 40 percent of the electoral college was safely in Jacksonian hands; only 13 percent was steadfastly National Republican. Another 27 percent of the electoral votes was within National Republican reach in Indiana, Kentucky, Louisiana, Ohio, and New York. If carried, these states could bring the parties abreast of each other. South Carolina, the seat of growing hostility to Jackson, remained firmly committed to Calhoun.

In seeking an *entente* with Calhoun, Clay modified his own high tariff position almost to the point of alienating Webster and the New England manufacturers. Clay at the same time endeavored to strengthen his hand in the West by proposing that revenue from

36

the sale of public lands be used for internal improvements. When Jackson, vetoing more bills than all his predecessors put together, vetoed the Maysville Road Bill designed to do this, Clay was furnished with a rallying cry. The veto became a banner against "executive usurpation" behind which all anti-Jacksonians could march.

Another issue for the 1832 campaign was the rechartering of the National Bank. Most anti-Jacksonians—Clay, Webster, even Calhoun—were supporters of the bank. Jackson's own position was one of mild opposition, held in the expectation that the rechartering matter would be handled by Congress quietly and in due course. Rechartering would ordinarily have come up after the 1832 elections. Instead, Clay urged Nicholas Biddle, the bank's president, to apply for rechartering early enough to throw the issue into the presidential campaign. Clay had Webster's strong support. The bank, with its array of officers and debtors, made up a considerable constituency in every state of the Union. In the absence of extensive local National Republican organization, the bank was also a substantial substitute for party organization. After careful consideration, Biddle decided to hurl down the gauntlet by asking Congress for an early renewal of the bank charter.

Jackson had pledged himself to a single term in the presidency. As Clay proceeded to mobilize the National Republican opposition and as Calhoun became a serious contender for the leadership of the Jackson party, Van Buren and the Kitchen Cabinet reached the conclusion that only renomination of the president himself could lay low both the Clay threat from without and the Calhoun faction from within the party. Early in 1830 two New York newspapers, the *Courier* and the *Enquirer,* opened the campaign for Jackson's renomination.

A major objective of the collaboration between Crawford's Richmond Junto and Van Buren's Albany Regency during Jackson's first term was to frustrate Vice President Calhoun's presidential ambitions. The Calhoun-Van Buren rivalry soon pervaded all aspects of national politics but manifested itself particularly in Calhoun's insistence upon tariff reduction and the implementation of his theory that any state could nullify a national law. As a consequence of the latter, in January 1830, Congress became the forum for a historic Webster-Hayne debate on the nature of the Union, on whether it was a union of the people or of sovereign states. Hayne propounded Calhoun's nullification doctrine. Webster made a classic appeal for union and patriotism.

By April 1831, Jackson began to take steps to remove Calhoun's supporters from his cabinet. Van Buren set off the process with his own resignation, giving the president a free hand to reorganize. Shortly thereafter Jackson gave Van Buren an interim appointment as ambassador to England, pending confirmation upon the return of Congress. Van Buren departed for England. The vote on confirmation in January 1832, however, produced a 23–23 tie. Vice President Calhoun broke the tie by voting against confirmation. The challenge to Jackson's authority was clear. Glaring at Calhoun, Senator Thomas Hart Benton thundered: "You have broken a minister and elected a vice president!" Writing to Van Buren, Jackson declared: "The insult to the executive would be avenged by putting you into the very chair which is now occupied by him who cast the deciding vote against you."[8] Jackson was now determined that Van Buren should replace Calhoun in the vice-presidency and eventually be his successor as the Democratic-Republican choice for president. The instrument he chose to accomplish this, undoubtedly at the suggestion of Van Buren and the Kitchen Cabinet, was the national nominating convention.

The short-lived Antimason party was the first to use a national convention for nominating a national ticket and held its only convention in 1831. The National Republicans, the loose coalition of Adams, Clay, and Webster followers, held their only national convention in the same year to nominate Clay. The first Democratic-Republican National Convention—and the first of those that later came to be called "Democratic"—was conducted in Baltimore on May 21, 22, and 23, 1832. Nearly three hundred voting delegates attended.

The basic decision-making rules adopted in its first convention prevailed at Democratic national conventions for the next century: representation apportioned in the same manner as the electoral college; two-thirds majority required to nominate; each state to cast its votes as a bloc (the unit rule). The Calhoun supporters were thoroughly overwhelmed by these procedures and never came close to the one-third necessary to veto Van Buren's nomination for vice president.

The National Republican campaign got under way promptly. Clay and Biddle mobilized the full resources of the National Bank throughout the country, spending the unprecedented sum of $80,000 for propaganda of all kinds. The bill to recharter the bank was sent to Jackson early in July. If Clay expected simply another veto against which he could cry "executive usurption," he seriously misjudged the president's political adroitness. On July 10 Jackson returned a shattering veto message placing the supporters of the bank squarely on the side of "the rich and powerful" against the interests of "the humble members of society." A bitter debate ensued and continued long beyond election day.

Clay had again erred in his estimate of the electorate. Compared to 1828, the Jackson-Van Buren ticket increased the Jacksonian pluralities in nearly every state, including Clay-Webster strongholds in New England. In Pennsylvania the Antimasons displaced the National Republicans as the principal minority party; in Vermont the Antimasons temporarily took the state entirely out of National Republican hands. Only in Clay's own Kentucky did the voters withstand the national tide and turn in a National Republican majority.

Shortly after the presidential election of 1832, the Nullifiers of Calhoun's South Carolina, through a state legislature controlled by them, called a special state convention to issue an Ordinance of Nullification. This proclamation declared that the federal tariffs of 1828 and 1832 were to be considered null and void insofar as enforcement within South Carolina was concerned. Unionist Democrats in the state held a separate convention to condemn the ordinance. On the same day, Jackson issued a proclamation declaring the national government sovereign and indivisible. No state could refuse to obey the law, he declared, and no state could leave the Union.

Jackson submitted a Force Bill to Congress which permitted military measures if necessary to preserve federal interests in South Carolina. During the crisis Henry Clay offered a compromise, soon accepted by all sides, which provided for gradual reduction of all tariff duties to a for-revenue-only level in exchange for abandonment of the protectionist principle. The compromise also accepted a Force Bill that empowered the president to use armed forces to execute federal law in South Carolina. However, when South Carolina repealed its Ordinance of Nullification, it at the same time also nullified the Force Act. The compromise was little more than acknowledgment of a stalemate. Over the next three decades this issue would divide the Democratic party and propel the nation into civil war. Meanwhile, the opposition to Jackson added the appellation "King Andrew" to their cries of "executive usurpation."

Hardly had the dust settled when Jackson set off another

storm by removing the public funds from the Bank of the United States in September 1833. Nicholas Biddle, president of the bank, had labored prodigiously during the summer and fall to foster a Clay-Calhoun-Webster alliance. With the withdrawal of the bank deposits, Biddle redoubled his efforts in order to forestall any Webster-Jackson rapprochement that could have been in the making during the nullification crisis. As Jackson withdrew federal deposits from the National Bank, Nicholas Biddle countered with a systematic contraction of the bank's loans, aimed at precipitating economic distress and developing popular pressure for rechartering the bank. In New York, however, Democratic Governor Marcy established a system of state credit for those banks put under duress by Biddle's move.

At a Fourth Ward political meeting in Albany, attended by former Antimasons and National Republicans, Thurlow Weed, founding genius, successively, of the Antimason, Whig, and Republican parties, denounced "Marcy's Mortgage" and Jackson's fiscal policies. The meeting was one of many inaugurating the Whig party. During the midterm congressional and local elections of 1834 many anti-Jackson candidates referred to themselves as "Whigs" thereby suggesting an analogy between their own battle against "King Andrew" and that of the British Whigs against Kings George III and William IV.

As Jackson's second term drew to a somewhat uneasy close, he and his fellow-Democrats could nonetheless look back over the many solid and historic organizational achievements of their party. His Kitchen Cabinet and his travels were, in effect, the beginning of modern presidential campaigning, whistle-stops and all. The popular vote, mobilized by his party colleagues, enabled him to capture winning majorities in the electoral college and also enabled him to become the first president to function openly as a party leader. Finally, his role in the creation of the Democratic national convention added the organizational capstone to a national institution that survives to this day.

The larger Jacksonian contributions included the broadening of the mass party-in-the-electorate through new suffrage laws, the substitution of popular for state legislative selection of presidential electors, the crystallization of the two-party pattern nationally, and the incorporation of the mass electorate into the national policy process as an integral part of the search for consensus. The nature and extent of this contribution are summarized by Robert A. Dahl:

Jackson's presidency marks the effective end in this country of the classic identification of democratic rules with legislative supremacy. . . . Jackson . . . developed a new pattern of relationship, a new constitutional system, and since his day that system has largely prevailed, rather than the Jeffersonian, the Madisonian, or the Revolutionary. The Jacksonian system may be interpreted as asserting that:

1. Groups not effectively represented in the legislature or judiciary may be effectively represented by the executive.

2. The election process confers at least as much legitimacy on the executive's representativeness as on that of the legislature.

3. The President has perhaps a better claim to represent a national majority.

It is the growth of the third principle that, I believe, sets off the period after Jackson from that preceding it, for the idea that the elected executive might be the true representative of the majority was revolutionary in import.[9]

3

Broken Party, Broken Nation

DURING their first century as a political party, Democrats learned two fundamental operating lessons. The first pertained to their search for consensus, that is, "the consent of the governed." This search required a party open to the influx of newly politicized constituencies and capable of holding together vigorous and often extremely disagreeable factional groups. The second lesson, closely related to the first, concerned the construction of creative and effective organizational tools for soliciting and mobilizing the existing consensus. When the party's factions become irreconcilable and its organizational tools neglected, Democrats were likely to pay the price of defeat, and the nation to share in the cost.

States' Rights versus Union in the Van Buren Era

Differences among Democrats during the 1830s tended to magnify sectional issues. The strains between pro-Calhoun Nullifiers and pro-Jackson Unionists in South Carolina had repercussions throughout the South. Abolitionist positions on slavery began to win important adherents among northern Democrats and to aggravate the anxieties of southern Democrats. Political support for the annexation of new territories began to hinge mainly on whether a new territory lay in the free Northwest or the slaveholding Southwest. The Compromise of 1820 became unstuck and the slavery problem rode close upon the heels of the extending frontier.

As these issues became intense during his second term, Jackson straddled. Thus, when the question of annexing Texas came up in 1835, he delayed action until after the election of 1836. Vice

President Van Buren, who was the Democratic nominee for president in that election, could be thankful for the postponement, but his difficulties were hardly ended.

Unable to bring the anti-Jacksonians together behind a single national ticket, Nicholas Biddle and the *Intelligencer* advocated the strategy of running several regional leaders—Daniel Webster in New England, Hugh L. White in the South, William Henry Harrison in the West—strong enough to prevent a Democratic majority in the electoral college. Van Buren could be beaten in the House of Representatives, thought Biddle. Clay debated the prospects of his own candidacy for some time before he concluded that the popular tide was not with him, whereupon he fell in with the Biddle strategy.[1] With his perceptions of national political life so steeped in the roles of legislative opposition and congressional caucus, Clay probably felt that a stalemated House of Representatives might yet turn to him, its former Speaker, as its final choice. But the Whig strategy was to no avail. The Jacksonians swept Van Buren into office with decisive popular and electoral college majorities.

The winning coalitions that Van Buren had gathered on behalf of Jackson became increasingly difficult to hold together during his own tenure. This was particularly evident in the growing breach between the Albany Regency and the Richmond Junto. The Regency was based upon the state legislative party in Albany, New York, fanning out to allies in other Mid-Atlantic and New England states. It had served as the springboard of Van Buren's rise to power. The Junto, on the other hand, was the operating base of the "Virginia Dynasty"—Jefferson, Madison, and Monroe—that controlled the presidency from 1801 to 1825, and their successors. In addition to this breach, the Democratic party had been developing a new generation of astute professionals eager to gain influence in the presidential party; some of these became Van Buren's most ardent adversaries.

The Little Magician, however, was himself a professional politician not easily persuaded to retreat or retire. For Van Buren the creation of a national political party was essential and honorable work:

But knowing, as all men of sense know, that political parties are inseparable from free governments, and that in many and material respects they are highly useful to the country, I never could bring myself for my part to deprecate their existence. . . . The disposition to abuse power, so deeply planted in the human heart, can by no other means be more effectively

43

checked; and it has always struck me as more honorable and manly and more in harmony with the character of our People and of our Institutions to deal with the subject of Political Parties in a sincere and wiser spirit.[2]

In the Northeast and the West, the exertions of Van Buren and his allies had produced impressive Democratic state organizations. Federal patronage had been used with skill for purposes of party discipline. The *Globe,* as the official party newspaper, gave unity to party policy orientations and to party affairs generally. Van Buren was indefatigable in his personal contacts and correspondence. In keeping with this organizational thrust, Democrats, for a second time, turned to the national convention as a means for tightening party lines behind a single national ticket. To capture the initiative in a divided field, the national convention was held early, on May 20, 1835, in Baltimore. The purpose of the convention as a political instrument was stated clearly enough by its chairman, Andrew Stevenson of Virginia, former Speaker of the House of Representatives (1827 to 1834):

Efforts will no doubt be made to . . . put in jeopardy, and possibly defeat the election of a president by the people, in their primary colleges. . . . The democracy of the union have [*sic*] been forced to look to a national convention, as the best means of concentrating the popular will, and giving it effect in the approaching election. It is, in fact, the only defense against a minority president.[3]

Roll call showed 612 delegates present, representing twenty-two states. Most of this large number, however, were from Maryland, giving the convention more the character of a mass rally than a representative assembly. Van Buren received the presidential nomination without opposition. The Jackson-Van Buren managers then proposed Richard M. Johnson of Kentucky, hero of the Indian wars of the West, as vice president. The South, particularly Virginia, had strong objections. To smooth Johnson's way, the Jackson-Van Buren managers attempted to change the nominating rule from a special two-thirds to a simple majority. The first of a century-long series of attempts to repeal the two-thirds rule was defeated. Johnson was nevertheless nominated by a bare two-thirds and at the cost of Virginia's support. Virginia refused to pledge itself to campaign for the full national ticket. Virginia, in fact, after the convention, nominated its own vice-presidential candidate, John Tyler.

Possibly the greatest "adversary" of President Van Buren was the Panic of 1837. Economic depression dominated his entire administration. The panic was preceded by speculation in canal and land investments, crop failures, and unsettled farm credit arrangements. Jackson's distribution of public funds—previously deposited in the National Bank—among state banks had, unfortunately, encouraged speculation. Van Buren responded to the crisis with a plan to establish an independent treasury system, but this was resisted in the House of Representatives. Senators Thomas Hart Benton and Silas Wright were able to muster enough votes to pass the Independent Treasury Bill through the upper house, 26 to 20. However, the crack in the Democratic lines soon became intense and obvious. In the House, a combination of Whigs and conservative Democrats succeeded in tabling the bill, 119 to 107. This defeat weakened the Van Buren Democrats for the duration of that Congress. The nation's economy never recovered while Van Buren was in office.

Slavery was another deepening wedge in the Democratic ranks, made deeper by the opposition party. John Quincy Adams, former president-turned-congressman, presented a petition on December 12, 1837, calling for the abolition of slavery in the District of Columbia. Six days later the southern members walked out en masse to deliberate upon their line of conduct.

In the Senate, Calhoun introduced a series of resolutions defining the character of the federal system and the rights of the "slave states" within it. This included the right to possess slave property as a local matter guaranteed under the Constitution. One Calhoun resolution placed the question of abolishing slavery in the District of Columbia and the territory of Florida (the only slave territory at the time) into the hands of Congress, but concluded by forbidding such abolition for "high expedient reasons." Thus, Calhoun sought to avoid the slavery issue by making an affirmation of congressional prerogative.

Southern leaders pressed Van Buren for his views. He took the position that a state had jurisdiction over slavery only within its own boundaries and that the Constitution did not give Congress the power to interfere either in the states or in the District of Columbia. Thereupon, to reduce the divisiveness of the slavery question, nearly all Democrats—Van Buren and Calhoun supporters alike—united to defeat the Adams petition for the abolition of slavery in the District of Columbia.

45

Another important attack on Van Buren's prestige came with the problem of electing a Speaker of the House in 1839. The House divided between 119 Democrats and 118 opposition members, with 5 members from New Jersey unable to be seated because of seating contests. The chief candidates were John Bell of Tennessee from the Whig side, and George W. Jones of Virginia for the Van Buren men. Neither Bell nor Jones could win the whole vote of their respective parties. Nor could the Calhoun man—Dixon H. Lewis of Alabama—get all the Democratic votes. In the end, Whigs and conservative Democrats united on Robert M. T. Hunter and elected him, 119 to 55 for Jones, 24 for Keim of Pennsylvania, and 34 votes spread among ten other candidates. Van Buren's influence sagged even more as the third Democratic-Republican National Convention, the convention that simplified the party's name to "Democratic," prepared to meet on May 5, 1840.

Titular Leader and Dark Horse

Van Buren characteristically began preparing for 1840 sometime before the party conventions. On February 8, 1840, Silas Wright received from Van Buren a draft of "hints" which contained 103 handwritten pages. This collection included principles upon which the party should run, organization strategies for the various states, and other guidelines. Van Buren evidently felt that his greatest opponent was fraud in the elections. This alluded to the early manifestations of urban machine practices that were to disturb the electoral process more seriously later in the nineteenth century. He strongly urged organization within the Democratic Party to offset the frauds of the opposition.[4]

Administration managers worked diligently to keep the factional ferment to a minimum. Preferring not to risk divisions on the floor of the national convention, the Van Buren men moved that a committee of one representative from each state consider the subject of nominations. This committee reported that, first, no opposition to Van Buren's renomination had been found, and, second, it had been agreed that no single vice-presidential candidate be chosen. The committee's report was adopted by simple majority circumventing the two-thirds rule, and this constituted the entire nominating procedure. Three Democratic vice-presidential candidates subsequently entered the field: Vice President Richard Johnson, Littleton W. Tazewell of Virginia, and James K. Polk of Tennessee.

As the 1840 presidential election approached, the new Whig party gathered itself under the guidance of Thurlow Weed of New York, a talented politician. The Whigs put the perennial Henry Clay's aspirations aside, nominated General Harrison, the hero of Tippecanoe, and enlisted John Tyler, an erstwhile Richmond Junto Democrat, as his vice-presidential companion. The singing and marching "Tippecanoe and Tyler, too" campaign defeated Van Buren by a relatively close margin of 147,000 votes in 2,404,000 cast. This election inaugurated an era of closely competitive presidential races.

Beaten, Van Buren nevertheless continued to see himself as his party's leader. He therefore assumed the responsibilities of "titular" leadership, the first Democratic presidential nominee to do so. He saw party organization as the greatest need of a party in defeat.[5] Lindenwald, Van Buren's home in New York, became something of a national party headquarters as plans for assisting Democrats in various key local elections in 1841 and in the congressional elections of 1842 proceeded apace. Democratic gains in these elections were generally credited to these efforts.

A personal comeback for Van Buren within the Democratic party, however, was not in the cards. President Harrison's death elevated to the presidency a former states' rights Democrat devoted to the permanent retirement of such nationalists as Henry Clay in the Whig party and Martin Van Buren in the Democratic. As president, John Tyler, an ambiguous figure in most history books, proved himself a match for the two principal party leaders of his day, Clay and Van Buren. In devoting himself to achieving the retirement of those two men from presidential politics, Tyler had the assistance of another little known giant of American party politics, Senator Robert J. Walker, the "Wizard of Mississippi." Son of a Supreme Court justice, Walker migrated to Mississippi in 1826 to practice law. Within a half-dozen years, he became leader of the Jacksonians there, Mississippi's United States senator, and spokesman for the Southwest in congressional politics. Walker, in alliance with Calhoun, devised the strategy for denying Van Buren a renomination at the 1844 convention. Their winning issue was the question of immediate annexation of Texas.

Texans had been pressing for annexation to the United States, and President Tyler pursued negotiations eagerly. Tyler had also brought Calhoun into his cabinet as secretary of state, and it was Calhoun who signed the treaty with the prospective slave state on

April 12, 1844, subject to Senate approval. Andrew Jackson, Robert Walker, and southerners generally sought immediate admission. Clay, Webster, and other nationalists resisted the admission of another slave state to the Union not only on abolitionist grounds but also because the balance of power between North and South in the Congress and the electoral college would be threatened. Annexation thus became *the* political issue of spring 1844. As titular leader of his party, Van Buren was, of course, expected to speak out on the issue. When he was slow in doing so, Congressman W. H. Hammet of Mississippi, a Democrat, asked him publicly to reveal his position. On April 27, Van Buren published a reply in the *Globe*. The annexation of Texas was clearly constitutional, he said, but "inexpedient" at this time on grounds that it could lead to war with Mexico. He also expressed concern with early annexation as a further provocation of sectional bitterness between North and South. Southern enthusiasm for Van Buren's renomination quickly cooled.

The array of candidates for the Democratic presidential nomination in 1844 was impressive. The Van Buren supporters acknowledged no alternative to the party's former president and current titular leader. Calhoun had given indications in 1841 that he would seek the nomination, but withdrew by mid-1844. Tyler, as the incumbent president, was well situated but held the loyalty of only a small number of Democratic state leaders, enough, however, to be pivotal at the national convention. Vice President Johnson, Lewis Cass of Michigan, and James C. Buchanan of Pennsylvania were other prospective contenders. Border state Democrats, straddling the annexation issue as best they could, were led by Cave Johnson of Tennessee, who was also managing the only campaign for the *vice-presidential* nomination. His candidate was Tennessee's Governor James K. Polk, who had been one of the three Democratic vice-presidential candidates running with Van Buren in 1840.

The Van Buren forces came to the convention in strength; fourteen state conventions, four congressional district conventions, and one state legislative caucus had instructed their delegates to support the former president for a third nomination. These committed votes came to 159, which was 18 short of the two-thirds needed to nominate, that is, if the two-thirds rule (originally designed to eliminate Van Buren's opponents in 1832) were again adopted.

Senator Walker moved readoption of the two-thirds rule as soon as the delegates convened. Debate raged for two days. On the roll call, the two-thirds rule was readopted, 148 to 118. The critical votes were Virginia's 17. George C. Dromgoole, head of the Virginia delegation, Speaker of the House of Representatives, and a Van Buren supporter of long standing, was the principal decision-maker in the important vote and clearly under pressure from Walker and his fellow-Virginian, President Tyler. Virginia withdrew from the floor of the convention to deliberate. The delegation cast its decisive ballot at the end of the roll call. The possibility of a renomination for the party's first titular leader ended there. Twenty-nine of the 159 votes pledged to Van Buren subsequently failed to vote for him, but 16 uninstructed delegates did support him, for a net loss of 13. Van Buren received 146 votes on the first ballot, 31 votes short of the necessary two-thirds.

The Walker-Dromgoole maneuver created a stalemate for seven nominating ballots. The supporters of Johnson, Cass, and Buchanan were unable to unite among themselves, nor was any one of them able to draw off any of the Van Buren votes. Polk's name was added to the candidate roster on the eighth ballot, most of his 44 votes coming from the Van Buren wing of the Massachusetts delegation. A bandwagon moved on the ninth ballot at the end of which Polk was nominated amid an uproarious ovation. The Democratic National Convention proved itself an institution capable of producing a special solution to a stalemate among its factions.

In retiring Van Buren and achieving the nomination of Polk, whose name was not even before the convention when it opened and who clearly was the second choice of many and a compromise candidate in the end, Democrats, under the leadership of Senator Walker, created a new form in American party history: the "dark horse" candidate. Polk was the first of many to come. The dark horse has proved to be a distinctive approach to factional stalemates in the nominating process. In sharply contested nominating conventions, the dark horse solution is always the hope of minor candidates who have carefully avoided offending major factional constituencies but who are well enough known among party professionals to be their second or third preference after their own candidate. The principal consideration in dark horse situations is the achievement of the intraparty consensus that is necessary before an effective search for the consensus in the presidential party-in-the-electorate can be launched.

As Senator Walker and President Tyler realized, Polk's nomination would be meaningless without mounting an effective campaign against Clay and the Whigs. Hence, promptly after Polk's nomination, Walker moved to reconcile the Van Buren forces. He personally proposed that Silas Wright of New York, a close associate of Van Buren, be nominated for vice president. Wright declined, and second place on the ticket went to Walker's brother-in-law, George M. Dallas of Pennsylvania.

President Tyler, without a chance for receiving the regular Democratic nomination himself, was at all times in the background and observed the results with satisfaction. Having removed Van Buren, he next targeted Clay, who had just received the Whig nomination. Tyler's principal strategist and field director was again Senator Walker, who now managed the Polk campaign with outstanding success.

At the end of the Democratic convention, on Congressman Dromgoole's motion, a central committee of fifteen was authorized.[6] This number left more than a third of the states unrepresented. The appointment of members to the central committee, to be resident in Washington, was left to a caucus of Democratic members of Congress, but no one was willing to call the caucus for fear of alienating those who would remain uninvited and unrepresented.[7] Finally, Walker assumed the initiative and organized the central committee.

Throughout June, July, and August, Walker labored prodigiously writing the address (as the platform was then called) of the Democratic convention to the people of the United States, serving as go-between in the negotiations to bring President Tyler's supporters behind Polk, and convincing Tyler and Calhoun newspapers to support the Polk-Dallas ticket. Walker was chosen chairman of the central committee, probably during June. He expected to serve in that capacity only temporarily: "I was chosen chairman, and consented to remain here [Washington] and discharge the duties of that office, until relieved by a substitute who was expected to take my place during the present month [August], and enable me before the close of August to return to Mississippi. In this expectation I have been disappointed."[8]

Sometimes referred to as the first Democratic national committee chairman, Walker was actually chairman of a *central* committee on which less than two-thirds of the states in the Union were represented.[9] He used the central committee to draw together many factional elements for the Democratic campaign. He asked Polk for a letter "to use discreetly" to win the support of the conservative Democrats whose votes would influence results in Maine, Connecticut, New York, and New Jersey.[10] President Tyler expressed the hope that his "friends"—some 150,000 of them—would be treated as equals in the event that Polk should be elected. In response, Walker asked Andrew Jackson and Polk for letters "of a character to put Tyler's friends at perfect ease."[11] Polk made pledges with respect to Tyler's "friends." The *Globe* ended its campaign against Tyler. Tyler publicly withdrew his own candidacy. The Calhoun press fell in behind the Polk-Dallas ticket. Thus, Walker successfully concluded all of the requirements of coalition-building.

The "address to the people" was another delicate task. A misstep on the annexation issue could be fatal. To please both the North and the South, Walker prepared two versions of the same address. One version, entitled "The South in Danger," seemed to put the Democratic party on record favoring the extension of slavery into Texas. This version was widely distributed in the South. The second version, substantially the same as the first but with a few key phrases altered, was distributed in northern constituencies. This distribution took place early in October. Communication in that day was too slow for prompt comparisons between the two versions. The differences never reached the attention of most voters until after the November elections. The post-election uproar about the deception was lost in the clamor about Polk's victory over Clay.[12]

Hoping to bring the party together to make a strong and stable administration, Polk staffed his cabinet with men experienced in party matters: James Buchanan in the State Department, Robert J. Walker in Treasury, William L. Marcy in War, George Bancroft in Navy, John Y. Mason as Attorney General, and his pre-nomination manager, Cave Johnson, as Postmaster General, an increasingly powerful patronage position. Walker and Johnson had guided the national convention of 1844 in its unprecedented course. Mason's colleagues in the Virginia delegation had put an end to the Van Buren candidacy. Bancroft's wing of the party in Massachusetts was responsible for starting the bandwagon to Polk. Marcy and Buchanan represented what had become the two most powerful states in the electoral college, New York and Pennsylvania.

By the 1840s and early 1850s, federal job patronage had become a major prize and source of "muscle" for the national parties. Hence, President Tyler's numerous (150,000) "friends." Overall, the patronage is estimated to have been worth over $50 million (in 1850 dollars).[13] Postmaster General Cave Johnson, therefore, promptly engaged himself in removing or accepting the resignations of eleven thousand of the fourteen thousand postmasters. This eleven-in-fourteen ratio compared with the one-in-eight removals under Andrew Jackson.[14]

The economic resources of the federal government were also expanding dramatically in size and influence, particularly with respect to the letting of contracts for supplies to be used in frontier policing and, later, in the Mexican War. New lands, acquired in the Mexican War, and the discovery of gold in California added to the resources controlled by party leaders in the presidency.

With a powerhouse of politicians surrounding him, President Polk made an unfortunate categorical commitment to serve only one term. Consequently, every policy decision of his lame-duck administration was fraught with implications for the succession. "I am left without any certain or reliable support in Congress, and especially in the Senate. Each leader looks to his own advancement more than he does to the success of my measures."[15] But there were successes for the coalition that Walker built. For example, to handle the public monies in the Jackson-Van Buren tradition, the Polk administration, under the guiding hand of Secretary Walker, restored the independent treasury. To start the tariff rate down, for years a Calhoun objective, a Walker-designed tariff law was enacted. Annexationists, North and South, were delighted by the settlement reached with the British bringing Oregon under American jurisdiction. The Oregon settlement stretched American boundaries to the Pacific for the first time and added a free territory. The war with Mexico put over $100 million in military spending into circulation and acquired all of the land from the Rio Grande through New Mexico to upper California.

By most political standards, the Polk administration would be regarded as activist and eminently successful. The acquisition of so much new territory, however, revived and aggravated the issue of extension of slavery. Democrats began to call each other "Barnburner" (like the Dutch farmer, so opposed to slavery as to be willing to burn the barn in order to rid it of rats) and "Hunkers" (whose hunger, or "hunker," for officeholding was so intense as to compel them to cooperate with slaveholders).

There was hardly an issue before the country that did not accentuate the differences between northern and southern Democrats. The northerners saw the Mexican War as threatening to bring more slave states into the Union. The southerners saw Oregon as another antislave state. Even raising the funds for the conduct of the Mexican War had turned out to be a great juggle between northern and southern financial centers, although not beyond the talents of Secretary of the Treasury Walker. Walker turned for assistance to the head of the Rothschild banking firm in New York, August Belmont, and William W. Corcoran, a Washington financier. Belmont, a nephew-in-law to John Slidell of Louisiana, was able to win the cooperation of southern bankers. Belmont in the North and Slidell in the South later worked together for Buchanan's election in 1856. (Slidell eventually became a leader of the secession movement. Belmont was Democratic national chairman from 1860 to 1872 and helped bring northern Democrats behind President Lincoln's war effort.)

As the Democratic National Convention of 1848 approached, Gideon Welles of Connecticut set down an estimate of the candidate situation in a memorandum to himself. Welles thought Cass of Michigan was in the lead with Levi Woodbury of New Hampshire next and Buchanan trailing, notwithstanding the optimism of the last's followers. Welles did not mention Silas Wright, probably because New York was divided to the point of sending two delegations—the antislavery Barnburners and the pro-South Hunkers. "The decision in the New York case and that of the two-thirds rule will be likely to affect the result." Then, alluding to the organization-conscious Polk leadership, Welles continued:

Unfortunately, we have no great and master minds which draw to them general confidence, and give to things a right direction. Nor have we any absorbing questions generating a wholesome distinction or correct party principles. The administration has endeavored to acquire for itself a strong party character, but has failed to create a party attachment. It has trusted too much to organization, and [has] not [been] sufficiently mindful of principles.[16]

In short, a party consensus in 1848 would be difficult to reach.

Uneasy Coalitions, 1848–1852

On January 24, 1848, a caucus of Democratic senators and representatives, with Senator Sam Houston of Texas as chairman, set the time and place of the convention call. Congress was still influential in presidential politics. At the convention, Senator Jesse D. Bright of Indiana, the leading parliamentarian in the Senate and a trusted ally of President Polk, provided floor leadership, particularly on matters of agenda, parliamentary procedure, and organization. Assisting Bright was Benjamin F. Hallett, former Antimason leader who was now chairman of the Massachusetts Democratic state committee and a spokesman for most of the New England delegations.

The convention readopted the two-thirds rule, which gave some candidates hope of stopping Cass. Both New York delegations were seated and required to share that state's vote. The first nominating ballot gave Cass 125, Woodbury, 58, Buchanan 55, and Dallas 3. Hallett led the New England swing from Woodbury to Cass. Buchanan supporters, willing to await another opportunity, joined the Cass parade. The nomination went to Cass on the fourth ballot. The platform committee's northern majority, under Hallett's guidance, wrote a plank on the slavery-abolition issue that was conciliatory to the South. The party's leaders were still trying to solve that problem as an exercise in language.

Senator Bright, now Polk's personal representative at the convention, then moved the creation of a national committee, the first of its kind. The national committee was to be a permanent standing committee to serve as an organic link between conventions. He also recommended the selection of the first Democratic national chairman, Benjamin F. Hallett. From the point of view of regional representation in the national organization, Hallett contributed to an overall balance. The nominees came from the Northwest and the Southwest, Hallett from New England, the two national committee secretaries from the Middle Atlantic area and the South.

Northerners and southerners alike had been rushing to settle the West, and with them went the fundamental economic issue: should the economy of the new territories and states be built on a foundation of slave or free labor? Hanging heavily upon this issue was the future influence of the Democratic South upon the presidency and Congress. In the latter, the South was already becoming a permanent minority.

The Democratic nominee, Senator Cass, and National Chairman Hallett were Hunkers, that is, conciliatory to the southern positions on the slavery issue. Both men, together with William R. King of Alabama, Stephen A. Douglas of Illinois, James Buchanan of Pennsylvania, and Levi Woodbury of New Hampshire, did their utmost to keep the party on a middle course. On the other hand, the abolitionist and free-soil wing was being led by such experienced politicians as former President Van Buren, his son John, Thomas Hart Benton, David Wilmot, and Francis P. Blair. At the other extreme were states' righters led by Robert M. T. Hunter and John Y. Mason of Virginia, Jefferson Davis, and others.

Van Buren, still a power in New York, felt that the slavery issue could no longer be straddled. He led a substantial Barnburner following into a new Free Soil party, whose presidential nomination he accepted. The defection cost the Democrats the election. The 300,000 votes he received were enough to deny to the Democrats the electoral votes of New York, Massachusetts, and Pennsylvania. The election put a Mexican War hero, General Zachary Taylor, into the White House.

Thus began a critical decade which, as the Whig party disintegrated, found the Union's future resting heavily in the hands of divided Democrats. It was an era in which the Democratic presidential candidates were "northerners with southern principles." Those who became president—Franklin Pierce and James Buchanan—were so cross-pressured by sectionalism that their administrations have often been evaluated as models of inertia and straddling. Their lack of motion, however, reflected the stalemate within the nation. They and their Democratic colleagues managed to hold the nation together one decade longer than might have been expected.

Most of the partisan political action during the 1850s took place in Congress, precipitated by the territorial gains of the Mexican War and the discovery of gold in California. Talk of secession now became serious among southern Whigs and southern Democrats in states from South Carolina to Mississippi. California was asking for admission as a free state. New Mexico was ready for territorial government. Abolitionists were again demanding the end of the slave trade in the District of Columbia. Southern slaveholders were insisting upon a more severe fugitive slave law. Debate in Congress on these issues occupied the attention of the nation for most of 1850 and brought forth the best oratorical efforts of the political giants of that day: Calhoun, Clay, Webster, Benton, Cass, Douglas, Seward, and others.

In a message to Congress, President Taylor recommended the admission of California and New Mexico under conditions that would allow each to make its own determination whether or not to admit slavery. This came to be known as "the President's Plan." Since the legislatures of the two territories were predominantly antislavery, the President's Plan would have tipped the balance of power in Congress in favor of the free states. The President's Plan had the support of Seward of New York and most northern Whigs. It provoked hot words from southern Democrats and southern Whigs. Men on both sides of the issue awaited a statement from Henry Clay, who was once again back in the Senate.

Clay offered a grand compromise in the tradition of his Compromise of 1820. To the North he offered: California free of slavery and the abolition of the slave trade in the District of Columbia. To the South he offered: territorial governments in New Mexico and Utah, leaving the slavery question to the future; tighter federal enforcement of the fugitive slave laws; and a generous cash settlement in the Texas-New Mexico boundary dispute. Vice President Fillmore, Webster, and the southern Whigs, joined by such Democrats as Senator Stephen A. Douglas of Illinois, supported the Clay Compromise. Congress seemed to favor Clay's Compromise over the President's Plan but feared the prospect of a presidential veto.

In the midst of it all, President Taylor died, putting Vice President Millard Fillmore, a Whig of narrow vision and nativist tendencies, into power. Whig factions became so extreme on the Clay compromise proposals that only the best efforts of a leading Democrat, Senator Stephen A. Douglas, carried the Compromise of 1850 through Congress. However, none of the factions was long satisfied with the deal. The Whigs, as a political party, never survived the strain of the slavery issue, a warning to the equally torn Democrats.

Party Division and National Disaster

In many localities, Democratic organizations were disappearing or drifting into a movement calling for a new "Union party" willing to defend the Compromise of 1850. National Democratic leaders, on the other hand, sought a truly "national" candidate for the presidency. At the 1852 national convention a three-way deadlock developed among Cass, Buchanan, and Douglas and lasted for thirty-four ballots. Among Buchanan's supporters were leading southerners. Douglas spoke for the Northwest. Following dark horse practice, a new name—General Franklin Pierce, whose political advancement was largely by virtue of the friends he made during the Mexican War—was introduced. Pierce was nominated on the forty-ninth ballot, retiring Cass and postponing the aspirations of Buchanan and Douglas for future years. Again, unity brought electoral success to the party.

The Pierce administration, however, was almost totally immobilized by the near-equal pressures of northern and southern Democrats. The impulse of every Democratic politician was to retreat from or somehow conciliate the issue of slavery. In this spirit, Senator Douglas introduced a bill into Congress authorizing the organization of the Nebraska territory, without making reference to slavery. Before the bill could pass, however, Congress converted it into an authorization for *two* territories, Kansas and Nebraska, each to decide according to the principle of "squatter sovereignty," that is, local option, whether it would be free or slave.

Northern Democrats, northern Whigs, northern "Know-Nothings," and the Free Soil party were outraged by the Kansas-Nebraska Act. They began to promote a mass migration of settlers from the East aimed at saving at least Kansas from slavery. Southerners started a countermigration. Local civil war raged within the territory. "Bleeding Kansas" put President Pierce and Senator Douglas out of the presidential running for 1856.

Another three-way battle developed at the 1856 national convention. John Slidell, with the help of August Belmont, led the Buchanan forces with great skill to defeat a Pierce-Douglas alliance on a test vote. On the sixteenth ballot, Buchanan had 168 and Douglas 122 votes, with Buchanan still short of the necessary two-thirds. At this point, Douglas, twenty-two years Buchanan's junior, withdrew his name. Slidell's victory was capped by the addition of a young southerner, John C. Breckinridge, to the ticket.

Buchanan was elected with only five of the sixteen "free" states supporting him; fourteen of the fifteen "slave" states, on the other hand, gave him their electoral votes. Having exercised such influence in the 1856 convention and election, Slidell and other southerners, abetted by a friendly president, were not likely to concede party leadership to Douglas four years later.

Senator Slidell was a dominant influence in the Buchanan administration. The southern view was further reinforced by the Dred Scott decision, in which the extreme southern position on slave property was endorsed by the Supreme Court. The Constitution recognized slave property, said the Court, and Congress had no right to discriminate against the property, slave or otherwise, of citizens simply because that property happens to be in a territory.

President Buchanan, anticipating the admission of Kansas under extremely difficult conditions, appointed politically seasoned Robert J. Walker as its governor. Through a ruse, a draft constitution was written locally at LeCompton, Kansas, which protected

57

slave property already in that territory. Buchanan and Walker urged upon Congress the admission of Kansas under this LeCompton constitution, but were overridden by the House. During this debate, Douglas broke with President Buchanan, thereby clearly establishing himself as the leader of the antislavery wing of the party.

The pace and intensity of the struggle over the slavery issue became grim by 1858. Slidell tried to read Douglas out of the party, urging the administration to withdraw patronage from Douglas supporters in Illinois. Such pressure notwithstanding, Douglas, in his famous debates with Abraham Lincoln, asserted his Freeport Doctrine, denying that Congress had power to force slavery upon a territory against the will of its people.

Meanwhile, the Republican party was emerging from the shambles left by the Whigs and adopted a hard antislavery position. Hinton Helper published *The Impending Crisis,* showing how the underprivileged whites of the South were also victims of slavery. John Brown made his futile attempt to arm the slaves. The Thirty-sixth Congress (1859–1860) met amid scenes of tumult. On the first day of the session a resolution was proposed in the House of Representatives declaring anyone sympathetic to the views of Helper as unfit to be Speaker. Republican John Sherman of Ohio, a principal candidate for Speaker, had been one of several members who had signed an endorsement of Helper's book. Debaters engaged in personal invective. The galleries participated loudly in the excitement. Observers speculated how many and which of the members were armed. The extremists were the loudest voices.

The Slidell-Douglas feud moved directly into the 1860 Democratic National Convention at Charleston. During the proceedings, the margins of factional victory were narrow and costly. A one-vote margin in the national committee put a Douglas man into the temporary chairmanship, but a Slidell man, Caleb Cushing, won the permanent chairmanship. The Douglas forces won a modification of the unit rule for delegation balloting, but Slidell's proposal for completing the platform before the nomination carried in another debate. Out of the southern-dominated platform committee came a majority report promising congressional protection of slave property. The Douglas men wrote the principal minority report reiterating the squatter sovereignty position. The Buchanan delegates and the more extreme southerners joined forces to send both reports back to committee, 152 to 151.

The platform committee, with great but belated candor, drafted a statement acknowledging publicly that a difference of opinion existed within the party with respect to slavery. On the floor of the convention, this version, a revision of the Douglas minority report, carried, 165–138. The Douglas manager rose to make a peace offer, but a southern walkout had already begun, Alabama in the lead. The seceders included most of Mississippi, Louisiana, South Carolina, Florida, and Texas delegations, who immediately organized their own Constitutional Democratic National Convention.

Chairman Cushing soon after ruled that the two-thirds needed to nominate would have to be based upon the full 303 votes originally sent to the convention rather than the 252 delegates remaining after the walkout. After fifty-seven ballots, Douglas was still short of the necessary 202 votes. The weary convention adjourned, to meet in Baltimore six weeks later.

During those weeks a great struggle for moral and numerical advantage took place in Congress. Jefferson Davis repeated the demand of the southern extremists for a "Congressional Slave Code." Douglas argued that only a majority at the national convention and not a minority in the Senate could properly prescribe what would be the test of party loyalty.

At Baltimore the decisive vote was on the credentials committee report. The Douglas men were ready to readmit all of the bolters except those from former Vice President King's Alabama and Slidell's Louisiana. This was upheld in a 199–150 floor vote. The exclusion of Alabama and Louisiana prompted the Virginia delegation to head the bolters. Departing Democrats included the delegates from North Carolina, Tennessee, California, Oregon, most of Maryland, most of Kentucky, Missouri, and Arkansas. With them went Permanent Chairman Cushing.

A "Seceders" convention, with Cushing in the chair, composed itself of some 230 delegates, 115 of whom had been among the membership of the original convention. Of these, approximately 58 were Buchanan appointees. Breckinridge became the nominee of the southern Democrats. In the southern view, the Breckinridge candidacy was launched from a position of great strength. He was, after all, the incumbent vice president and had the support of the president and the largest number of normally Democratic states. Douglas, on the other hand, had to face the new Republican party in the Northeast and the Midwest.

In the regular Democratic National Convention, Douglas prevailed. From the Douglas point of view, two decades of compromise on the slavery issue had given the southerners a disproportionate influence in the presidential party. If the southerners would not accept Douglas, to whom they would have access in the presidency, they might get an inaccessible antislavery Republican like Lincoln. Miscalculation followed misperception. Although moderates on both sides spent most of the campaign months trying to negotiate reconciliation or combined electoral slates, the extremists prevailed.

Lincoln's election promptly generated talk of southern secession. Head of a repudiated party, President Buchanan could do little to restrain his southern colleagues. As a president-elect without official power, Lincoln, in the four months between election and inauguration, could do nothing to head off catastrophe. The situation was ideal for extremist maneuvers, and these took place soon enough with the firing on Fort Sumter.

Thus, the Democratic party's inability or unwillingness to use the available "method of numbers" in its nominating process in order to find some basis for intraparty consensus led to electoral and military outcomes that plunged the nation into a devastating civil war. The nation's political party institutions were not yet strong or stable enough to surmount the bitter ideological, economic, and cultural differences between North and South.

4

Partisan War
and the Liquidation of
Reconstruction

AS the 1850s came to their tragic close, the Whig party disappeared, northern and southern Democrats tore their party in two, and a sectional Republican party was created out of Whig, Free Soil, and abolitionist remnants. The nation, its consensus-measuring institutions incapacitated, floundered into civil war. Party alignments and coalitions were confused and almost meaningless for the twelve years from 1860 to 1872.

The struggles that took place in Congress may have been less bloody than those on the battlefields but were hardly less intense. Republicans split into radical and conservative factions. The Radicals gave no quarter to Lincoln, conservative fellow-partisans, or Democrats as they mounted their campaigns to exclude the postwar South from the political process, impeach Andrew Johnson and thereby capture the presidency, and keep the Democratic party divided and disabled. The disputed Hayes-Tilden election of 1876 brought these developments to a climax that verged upon civil war. Democrats backed away from the "method of violence" and gave up their claim to the presidency in 1876 in exchange for Republican promises to liquidate the oppressive Reconstruction policies inaugurated by the Radicals. Overall, the Democratic party's search for consensus during the generation from 1860 to 1880 was a series of failures, and, as a consequence, so was the nation's.

War Democrats versus Peace Democrats

From 1829 to 1859 Congressional Democrats held majorities, often very large ones, in twelve of fifteen sessions of the House of

Representatives. However, probably because the nation's rapid physical expansion brought so many new and inexperienced members into the House and because the oldest and most influential party leaders were in the Senate, the party-in-the-House had relatively minor impact on national politics during these decades. In the Senate, on the other hand, while the size of Democratic majorities in thirteen of the fifteen sessions was somewhat smaller, dramatic and effective political personalities were decidedly more numerous. Between 1840 and 1860, the main political scenes were played in the Senate, where the great debates on the federal system, slavery, and executive-legislative powers were conducted and great compromises were hammered out.

From 1860 to 1876, however, party labels and loyalties in both houses of Congress were in profound disarray. Perhaps the most cohesive force in the legislative process was the Radical Republican faction. Its influence was to be felt for decades. Radicals hamstrung Lincoln's conduct of the war, demanding, among other things, the appointment of Republican generals. They forged the Reconstruction policies that kept the South incapacitated for generations and generated the white backlash that left blacks electorally powerless until the civil rights movement of the 1950s and 1960s. The Radicals also brought General Ulysses S. Grant to the presidency from 1869 to 1877. Calling themselves "Stalwarts," they surrounded Grant with a Senate cabal that directed his policies and eventually corrupted his administration. In achieving all this, the Radicals often had the deliberate or unwitting help of individuals from one or another of the other fragmented parties: former Whigs, former Free-Soilers, abolitionists, and some Democrats, particularly those in the predominantly midwestern faction known as "Peace Democrats."

With the departure of the South from the Union in 1861, the Democratic presidential party was deprived of some hundred usually reliable electoral college votes. Fully half of the party's popular vote had been in the southern states, and these were lost with secession. If the party had any future at all, it rested upon three clusters of competitive two-party states: New York and New Jersey in the East, Ohio, Illinois, and Indiana in the Midwest, and California and Oregon in the West. The biggest were New York (35 votes) and Ohio (23 votes). Those two states, however, became opposite poles in a wartime factionalism within the party: "War Democrats" versus "Peace Democrats."

The unexpected death of Stephen A. Douglas in 1861 left northeastern and western Democrats leaderless and at the point of following the Whig party into limbo. The western and eastern wings had been held together by Douglas (Illinois) and National Chairman Belmont (New York), respectively. With Douglas gone, formal leadership devolved upon Chairman Belmont, who promptly placed war Democrats behind Lincoln's efforts to preserve the Union. Meanwhile Peace Democrats, including Breckinridge and Bell supporters of the states' rights position, began to look for leadership from Mayor Fernando Wood of New York and Congressman Clement L. Vallandigham of Ohio. Taking advantage of the usually close margins of New York's election outcomes, elements in Tammany Hall, including Wood, established a tradition of opposition to the rest of the party within New York State, a threat to state and national Democratic candidates that frequently resulted in deals favorable to Tammany.

A member of the House of Representatives and a manager of the Douglas presidential campaign, Vallandigham saw himself as the successor to the mantle of the deceased "Little Giant." In Congress he devoted much time in search of a compromise for the sectional conflict. His own plan, Calhounian in concept, was premised upon a division of the nation into four sections. A majority of the electoral college votes in *each* of the four sections would be necessary to elect a president. Certain laws could be passed only with the assent of the senators of each section. Secession would be a legal right, but only with the consent of all the state legislatures of a section.

The Vallandigham plan for a new constitutional "method of numbers" to end the violence of the Civil War never caught on. By 1863 many of the more extreme Peace Democrats, or "Copperheads" as the Republicans called them, were resorting to secret organization in an effort to supplement or replace the regular party machinery. The Knights of the Golden Circle and similar societies evolved into the Order of American Knights, and, subsequently, into the Sons of Liberty. These clandestine political societies maintained military subsidiaries. The judge advocate general of the United States reported that some 340,000 of their half million members were persons trained for military service. The southern press and some of the South's military leaders sympathetically suggested a separate "Northwest Confederacy." War Democrats and Unionists in the Northwest countered with clubs called "Loyal Leagues."

Peace Democrats were not alone in their efforts to bring about a negotiated peace. The British and the French, with substantial economic interest in both the North and South, maintained various types of pressure in order to end the devastation of the Civil War. Democratic National Chairman Belmont, a War Democrat, offered President Lincoln specific proposals for a negotiated peace, recommending general amnesty for political offenses, a national constitutional convention to reconstruct the federal compact, and review of the constitutionality of slave property-holding. Belmont proposed federal assumption of both northern and southern war debts, a plan similar to Lincoln's, in which all Americans would participate in rebuilding the southern battlegrounds.

Belmont also suggested that a large national standing army and navy be maintained after the cessation of hostilities. At the time of the attack upon Fort Sumter, fully nine-tenths of the federal army was in the Midwest and on the frontiers of the Far West; only about a thousand troops were stationed around the District of Columbia, an easy prey. Only New York and Massachusetts *state* militias in the North and Virginia and Louisiana *state* militias in the South could, in 1861, be considered equipped and manned for combat. As a consequence, southern extremists, pressing for military action, had reasonable grounds for believing they had a better-than-even chance of winning. What the southern extremists did not anticipate was Lincoln's and the North's willingness to pay a very high price for the preservation of the Union. Belmont's proposal, implemented in the postwar period, was important for the political integration of the United States and possibly a factor in preventing the outbreak of another civil war during the Hayes-Tilden crisis in 1876.

Two events importantly shaped the fortunes of the Peace Democrats: (1) the transfer of General A. E. Burnside from the Army of the Potomac to the Department of the Ohio and (2) the defeat of Congressman Vallandigham for reelection to Congress in 1862. Burnside arrived at his new post hoping somehow to erase the humiliating circumstances of his transfer. Vallandigham, for his part, returned to Ohio eager to compensate for his recent defeat by running for governor. In the course of the campaign, Burnside ordered the arrest of all persons declaring sympathy with the southern Confederacy. Vallandigham interpreted the order as a direct personal challenge. On May 1, 1863, to overflow audiences, Vallandigham delivered two "disloyal" campaign addresses. He was arrested on May 5, denied a writ of habeas corpus, tried, and convicted of treason by a military court.

The case was appealed to President Lincoln, who commuted the sentence and instructed the military authorities to send Vallandigham into exile in the Confederate states, subject to the original sentence of imprisonment if he returned. The Democratic party of Ohio, at its June state convention, however, defiantly nominated the exile as its candidate for governor. Before another month had passed, Vallandigham set up headquarters on the Canadian side of Niagara Falls, whence he conducted a campaign notable for its brazenness. His defeat by a vote of 247,000 to 185,000 did not end his political activity, but it did mark the beginning of a decline in the influence of the Peace Democrats.[1]

August Belmont, the party's national chairman, interpreted the 1860 election results as a repudiation of President Buchanan rather than a certification of Abraham Lincoln.[2] From 1860 to 1872, his tenure in the Democratic national chairmanship, Belmont's home in New York City served as something of a permanent national party headquarters.[3] Belmont's influence was important in the war effort. To Baron Rothschild in the House of Commons and to Lord Dunfermline in the House of Lords, he wrote letters emphatically predicting victory for the northern states and deploring the British government's contemplated recognition of the Confederacy as a full belligerent. Belmont saw the seceding states as a rebellious minority, pure and simple, and the British, he averred, had no business interfering in the domestic affairs of the United States. Belmont's influence in the court of France's Louis Napoleon was also a decisive factor in frustrating the efforts of his wife's uncle, John Slidell of Louisiana, to bring the French Empire to the side of the Confederacy. Largely through Belmont's efforts, War Democrats were able to maintain their significant role in the Democratic party and in national affairs during this tumultuous period.

The Radical Republican Assault on Presidential Government

Having been elected in 1860 by only 40 percent of the vote, less than a popular majority, President Lincoln had an uncertain mandate for his efforts to carry on the war and preserve the nation. The new Republican party, whose nominee he was, was itself a loose coalition of northern Whigs, anti-Nebraska Democrats, Free-Soilers, abolitionists, and others. The coalition held the traditional Federalist-Whig commitment to legislative supremacy among the branches of government, a view that was aided by the absence of southern

Democratic delegations in Congress during the Civil War. The doctrine of congressional supremacy had its most effective advocates among Radical Republicans.

The Congress that was elected with Lincoln was, in name at least, overwhelmingly Republican: in the Senate, 31 Republicans, 10 Democrats, and 8 from other parties; in the House, 105 Republicans, 43 Democrats, and 30 others. The lopsided Republican majorities, the varied party backgrounds of different Republican members, the doctrine of congressional supremacy, and the problems of a nation in civil war promoted factional strife. This propensity was reinforced by conditions in the electorate.

Most safe one-party Republican states were in New England, home of federalism and abolitionism. Radical Republicans in Congress drew some of their more dignified leaders from this region: Charles Sumner of Massachusetts, William Pitt Fessenden of Maine (principal philosopher of proposals to substitute a parliamentary for the presidential system), and John P. Hale of New Hampshire, former presidential nominee of the Free Soil party. Republicanism in the Midwest, on the other hand, was of two general types. The older states—Illinois, Indiana, and Ohio—had been competitive states since 1824 and enjoyed the kind of ideological moderation associated with competitive politics. The new states—Iowa, Michigan, Minnesota, and Wisconsin—had participated, on the average, in only three presidential elections and were for the most part populist frontier democracies with electorates created by democratic suffrage laws; these had a less competitive and more ideological politics than the older states. Out of the older states came the Lincolnian ambivalence about dealing severely with the South. From the newer states came the vindictive demagoguery that was a mark of Radical Republicanism, as exemplified by Zachariah Chandler of Michigan.

The two most rabid Radicals in Congress during the critical months between election and inauguration in 1860 were Senator "Zack" Chandler of Michigan and Representative "Bluff Ben" Wade of Ohio. In February 1861, Chandler created a sensation by asserting in a letter to Michigan's Governor Austin Blair: "Without a little blood-letting, this Union will not, in my estimation, be worth a rush."[4]

The second session of the Thirty-sixth Congress convened December 1860. There was a general inclination to view the secessionist crisis as a "flurry" that would soon dissipate itself. Both houses of Congress undertook to find *the* compromise that would, once and for all time, settle the troubled waters. The House had a Committee of Thirty-three, the Senate a Committee of Thirteen, for this purpose. The President-elect, however, began making known his resistance to compromise. Lincoln believed that the secession movement could and would be suppressed within the South itself, without blandishments from the federal government. Lincoln's attitude was made public in Horace Greeley's *New York Tribune* on December 22. Lincoln asked the senior Republican in the Senate, William H. Seward of New York, to introduce certain anticompromise resolutions to the Committee of Thirteen. Seward complied, with reluctance, making his own modifications in the resolutions.

The selection of Lincoln's cabinet set the occasion for the first intraparty drama to take place between Lincoln and Seward. Seward had been a leader in national politics long before Lincoln. Immediately after the election, Thurlow Weed, head of the New York Republican organization, suggested that President-elect Lincoln pay a visit to Senator Seward at Auburn, New York, to discuss the policies of the new administration and the selection of the cabinet. This display of superiority was brushed aside by Lincoln. Weed suggested a neutral place and was again rebuffed. On December 10, Weed received an invitation, sent indirectly, to come to Springfield. Nine days later, he presented himself to the President-elect and was told of Seward's nomination as secretary of state.

Shortly after his appointment Seward gave indications that he intended, in the Hamiltonian tradition, to be "prime minister" of the new administration. On April 1 he sent "some thoughts for the President's consideration," an unsolicited communication that listed what Seward believed should be the administration's foreign and domestic policy and urging that, whatever policy is determined, it should be energetically prosecuted either by the president or "some member of the Cabinet." Although their ideological orientations were fairly close, Lincoln's patient reply, written the same day, completely rejected Seward's application of parliamentary theory to the American presidency and firmly asserted that the president alone would decide and prosecute administration policy. The reply made official relations between the two men clearer; the personal relationship also tended to improve. Throughout the Civil War and Lincoln's campaign for reelection, Seward remained the ranking member of the cabinet and, eventually, a staunch Lincoln supporter.[5] But the parliamentary theory of government gained advocates in another quarter and upon a far more serious scale.

Congressional leaders and most members of the cabinet soon realized that Lincoln was disinclined to consult with them. Regular meetings of the cabinet were dropped entirely after a brief but futile attempt to make them meaningful. Fort Sumter was attacked on April 12, 1861. Three days later, upon his own authority as commander-in chief, Lincoln ordered General Winfield Scott into action, called up the state militia in the national defense, and called a special session of Congress for July 4. For many members of Congress Lincoln's military actions, taken while Congress was absent from Washington, posed the question: Is not Congress the only constitutional agency authorized to declare war? Was Lincoln dealing with "war" or "insurrection"? The Radicals preferred to call it "war" and spoke of the South as "the enemy." Congressmen and senators at the special session of Congress, convened nearly three months after Sumter's fall, did not relish being confronted with the *fait accompli* of military engagement. Lincoln's executive acts placed severe constraints upon congressional choices. Congress could do little else but approve Lincoln's proclamations.

Meanwhile the Union forces met their first catastrophe at Bull Run. The only good news came from General George B. McClellan's command, which saved West Virginia for the Union. McClellan displayed consummate skill in organizing and directing his forces. On July 25, Lincoln gave him full command of the defense of Washington. By fall, General Winfield Scott—Whig turned Republican—was retired, and McClellan—a Democrat—was made chief of military operations.

According to one source, 80 Democrats were among the 110 generals of the federal army of 1861. The principal among them—McClellan—was a former supporter of Buchanan and held avowed proslavery sentiments. Why, asked the Radicals, were there not more Republican generals and why was not that great Republican, General John C. Fremont, that party's first nominee for president in 1856, put in charge? In a nation accustomed to elevating its successful generals to the presidency, the military motivations for Lincoln's selection of McClellan were lost among Radical charges of "treason" to the Republican party.

When Congress reconvened in December 1861, Zachariah Chandler proposed a committee of three to investigate the "disasters" of Bull Run and Edward's Ferry. From this proposal came the controversial Committee on the Conduct of the War, original members of which were Benjamin F. Wade, Zachariah Chandler, and Andrew Johnson, two Republicans and one Democrat representing the Senate, and Daniel W. Gooch, John Covode, George W. Julian, and Moses F. Odell, three Republicans and one Democrat representing the House. It was basically a Radical committee, with Wade and Chandler furnishing active leadership, assisted by George Julian, son-in-law of abolitionist Joshua Giddings, as principal spokesman for the Radicals in the House. Andrew Johnson's activities as a Democratic minority member undoubtedly had much to do with his subsequent difficulties with the Radicals when he became president.

In his Emancipation proclamation of September 1862, Lincoln once again acted during the absence of Congress on a highly political matter in his role as commander-in-chief. The proclamation took some of the wind out of Radical sails during the midterm campaigns. Radicals, who should have been the most pleased, presented the gloomiest countenances.

The November 1862 elections proved unfavorable for the Lincoln administration. The time now seemed ripe for demonstrations of Radical strength. Their next blow was aimed at Seward, whose removal had by now become an important Radical objective. After a secret caucus on December 16, 1862, nine Republican senators were chosen to present their case against Seward to the president. Known as the Collamer Committee, it prepared a statement to the chief executive in effect instructing him to remove Seward and all the Democratic generals, blaming them for most of the Union's military disgraces and for Republican defeats at the polls. The committee also cautioned the president that his official political theories and policy would have to be based upon the "combined wisdom and deliberation" of himself and his "cabinet council."

This statement was a clear challenge to Lincoln's presidential powers and a Radical interpretation of the constitutional functions of the cabinet. Anticipating the crisis, Seward handed an undated resignation to the president. Lincoln's dilemma was a serious one. How was he to keep one faction from destroying his coalition cabinet and yet himself remain master of the situation? His response was to create a counter-dilemma for Chase. Lincoln invited the Collamer Committee to return on the following evening and asked all members of the cabinet, with the exception of Seward, to attend. In the course of the conversations, Secretary of the Treasury Salmon P. Chase, the leading opponent to Lincoln and Seward in the cabinet, was put in the position of either agreeing with the complaints of his Senate cohorts or remaining loyal to his chief. He did neither too well and the next day submitted his resignation. Triumphantly, the president, with two key resignations in his hands and a show of great impartiality, asked both Seward and Chase to remain in office "in the public interest." Lincoln had again frustrated a Radical scheme to revise the presidential system.[6]

The state and congressional returns of fall 1862 made it evident to Lincoln that he would have to find support for the war through a political coalition of War Democrats and conservative Republicans. Henceforth he systematically avoided reference to the Republican party. Meanwhile, in local politics, the term "Union" began to replace "Republican."[7] When the Sewardites, for example, found themselves no longer in control of the Republican party in New York, they energetically began to build a new "Union" organization. Early in 1864, Thurlow Weed wrote to Republican Senator Morgan that he had been in consultation with prominent New York War Democrats. All were convinced that an immediate reconstruction of parties, excluding Radicals and Copperheads, was feasible.[8] The new Union party emerged elsewhere as well, and eventually the Republican National Committee referred to itself as the Union National Committee, with Senator Morgan of New York as its chairman.

Despite his defeat in 1856, the name of General John C. Fremont of California appeared regularly among those considered presidential possibilities. He became a favorite of the Radicals. A Fremont-for-President movement started in Missouri in 1861, despite Lincoln's removal of the inept general from his command of the western military districts. Fremont then moved to New York. Fremont clubs, particularly those in Illinois and New York, sent delegates to a special nominating convention in Cleveland. About four hundred delegates attended, but none were leading Radicals. A small group from the East came to work for the nomination of General Grant. The Cleveland convention nominations: John C. Fremont of New York for president and former Tammany Congressman John Cochrane of New York for vice president. The ticket was of dubious constitutionality in view of the fact that both candidates were from the same state.

As the candidacies of Secretary of the Treasury Chase and Fremont developed, the fortunes of a Lincoln renomination seemed uncertain. Since the beginning of the national convention nominating system, no incumbent president had won a renomination followed by electoral success. Anti-Seward factions in New York were opposed to Lincoln. During the early part of 1864, even though "Union Lincoln associations" were growing in number, the entire New York press, with the notable exception of Henry J. Raymond's *New York Times*, was skeptical about the desirability of the president's renomination. Most of the 1864 Union National Convention delegates nevertheless were friendly to Lincoln. Its first ballot showed 484 for Lincoln and 22 Missouri votes for General Grant.[9]

A scramble for second place ensued, focusing around a New York factional fight. Hannibal Hamlin of Maine, Andrew Johnson of Tennessee, and Daniel Dickinson of New York were the principal candidates. Weed opposed his fellow-New Yorker, Dickinson, arguing that Andrew Johnson, a War Democrat, was the man needed to balance a Republican president on a Union party ticket. Speeches pointed to Johnson's humble origins, war record, pure character, and ability to unite the New York Unionist factions. These arguments and the Lincoln influence proved effective. Johnson was named on a single ballot. Johnson's antislavery letter of acceptance later helped remove the troublesome Fremont candidacy.[10]

Union Republican, Union Democrat, and Reconstruction Plans

In fall of 1862, Horatio Seymour, governor of New York, won a spectacular reelection victory over James S. Wadsworth and entered upon his second term. Seymour had long been one of the principal figures of the New York Democracy: governor in 1853; considered a dark horse prospect during the Charleston impasse of 1860; a promoter of Democratic fusion tickets in the 1860 campaign. In 1862, Seymour was viewed as the best man to return the state to the Democrats in time for the 1864 presidential contest. He was the choice of old-time Whigs in the Constitutional Union party, former Hunker Democrats, and Van Buren-Tilden Barnburners. His campaign speeches even won occasional endorsement from Thurlow Weed. Seymour's election gave New York Democrats a candidate for the presidency in 1864. In fact, two-thirds of Seymour's 1862 inaugural address was devoted to national affairs and hit the Lincoln administration at all of its constitutional weakpoints.

By spring of 1864, however, both Seymour and Vallandigham of Ohio had run into enough political mishaps to keep both out of the nomination race. Seymour's opposition to the conscription law led the Republican press to blame him for the New York draft riots of July 1863. He had favored volunteer recruiting as a more desirable method for filling all the needs of the military. This position pleased neither War Democrats nor Peace Democrats. Vallandigham, as we have seen, was in exile.

The other major Democratic presidential possibility was General George B. McClellan, whose in-and-out adventures at the head of the Union armies and political persecution at the hands of the Radical Republicans had made a popular martyr of him. McClellan had also become a severe critic of Lincoln's war management. As early as June 1863, Thurlow Weed asked McClellan to participate in a New York war rally; Weed's object was to push "Little Mac" to the fore as a Union party candidate. Democratic National Chairman Belmont was also trying to recruit McClellan.[11]

The Democratic leadership situation was further unsettled by the activities of such Republicans as Seward, Weed, Morgan, and others who were arranging to drop the Republican designation. Their effort was to gather Democrat and Republican alike under a "Union" banner, keep Lincoln in office, save the country from the Radicals and the Copperheads, and prevent defeat at the hands of the Confederacy. Their plan presented a substantial temptation for many War Democrats. When the Union Lincoln Association of New York was organized, National Chairman Belmont, addressing an audience at Cooper Union, found it necessary to warn Democratic leaders against being drawn into the new organization.[12]

During July and August the factional maneuvering continued. Samuel J. Tilden, a major figure in the New York Democratic party, openly opposed Vallandigham's nomination and refused to commit himself to McClellan. An original Jacksonian, Frank Blair, tried to dissuade McClellan from running against Lincoln. By the time Belmont called the national convention to order, however, it was fairly certain that McClellan would be its nominee.

Governor Seymour was elected permanent chairman. Tilden went onto the resolutions committee, where, by the close vote of 13 to 11, he managed to defeat Vallandigham's bid for its chairmanship. Despite this, Vallandigham was able to get the committee to approve, again by a narrow margin, a plank condemning the "experiment of war" and demanding immediate cessation of hostilities. Tilden and Belmont, with bitter memories of 1860, backed away from a floor fight on this plank, and the convention roared its approval. Then, with obvious inconsistency, the convention went on to nominate for president a general, who, by his vigorous prosecution of the war which it had just disapproved, had become its hero. War and Peace factions had their imprint upon ticket and platform. The more extremist War Democrats, however, remained unreconciled and, in the last days of the fall campaign, conducted a convention in New York to announce their support of the Lincoln administration.[13]

Months earlier, on December 8, 1863, Lincoln had presented to Congress his plan for post-hostilities reconstruction in the South. The plan offered full pardon, with a few exceptions in the higher ranks, to all who fought in the armies of the Confederacy, on condition that they take an oath of allegiance to the United States and agree to accept the presidential proclamations and congressional enactments relative to slavery. Whenever 10 percent of the citizens of a southern state formed a government and applied for readmission, that state could again become a part of the United States.

The president's premise was that the states of the Confederacy never departed from the Union but were conducting an "insurrection." The Radicals, on the other hand, considered the breach between the sections complete; readmission of the South was to be allowed only under the most stringent conditions. Bound up in this disagreement was the equally fundamental issue of the constitutional relationship between the Executive and Congress in arriving at these momentous decisions. The Radicals brought forward a "Congressional Plan" which declared that Confederate readmission was a matter for Congress, not the president, to decide.

Henry Winter Davis and "Bluff Ben" Wade were the spokesmen for the Congressional Plan. Their Wade-Davis Bill passed on July 2, 1864. Lincoln killed it with a pocket veto and, by presidential proclamation, put his own reconstruction plan into effect six days later. The Radicals were incensed. On August 5, 1864, a "Wade-Davis Manifesto" declared Lincoln's proclamation a "stupid outrage of the legislative authority of the people," a gross encroachment of executive power, and an attempt to win rebel electoral votes for Lincoln. The manifesto came in the midst of the presidential campaign.

On August 14, the anti-Seward contingent in New York started a movement to have Lincoln abdicate the nomination and call another nominating convention for September. Horace Greeley's *Tribune* supported the abdication proposal. National Chairman Raymond, in communication with Union party state leaders, began expressing the view that "we don't stand the ghost of a chance in November."[14] Even Thurlow Weed was telling the president that his reelection seemed an impossibility. Lincoln-Johnson prospects were at their lowest when the news came, on September 2, that General Sherman had marched into Atlanta. The emotional lift was enough to end talk of a negotiated peace and carry the Lincoln administration back into office.[15]

Lincoln's reelection and the congressional returns caused widespread demoralization in the Democratic party. McClellan's departure for a stay of several years abroad left the party without a titular leader. The only Democrat holding a major national office was Vice President Andrew Johnson. But who could be sure how much of a Democrat the "Union" vice president would continue to be? Operation of the frail machinery of the national party once again devolved upon its national chairman, August Belmont.

According to James G. Blaine's analysis of the political complexion of the Thirty-ninth Congress, the Senate that was elected with Lincoln in 1864 had 34 Republicans, 11 Democrats, and 5 "Administration Republicans." The House had 135 Republicans, 41 Democrats, and 8 "Administration Republicans."[16] These were uncertain categories. The period was one in which party labels were lightly held. Not even the *Congressional Directory*'s editor, Ben Perley Poore, presumed to record who was a Radical Republican, Conservative Republican, Administration Republican, Unionist, War Democrat, or Peace Democrat.

By Blaine's count, 34 Republican senators were classifiable as non-Administration Republicans, that is, susceptible to pressure from the Radical faction. Only 26 of the Senate's 50 members were needed for an absolute majority. Similarly, in the 184-member House, 93 was the number needed for a majority, with 135 non-Administration Republicans available to make it up. The political goal of the Radicals was, arithmetically speaking, simple enough. The eleven southern states that went into the Confederacy had had twenty-two votes in the United States Senate and fifty-eight in the House, nearly all in the Democratic column. So long as the southern Democrats were not among those counted in Congress, the Radicals could maintain their control over national politics. Thus, for example, the speakership of the House of Representatives remained in Republican hands until 1875, and the Senate had a Republican majority until 1879.

With political and military victories behind him, Lincoln proceeded to put into effect the Presidential Plan for southern reconstruction. For this he had, for the moment, sufficient congressional support. In February 1865, his supporters were able to bring about the defeat, 80 to 65, of a Radical bill declaring that no congressional representative should be admitted from the rebel states until Congress had given its approval.

On the evening of April 14, Lincoln was assassinated. The following day Andrew Johnson became the third vice president to succeed to the presidency. On May 26, 1865, the last Confederate army surrendered. Between May and December, Johnson appointed provisional governors for all the Confederate states. Conventions were held, state legislatures elected, senators and representatives chosen, and civil government restored.

"Johnson's Party" versus "The Directory"

It was not an easy time to search for national consensus. Partisan anomaly was now heaped upon factional paradox. With the cessation of hostilities, would Johnson be Democrat, Unionist, or Republican? Johnson's endorsement of Lincoln's reconstruction policy, the glorification he received from the Democratic and southern press, and the support given him by the conservative Republican *New York Times* was sufficient to convince the Radicals, particularly such Radical leaders as Ben Wade and Zachariah Chandler who had served with Johnson on the Committee on the Conduct of the War, that the new president would never be one of their fraternity.

As early as August 1865, the Radicals began planning to win control of their party machinery in Congress. The wiser men among Republican conservatives had no illusions about the quality of the Radical foe. Morgan and Raymond wrote to their mentor, Thurlow Weed, warning that the Radicals would not have peace except on their own terms.[17] Throughout 1866, the *New York Times* did all it could to dissociate President Johnson from the Democratic party, but the Democratic press clung resolutely. Raymond, in addition to his activities as editor of the principal pro-Johnson newspaper and chairman of the Union National Committee, was now a freshman congressman leading the meager administration forces in the House.

Just prior to the opening of Congress, a caucus of Union party members—conservative and Radical—was held. A committee of seven was appointed to prepare appropriate resolutions for the caucus; most of the members of this committee were Radicals. Thaddeus Stevens was elected chairman; Raymond was one of an unsuspecting minority. Stevens then offered a resolution calling for the appointment of a joint congressional committee of fifteen to inquire into the condition of the seceded states and to report at any time whether all or any of them were entitled to representation in either house. The Union caucus unanimously approved the resolution, and it was voted into effect on the first day of the new Congress. Eight of the fifteen members of this joint committee, soon to be known as "The Directory," a reference to the radical committee of the French Revolution, turned out to be Radicals.

Raymond and the conservatives had been taken in. The conservative Republican and the Democratic views had been that the southern states never left the Union; hence there could be no doubt that they were entitled to representation in Congress. The Union caucus resolution, however, reopened the entire question. The Radical Directory kept it open. Raymond and his colleagues attempted to have all matters pertaining to representation referred to the Committee on Elections, but the Radicals were not about to compromise. On December 18, Thaddeus Stevens, in a speech before the House, served notice that southerners would not be readmitted to Congress until the supremacy of the Republican party had been assured.

It was no longer Republican *versus* Democrat, Unionist *versus* Copperhead, but president *versus* The Directory. Realizing this, those inveterate party-builders, the Blairs, once again assumed the task of party reorganization, this time aimed at an alignment which would be moderate on southern reconstruction and general economic policy and favorable to Andrew Johnson.[18] Wisconsin Senator James R. Doolittle, long an ally of the Blairs, became the midwife of the new movement.

Meanwhile, the United States Congress was experiencing a game of political ping pong: the Radicals legislating and the president vetoing. In March, after several vetoes, a Civil Rights Bill, making Negroes citizens and conferring large powers upon United States marshals, district attorneys, and judges to enforce equal rights before the law for Negroes, was sent to the president. Johnson returned it with his usual veto. This time the Radicals moved with design and determination. A pair was broken; a pro-Johnson senator was unseated; persuasion and a relentless party whip were employed. Most important, three fence-sitting Republican senators finally were shoved into the Radical line-up: Stewart of Nevada, Willey of West Virginia, and Morgan of New York. The most influential of these was the former Republican national chairman, Morgan of New York, whose shift was greeted with great applause. Although an associate of Seward, Raymond, and Weed, all of whom were supporting Johnson, Morgan also had been a consistent champion of Negro rights. Confronted with a choice between factional and philosophical loyalties, he decided in favor of the latter.

During spring of 1866, president and Directory were moving into extreme positions. Union National Chairman Raymond wrote to Thurlow Weed asking the venerable politician to exert a moderating influence upon Johnson.[19] Senator Doolittle, on the other hand, was busily at work with the Blairs building a Johnson political organization and preparing for an unprecedented midterm national convention. Should it be an organization within the Democratic or the Union Party? Should it be a third party? Some former War Democrats had indicated their willingness to give way to Republican leadership in a new third party. Johnson Republicans, such as Raymond and Seward, would support a Johnson party only if it grew up within the Union party organization.

Union midterm convention sponsors agreed that it was essential for Union National Chairman Raymond to attend. Seward, after some tardiness in becoming a backer of the convention, advised Raymond that, since the object of the meeting was primarily consultation, Union men should probably attend in order to prevent its falling into the hands of the Copperheads. Raymond visited the president to tell him that he himself could have nothing to do with the formation of a new party. However, if the convention were simply to seek the election of members of Congress favorable to the admission of loyal southern representatives—War Democrats in some places, Union men in others—Raymond thought much good might be accomplished. President Johnson replied, according to Raymond's version of the interview, that this was precisely what he desired: a loyal Congress, but no new party. The Union national chairman was thus prevailed upon to participate in the novel midterm convention.[20]

William B. Reed of Philadelphia, working with Montgomery Blair and Senator Doolittle, took special pains to urge such Democrats as August Belmont and Fernando Wood to attend the forthcoming Johnson convention. For National Chairman Belmont, the proposed convention may have been an excellent opportunity to keep the president from going completely over to the Republicans. But Belmont recognized the opportunity as more apparent than real.

Seward was backing the convention. The president was unwilling to commit himself politically that year to anything more than the election of a pro-Johnson Congress. Union National Chairman Raymond would be attending in a leading capacity. In short, there would have been few rewards and many risks for Democratic leaders at the Johnson convention. Belmont decided to stay away from Philadelphia.

The Johnson convention was called for August 14 by the "National Union Executive Committee of Washington," a merger of the District of Columbia National Johnson Club and the National Union Club. Neither was connected with the Union party's national committee. Raymond attended the Johnson convention as an influential individual, not as representative of the Union National Committee. Senator Doolittle was chairman of the convention; Raymond participated actively. His leadership prevented the admission of three famous "Copperhead" Democrats as delegates: Clement L. Vallandigham, Fernando Wood, and Henry Clay Dean. Raymond was also chief draftsman of the convention's declaration of principles and its address to the people.

For the Radicals, the Johnson midterm convention was perceived as equivalent to the organization of a new political party.[21] They moved to the attack. Dennison, Harlan, and Speed resigned from the cabinet. A Southern Loyalist Convention was set for September 3, to be held in Philadelphia. To give the impression of independent sectional action, a separate convention of Northern Radicals was called for the same date in the same city.

On August 20, Samuel A. Purviance of Pennsylvania wrote to New Jersey's Radical-leaning Governor Marcus L. Ward suggesting that "our Committee" meet simultaneously with the Southern Loyalist Convention in September to determine what action ought to be taken now that Union National Chairman Raymond had attached himself to the "new party." Purviance was fearful that the public might think the Union National Committee "had gone over" to the enemy along with Raymond. "Mr. Raymond may possibly deserve to meet with us for the purpose of making a formal withdrawal."[22] Purviance did not make clear whether "our Committee" referred to the entire Union National Committee or to its executive committee. It was the Union Executive Committee that was called to meet in Philadelphia on September 3, the day of the Radical conventions. The call was issued by four Union national committeemen. The initiator was a Radical but at least one of the others later denied that he had authorized the use of his name. Horace Greeley's *New York Tribune,* with unusual speed, publicized the call. Greeley's long-standing feud with Raymond and the *New York Times* was apparently heading for a new confrontation.

Raymond comprehended what lay ahead and on August 24 issued his own notice as national chairman for a meeting of the National Union Executive Committee on the same day fixed by the Radicals but to take place in *New York City* rather than Philadelphia. This immediately brought a cutting public rebuke from Governor Marcus L. Ward, who wrote Raymond:

You have deemed it wise and proper to abandon the great union Republican party [*sic*] of the country, and to connect your name and influence with a new organization designed to destroy and defeat the cause with which I sympathize, and of which I am, in some small degree, a representative. Your public action has been such that I cannot acknowledge your right to use the title, under which the meeting has been called. . . . All who would respond to your call would be regarded as betraying the party they have ceased to represent.[23]

The two Radical conventions met on September 3 and both issued declarations supporting Congress against the president, that is, The Directory against the Johnson party. In New York, Chairman Raymond met with a handful of members of the executive committee of the Union National Committee and, lacking a quorum, adjourned. At the Radical-sponsored meeting in Philadelphia, some fifteen committeemen appeared and proceeded to expel Raymond for "affiliation with the [Union party's] enemies." Governor Ward of New Jersey was elected as new national chairman. An address to the nation, prepared by Horace Greeley, was issued by Ward. Two days later, a Union state convention meeting at Syracuse, New York, endorsed Raymond's expulsion and named Greeley as New York's new national committeeman. Thus, the Radicals had succeeded in removing the Republican conservatives' national chairman and capturing the national machinery of the Republican party.[24]

After the pro-Johnson midterm convention, President Johnson embarked upon his unprecedented "swing around the circle," a campaign tour of the entire country, lasting from August 28 to September 16, during which he urged the voters to return a Congress that would support his programs. Election odds then, as they do to this day, ran against the incumbent president's party (presumably

Democratic in Johnson's case) in congressional midterm races. The Radical Republicans returned as numerous as before, determined to deal with their Democratic "enemy" in the office of Chief Executive.

The Radicals enjoyed impressive victories in the 1866 midterm elections. Before it ended, the Thirty-ninth Congress placed on the statute books a host of Radical laws: the first Reconstruction Act, the Tenure of Office Act, the Conduct of the Army Act, the second Reconstruction Act, the third Reconstruction Act, the Act admitting North Carolina, and the joint resolution setting aside the 1868 electoral vote of Louisiana and other states.

The vice-presidency had, of course, remained vacant after Johnson became president. The 1866 election returns were still coming in when John Forney, the Radical secretary of the Senate, proposed to "Zack" Chandler a plan to elect "Bluff Ben" Wade, now a senator, as presiding officer of the Senate, thus next in line for succession to the presidency. In order to capture the presidency itself, Forney suggested impeachment proceedings against Johnson.[25] The Directory agreed.

The Tenure of Office Act, curbing the president's power of removal by requiring the "advice and consent" of the Senate, was intended to protect Radical officeholders. In December 1867, Secretary of War Stanton, a Radical sympathizer, provoked a dispute with Johnson and was subsequently removed without the "advice and consent" of the Senate required by the recently enacted Tenure of Office Act. Johnson named General Grant as Stanton's successor. The president was charged with violation of the Tenure of Office Act, the basis for impeachment proceedings that followed.

The trial lasted from March 13 to May 26, 1868. The critical test vote was taken on May 16, only four days prior to the "Union Republican" National Convention. Thirty-six votes were needed to convict. Thirty-five voted for conviction. A single vote prevented the capture of the presidency for Ben Wade and The Directory.

Failing in their impeachment strategy, the Radicals turned to the Union Republican National Convention as their next shot at the presidency. The new party name marked a step back to Republicanism from Lincoln-Johnson unionism, a step that was encouraged by Horace Greeley. Radicals were now adamant about dissociating themselves from Democrats.

As the hero of the Civil War, General Ulysses S. Grant was everybody's choice. Early in 1866, New York Democratic leaders quietly launched a Grant-for-president movement. Thurlow Weed, hoping to get the jump on the Democrats, conducted a huge public meeting and demonstration for the general. Grant, leaning toward the Radicals as early as 1866, aided their cause by refusing to assume Secretary of War Stanton's portfolio when appointed to it by President Johnson. When the Radicals captured the Union party national chairmanship, it was clear that The Directory would control the national nominating convention in 1868. Union National Chairman Ward was one of the most zealous in marshaling Grant delegates. The Union Republican Convention nominated Grant without opposition. The general was elected by 52.7 percent of the popular vote; 214 electoral votes to Horatio Seymour's 80.

The Directory had conquered the Johnson party and now controlled the Congress, the presidency, and the principal organs of the Union Republican party. Their success was attained by obstructing Johnson's attempts to reconstruct the national consensus. Commenting on the Johnson impeachment episode, Walter Bagehot wrote:

A hostile legislature and a hostile executive were so tied together, that the legislature tried, and tried in vain, to rid itself of the executive by accusing it of illegal practices. . . . This was the most striking instance of disunion between the President and the Congress that has ever yet occurred, and which probably will ever occur. Probably for many years the United States will have great and painful reason to remember that at the moment of all their history, when it was most important to them to collect and concentrate all the strength and wisdom of their policy on the pacification of the South, that policy was divided by a strife in the last degree unseemly and degrading.[26]

Reconstruction of Democratic Factions

Frustration marked the efforts of Democratic presidential politicians at every turn in 1868. McClellan, hardly cut out for practical politics, was abroad. President Johnson had never decisively grasped the party helm and was destroyed by the impeachment proceedings. Vallandigham and George Pendleton had become locked in a bitter feud for control of the Ohio Democratic organization. Governor Seymour, over the protest of New York State Chairman Samuel J. Tilden, took himself out of the race. Robert J. Walker wrote about the availability of Winfield Scott Hancock, a popular but politically inexperienced Union general. Senator Thomas A. Hendricks, a "sound money" midwesterner, was proposed because questions of currency and credit had come into prominence along with postwar inflation and agricultural depression.

After twenty-two ballots at the Democratic National Convention of 1868, Hancock and Hendricks were stalemated. A compromise delegation gave Ohio's vote, in a surprise maneuver, to Seymour. New York followed, and Horatio Seymour became the reluctant "hard money" nominee. The convention, reflecting the party's division, wrote a greenback platform. The ensuing campaign was also reluctant, divided, and unsuccessful.

What did emerge from the 1868 campaign was a new force in presidential politics, Samuel J. Tilden. A corporation lawyer who had accumulated substantial wealth, Tilden had been active in New York politics since the 1830s. In time, he became a political associate of Horatio Seymour. Tilden was able to work with or against Tammany Hall as the situation demanded. Cultured, aloof, and frequently in poor health, Tilden never quite achieved a large popular following. He was a party organizer and a politician's politician. As Seymour's campaign manager in 1868, Tilden succeeded in supplementing the lethargic and divided official party machinery with a vigorous new organization called "The Order of the Union Democracy." Like Van Buren's before him, Tilden's efforts would be felt across Democratic national politics for more than a generation.

His cabinet crowded with personal friends as ill-experienced as he, President Grant was soon surrounded by The Directory, now known as the "Stalwart Cabal." The Cabal kept a tight hand on the distribution of patronage, maintained a high tariff, and administered the Radical reconstruction program for the South. New England and Midwest Republican moderates like Charles Sumner and Carl Schurz found that they enjoyed little access to their president and had less luck with their program for civil service reform and a moderate southern policy. By 1871, even erstwhile Radical Horace Greeley, still publisher of the *New York Tribune,* joined a factional bolt that created the Liberal Republican party.

New York's ascendancy in the national Democratic party was at this time threatened by Horatio Seymour's political retirement and the growing influence of the Tweed Ring. Boss Tweed dominated both city and state governments by 1870. Popular reaction to the *New York Times* exposures of Tweed's corruption was heated. During 1871, Samuel J. Tilden began a campaign to break the hold of the Tweed Ring. Through public investigations and legal suits, aided by a number of distinguished Democrats, the movement was extremely effective. The Ring lost its grip in the elections of 1871. Its leaders dispersed or faced trial. As a consequence, Tilden was on his way to becoming a Democratic reform governor and a reform candidate for president.

In 1872, however, uncertainty prevailed among New York Democratic leaders. This left the national party in a leadership quandary. The nominee of 1868, Seymour, had retired. Belmont was in his twelfth year as national chairman. Democratic confusion was compounded by the exodus of reform-minded Republicans from that party to form a new third party. For the leaderless Democrats, still incapacitated by the absence of their southern wing and facing a second-term campaign against a popular incumbent, a gnawing dilemma presented itself: Could an alliance with the new Liberal Republican party produce victory? Could the Liberal Republicans later be absorbed into the Democratic rank-and-file? Would the combined reformist elements in the Democratic and the new third party make possible an effective attack on corruption in the Grant administration?

The Liberal Republicans met in 1872 to put together their national ticket. As they watched the proceedings, Democrats generally expected Supreme Court Justice David Davis, Lincoln's close political associate, or Charles Francis Adams to be the Liberal nominee. Either man would have been acceptable to a majority of the Democratic leadership. Instead, after a tough nominating fight, the Liberals came up with Horace Greeley.

The unanticipated Liberal Republican nomination of the Democrats' old foe, Horace Greeley, left the Democratic party in a dilemma. With no candidate of their own, the Democratic leaders had already paved the way for an endorsement of a Liberal Republican nominee. Although opposition to endorsement of Greeley was pronounced in New York, New Jersey, Pennsylvania, and Delaware, the Democrats had no direction in which to retreat. Furthermore, there were also important elements in the party willing to endorse Greeley. The South particularly saw Greeley as a friendly candidate, and the Democratic press of that section rallied behind him. Tilden's political associate, Augustus Schell, took on the management of the ill-fated Greeley campaign and did as much as he could with the opportunity to strengthen ties with the reemerging Democratic leadership in the South.

The election of 1872 was disastrous for the Democrats in terms of votes. In other respects, the campaign brought a substantial part of the South back into active participation in Democratic presidential politics, recruited large numbers of Republican liberals into the Democratic fold, elevated the reform issue on the agenda of national politics, and put the Tilden forces in control of the presidential party machinery. Tilden, as governor of New York in 1874 and destroyer of the New York Canal Ring in 1875, became the front-runner for the presidential nomination in 1876.

Although the Democrats had been losing the contests for the presidency, they did enjoy steady improvement in their congressional position throughout the Grant administration. Off-year successes in 1874 enabled the Democrats to choose their first Speaker of the House of Representatives since the beginning of the Civil War. They did this with unusual care. Samuel J. Randall of Pennsylvania was, for all practical purposes, the leader of House Democrats, but the party chose M. C. Kerr, a congressman with fewer political scars. Kerr projected a fresh image of the party before the nation, as did a vigorous first-term congressman from New York City, Abram Hewitt, son-in-law of the famous Peter Cooper and political associate of Governor Tilden. Tilden and Hewitt had worked together in driving Boss Tweed and the Canal Ring from New York.

Hewitt, serving as Tilden's advance scout in Washington, frequently addressed himself to the two issues dividing the Democratic party at that time: the currency and the tariff. Northwestern agrarian elements in the party, reacting to the farm depressions that afflicted their region, had been advocating a soft-money, greenback currency policy for several years. Eastern business Democrats were for hard-money and tight credit policies, and these were Hewitt's preferences. On the tariff issue, Hewitt, an antiprotectionist, favored tariffs for revenue only.

The Panic of 1873 made the currency shortage a critical national issue, yet one which Congress refused to face. In 1874, a bill setting January 1876 as the date for redemption of greenbacks was vetoed by Grant. In 1875, payments were officially deferred until 1879. The Greenback party was organized in 1876 to try to mobilize popular opinion where Grangers, Liberal Republicans, and the independent farmers' parties had failed. Although the main Greenback strength was in the Old Northwest and in most parts of the South, influential easterners like Peter Cooper were also actively in accord with its expansionary objectives.

The New York Democratic convention proposed Tilden for the presidency on April 26, 1876. The lack of applause confirmed that the state organization would support Tilden only grudgingly. Tilden proceeded to create his own campaign and publicity agencies, as he had for Horatio Seymour in 1868. A Newspaper Publicity Bureau was established, shortly followed by a Literary Bureau. Tilden sank some unnamed amount of money into the latter, and Edward Cooper, his father's Greenback politics notwithstanding, gave $20,000. A private advertising agency was hired to do part of the pre-convention work.

Anti-Tilden Democrats were heartened when Tammany's John Kelly openly joined them. Prior to the national convention, 120 prominent Democrats signed a circular declaring themselves opposed to Tilden. At the convention itself, Kelly placed a banner over Tammany headquarters stating: "New York, the largest Democratic city in the Union, is uncompromisingly opposed to the nomination of Samuel J. Tilden because he cannot carry the State of New York."

Tilden was nevertheless nominated on the second ballot; Hendricks, his runner-up for first place, was given the vice-presidential nomination. Hard- and soft-money elements submerged their differences by uniting on a reform platform. Congressman Hewitt became national committeeman from New York, "doubtless by the wish of Mr. Tilden."[27]

A Second Civil War?

The Republican campaign was completely in the hands of Zachariah Chandler, having just been elected Republican national chairman. His experience and talent were great resources for nominee Rutherford B. Hayes. Despite Hayes's subsequent conciliatory position on the southern question, during the campaign he heartily endorsed Chandler's waving of the "bloody shirt." This was possibly one of the hardest campaigns in Zack Chandler's long and rough career, for the South was restive and Tilden was too much of a politician to be easily rattled or beaten.

The October elections in Ohio, Indiana, and West Virginia seemed to forecast a return to power for the Democrats. The November presidential count gave Tilden 250,000 more popular votes than Hayes. The electoral college votes seemed to give the election to Tilden, 203 to 166. However, returns from Louisiana (8 electoral votes), South Carolina (7 votes), Florida (4 votes), and Oregon (one elector of doubtful legality) were tardy and uncertain. Democrats could be sure of only 184 electoral votes; they needed 185 to elect

Tilden. The outcome hung on one vote and awaited validation of the returns from three southern states.

This crisis came at the end of a campaign in which Republicans had waved the "bloody shirt" with special intensity, telling the voters that the Democratic South had been chiefly responsible for the bloody ordeal of the Civil War and hence Democrats were not fit to govern. It was eleven years since the termination of Civil War hostilities, yet the South was almost as torn by "salvation" and "reconstruction" as it had been by cannon and shell. The Negro, as postwar voter and militiaman, was the foundation upon which Republican state governments had rested. Carpetbaggers and scalawags had been everywhere. The terror of the Klu Klux Klan and anti-Republican rifle clubs were part of a subterranean white resistance. Southern despair brought strikes, riots, massacres, and the rise of demagogues of the style of "Pitchfork" Ben Tillman. The ballot box in the South was regularly drenched in blood and fraud, and President Grant often augmented federal troops there to preserve order.

The two parties, through their press and local organizations, were arrayed as hostile armies during the four months from November until inauguration in March, many elements in each ready, even eager, to take up armed conflict once again. President Grant appreciated the imminence of another civil conflict and declared that he would accept *any* solution worked out in Congress so long as this solution was nonmilitary. The two candidates, Hayes and Tilden, were men of moderation even in this exceptional conflict. Both had conducted themselves with dignity and reserve during an otherwise rough political campaign. The push for another civil war came from others than Grant, Tilden, and Hayes.

Hewitt, as congressman and national party chairman, was in the midst if not at the head of the Democratic response. A Democratic congressional caucus organized a permanent advisory committee consisting of eleven representatives and six senators. This committee met frequently during the crisis and devoted itself to the definition of a compromise. According to Hewitt's later testimony, Tilden was constantly consulted. Tilden used several agents—Chairman Hewitt, Speaker Randall, and Colonel Pelton—designating no particular one as his sole spokesman. Tilden sent most of his messages through Pelton, but his final views were announced through Randall. Hewitt, with his usual independence, leaned heavily upon his Democratic associates in Congress for advice and seemed to become more a spokesman for Democratic legislators than Tilden's agent. During December, Hewitt's zeal got the better of him, and he wrote an address intended to signal mass rallies on January 8 throughout the nation. Tilden, wary of the incendiary character of such meetings, refused to approve the address.

Pressures for solution of the presidential impasse also came from outside the Congress. As Republican Representative James A. Garfield of Ohio put it to Governor Hayes, the nation's Democratic businessmen were more anxious for peace than they were for Tilden.[28] Certain businessmen in particular were instrumental in the outcome. Thomas Scott of the Texas and Pacific Railroad and Collis Huntington of the Southern Pacific and Central Pacific lines were bitter protagonists for a congressional subsidy to build a southern railroad route to the Pacific. The *quid pro quo* for supporting the subsidy were votes to help seat Hayes. The debate over the proposed subsidy revived North-South divisions among Democrats and facilitated the eventual election of Hayes.[29]

The Democratic majority in Congress established a special fifteen-member Electoral Commission to determine which sets of disputed returns would be accepted in Louisiana, South Carolina, Florida, and Oregon. To serve on the Electoral Commission the Senate placed three Republicans and two Democrats, the House three Democrats and two Republicans, and the Supreme Court two Democratic and two Republican justices. The fifteenth "nonpartisan" member was chosen from the Supreme Court by the other four justices.

Speaker Kerr had died before the election, and Samuel J. Randall had been chosen to succeed him in that post. It was Randall who presided over the House of Representatives during the disputed Hayes-Tilden election. Partisan Democrat though he was, Randall insisted upon following to the letter the procedures set down in the Electoral Commission Act.

The commission made eight-to-seven decisions in favor of Hayes on each set of returns. What had been a "Democratic compromise" (the Special Commission) produced a Republican president. Hayes was elected. In return for Democratic constraint and moderation, Congressman Hewitt was able to elicit an indirect Republican commitment to withdraw federal troops from the disputed southern states, allowing their return to the Democratic fold.

As inauguration day approached, popular passions were a growing concern for responsible leaders and armed conflict became a near reality. To avoid popular demonstrations and to minimize the chances of a violent transition, Hayes was sworn in as president secretly on March 3 and publicly the next day.

As president, Hayes inaugurated a policy of troop withdrawal, nonintervention, and conciliation to the extent of appointing southern Democrats to important federal posts in the South. Hayes hoped that enough conservative Democrats in the South would be converted to the Republican party to lead to a "natural" two-party division in that electorate. If this could be brought about, he thought, it would be worth abandonment of carpetbaggers and Negro leaders. But bitterness, populism, and racism did not let it come about. Republican congressmen, governors, and other state officers were roundly defeated in the southern elections of 1878 and 1880. The South's political agonies were not yet past. It would require another hundred years for the Democratic party to bring the South fully back into the Union and to a more "natural" and national place in the American consensus.

5

Fighting Factions of the Tilden-Bryan Period

DURING the final quarter of the nineteenth century, the nation experienced growing pains of many kinds. The return of the South to the Union went poorly. Poverty, populism, and racism cut off most efforts to achieve broad consensus within the South and between the South and the rest of the nation. Migration westward changed the United States into a continental community, brought in new states, altered the balance of power in Congress and the electoral college, and put the Pacific Ocean and the Far East onto the popular agenda. The Civil War left an arms industry that became the basis for an era of dramatic growth in corporate enterprise and a national military establishment that became increasingly involved in peace-keeping operations in the South and West and in foreign affairs. Large-scale immigration began to burden the economic and Americanizing capacities of large cities. The Democratic party found itself sorely tested by the many contentious interests that came under its political tent. It was more often an out-party under the leadership of men like Tilden and Bryan than an in-party headed by a President Cleveland. It was a difficult quarter century for its consensus-seekers.

In retrospect, the vitality that Jackson and Van Buren had given to the office of President and to the presidential wing of the party had been sustained by Polk but dissipated by Pierce and Buchanan. As the out-party during the Civil War and Reconstruction, Democrats were in no position to employ the resources of the presidency to reunite either the party or the nation. The great achievement of Tilden, whose political career and contributions to the party have

89

largely gone unrecognized, was to rebuild the party and its organizational components sufficiently for the near-victories in 1876 and 1880 and for its return to presidential office under Cleveland in 1884.

Retiring Tilden and Recruiting Cleveland

Over sixty, afflicted with arthritis and other ailments, a defeated nominee in 1876, Tilden went into semiretirement. His associates, however, kept alive his political availability, arguing that he had been a victim of fraud at the hands of his enemies and stupidity among his friends. This is how it appeared before the *New York Tribune* revealed a series of telegrams sent between Tilden's nephew and a Tilden manager revealing that there had been bribery negotiations for the purpose of purchasing votes for Tilden. A congressional committee, the Potter Committee, investigated and confirmed the story but exonerated Tilden. The revelations nonetheless destroyed Tilden's political future. Overnight, forty years of Tilden's devotion to political reform were forgotten under the brush of scandal among his associates.

Ironically, it was an era in which machine politics, sharp campaign practices, and election frauds were common in both major parties and were extending from city and state to national contests. The same Potter Committee also uncovered a host of illegal acts perpetrated by the Republicans under Zachariah Chandler's management in the 1876 campaign. Republican state machines were as common as Democratic city machines. "Floaters," that is, voters who cast ballots in more than one precinct in the same election, were being transported in substantial numbers from city to city to help carry elections. Coffee was poured on election records to give them the appearance of age and handling. Money was used for the outright purchase of votes. Politically appointed government employees were expected to make substantial party campaign contributions. In short, the drive to win and the prizes in patronage were inviting distortion in the measurement of community consensus by both major parties.

Among the politicians close to Tilden over the years were some of both political styles, that is, some reformers and some manipulators. One of the former was Abram S. Hewitt. A poor young tutor who gave college instruction to Edward Cooper, son of Peter Cooper, the mechanical genius of the new age of iron, Hewitt was subsequently brought into the management of one of Cooper's iron mills and married Edward's sister. Weak eyes kept Hewitt from completing his law studies which, meanwhile, had brought him in touch with another law student, Samuel J. Tilden. The Tildens and the Hewitts became neighbors and friends, and, in 1871, Hewitt joined Tilden and Edward Cooper in their campaign to rid New York of the Tweed Ring. At Tilden's behest, Hewitt successfully ran for Congress in 1874, became Democratic national chairman in 1876, and, as we have seen, was a Tilden spokesman in Congress during the Hayes-Tilden electoral negotiations.

Another Tilden associate on the reform side was William C. Whitney, who, in 1876, was the thirty-five-year-old corporation counsel of New York City. Of Puritan stock and educated at Yale and Harvard, Whitney married the sister of a college classmate, Oliver H. Payne (later treasurer of Standard Oil Company). Whitney began his law practice in New York in 1865 where he met Tilden and aided him in the anti-Tweed crusade. Whitney's father-in-law, Henry B. Payne, was a leading Democrat in Ohio who had placed James Buchanan in nomination at the national convention of 1856. Elected to the House of Representatives in 1874, the elder Payne, at Tilden's request, was named chairman of the House committee on the electoral count in 1876–1877. Whitney was still New York corporation counsel in 1882 when he began to devote full time to placing the Tilden following behind Grover Cleveland's campaigns for the governorship and the presidency.

Samuel J. Randall, an old hand at the rough-and-tumble of Pennsylvania politics, was leader of the pro-Tilden faction in that state's Democratic party and came closer to the manipulator type. As Speaker of the House of Representatives during the Hayes-Tilden electoral count, however, Randall was meticulously correct in all his actions. He continued as Speaker until 1880 when House Democrats lost their majority. Randall was the first of the modern "strong" Speakers, credited with substantially increasing the influence of the speakership through modifications and interpretations of the House rules. Two of Randall's Democratic successors, Carlisle and Crisp, and two Republicans, Reed and Cannon, later built upon the precedents established by him.

Also of the manipulator type was William H. Barnum of Connecticut. Barnum's wealth was derived from his father's iron foundry, investment in land companies, and manufacture of car wheels. Barnum first ran for Congress in 1866 against another wealthy man, Phineas T. Barnum of circus fame but no relative, and won after a heated contest. He served in the House for the next ten years. In 1868, as treasurer of the Democratic congressional campaign committee, he developed friendships with National Chairman Belmont and New York State Chairman Tilden. Through Tilden, Barnum came to know Hewitt, and subsequently the three men invested jointly in Michigan iron mines. When Connecticut's Senator Orris S. Ferry died in 1875, Barnum reputedly consummated enough political deals in the state legislature to win that body's election to the vacancy despite the governor's nomination of another person.

When Abram Hewitt resigned from the Democratic national chairmanship in 1877, Senator Barnum succeeded him and remained in this position against all challengers for a dozen years. A match for even the Republican's Zack Chandler, Barnum, during the 1876 campaign, carried his oratorical gifts and some $60,000 for literature and speakers into the intense contest for Indiana's electoral votes and helped carry that state by five thousand votes. It was here that Republicans tagged him "The Mule-Buyer," a reference to an alleged dispatch in which National Chairman Hewitt advised him to "buy seven more mules," that is, draw $7,000 in additional campaign funds.[1]

Hewitt, Whitney, Randall, and Barnum were leading actors in national party affairs for much of the Tilden period.

As Tilden suffered his semiretirement, President Hayes was beginning to have troubles of his own. Hayes appointed liberal Republicans to his cabinet and encouraged their civil service reform efforts; this alienated Republican Stalwarts. To win over southern conservatives, he made an ex-Confederate and Democrat his Postmaster-general. Hayes withdrew troops from South Carolina and Louisiana; this offended James G. Blaine's "Half-Breed" Republicans.

Democrats won control of both houses of Congress in 1878. The executive and legislative branches became bogged down in partisan antagonism, particularly in connection with currency policy. The expanding American economy continued to demand more and more currency to carry on its business. To the money-needy, the nation's newly plentiful silver supply from the Mountain States seemed a good supplement to the short supply of paper and gold currency. In 1876, Richard P. Bland, a Democratic representative from Missouri, and William E. Allison, a Republican senator from Iowa, stepped into the leadership of a silver coalition in Congress. Hayes's veto of the Bland-Allison Bimetallism Bill elevated the silver issue alongside the tariff as a long-term national issue.

Tilden's misfortunes and silence regarding his plans as titular leader invited factional contention as candidates moved into position for the 1880 national convention. When John Kelly's anti-Tilden maneuvers were defeated in the New York Democratic convention of 1878, Kelly bolted the party, had himself nominated for governor on a separate ticket, and thereby helped defeat the Democratic state slate. Loss of the governorship was a telling blow to the Tilden forces and encouraged a protectionist outsider, Senator Thomas F. Bayard of Delaware, to seek national convention delegate support in Tilden's own home state.   .

Bayard was also a factor in Pennsylvania factional tensions where Tilden men were led by Speaker Randall and their opposition by Senator William A. Wallace, a Hancock manager. "Coffee-pot" Wallace was an aggressive operator who seems to have been the principal source of rumors that he might soon be elected to replace Barnum as national chairman. Chairman Barnum, for his part, was receiving urgent requests to mediate the factional fights in Pennsylvania, New York, and Ohio. Barnum, however, was able to do very little to calm the waters.[2]

Democratic leaders were of three views about the 1880 presidential nomination. First, there were those who believed that Tilden wanted the nomination but would do nothing overt to get it. Second, there was the group who thought that Tilden would not run but did expect to name the candidate. This group saw Tilden's preference as either Henry B. Payne, father-in-law of William C. Whitney, or Speaker Randall of Pennsylvania. Kind words were also circulating about National Chairman Barnum, whose Senate term would end in 1879. A third group was distinctly anti-Tilden. Among these were supporters of Ewing, Thurman, Bayard, Hendricks, and Hancock, names that had been considered at previous Democratic national conventions. Ewing had little organized strength. Tilden was firmly opposed to Thurman, Bayard, and Hendricks, all soft-money advocates. General Winfield Scott Hancock of Pennsylvania, famous for repulsing the Confederate armies at Gettysburg and one of the two principal candidates in the deadlocked convention of 1868, was the remaining alternative to Tilden himself.

Tilden's ambivalence and status as titular leader left most Democratic delegates in confusion as they arrived in Cincinnati for the nominating convention. Before his colleague, Daniel Manning, set out for the convention, Tilden told him that he would not accept the nomination unless it were unanimous but, since unanimity seemed unlikely, his first choice was Payne and his second Randall. Almost simultaneously Tilden sent a telegram to Payne asking him to accept second place on a Tilden ticket. To this, Payne agreed.[3] Tilden also gave Manning a letter that hinted that his health might not permit him to accept the nomination even if it should be offered. Dated June 18 and addressed to the New York delegation, the letter was to be read to the delegation at an appropriate time. The letter was long and ambiguous. In it Tilden asked for "an honorable discharge." He said that he wished to "lay down the honors and toils of even *quasi* party leadership, and to seek the repose of private life."[4] The New York delegation decided to consider the letter, when it was read to them, a firm withdrawal.

The first ballot put Hancock in the lead with 171 votes, Bayard second with 153½, Payne third with 61, Thurman fourth with 68½, and the rest scattered over a large field. During an overnight adjournment, a Hancock boom developed out of shifts among Bayard and Hendricks supporters. Pennsylvania, in the midst of the morning roll call, threw all its votes to Hancock; "Coffee-pot" Wallace had succeeded in uniting the divided delegation. Before the second ballot ended, Hancock had 705 votes and the nomination.

Bayard and Hendricks supporters had been mainly southern and midwestern soft-money men. Tilden and Payne followers were for hard-currency policies. Hancock had straddled the issue and thereby attracted Bayard-Hendricks votes as neutral ground. William C. Whitney, acting as a Tilden lieutenant, observed to a friend after the convention: "Yes, it has gone as I foresaw, but not as I hoped. If Mr. Tilden had been frankly out two weeks before the Convention, we could have nominated Payne."[5] But Tilden apparently did not want to be out of his own volition and might not have been if his letter had been read to the convention instead of to the New York delegation.[6]

With Hancock as nominee and Tilden still a major power in the Democratic Party, the selection of a national chairman raised an issue of intraparty accommodation. Control of the chairmanship had come to mean large influence in the campaign and in preparations for the next national convention. Despite his wretched health, Tilden was apparently determined to remain in the political picture. Smith M. Weed, a Tilden aide, and Barnum had conversations with Hancock's supporters, who were glad to do whatever was necessary to enlist the support of Tilden.[7]

"Coffee-pot" Wallace was Hancock's first choice for Democratic national chairman. Hancock-Wallace supporters argued that there was no precedent for disregarding the wishes of the nominee. Nor did precedent dictate that the nominee's choice should invariably prevail, retorted the Tilden followers, noting also that they remained a powerful sector of the party deserving of recognition. In addition, argued the Tilden men, Barnum was a far better fundraiser than Wallace. Speculation continued until Wallace announced his own ineligibility because of nonmembership on the national committee. The chairmanship went to Barnum "unanimously."[8] The Tilden men would still control the national machinery in 1884. Some observers went so far as to conclude that Barnum's reelection meant that Tilden would also control a Hancock administration.[9] Hancock subsequently did pay a visit to Tilden's residence at Greystone, New York, to solicit advice and support.

While Tilden made some speeches, his skilled hand was absent from active direction of the Democratic campaign. Hewitt, who was on the national executive committee, did not have his heart in his work. In midsummer he went to Europe, and falling ill, was detained in London for some time. The campaign finale saw Barnum having extreme difficulty raising funds, General Hancock still uncommitted on any public issue, and Tilden uneasy about the vigorous support Tammany's John Kelly was giving the national slate.

On election day, 4,449,053 voters preferred James A. Garfield and 4,442,030 Hancock. The popular vote divided 48.3 percent to 48.2 percent. The electoral vote was 214–155 in favor of Garfield. Barnum and Kelly, in a rare display of unity, charged that 20,000 Republican votes had been cast illegally in New York alone, but no legal action was taken. General Hancock went to his grave convinced "that he had been really elected and then defrauded."[10] Twenty years of defeat in presidential contests left Democratic leaders in deep gloom.

With election day past, old reform alliances in New York were refurbished for an effort to drive out John Kelly and to rein in Tammany Hall. In New York City, Abram Hewitt and William C. Whitney organized the "County Democracy" as a grass-roots alternative to Tammany. Tilden's upstate organization, under State Chairman Daniel Manning, was pleased to help. The County Democracy favored Abram Hewitt for the 1882 gubernatorial nomination. Tilden, who would control the state convention, failed to respond favorably; the old friends had fallen out after the crisis of 1876. Hewitt refused to allow his name to be used unless he had

Tilden's explicit support. The County Democracy proposed Edward Cooper instead. As second choice to Cooper, Whitney recommended Grover Cleveland, the incumbent reform mayor of Buffalo, to receive the County Democracy vote "at the proper time." The proper time came on the state convention's second ballot when the two front-runners in a field of seven candidates were deadlocked with 123 votes each and Cleveland was third with 71 votes. The County Democracy vote, plus others controlled by Manning, started a stampede for Cleveland. David B. Hill, mayor of Elmira and in later years a thorn in Cleveland's side, was nominated for lieutenant-governor.[11] Cleveland won the governorship, and the Tilden organization had an heir-apparent.

With Hancock completely retired from politics, Tilden was again the principal elder in the Democratic clan. However, he was becoming more and more of a recluse at his Greystone estate, and most of his influence was felt through his younger colleagues: State Chairman Daniel Manning and Colonel Daniel Lamont. National Chairman Barnum, always a loyal Tildenite, however, continued to talk of Tilden's "inevitable" election to the presidency. Governor Cleveland, an admirer of Tilden, frequently sought his advice. To the delight of Tilden and the County Democracy, Cleveland left Tammany completely out of the state patronage in 1883 and embarked upon an explosive public quarrel with John Kelly.

Money Issues: Patronage, Tariff, Silver

When nominated by the Republicans, James A. Garfield of Ohio had beaten a solid phalanx of Republican state bosses whose strategy had been to promote a third nomination for former President Grant. The alliance of Stalwart bosses was led by Roscoe Conkling of New York, one of whose lieutenants, Chester A. Arthur, received the vice-presidential nomination. Two months after inauguration President Garfield died of wounds from the gun of an angry Stalwart office-seeker. Arthur became president, and the event heightened popular concern over the problem of federal patronage. The fear among Republicans was that President Arthur would give the bulk of the growing patronage to his Stalwart associates.

Instead, Arthur reassured the reform element in his party by endorsing civil service legislation. He then dropped Hayes's policy of trying to conciliate conservative southern Democrats and used the patronage to strengthen the diminishing number of southern

Republicans with an eye to influencing their delegations to future Republican national conventions. Arthur's southern policy began a process of converting the Republican party in the South into a tiny collection of federal jobholders, thereby reinforcing the aberration occurring on the Democratic side as the latter became more and more a white party in a one-party region.

Nationally, the tariff issue was gaining public attention, rapidly becoming the principal issue between the parties and between their respective factions, the latter particularly true within the Democratic party. Rapidly increasing foreign trade made customs receipts heavy, creating a bulging Treasury surplus. Disposition of the surplus was a matter of growing congressional interest. The Republicans, finding the "bloody shirt" issue a somewhat worn garment early in the campaign of 1880, had begun to attack the Democratic platform phrase "tariff for revenue only" in the hope of thereby winning support from both business and labor. Hancock's foolish remark in the campaign that the tariff was a "local issue" helped the Republican stratagem.

In the House of Representatives, two Tilden men were becoming principal spokesmen on opposing sides of the tariff question: Abram Hewitt for reduction and Samuel J. Randall supporting protection. Pennsylvania became the seat of protectionism, with Randall Democrats and Simon Cameron Republicans able advocates in each party. From Maryland came another frequently heard Democratic voice on the tariff issue: Senator Arthur Pue Gorman, who styled himself as an "incidental protectionist." Gorman, like many of his Senate colleagues, was not a protectionist on every commodity. For example, he favored the reduction of tin ore duties. Maryland, not coincidentally, was one of the major centers of the canning industry in the country at that time. Another center of protectionist influence was Connecticut, whence came Democratic National Chairman Barnum, a leader in the protectionist iron industry. When the Democratic National Committee met on February 22, 1884, Chicago was chosen over St. Louis as the national convention city by 21–17 on a third ballot. The press interpreted the vote as a victory for the protectionist wing of the party, evidence of the importance attached to the issue.

The 1884 Democratic presidential favorites were Thomas F. Bayard, Allen G. Thurman, and Grover Cleveland. Manning, Hewitt, and Whitney were operating Cleveland headquarters, doing their utmost to counteract Tammany threats of bolting should Cleveland be the nominee and denying rumors that Randall was

Tilden's real favorite. Tammany's John Kelly tried to have the unit rule abolished in order to break Manning's control of New York's 72 votes, but lost in a 463 to 322 convention vote. Cleveland's strength appeared on the very first ballot, his 392 votes well ahead of Bayard's 170, Thurman's 88, and Randall's 78. When Pennsylvania's protectionists, led by those old adversaries Randall and Wallace, climbed onto the bandwagon, Cleveland had the nomination.

Cleveland wanted Daniel Manning to be his national chairman, but Barnum, Gorman, and Wallace were also major contenders for the position. Barnum, now sixty-six and a protectionist, had declared his wishes to retire, but he also was a key link to Tilden allies. Wallace, a protectionist, had been Hancock's preference for chairman in 1880 and was now the second choice of many members of the national committee. Next was Gorman, perhaps the most skillful political manager of the three, as demonstrated while he was a member of the congressional campaign committee. In a display of deference to Tilden, Barnum was elected by acclamation.[12] However, the principal management of Cleveland's campaign rested with Manning, Whitney, and Gorman. Barnum's main responsibility was to make supervisory trips to western states. He also was the largest financial contributor to the Cleveland campaign.

The Republican nominee, James G. Blaine, sought to make the tariff the main issue of the campaign. Gorman, however, launched an attack on Blaine's personal integrity. Mugwump revelations of new Mulligan Letters helped. The Mugwumps were a reform faction of the Republican party supporting Cleveland. The Mulligan Letters, so named for the railroad bookkeeper who brought them to light, were written by Blaine while Speaker of the House of Representatives advising a group of railroad promoters how to bring about legislation giving them land grants and suggesting that they bring him into their enterprise.

Integrity issues, however, have a way of becoming double-edged swords. On July 21, a Buffalo, New York, newspaper broke the story of bachelor Cleveland's affair with a woman named Maria Halpin and the illegitimate son presumably resulting from this union. Cleveland took on the scandal personally and directly, urging his colleagues to "tell the truth." Expressing doubt that the child was his, Cleveland indicated his willingness to assume responsibility for the child's support. The storm subsided for Cleveland, but not for Blaine.

Gorman, almost completely in charge of the Cleveland campaign, sent a stenographer to trail Blaine about New York City during the last days of the campaign. Reading the stenographer's notes, Gorman caught the implications of Reverend Burchard's reference to the Democrats as the party of "Rum, Romanism, and Rebellion." It was also Gorman who appreciated the affront to the common man represented by a semi-secret "prosperity dinner" tendered Blaine at Delmonico's Restaurant by the New York business community. Both events were widely reported in Rum-Romanism-Rebellion handbills and in "Royal Feast of Belshazzar Blaine and the Money Kings" cartoons.

The election returns were so close, particularly in New York, that both parties formally claimed victory. It seemed to be 1876 over again. Mobs swirled around the streets of New York and Boston. Riots-in-the-making were everywhere. The final official returns showed that Cleveland had carried New York's 36 electoral votes by the bare margin of 1,200 popular votes, and the electoral college by 219 to 182.

The Cleveland victory marked the return of the Democrats to control of the White House after twenty-four years. It was a mixed blessing. Federal patronage had become a burden instead of a partisan asset. The tariff was becoming a logrolling exercise for domestic economic interests rather than a source of revenue. The mining of silver was becoming a challenge to the stability of the monetary system rather than a new source of national wealth.

So great had the presidential job patronage become and so overflowing the federal treasury from custom revenues that the dilemmas of affluence quickly became major preoccupations for the new president. In postmasterships alone, there were more than fifty thousand appointments to be handled. Tens of thousands of other federal jobs were also to be filled. Every presidential appointment produced at least one disappointed Democratic applicant and several offended civil service reformers.

Money issues, in one form or another, began to consume the attention of Cleveland and national politicians generally for more than a generation. The tariff, a matter that had subsided since the days of Clay and Calhoun, became salient as customs receipts increased due to national industrial growth and greater foreign trade. The Treasury, in fact, now found itself with an embarrassing surplus. Should the surplus funds be used to retire the public debt? Such a move would rocket the market price of government obligations beyond any figure that the secretary of the treasury could pay.

99

So Congress turned to such solutions as veterans' pensions, rivers and harbors appropriations, and, somewhat more reluctantly, aid-to-education programs. Basically, however, the issue was whether the tariff should be reduced to a level producing revenue only or be maintained at high levels for the continued protection of American industry from foreign competition.

Most Republicans leaned toward protectionism, although some midwestern Republicans, representing agricultural communities, favored reduction. The Democrats, on the other hand, were more evenly divided. A congressman's position on the tariff depended upon his place of residence. Given the number of places and the number of commodities to be imported or protected, the tariff became one of the greatest sources of confusion and logrolling in congressional politics.

Monetary policy was closely related. Should a large supply of currency and easy credit (soft money) be made available to the commerce of the country? Or should credit be given only to the best risks at high prices (hard money) so that the nation's currency circulation could be kept close to the amount of the gold and silver supply that was its underpinning? Political leaders from the banking centers of the East were for the hard-money solution. Representatives from the agricultural Midwest and the South were for the soft-money alternative. Farmers were among the major buyers of credit, yet seemed unable to borrow their way out of their economic depression.

Bimetallism was another aspect of this same currency problem. Proponents of bimetallism argued that if the gold and paper currency were not in sufficient supply to handle the needs of a rapidly growing business and agricultural economy, silver, always in plentiful supply and even more so during the 1880s as mining output in Nevada, Colorado, and other Mountain States increased, ought to become a companion to gold as the specie basis for currency. Should the Treasury pay out millions in gold bullion in order to purchase the annual fixed amount of silver for coinage as required by the Bland-Allison Act? Cleveland favored dropping silver coinage entirely in order to protect the government's gold stocks. Within a decade this "anti-silver" position isolated him from the mainstream of his party.

In Congress, almost irresistible pressure was being placed on Democratic leaders to heed the demands of proponents of easy credit, plentiful currency, silver specie, tariff-for-revenue-only, and the reduction of the federal Treasury surpluses. In extreme form, these had been the demands of the Greenback party. The Greenbackers experienced their heyday through the 1874–1884 decade, in 1876 running their first candidate for president. In the congressional elections of 1878 they pulled more than a million votes. In 1880, the Garfield-Hancock contest, the Greenback candidate for president received as much as 3.4 percent of the popular vote, enough to hurt the Democrats severely. Greenback strongholds lay in some 306 agricultural counties across about 15 states, the most important of these: Iowa, Kansas, Michigan, Missouri, and Texas. Although the Greenback party disappeared after 1884, many of its elements reappeared in the Populist party of the 1890s. Democratic responses to the Populists were to be greatly influenced by the party's experience with the Greenbackers.

Even before Cleveland had departed Albany, Senator Gorman, fearful that the new president might neglect the party organization in the distribution of patronage, took it upon himself to provide a list of party leaders who should be called to Albany for consultation.[13] Cleveland preferred to keep his own counsel on patronage, but, before the year had passed, found himself up against rebellious organizations in New York, where David B. Hill was now governor, and in Gorman's Maryland. Changes in Cleveland's appointment policies soon followed.

In his first annual message of December 1885, the president asked that the Bland-Allison Act, requiring the annual coinage of a fixed amount of silver, be terminated. The Treasury was paying out millions in gold, the long-standing basis of the nation's currency, in exchange for millions of the more slowly circulating silver coin. This policy presented a constant threat to the Treasury's stock of gold, to business confidence, and to the savings of the thrifty, Cleveland argued. Congress declined to act on the president's recommendations.

Another money issue that could no longer be ignored was the Treasury surplus created by customs revenues. Cleveland decided in 1887 to devote his entire annual message to the one issue of tariff revision. As he prepared the message, Cleveland heard important voices pro or con, cautioning or encouraging: Randall, Gorman, and Barnum arrayed against Carlisle, Hewitt, and Scott. William C. Whitney, with an eye to the forthcoming presidential contest, advised the president to "take it easy" or to postpone the issue. Cleveland refused to delay.

Cleveland's tariff message of December 6, 1887, set the entire tone of politics for the upcoming presidential year. It was Jacksonian in its broad appeal to the masses to unite against the special interests. The tariff message put Cleveland in position for renomination in 1888 without his seeking it. The message gave the president the political initiative, and the national debate proceeded on his terms and around his name. Reluctantly, Whitney admitted that "it was a winning issue." "Your position," he told the president, "has been greatly raised."[14] To implement Cleveland's views, the Mills Tariff Reduction Bill was introduced into Congress.

The protectionists in the Democratic party were not idle before the challenge. Senator Gorman, one of the leading protectionists, had a great deal to say during the next meeting of the national committee on February 22, 1888, and, with Barnum in the chair, the opportunity to say it. Nothing was said about the tariff message, but the debate over the choice of national convention time and place was unusually protracted. Gorman moved that the convention be held late, July 3. Several other dates were proposed. William L. Scott of Pennsylvania, as the new committeeman replacing Samuel Randall and closest to the Cleveland administration, tried to prevent a clear demonstration of Gorman's strength in the committee. When the final ballot was cast, however, Gorman's July 3 was preferred over June 5 by a vote of 28 to 19. The protectionists seemed to have the votes.

The choice of a convention city came next and required *fourteen* ballots. The committee was evenly divided over three cities: San Francisco, Chicago, and St. Louis. Gorman led the fight for San Francisco, Scott for Chicago. An overnight recess was taken after the eleventh ballot. When the sides remained unchanged next morning on the twelfth ballot, Scott moved to reconsider the convention date, but lost 24 to 23. On the thirteenth ballot it was still San Francisco 17, Chicago 16, and St. Louis 13. However, on the fourteenth, 3 Chicago votes shifted to St. Louis and, giving up, nearly all Gorman's San Francisco votes followed. Scott then moved to reconsider the date, and June 5 was chosen, 29 to 17. The Cleveland forces had their way, but the size of the protectionist opposition had become clear. Gorman now acknowledged that Cleveland's renomination was a foregone conclusion. However, there were platform, campaign management, and post-election patronage over which to battle and bargain.[15]

The protectionist-reductionist dispute went forward in the

committee on resolutions as soon as the convention met. Editor Henry Watterson, leading the low tariff group, ran against Gorman for the resolutions committee chairmanship and was elected by a close vote, 22 to 20. Gorman now cast himself in the role of negotiator between the factions. Cleveland had privately given him a tariff plank which avoided reference to the Mills Bill still pending congressional decision. The draft plank was written in such moderate language as not to put the president out on a limb as a free-trader. Gorman, without revealing its authorship, showed it to Samuel J. Randall, now leader of the more extreme protectionists, who remarked that it suited him but that "the Cleveland crowd would kick." Gorman said he thought he could manage them.[16]

The convention took the unusual step of renominating Cleveland before receiving the report of the platform committee. Notwithstanding the moderation displayed by Cleveland and Gorman, the reductionists had the votes to put a strong tariff reduction plank into the platform, and, by separate resolution, endorse the controversial Mills Bill.

Factionalism now projected itself into the organization of the national campaign. William C. Whitney continued to be at hand to serve as Cleveland's unofficial spokesman. Barnum and Gorman, their protectionist views well known, declined the national chairmanship. The vice-presidential nominee, Allen G. Thurman of Ohio, longtime Democratic associate of Whitney's father-in-law, Henry B. Payne, suggested for the chairmanship another Ohio colleague, Calvin Brice. Brice was acceptable to Cleveland and the factional leaders. Probably the most significant fact about the selection of Calvin Brice as national chairman was the search for a "neutral" man that preceded it. The factions within the Democratic party were constrained to present a united front against the Republican opposition.

Factional adjustments should have ended with the appointment of Brice, but the problems ran on into the campaign during which vigorous leadership continued to be lacking. Brice set up New York headquarters practically alone. It soon became evident that he was not familiar with state factional matters, particularly in the eastern states, that he himself was waiting for signals to be called, and that, in the last analysis, he had little interest in running a publicity bureau. Most persons connected with the campaign organization looked to Cleveland's secretary, Colonel Lamont, as the team's quarterback. Barnum did some field work, but, according to certain

Connecticut Democrats, he grossly neglected the campaign in his own state. Gorman and his state organization sat on their hands. "Gorman's obvious, apparent apathy even leads us to hope we may carry Maryland," reported one Republican state leader to that party's nominee, Benjamin Harrison.[17]

On July 21, 1888, the Mills Bill, following the reductionist position of the president, was passed in the House, 162 to 149, in a partisan vote. Only 4 Democrats voted against the bill; 3 Republicans and 3 Independents crossed lines to vote in support. The president's prestige was greatly enhanced, although the Senate subsequently followed a strategy of delay and substitution.

Cleveland received a hundred-thousand-vote popular plurality, but these votes turned up in the wrong places. New York went Republican by only thirteen thousand votes. Its pivotal electoral college votes put Benjamin Harrison into the White House. In an era when local registration and voting safeguards were almost nonexistent, the Republican National Committee was able to mobilize three important "movements" of voters from Pennsylvania to New York City. It is estimated that some fifty thousand Republican "floaters" were contracted for, although a much smaller number were actually delivered to New York City precincts.

Cleveland retired to the practice of law in New York and for some time remained silent on public policy and his availability for renomination.

Awkward Coalition: Bankers and Populists

Benjamin Harrison's administration also grappled with the tariff, currency, and civil service reform issues. During 1890 there were a number of congressional enactments related to these matters. The McKinley Tariff raised customs duties to new highs in keeping with the Republican protectionist position. The Sherman Silver Purchase Act made a stride toward bimetallism in the interest of easing the currency shortage. Civil service reform remained at a standstill, with forty-nine thousand of the fifty-six thousand available postmasterships changing hands.[18] Two other issues were gaining prominence: the growth of monopolistic business enterprise, to which the Sherman Anti-Trust Act was a response, and the aberration of party politics in what was rapidly becoming "the Solid South."

The southern policies of Hayes, Garfield, and Arthur and the anger of southern whites over Reconstruction's Black Republicans combined to spur white supremacy practices and legislation aimed at completely disfranchising the Negro. The trend also meant a continued loss of Republican strength and prospects in the South. Harrison, after long study of the problem, concluded that a federally protected ballot box, including the possibility of using troops, was the only solution. Henry Cabot Lodge of Massachusetts introduced what came to be known as the "Force Bill" into the House of Representatives where it passed on July 2, 1890, by a bare margin of 155 to 149. The bill never came up for full consideration in the Senate where a filibuster against it threatened to impede enactment of the protectionist McKinley Tariff. This led to the tabling of the election bill.

As Congress debated these issues, severe agrarian unrest in the South and West swept in a number of representatives and at least two senators running on Populist and Independent tickets in the fall elections of 1890. A substantial number of Democrats pledged to Populist programs were also elected. The Populist party became a national organization during the following year and proceeded to pursue those parts of the southern and western electorates that were not yet integrated into the two major parties. Populist and Democratic organizations found themselves competing in some places and cooperating in others to bring new voters into the national consensus.

The issue upon which Cleveland eventually chose to break his silence and take a public stand was hardly calculated to bring fellow Democrats in certain sections of the country running to his support. The potent silver interests in the Mountain States and the aggrieved agricultural interests in the South and Midwest were insisting upon the maintenance of a bimetallic currency, the former to dispose of the growing supply of silver and the latter to make currency and credit more readily available. The depressed agricultural economy, which had excited a vigorous populism and, along with it, a Democratic sweep in the congressional elections of 1890, suggested that the party was on the verge of being overwhelmed by the silver forces. The former president, early in 1891, put his political future on the line by declaring unqualifiedly that free coinage of silver was a "dangerous and reckless experiment." The newspapers of the South and the West went into a fury in condemning him.

Opposition to a possible Cleveland renomination gathered momentum. Protectionists such as Senator Arthur Pue Gorman of

Maryland were active. In New York, Governor David B. Hill stepped up his old feud with the former president. Even National Chairman Calvin Brice expressed doubt that Cleveland could muster the necessary two-thirds for renomination. The principal exponent of a Cleveland renomination, William C. Whitney, however, was not deterred. The wealthy corporation lawyer, political adjutant to both Tilden and Cleveland over so many years, assumed a quiet leadership that overcame every obstacle. The 1892 national convention renominated Cleveland on a single ballot.

A major threat to Cleveland's election chances was Populist enmity. In the South and Midwest, Populist appeal was mainly agrarian. However, the farther west one traveled, the greater the Populist emphasis upon free and unlimited coinage of silver. James Weaver was the Populist nominee for president.

At the beginning of the 1892 campaign, leaders in both major parties were indifferent to the Populists. Democratic national leaders, however, recalling their problems with the Greenbackers, attempted a fusion of forces with the Populists wherever such action gave some promise of knocking a normally Republican state out of the Harrison column. Such efforts in Washington, California, and Montana came to naught. In Colorado, Idaho, Minnesota, North Dakota, South Dakota, Nebraska, Kansas, and Oregon, Democrats either endorsed Populist electors, offered their own electoral lists but campaigned for the Weaver electors, or apportioned Weaver and Cleveland electors on anti-Harrison tickets. In Nevada, a Silver party was organized and endorsed Weaver, its ranks thick with silver Republicans. The Democratic National Committee advised local Democratic leaders to help the Silver party carry the state for Weaver and prevent its going to Harrison.

In the South, the Republicans, as the minority party, played a similar game. Southern Republicans in Arkansas, Texas, Louisiana, Florida, Alabama, and Georgia gave either tacit or express endorsement to Populist electoral tickets. Among southern Democratic factions as well, pro-Populist Democrats were winning in primaries or bolting to run as independents.

For advice on Democratic silver statements, Whitney turned to Benton McMillin of Tennessee and William Jennings Bryan of Nebraska.[19] McMillin was in his seventh term in Congress and knew the politics of the border states thoroughly. Bryan, just turned thirty-two, had a good knowledge of midwestern affairs. Whatever advice McMillin and Bryan gave Whitney, however, Grover Cleveland heeded none of it. Cleveland stood firm against "doubtful experiments" with the nation's currency.

Once again the major-party popular vote was evenly divided, 5,554,000 for Cleveland to 5,191,000 for Harrison. This time well over a million votes had been drawn off by the Populist nominee. Through their numerous local alliances with Democrats, the Populist leadership found itself in substantial position to influence Democratic party decisions in the next several years, particularly 1896.

As Cleveland awaited his second inauguration, the economic horizons filled with signs of impending collapse. Financial and congressional leaders spoke with unprecedented urgency about the need to repeal the Sherman Silver Purchase Act, upon which they placed blame for the precarious conditions of the gold supply, credit, and price structure. By May, the Panic of 1893 was upon the nation.

Congress convened in August in special session, at the president's call, and fought over the repeal issue until November. From the southerners and the westerners came charges that the president was "the tool of Wall Street." Reviewing the 1892 election results, Democratic leaders noted that a million votes—nearly 9 percent of the national total—had been cast for Weaver, the Populist nominee. For most of these voters, "free silver" was a throbbing issue. In the House of Representatives, however, there were approximately 173 anti-silver men, 114 silverites, and 69 doubtfuls. Former Speaker Tom Reed, Tammany's Bourke Cockran, and William L. Wilson eloquently represented the administration's position favoring repeal. The greatest pro-silver speeches came from Congressman William Jennings Bryan, supported by Richard P. Bland and Joseph W. Bailey. In the Senate James K. Jones of Arkansas led such eminences as George Vest, Henry M. Teller, Fred T. DuBois, and others. When Cleveland's repeal measure passed, silver leaders in the Democratic party, with an ear to their Populist allies, began to reevaluate their allegiance to the Cleveland administration.

These reevaluations became decisive during the battle over tariff legislation in the following year. Congressman William L. Wilson was in charge of the administration's reductionist proposal in the House, and Senator Jones was designated to shepherd it throught the Senate. The House bill, although moderate in its reductions, met stubborn resistance in the Senate, where it was padded with over six hundred amendments. Senator Gorman, whom Cleveland already viewed as a "traitor" for having sought a compromise on the silver repeal bill, was at the head of "the Amenders," whose work converted the reductionist Wilson-Jones Bill into the protectionist Wilson-Gorman Tariff Act.

As the heat of the tariff debate reached a climax, President Cleveland, in a public letter to Congressman Wilson, denounced the failure of "certain Democrats"—referring to Gorman and his followers—to keep the party's pledges. Gorman delivered a stinging reply from the Senate floor, while Senator Jones sat silent and unwilling to defend the administration he presumably represented. It was Jones's opinion that Cleveland had sufficient information about the legislative negotiations to have taken a firmer stand privately before resorting to a public fight. The Senate version of the tariff was passed and became law without Cleveland's signature.

Cleveland's second administration was a thoroughly troubled one. The depression had aggravated the party's internal differences on currency as never before. Labor unrest led to such crises as the Pullman strike in Chicago in 1894, broken by Cleveland's dispatch of federal troops. The protectionists in both parties, as described above, undid the administration's tariff bill. The party's factions raced toward a showdown. The president became a target for all who were riding the tides of discontent. Ben Tillman promised to stick a pitchfork in Cleveland's "old ribs." Missouri's Champ Clark spoke of Cleveland, Benedict Arnold, and Aaron Burr in the same breath. The 1894 midterm election gave Republicans and Populists such impressive margins that the president's prestige never recovered.

The congressional election was generally damaging for Democrats. The party limped into the House of Representatives with only 104 to the Republicans' 284 seats. The one issue that transcended all others in symbolizing popular discontent was free silver. The issue split both major parties, the Democrats far more seriously than the Republicans. An analysis of the resolutions adopted by state party conventions during spring of 1895 showed that Republicans could expect 322 free-silver delegates and 584 sound-money men at their 1896 national convention. The Democrats, on the other hand, could expect 433 silverites against a slim majority of 473 sound-money votes.[20]

Bryan's Silver Coins and Cross of Gold

In both parties, free-silver organizers were on the move. Silver Democrats launched the American Bimetallic League. Silver Republicans promoted the National Bimetallic Union. Both merged to become the American Bimetallic Union. In July 1895, a conference of bimetallic Democrats, intent upon capturing the next national convention, met in Washington and organized the Bimetallic Democratic National Committee.

President Cleveland remained silent about his renomination intentions, thus keeping his own sound-money supporters off balance. Whitney based the Cleveland convention strategy on the expectation that the president could control one-third of the votes, that is, 312 of the 930, enough to veto a free-silver nomination. A test vote on the temporary chairmanship of the convention, however, revealed a majority on the side of the silverites: 556 to 349, that is, a 60–38 percent division. Whitney began to doubt that he could hold the 37-vote margin he needed to veto. A free-silver leader would be nominated. The question was: which one? The strongest contenders were Richard P. Bland and Horace Boies. Another well-known name in the silver cause, but a minor prospect as presidential timber, was thirty-six-year-old William Jennings Bryan.

The draft platform featured a silver-gold ratio of 16-to-1 and full repudiation of "government by injunction," that is, Cleveland's handling of the Pullman strike two years earlier. When the resolutions committee completed its work, its chairman, Senator Jones, invited Bryan to arrange the floor debate on the platform. Bryan's version of this request describes it as an "unexpected stroke of luck":

My ambition had been to be chairman of the Committee on Resolutions, but I found that Senator Jones aspired to that place, and as he was a much older man, and the president [sic] of the bimetallic organization formed at Memphis, I did not care to be a candidate against him, and gave up the thought of that place. . . . The request came as a surprise. . . . After the Convention was over and Senator Jones had been made Chairman of the National Committee at my request, I asked him how he happened to turn the defense of the platform over to me. I know that it was not with any thought of favoring me as a candidate, because he was a supporter of Mr. Bland and too loyal to him. . . . Senator Jones answered my question by saying that I was the only one of the prominent speakers who had not had an opportunity to address the Convention. . . . He knew of the part I had taken in the organizing of the fight and how I had traveled over the country for a year helping in many states and said that his invitation to me was due entirely to a sense of fairness.[21]

109

As Bryan arranged it, Senator Jones was to read the platform. Tillman would open the debate for the silver side. Hill, Vilas, and Russell would follow with the sound-money arguments. Bryan would close for silver.

The preceding evening, at his hotel room, as Bryan wrote a news dispatch for the *Omaha World-Herald*, a delegation of Silver Republicans called upon him to present the claims of Senator Henry M. Teller for the Democratic nomination the following day. Could Mr. Bryan be enlisted in favor of Teller? Bryan quietly replied:

I am perfectly willing to vote for Senator Teller myself because I regard the money question as the paramount issue, but the silver Democrats have won their fight, while the silver Republicans lost in their convention, and it will be easier to bring the minority silver Republicans to us than to take the majority silver Democrats over to a Republican nominee.

Then, with disconcerting candor, Bryan concluded that he felt he himself could make a stronger fight than any lifelong Republican. "I expect to be the nominee of the convention," he told the stunned delegation.[22]

When the "Boy Orator" rose to make his platform speech next day, he was aware of several facts: (1) Within the silver faction, the Bland and Boies candidacies were about to stalemate each other. (2) Because of their narrow nominating majority, the silver leaders could not afford a drawn-out nomination contest. (3) Many southern delegations were either uncommitted to any candidate or supported Bryan as their second choice. (4) No silver Democrat could as readily win endorsements from the Populists, the Silver Republicans, and the National Silver party as Bryan himself. (5) Among the major silver leaders, Tillman was friendly, Daniel uncommitted, and Altgeld influenced by a strong pro-Bryan group in the Illinois delegation. Above all, (6) the one question upon which at least 626 of the delegates were resolutely united was free silver. It was Bryan's ringing final words that shifted the undecided votes to him: "We shall answer their demands for a gold standard by saying to them, you shall not press down upon the brow of labor this crown of thorns. You shall not crucify mankind upon a cross of gold." The nomination was his on the fifth ballot. Senator James K. Jones of Arkansas, although not a member of the national committee, became its chairman as the youthful Bryan sought to make a gesture to the party elders.

The Democratic search for a winning coalition was never more complex than during the 1896 campaign. The campaign organization could not be filled out until the Silver Republicans, the National Silver party, and the Populists had acted on endorsements of Bryan's candidacy. It was also certain that the sound-money Democrats would create problems. Nor was it easy for the older silver leaders to be enthused over the "Boy Orator." Governor Stone was frank enough to tell Bryan: "I follow you because the party has made you its leader. I am glad the leader is a man I can respect and honor for his sincerity, his ability and his manhood; but I want it understood that I am not going to sneeze because you take snuff."[23]

Senator Teller soon sent word that he was about to confer with numerous Silver Republican leaders about an endorsement of Bryan. "I have written to all the Populist leaders . . . urging them to nominate you and I made it impossible for my name to be used."[24] The Silver Republican endorsement was promptly given.

The Populists, however, presented a different picture. Most of the 1,400 delegates to the Populist national convention in St. Louis were fearful of being "sold out" to the Democratic party. This was particularly true of southern Populists, whose six years of political activity had been largely, as they saw it, a wearying battle against southern Democrats. These anti-fusionists, however, were a poorly organized majority at the convention. The fusionists, led by James B. Weaver, were far better organized, aiming for endorsement of Bryan and fusion of the two parties. For three days prior to the Populist convention, Democratic Chairman Jones consulted and worked closely with the fusionists.

Senator Marion Butler came up with a compromise plan. Would the anti-fusionists go along if a radical southern Populist—Tom Watson—were substituted for Sewall as the Democratic vice-presidential nominee? Rumors circulated among convention delegates that the Democratic managers would withdraw Sewall in favor of a Populist if Bryan were endorsed. The compromisers made the unusual suggestion that the vice-presidential candidate be nominated first. This procedural change was approved 738 to 637, and Watson was nominated to their Bryan-Watson slate.

The following morning delegates read in the newspapers a telegram from Bryan asking Senator Jones to withdraw his name if Sewall were not endorsed. The papers also carried a statement by Senator Jones denying that he had agreed to the withdrawal of Sewall. Anti-fusionists charged that the convention's chairman, Senator William V. Allen of Nebraska, had withheld this information from the convention. Allen refused to take cognizance of the Bryan message and hurried the balloting along. The anti-fusionists caucused on a proposal to bolt but reached no decision. They departed from St. Louis in no mood to cooperate in the campaign with either the Democratic party or their own fusionist faction.[25]

The campaign activities of four political parties—Democrats, Populists, National Silverites, and Silver Republicans—now needed to be coordinated. This was partly accomplished by creation of an Advisory Committee to the Democratic National Committee, consisting of six Democrats and six representatives from the other three parties. The treasurer of the Democratic and the National Silver national committees was the same man. Organizational work proceeded very slowly. Chairman Jones at times lashed out impatiently at the troublesome southern Populists who, he said, "are out for nothing but spoils."[26] It was September before membership of the Advisory and other national committees was completed. It took weeks to accomplish fusion slates of presidential electors in twenty-eight states. The Republican press rejoiced over the tribulations of the "popocrats."

Meanwhile, conservative Democrats in the East decided to concentrate on congressional and local races or come out for a third party ticket in support of the gold standard. On July 23 and 24, a conference of sound-money leaders took place in Chicago. At an August 7 meeting, a national committee of thirty-five was organized and a nominating convention called. On September 2, the "National Democratic Party" was formally established. John M. Palmer and Simon B. Buckner were nominated, after President Cleveland had been offered first place and declined. The new party's finance committee constituted a formidable roster: Charles J. Canda (former treasurer of the regular Democratic National Committee) as chairman, William C. Whitney, former Democratic Chairman Abram S. Hewitt, August Belmont the Younger, George Foster Peabody, William R. Grace, John D. Crimmins, Roswell Flower, Don M. Dickinson, and others. This was a wealthy and politically expert group.

The campaign of the Gold Democrats was concentrated in about five midwestern states—Indiana, Kentucky, Michigan, Minnesota, and Kansas—to draw off enough Democratic votes from Bryan to secure majorities for McKinley.[27] President Cleveland and his cabinet supported the Palmer-Buckner ticket. Only the necessity of conducting further legislative business with Congress kept Cleveland from making a public campaign in behalf of the new ticket.[28]

In contrast with Democratic divisions was the unity achieved among Republicans by their decision on the gold plank and by Republican National Chairman Mark Hanna's extraordinary conduct of the campaign for William McKinley. Active in the campaign was former President Harrison, who spoke frequently in New York, Virginia, and his home state of Indiana. Never before had a presidential campaign been so thoroughly organized nor so much campaign literature and speeches communicated to the electorate, nor so much money raised and expended. Hanna's managerial achievements were unprecedented and have been fully documented elsewhere.[29]

Two complete Republican headquarters, one in Chicago and the other in New York, were established. There was a division of labor, under Hanna's direction, among the Republican National Committee, the Republican congressional campaign committee, and such nonparty groups as the Protective Tariff League.[30] Expenditures were without parallel to that date; some informed estimates put the figure as high as $7 million expended by the national agencies alone.[31] A complete commercial bookkeeping and auditing system was installed to keep track of the flow of funds. On October 14, the *New York Journal* revealed that Hanna had sent out a circular letter to several banks in Newark, New Jersey, assessing them one-eighth of one percent of their capital stock for support of the campaign. This was confirmed and was found to be the fund-raising procedure in several states. Standard Oil gave $250,000. Republicans produced hundreds of millions of pamphlets and other documents; estimates ranged from 120 million to 225 million.

While Governor McKinley and his multimillionaire campaign manager, Mark Hanna, were formidable enough opponents, once again the main elements of defeat lay within the Democratic party itself. Unable to mobilize the many parts of its coalition, the party succumbed to the Hanna steamroller. Once again, a defeated presidential nominee, this time William Jennings Bryan, became titular leader of the Democrats as the out-party. Like Van Buren and Tilden before him, Bryan would be a force to reckon with for almost a generation and would leave a lasting imprint on the party.

6

In the Wilderness
with
William Jennings Bryan

THE Bryan-McKinley contest of 1896 has
been characterized as a "critical election" in which there was a
sharp and durable realignment in the voting patterns of the electorate. The Panic of 1893 brought bank failures, railroad receiverships,
unemployment, strikes, populism, strife over the monetary system,
and great factional strain within both parties. The midterm setbacks
of the Democrats in 1894 swept on into the election of 1896 when,
across the board, voters in working-class as well as silk-stocking
wards, in the cities as well as the country, blamed the Democrats
for the nation's hardships and, in doing so, moved over to the
Republican party on a long-term basis.[1] The unfortunate task of
leading the party through the wilderness during this period fell
chiefly to William Jennings Bryan, who performed these duties with
more tenacity and skill than many of his colleagues cared to abide.
Not until Woodrow Wilson became the divided party's compromise
presidential nominee in 1912 did Bryan's domination of the party
fade and a new era begin.

Bryan's defeat was in many ways a less serious setback for the
silverite coalition controlling the Democratic party in 1896 than
were the discovery of new gold deposits in the Klondike and the
era of prosperity that arrived shortly after the election. The shortage of currency, which had been the economic justification for the
free-silver movement, was no longer a pressing problem. Yet, politicians found it difficult to give up this familiar issue and factional
touchstone.

The McKinley administration rode high with the nation's prosperity, self-confidence, and expansionist fervor. The land-space between the Atlantic and the Pacific was almost filled; only Arizona, New Mexico, and Oklahoma remained to be admitted to the Union. American free-lancers were prospecting in Alaska, upsetting a monarchy in Hawaii, selling supplies to Cuban revolutionaries, filibustering up and down Central America, investing in South American enterprises, proposing an interoceanic canal across Nicaragua, and reaching advanced stages of monopolistic industrial enterprise at home. The gold discoveries had, for all practical purposes, solved the bimetallic currency issue.

War with Spain in 1898 seemed almost a sideshow, yet it led to independence for Cuba, American acquisition of Puerto Rico and Guam, and, for $20 million, the purchase of the Philippines. A continent-wide nation with overseas possessions and investments, its citizens suddenly were world politicians, although for three or four more decades most would resist the thought and the action.

The Spanish-American War made imperialism the new grand issue of domestic politics. The annexation of the Philippines, Puerto Rico, and other distant islands was opposed by eminent figures in both parties. Democratic party leaders across the country debated the priority to be given to the imperialism issue in their legislative program and in the next presidential election. Had feeling on free silver abated? Was the growing antitrust sentiment in the country sufficient to warrant party attention? Complicating Democratic deliberations were new and well-organized pressure groups, for example, the bimetallists, the anti-imperialists, the antitrusters, and the prohibitionists. Divisions of opinion and the party's inability to produce dramatic new national leaders left congressional Democrats a squabbling minority in both houses during the opening years of the twentieth century.

Bryan: Activist Titular Leader

The national leadership of the Democratic party retired almost *en masse* after election day. President Cleveland retreated to Princeton. William C. Whitney, the financier, returned to his business interests. Arthur Pue Gorman suffered temporary banishment from his Senate seat in the fall elections of 1899 but returned in 1903. Tillman, Daniel, and Vest continued in the Senate, substantially deflated by the fading fortunes of the Populist and free-silver movements. Tom Watson became virtually a political recluse for eight years. Failing reelection in the Illinois gubernatorial race, John P. Altgeld ended active participation in politics, except for a brief return during the mayoralty race of 1899 in which he unsuccessfully challenged Carter H. Harrison's control of the Chicago Democratic organization. David B. Hill left the Senate to resume his law practice; his personal following in New York declined. William J. Stone returned to the practice of law at the end of his term as governor in Missouri succeeding George Vest as United States senator in 1903.

Bryan, on the other hand, made himself a full-time titular leader, writing an account of the 1896 campaign as *The First Battle*. Between 1897 and 1899, he traveled some ninety-three thousand miles on the lecture circuit and earned the nickname "Chautauqua King." His principal lecture topics were money, trusts, and imperialism. On the organization side, Bryan encouraged the development of local clubs whose parent organization became the National Association of Democratic Clubs (NADC). National Chairman Jones and leaders of the regular party organizations were slow to give their attention to the clubs. They finally did in 1900 when publisher William Randolph Hearst agreed to serve as NADC president.

Democratic factional struggles continued in state organizations across the nation, complicated by shifts and changes within the Populist and Silver Republican party organizations. Although there was little doubt that Bryan would receive a second nomination, anti-Bryan feeling manifested itself in a variety of forms: delays in public endorsements of Bryan's leadership, debates over the proper emphasis to be given the money issue in the 1900 platform, and arguments over party procedural questions. While there was no real challenger for the presidential nomination, there were great differences in enthusiasm for Bryan.

The Gold Democrats decided to establish a permanent headquarters in New York City and asked their national chairman, William D. Bynum, a former Indiana congressman, to take charge. In spring 1897, Bynum took on the job, producing sound-money literature and maintaining contact with many midterm candidates for Congress. However, by September 1898, Bynum was ready to recommend a dissolution of the Gold Democratic national committee and ordered the treasurer to refund money on hand proportionally to all contributors. The national committee, however, chose to continue and appointed a new chairman. Meeting again in July 1900, however, the committee decided that it had lost not only its principal leaders and main sources of financial support but also its issue. The committee voted not to name a third-party ticket but declared it the duty of all sound-money Democrats to join in defeating Bryan's second candidacy.[2]

The return of the Gold Democrats to the regular Democratic party revived the money issue and gave it a factional significance it might not otherwise have had in the nominating process of 1900. Perry Belmont spoke out on behalf of the sound-money "regulars" in a widely publicized address challenging the concept of the 16-to-1 coinage ratio. Buffalo leader Norman E. Mack observed sadly that the Gold Democrats were not coming back into the party as graciously as one might hope.[3] The Gold Democrats forced the money issue into the local New York factional battle between David B. Hill and Tammany's Richard Croker. Croker favored full reiteration of the 16-to-1 plank. Hill, on the other hand, held to mild demands for a "brief" reiteration of the 1896 platform, but urged top priority to new issues: imperialism and monopoly. "Give us the best quality of crow you can," he asked of Bryan.[4]

Chairman Jones's position did not help matters when, during 1898, various factional elements sought to negotiate greater intraparty unity. Writing to Bryan, Jones reported:

Many men approach me on this question of "getting together." My answer invariably to them is, that we would be very glad to have all Democrats squarely back in the fold; that the party will not deviate one hair's breadth from the line already marked out for us, and that it will be necessary either to come in without conditions or, in my opinion, join the Republicans. I always do this in as courteous a way as I can, and try not to be offensive.[5]

Bryan, on the other hand, was willing to move to other issues. This was especially true since the Spanish-American War had made imperialism a salient public question. He opposed imperialism but supported ratification of a peace treaty with Spain. Bryan remained somewhat aloof as the Senate struggled over the treaty's ratification. It was finally approved by a single vote more than the necessary two-thirds. Andrew Carnegie and the Anti-Imperialist League charged that one word from Bryan could have beaten the treaty. But Senator Jones regretted that Bryan had taken "so prominent and pronounced a stand in favor of ratification."[6]

By 1900, there was widespread confusion within the multiparty coalition that had favored free silver. The southern middle-of-the-road Populists left their party in 1897 and conducted a nominating convention in Cincinnati on May 11, 1900. The fusion Populists held their own nominating convention at Sioux Falls, South Dakota, on the same date. Large numbers of Silver Republicans attended the latter, which rededicated itself to Bryan and free silver.

For vice-presidential nominee of the Sioux Falls convention, Bryan and National Chairman Jones had suggested a little-known Populist so that the Populist nomination would seem less offensive to the subsequent Democratic National Convention. Bryan also hoped to make it simpler to arrange a Populist withdrawal in favor of the eventual Democratic vice-presidential nominee. The Populist convention, however, ignored the recommendation and nominated for vice president the popular national chairman of the Silver Republican party, Charles A. Towne. This action simply fueled the Democratic vice-presidential race, for which New York alone offered five candidates.[7]

Bryan's renomination assumed the appearance of a holding operation. David B. Hill, now U.S. senator from New York, voiced the demands of the eastern wing in strong opposition to those of the West and South. Selection of the convention's temporary chairman, various platform planks, and other convention decisions were decided by very close votes. Selection of a vice-presidential nominee became an awkward issue among Democrats, Populists, and Silver Republicans in the lobbies. Cleveland's 1892 running mate, former Vice President Adlai E. Stevenson, was settled upon as a compromise.

The management of the Democratic campaign, again in contrast to that of President McKinley's, was a repetition of 1896, perhaps with fewer factional and interparty complexities. The national organization lacked firm direction and enthusiasm. The issue of having a headquarters in New York City remained unresolved until mid-September. Senator Gorman and others waited until October to announce their support of Bryan. Such questionable techniques as the "endless chain" method of raising funds (each Democrat to solicit contributions from a half dozen or so other Democrats) left much to be desired.

Bryan, as usual, carried on his own individual operation. He had poor press and explored the possibility of launching a large daily newspaper in New York and Chicago. This was in part taken care of when William Randolph Hearst endorsed his candidacy and founded the Chicago *American* as the Bryan paper in the Midwest.[8]

The election of 1900 revealed the same one-party patterns in the electorate that had emerged four years earlier. Some fifteen states, mostly in the South, were overwhelmingly Democratic; another fifteen were as safely Republican. With thirty of the forty-five states functioning under one-party systems, only about ten of the remainder could be considered relatively competitive, and, in these, Bryan had few resources that could match the organization and funds of Republican Mark Hanna who was once again McKinley's campaign manager. Election day, 1900, brought another McKinley landslide, and Democrats continued as the disjointed out-party.

From Populism to Progressivism

In a matter of days after the election, discussion was under way regarding the next presidential nominee. Younger leaders expressed the hope that Bryan would continue "as the aggressive and forceful leader of the Party." National Chairman Jones went so far as to suggest a third nomination for Bryan.[9] Speaking as a leader of the former Gold Democratic party, Don M. Dickinson of New York expressed the hope that both elements of the Democratic party—the silver and the gold men—could effect a reunion soon. Then, with remarkable candor, he added: "It was only through Bryan's defeat that the desired reorganization could be brought about. Hence, it was that this year the gold men gave their strength to McKinley instead of setting up a candidate as in 1896."[10] Senator David B. Hill began to suggest the availability of fellow–New Yorker Judge Alton B. Parker. Prior to his appointment to the bench, Parker had been Democratic state chairman, winning a reputation for his leadership of the campaign of 1885 that swept the state ticket into office and Hill into the governorship.

While William Jennings Bryan, at forty, was the first presidential nominee to suffer defeat twice consecutively, he hardly viewed defeat in an election as synonymous with retirement from leadership of the Democratic party. The popular party leader who has suffered electoral defeat but wishes to remain active and influential may do so by threatening to become a candidate again. "I am not a candidate for any office," he said in 1901: "however, I would not enter into a bond never to become a candidate."[11] Bryan was not about to relinquish his titular leadership. Rather, Bryan "retired" to the publication of a weekly newspaper called *The Commoner*, wrote *The Second Battle*, lectured interminably, and, with increasing religious content, commented on the great issues of the day.

119

Assassination of President McKinley three months after his inauguration elevated Theodore Roosevelt of New York to the presidency in 1901. This gave the goals and platforms of progressivism a strong impetus throughout the nation. Republican progressives had evolved from the liberal, reformist, mugwump elements of that party during the 1890s. Philosophically close to most Democrats, Republican progressives believed that poverty was a social rather than an individual problem, that corporate monopolies were a threat to free enterprise and liberty, and that municipal government required reform. Honest and efficient municipal and state government was a principal goal to which Roosevelt, while governor of New York, not only subscribed but also added a long list of practical achievements. In the presidency, Roosevelt, a leading progressive, now gave new currency to many old Democratic postures: a Jacksonian attack on the "moneyed interests," a Tildenite concern for governmental reform, and a Cleveland-like challenge to political bossism. With a hostile Republican leadership in Congress, Roosevelt's presidential policy aspirations tended to be more symbolic than material.

The new environment of political discourse nicely suited William Jennings Bryan's brand of democratic philosophy and reformism. Lacking any other party rostrum, he expounded on these fully in *The Commoner*, his weekly newspaper. Bryan favored a federal income tax, direct election of United States senators, independence for the Philippines, prohibition, woman suffrage, a Department of Labor in the cabinet, publicity of election campaign expenditures, and other relatively radical reform proposals of his day. He persistently supported and reiterated the demands of agrarian and labor groups, themselves still relatively weak political organizations.

Some of Bryan's political philosophy, particularly with respect to achieving consensus by the method of numbers, was revealed in his advocacy of popular election of senators. Following a Madisonian line, Bryan firmly supported "the dogma," as he called it, of majority rule:

There is no reason to believe that a majority will always be right. There is, however, a reason to believe that the rule of a majority is more apt to be right than the rule of the minority. Truth has such a persuasive power that a minority in possession of the truth generally grows into a majority, but until it becomes a majority, it cannot insist upon recognition. . . . If we deny to the majority the right to rule, there is no basis on which to build. If a minority rules, it must rule by force, for the moment it secures the consent of the majority, it is no longer a minority.

In proposing direct popular election of senators, Bryan was confident that "the people can be trusted with the direct choice of their public servants." He was also confident that one of the indispensable instruments of that direct choice was the political party. Bryan supported Theodore Roosevelt's suggestion that public funds be made available for the legitimate expenses of parties, arguing that this could be justified on the same ground that the printing of ballots by the government had been in earlier years.[12]

In 1903, Bryan began an extended foreign tour under the auspices of the Hearst newspapers. With editor Henry L. Stoddard as his companion, he traveled for nine weeks to Cuba, Mexico, Europe, and Russia, writing dispatches about his trip for the Hearst syndicate. Meanwhile, William Randolph Hearst, fiercely antitrust and prolabor, prepared to solicit the help of Bryan supporters in winning the presidential nomination at the next national convention. He had Bryan's endorsement. As Hearst set out on the delegate-collecting trail, he encountered a tough coalition of state and local bosses: Roger Sullivan in Illinois, David B. Hill and Tammany's Charles Murphy in New York, Tom Taggart of Indiana, Gorman of Maryland, and others. With no notable candidate of their own, the anti-Bryan forces at first rallied around the name of former President Cleveland, but eventually settled upon Judge Alton B. Parker, the distinguished but little-known New York jurist.

In Chicago, on April 23, 1904, Bryan declared, somewhat gratuitously, that he was not a candidate for renomination. Elsewhere the Hearst boom, considered a stalking-horse operation for Bryan, was collapsing. At the national convention in July, a conclusive test of Bryan's diminished influence was his unsuccessful fight to seat the Hearst delegation from Illinois, the convention voting 647 to 299 against Hearst. Bryan led a more successful fight in the platform committee, where an anti-bimetallism plank was dropped in favor of silence on the currency issue.

After all the states had nominated, seconded, or passed, Bryan went to the rostrum and asked that the rule limiting speeches be suspended, a tactic that would be employed by him in future conventions. The rule was suspended without opposition. The peerless leader's speech revealed how much he considered the titular leadership an active responsibility. "Eight years ago a Democratic national convention," he said, "placed in my hand the standard of the Party and commissioned me as its candidate. Four years later that commission was renewed. I come tonight to this Democratic convention to return the commission." At his most spellbinding, Bryan continued: "You may dispute whether I have fought a good fight, you may dispute whether I have finished my course, but you cannot deny that I have kept the faith." He implored his listeners to nominate a man whom the West could accept. He mentioned several who would be acceptable. His list did not include Parker. The convention listened respectfully but did not accept his advice. Parker received 679 of the convention's 1,000 votes on the first ballot.

During the vice-presidential nomination, a telegram came from Parker which threw the convention into an uproar and caused it to recess. "I regard the gold standard as firmly and irrevocably established. . . . As the platform is silent on the subject, my view should be made known to the Convention, and if it is proved to be unsatisfactory to the majority, I request you to decline the nomination for me at once."

Bryan angrily told the infuriated and embarrassed delegates, "From the tactics they pursued, you should have known it was not compromise they demanded, but surrender." A reply to Parker was composed by the convention leadership. "The platform . . . is silent upon the question of monetary standard, because it is not regarded by us as a possible issue in this campaign, and only campaign issues are mentioned in the platform." A vote of 794 to 191 authorized the sending of the telegram.

The conservative, anti-Bryan character of the Democratic National Committee's executive committee, responsible for Parker's campaign, was further evidence of the victory of the eastern faction. Most of the executive committee members had been Gold Democrats in 1896. William F. Sheehan of New York was chairman. The members included: New York banker August Belmont; petroleum magnate James M. Guffey of Pennsylvania; Ohio multimillionaire John R. McLean, long a foe of Bryan; former Senator James Smith of New Jersey; Senator Thomas S. Martin of Virginia; and Timothy E. Ryan of Wisconsin. Although not on the executive committee, Senator Gorman of Maryland was virtually a member. George Foster Peabody, an outspoken sound-money man, was named treasurer; Delancey Nicoll, a noted New York corporation lawyer who had voted for McKinley in 1896, was appointed vice chairman. The Parker telegram and the composition of the executive committee left no doubt that the gold faction wished to deal Bryan a hard defeat within the party.[13]

The executive committee declared the campaign in New York

as the key to the election. Capture of New York's 39 electoral votes would probably carry with it, they reasoned, Connecticut, Delaware, New Jersey, Maryland, and West Virginia. Together with 151 certain southern electoral votes, these states would bring the Parker ticket within 12 votes of the electoral college majority needed to defeat President Roosevelt. In the course of the campaign, however, Democratic National Chairman Tom Taggart sadly observed that the contest was "apathetic" and attributed this to the fact that campaign documents had replaced torchlight parades and brass bands.[14]

Bryan came into the Parker campaign in mid-July with a bombshell. In *The Commoner*, he indicated that he would support Parker for four reasons: the anti-imperialism stand of the party; the platform declaration favoring reduction of the standing army; Roosevelt's agitation of the race issue; and Roosevelt's warlike postures. However, wrote Bryan, Parker was wrong on the money question, the antitrust issue, and the problems of labor. "The fight on economic questions . . . is not abandoned. As soon as the election is over, I shall . . . undertake to organize for the campaign of 1908."

A few days later, Bryan announced his program, reiterating that "immediately after the close of the campaign I shall start out to reorganize the Democratic Party along radical lines." Bryan, in effect, was publicly predicting Parker's defeat and readying himself to resume leadership of the party.[15]

"Democracy versus Plutocracy"

Roosevelt trounced Parker, 7,629,000 to 5,084,000 in the popular vote. Thirteen states—the Solid South and some Border States—voted Democratic. As though the lopsided defeat were not enough to put the gold Democrats in retreat, Bryan's *The Commoner*, on November 11, carried the headline "Prepare for 1908—Democracy versus Plutocracy—The Election's Lesson."

Bryan began preparations for a third nomination. He conducted a speech-making tour of the Mississippi Valley. He published pledge cards in *The Commoner* on which his followers could promise to take active part in local primaries. Meanwhile, it was becoming increasingly clear that the man in the White House, Theodore Roosevelt, seemed to have the political style and progressive policies which the public had associated with Bryan, a fact that Bryan himself more than once was compelled to acknowledge.

Surprisingly at first, several New York leaders began, somewhat ostentatiously, to note that Bryan could surely qualify as the party's leader in 1908. In part, these endorsements could have been recognition of Bryan's diminishing radicalism; in part, a reaction to Roosevelt's apparent capture of the progressive cause; in part, a way of heading off William Randolph Hearst's increasingly aggressive campaign to win over Bryan's radical following by taking strong stands in favor of public ownership of utilities.

Meanwhile, National Chairman Taggart was having problems at home in Indiana, where an unfriendly governor was conducting an investigation of gambling activities at Taggart's French Lick Springs Hotel. The hotel's casino was raided, patriotically enough, on July 4, 1906, and the national chairman faced a scandal. A move was initiated to have him ousted as national chairman; its prospects depended to a large degree upon Bryan's views, Bryan, however, refused to attack Taggart as national chairman and observed that the Hoosier's status as national committeeman from Indiana was a matter to be decided by the Democrats of that state, most of whom were, of course, in Taggart's corner.[16]

Bryan was less friendly to "Boss" Roger Sullivan of Chicago. Sullivan had been responsible for Bryan's defeat in the Illinois seating contest of 1904. Bryan took the occasion of Sullivan's election as Illinois national committeeman to demand his resignation on grounds that Sullivan was too closely allied with big corporations. The demand was not likely to produce a resignation, but it did create a furor in the newspapers and served to remind Bryan's followers that he was still anti-boss and anti-corporation.

Bryan's homecoming from a world tour at the end of August 1906 was celebrated by a mammoth Democratic rally at Madison Square Garden in New York City. Some eighteen governors, fifteen senators, and nearly every prominent Democrat in the country was in attendance. As Bryan came ashore, National Chairman Taggart was the first to shake his hand. Even Roger Sullivan stood close by with a host of other Democratic dignitaries. That night, in an overflowing Madison Square Garden, Bryan reviewed with particular eloquence the entire gamut of Democratic values and issues. The surprise, and presumably the issue for 1908, came when Bryan declared that the railroads "must *ultimately* become public property."

This was Hearst's issue, and the publisher immediately conferred with Bryan to determine the significance of the declaration for his own persidential ambitions. Dissatisfied with Bryan's responses, on May 3, 1907, Hearst founded a third party, the Independence League, in a strategy to draw radicals away from Bryan. Meanwhile Bryan backed off from the position taken at Madison Square Garden. By July 26, 1907, Bryan wrote in *The Commoner:* "Government ownership is not an immediate issue."[17]

Democrats, in one way or another, began divesting themselves of the big-money, conservative image acquired during Parker's campaign and tried to make political capital of post-election revelations that Standard Oil and the New York Life Insurance Company had contributed hundreds of thousands of dollars to the 1904 Roosevelt campaign. The national committee, for example, adopted a resolution extending the party's thanks to Perry Belmont, a leading hard-money advocate, for his leadership in the movement for legislation to require publicity of campaign finances.

The 1908 national convention at Denver conducted its business without a hitch. In a rare absence from the national gatherings, Bryan remained at home in Fairview, Nebraska, sending his brother Charles to represent him. After Bryan's nomination, the convention chose John W. Kern of Indiana, National Chairman Taggart's good friend, for second place on the ticket.

The national committee went to Lincoln, Nebraska, to consult with Bryan concerning the organization and leadership of the campaign. Bryan addressed the group and endorsed the convention's statements favoring publicity of campaign contributions and expenditures. The nominee asked the committee not to accept any contributions from any corporation, to make public all contributions above $100, set a maximum of $10,000 for contributions, and publicize committee finances before rather than after the election. Chairman Taggart, always a practical man, qualified Bryan's statements by observing that the principles applied to the national but not to local party committees.

Bryan evidently had given little thought to the selection of a national chairman. He intended to run his own personal campaign again and, on the basis of his behavior in three previous presidential races, viewed the chairmanship as an instrument for keeping the organization "regulars" loyal or, at the least, within bounds. At Lincoln, he had no nomination to make for chairman. The Nebraska national committeeman then moved that a committee of eleven be appointed to make the selection. Eleven days later, the committee of eleven met in Chicago to choose Norman E. Mack of New York as national chairman. Mack was probably the most "regular" Demo-

crat of all, having successfully served in the difficult role of intermediary between Parker and Bryan factions in New York in 1904.

The presidential campaign was dull. Very few of the experienced Democratic politicians expected Bryan to beat the formidable
combination of Republican nominee William Howard Taft and incumbent President Theodore Roosevelt. Although his new third
party was hardly a serious threat, Hearst did have a powerful chain
of newspapers interested in Bryan's defeat, and so Bryan sent Senator Pettigrew of North Dakota to Arthur Brisbane to see what could
be done about regaining Hearst's support. Hearst would have none
of it. Even Bryan's friend, Clarence Darrow, joined Hearst. The
Hearst party nominated a Connecticut unknown as its candidate,
and the publisher proceeded to use it as a platform to expose the
"corrupt moneyed interests" controlling both major parties.

Election day ushered in Bryan's third defeat, a distinction that
matched Henry Clay's. Characteristically, however, Bryan intended
to give the toga of titular leadership another hard wearing. He again
went on a newsworthy foreign tour, this time to South America.

Meanwhile, management of the nation's new overseas depen-
dencies was proving to be a sticky and expensive task for the Taft
administration. Monopoly-dominated industries were straining the
governing capacities of the states and the cities; demands for federal
intervention were increasingly vociferous. Muckrakers in the press
and congressional investigating committees were finding much to
criticize in the way the country was being run.

Still unaccustomed to its emerging role as a world power, the
nation hesitatingly gave attention to defense needs, particularly an
enlarged navy, mindful that there was a relationship between arms
production and domestic prosperity. Populism continued to fade as
progressivism took its place. Anti-imperialism became tinged with
isolationism. Antimonopolism acquired a tart Marxist idiom. Hostility to corruption and whiskey were somehow tied to demands for
governmental reforms in such areas as the city-manager system, primary elections, women's suffrage, and direct election of senators.

In the antimonopoly spirit of the day, House Democrats
launched a revolt against the monopoly powers that had accumulated in the office of Speaker. During the late 1860s, as we have
seen, the Radical Republicans built the congressional campaign
committee into an instrument of party discipline that succeeded in
dominating the Grant administration. By the 1880s the campaign
committees of both parties had become deeply involved in raising

and dispensing campaign funds, influencing policy and patronage, and maintaining the growing influence of the party leaders in both houses of Congress. In the House of Representatives, the office of Speaker became the principal center of power and the main prize in the factional and partisan contests for influence. In 1876, the year of the disputed Hayes-Tilden election, Samuel J. Randall, a Pennsylvania Democrat, became the first of a series of strong Speakers that included Thomas B. Reed of Maine (1889–1891 and 1895–1899) and Joseph G. Cannon of Illinois (1903–1911).

In addition to his prerogative of floor recognition, the Speaker had become chairman of the Committee on Rules, which enabled him to control the day-to-day agenda of the House. Party-line voting came to be expected of rank-and-file members, particularly in the Speaker's party where he had the support of his own appointees to his party's congressional campaign committee. Under "Uncle Joe" Cannon, however, the Speaker's powers became a personal rather than a party resource. Cannon practically dispensed with the Republican caucus. A small group of thirty progressive Republicans found themselves up against the more than 180 other Republican members beholden to Cannon.

In 1910, led by Democratic Congressman Champ Clark of Missouri, Democrats and progressive Republicans became allies in trimming back the Speaker's powers. On March 17, Congressman George W. Norris of Nebraska, a progressive Republican, offered a resolution calling on the House rather than the Speaker to appoint the Committee on Rules, from which the Speaker would be excluded from membership. Two days later, the resolution was adopted, 191 to 155, every Democrat and nearly every progressive Republican voting for it.

It was a spectacular victory whose consequences for party politics in Congress would be profound. It brought to an end the concentration of party power and responsibility in the hands of the Speaker and eventually dispersed that power among the standing committee chairmen entrenched by the seniority system. This dispersion of congressional party leadership contributed to the deep divisions within both major parties during the 1920s and to the emergence of a durable coalition of conservative Republicans and southern Democrats in the 1930s.

The Democrats, who assumed control in the next session, revived their own caucus as an instrument of party management. Democratic majorities in the elections of 1910 put Champ Clark into the speakership, where he gained sufficient popularity to make him a leading contender for the Democratic presidential nomination in 1912.

Progressive victories, both Democratic and Republican, in the 1910 congressional and gubernatorial races across the country gave "Titular Leader" Bryan the basis he needed to maintain his influence in presidential political developments during 1911 and 1912. The growing breach between conservative and progressive wings of the Republican party was dramatized by the alienation of former President Roosevelt from incumbent President Taft. Taft, for example, had solicited Roosevelt's advice on the formation of his cabinet, then failed to take most of it. Taft signed the highly protectionist Payne-Aldrich Tariff which offended Republican progressives. Taft's dismissal of Gifford Pinchot, chief forester of the Department of Agriculture and a hero of the conservation movement, worsened the split. Taft also failed to support the revolt against Speaker Cannon in 1910, and this was the final litmus test. Roosevelt and the progressive wing of the Republican party concluded that Taft must go.

These developments gave Bryan grounds for claiming that Democratic radicalism, of which he was the leading representative, still had much to accomplish. As increasing numbers of Democrats available for the presidential nomination appeared, Bryan appreciated the competition that would take place at the national convention. It was reminiscent of the many candidacies at the convention of 1896, and Bryan was a past master in maneuvering divided conventions.

Among the principal names in the Democratic ring was Speaker Champ Clark of Missouri. With wide connections and support in the party, Clark had been chosen permanent chairman of the national convention that nominated Parker. Clark was particularly well liked by regulars.

A second prospect was Oscar Underwood of Alabama, a southern conservative who had served many years as Democratic floor leader in the House of Representatives. Another conservative was Governor Judson Harmon of Ohio, attorney general during Cleveland's second term. Harmon had substantial support in the Northeast.

A fourth candidate was Woodrow Wilson, a Virginian, political science professor, and president of Princeton University from 1902 to 1910. Although his origins were conservative, Wilson took on the mantle of progressivism soon after he was nominated for the governorship of New Jersey in 1910.[18]

For William Jennings Bryan the progressive choice lay between Speaker Clark and Governor Wilson. Bryan made this clear in a speech delivered August 14, 1911, at Columbus, Ohio, in which he eliminated Harmon, whom he considered suspiciously close to Wall Street. But Bryan refused to take a firm position favoring either Clark or Wilson. He relished his new king-maker role, which held all kinds of possibilities: his own renomination, the prospect of naming his successor, influence in choosing the campaign issues, etc.

Bryan sent questionnaires to the candidates to test their orthodoxy as progressives. During much of 1911 and 1912, he published in *The Commoner* letters from his readers urging him to run again but he himself denied that he was a candidate. When specifically asked by Champ Clark if he meant to run, Bryan said "No." Yet, Bryan kept himself in the public eye. On one occasion he devoted a speech to the praise of Speaker Clark, on another he commended the new progressive governor of New Jersey. As the national convention approached, it was clear to all that William Jennings Bryan intended to have a major part in it.[19]

Wilson: Progressive Nominee, Minority President

After assuming the presidency of Princeton University, Woodrow Wilson spoke frequently on public affairs. His personality and the content and style of his presentations caught the attention of George Harvey, one of William C. Whitney's chief lieutenants during Cleveland's administration and now publisher of *Harper's Weekly* and *North American Review*. In 1906 the world of higher education was deeply impressed by the adoption at Princeton of one of Wilson's greatest academic reforms, the preceptorial system. Editorials in Harvey's publications began to speak of Wilson as presidential material.

Before 1908, Wilson was generally perceived as a conservative intellectual, Virginian in origin and northeastern in residence. The "progressive" Wilson began to appear during his struggles with the trustees of Princeton, the conduct of his campaign for governor, and his successes in pushing through the New Jersey legislature substantial government reform proposals.

George Harvey was instrumental in persuading the New

Jersey Democratic leaders that they ought to nominate Wilson for governor. Prior to 1910 Harvey also began to launch a Wilson-for-president campaign. When Wilson's growing progressivism threatened to embarrass Harvey, a conservative, the Harvey operation came to an abrupt end.

In its place arose another group of Wilson enthusiasts, united around the fact that Wilson was a southerner. Their names appear frequently during the Wilson era. Among the members of this group were two New York lawyers, William F. McCombs of Arkansas and Walter F. McCorkle of Virginia, and one editor, North Carolinian Walter Hines Page of *World's Work* magazine. McCombs had been an honor student under Wilson. Page, an ardent advocate of educational and agrarian reform in the South, had been a personal friend since 1882. William Gibbs McAdoo of Georgia joined shortly afterward. McAdoo was reared in Tennessee and became a prominent New York lawyer. In 1911, he was president of the Hudson and Manhattan Railroad Company which handled the building of the Hudson Tunnel between New York and New Jersey.

Wilson was eager to have the support of Democratic organizations in neighboring states. This was particularly true for Pennsylvania where a progressive faction was giving the established party leadership, led by Joseph M. Guffey, a rough contest. Leading the newly organized progressives were Vance C. McCormick, A. Mitchell Palmer, and Representative William B. Wilson. After futile attempts to reshuffle the party machinery to accommodate both factions, the two wings went their separate ways, creating two Democratic state committees. But both factions, in response to overwhelming popular sentiment in the state, endorsed Wilson's candidacy. This was Wilson's first organizational endorsement and his largest single bloc of delegate votes throughout the 1912 nomination contest.

Another southern recruit to the Wilson bandwagon was Colonel Edward M. House, a reform-minded Texan who had been involved in several party campaigns in his home state and was at this time a resident of New York City. A man of means and deeply fascinated by presidential politics, House at first backed Mayor Gaynor of New York for the 1912 nomination. Wilson and House met through George Harvey at House's New York apartment on November 24, 1911, and this was the beginning of a famous political friendship.

During October 1911, Wilson formally designated McCombs as

his campaign manager. McCombs had already become *de facto* leader of the Wilson campaign, having devoted the greatest amount of time and energy and having raised, with much success, the necessary funds. Energetically pursuing the creation and coordination of Wilson organizations in other states, McCombs methodically went about the business of establishing direct contact with newspaper editors and well-known public figures who might be sympathetic to the Wilson cause. McCombs also made himself the main liaison with Democratic bosses and regulars despite the fact that Wilson had all too successfully fought bosses in New Jersey.

Theodore Roosevelt's Bull Moose bolt from the Republican party offered the Democrats their best chance in two decades to capture the presidency. The Democratic National Convention, still operating under the two-thirds rule, was sufficiently divided to give nearly every major candidate a veto over the others. The situation was made to order for Bryan.

When Bryan declined a Democratic National Committee offer that he serve as temporary chairman and keynote speaker at the 1912 national convention, the committee turned to Alton B. Parker, the second senior man in the party. Bryan used this choice as the issue upon which to test conservative and progressive alignments. He nominated his 1908 running mate, John W. Kern of Indiana, as an alternative to Parker. Kern took the podium to decline and to appeal to the New York leaders to accept some compromise. When the latter gave no response, Kern nominated Bryan for the temporary chairmanship. Parker, however, won the chair, 579–508, with the support of Underwood and Harmon votes. The Clark following was evenly divided, and this proved fatal to Clark's candidacy. Wilson votes went to Bryan solidly. Over a hundred thousand telegrams descended upon the convention decrying the conservative tactics. Bryan was still in the saddle.

Bryan's next maneuver was to isolate the New York leaders. He introduced a resolution asking the convention to declare itself "opposed to the nomination of any candidate for President who is the representative of or under obligation to J. Pierpont Morgan, Thomas F. Ryan, August Belmont, or any other member of the privilege-hunting and favor-seeking class." A second part of this resolution demanded the "withdrawal from this convention of any delegate or delegates" representing these interests.

According to contemporary accounts, delegates "screeched," "frothed at the mouth," and one even proposed the assassination of

Bryan. During the debate Bryan withdrew the second section. The first section was adopted by an overwhelming majority. Any nominee now obviously had to win the endorsement of *both* Bryan and the New York leaders.

Choosing such a nominee was not easy. With 726 votes needed to nominate, the first ballot showed Clark with 440½, Wilson 324, Harmon 148, Underwood 117½, and the rest scattered. On the tenth ballot Clark had a simple majority. Up to this point Nebraska's (Bryan's) votes had been for Clark. On the fourteenth ballot Bryan rose to explain that, since a few ballots earlier New York had shifted its votes to Clark, he was changing his vote from Clark to Wilson. The stalemate was prolonged, until finally Wilson was nominated on the forty-sixth ballot. The Bryan era in the Democratic party was thus brought to an end as dramatically as it had begun, on the basis of a new consensus within the party.

In view of his position in the pre-nomination campaign, McCombs was the logical choice for national chairman. Bryan was reportedly in favor of retaining the incumbent, Norman E. Mack. Joseph E. Davies of Wisconsin was promoted by many midwesterners. McAdoo, whose relations with Wilson had grown increasingly cordial during the previous weeks, would probably have been the nominee's personal choice. Many of the national committeemen, thinking of the public impression if Wilson *failed* to choose McCombs, strongly recommended the nominee's former Princeton student. After two weeks of hesitation, Wilson agreed to the selection of McCombs.

Wilson hardly intended that McCombs would run his campaign. Using National Committeeman Hudspeth of New Jersey as his channel of communication, Wilson embodied his own plans for the campaign in a long memorandum. Wilson also named the other officers of the national committee: McAdoo as vice chairman, Joseph E. Davies as secretary, and Henry Morgenthau as chairman of the finance committee. McCombs was bitterly opposed to McAdoo in so prominent a position and preferred that experienced leaders such as Charles F. Murphy, Tom Taggart, William J. Stone, and others be on the campaign executive committee.

There were few surprises in the election outcome. The campaign reduced itself to a battle between progressives: Wilson versus Theodore Roosevelt. President Taft's candidacy had the principal consequence of denying victory to Roosevelt. Wilson received less than a majority of the popular vote, but carried 42 of the 48 states.

Roosevelt's 4,216,000 votes and Taft's 3,484,000 together would have beaten Wilson's 6,286,000 plurality. It was a shaky national consensus that enabled the Democratic party once again to control the White House after sixteen years in the wilderness with Bryan. A new generation of Democratic leaders collected around Woodrow Wilson and dominated party affairs well into the New Deal era.

7

Wilsonians, Bosses, and Bigots

NOT since Madison and Van Buren had a president analyzed and written so extensively about presidential party leadership as Woodrow Wilson.[1] There were important differences among the three writers. Madison and Van Buren had been party politicians long before reaching the presidency; Wilson had not. Further, each man wrote during distinct periods in the institutional development of the executive and legislative branches. Madison considered party organization essential in Congress and in campaigns for the presidency, but he never advocated affirmative party leadership by the president *after* election to the office. Van Buren agreed with Madison but added views favoring the strong exercise of party leadership in the presidency.

Wilson carried institutional growth a step further. Party is indeed vital in congressional affairs, he wrote, but mainly insofar as Congress follows executive leadership, as in the British parliamentary system. Party is important during presidential campaigns, but only insofar as it follows the nominee's lead and not that of party bosses. Party leadership is most demanding in the conduct of the presidency itself, for in that position a person is the spokesman for both his party and the nation at the same time as well as molder of public opinion on the basis of which the nation makes its policies.

Another major difference between Wilson and his two predecessors lay in their personalities. Madison and Van Buren, particularly before the latter's retirement by the national convention of 1844, were negotiators, compromisers, and builders of political alliances. The skills these men possessed were necessary to a system of divided governmental powers. Wilson, on the other hand, was "burdened with serious, at times crippling, temperamental defects" which often only fortuitously fitted the requirements of governmental leadership in his day. As the Georges have observed:

Though forced to operate within a governmental system of divided powers and checks and balances, Wilson's driving, essentially autocratic, leadership was for a number of years politically acceptable and successful. This achievement was due in large measure, of course, to the character of the situation at the time, which favored political reforms and strong leadership. [2]

Wilson's first book, *Congressional Government*, published in 1885, concluded that the principal political power in the nation rested with Congress, particularly the Senate. The ultimate repository of power lay in the committees of Congress, according to Wilson. Despite his veto power, the president could establish his influence over Congress only by great exertions and strong acts of will.

Wilson's enthusiasm for the British cabinet and parliamentary system was articulated early. A major advantage of the British system, he argued, was that both executive and legislative authority are vested in the leaders of the dominant party. The prime minister and his cabinet participate directly in the legislative process, initiate all important legislative propositions, and can be held accountable for their legislative program. The keenest criticism of that program is forthcoming from the opposition, and the ensuing debate clarifies the issues and informs public opinion. Wilson's behavior in the presidency, particularly his presentation of entire legislative programs (reminiscent of Alexander Hamilton's approach) and his tactic of "taking issues to the people," was undoubtedly premised upon his assumption that the American system could more closely imitate the British.

Wilson's later views on the presidency, possibly a consequence of his own personal interest in the office, differed from his earlier acceptance of congressional ascendancy. In *Constitutional Government in the United States*, published in 1908, Wilson took the position that the president was the main seat of governing power in the nation. Wilson had, of course, been watching Theodore Roosevelt operate as an activist president.

Wilson had already been publicly mentioned as a presidential prospect when he wrote in *Constitutional Government* that the president automatically becomes the leader of his party through his selection by a nominating convention; that is, the agency for conferring titular leadership is the national party convention. Once a nominee is chosen, he stands before the country as the symbol of the party. It is inevitable that the party must be led by its presidential candidate during the campaign.

Once a president is elected, "he cannot escape being the leader of his party except by incapacity and lack of personal force, because he is at once the choice of the party and the nation. He is . . . the only party nominee for whom the whole nation votes." It then is entirely up to the president himself whether he becomes the leader of the nation. "His is the only national voice in affairs. Let him once win the admiration and confidence of the country, and no other single voice can withstand him. . . . If he leads the nation, his party can hardly resist him."

Through the exercise of persuasion and appeals to public opinion, according to Wilson, the president may also exercise leadership over Congress. The presidency, he wrote, is no longer a mere executive office but rising rapidly as a political office. Wilson's basic position, in sum, was that the American political system could not operate effectually without vigorous presidential leadership. When the power of initiative and direction of public policy lies in a single person leading a disciplined party, he believed, the people can rest assured that the power will be used responsibly. Such unification of power could bring to an end the irresponsible "hide-and-seek" government that unfortunately exists in periods of legislative supremacy.

Wilson's "Parliamentary" Presidential Party

The first tests of Wilson's theory of party government came with the appointment of his cabinet and the distribution of federal patronage. Wilson's views on the selection of a cabinet were summarized in a paragraph of his book on *Constitutional Government in the United States*:

Self-reliant men will regard their cabinets as executive councils; men less self-reliant or more prudent will regard them as also political councils, and will wish to call into them men who have earned the confidence of their party. The character of the cabinet may be made a nice index of the President's theory of party government; but the one view is, so far as I can see, as constitutional as the other.[3]

When Democratic National Chairman McCombs appeared in Princeton the day after the election in order to discuss patronage matters, he found Wilson unreceptive, even unwilling to dismiss his stenographer from the room during their conference. According to McComb's probably biased account, Wilson said: "Before we proceed, I wish it clearly understood that I owe you nothing. . . . Remember that God ordained that I should be the next President of the United States. Neither you nor any other mortal or mortals could have prevented that!" McCombs finally observed that he had been "commissioned by members of the national committee" to leave appointment suggestions with the president-elect, which he did and departed.[4]

Wilson conducted lengthy interviews with the regular party leadership, but, basically, he distrusted them and collected most of his information about prospective cabinet officials through Colonel House, Walter Hines Page, and Joseph Tumulty. In the end, the Wilson cabinet was something of a cross between a "political council" and an "executive council." Bryan was the only member with a national following, and his appointment as secretary of state was a major gesture to progressivism. Wilson's preference for McAdoo over McCombs for Treasury made clear to whom he would be turning for advice on party affairs. For postmaster-general he chose Albert Burleson, who had been chairman of the Democratic caucus of the House of Representatives, and for secretary of the navy, Josephus Daniels, who had been director of publicity for the Democratic National Committee during the campaign. Most of the others in the cabinet, specifically McReynolds, Lane, Houston, and Garrison, were appointed on the basis of experience, merit, or some similar nonpartisan criterion.[5]

Wilson's strong predilection for the civil service merit system was severely tried in the distribution of presidential patronage. About 40 percent of the 470,000 civil employees of the federal government at this time were subject to appointment without examination. More than 50,000 of these were postmasters, district attorneys, collectors of customs, and other officials to be appointed directly by the president. Wilson's initial preference was to review the file for each nomination. He began to do this in the case of postmasterships during his first days in the White House. Dissatisfied with the qualifications of a substantial number of the candidates, Wilson seemed inclined to set aside completely all the traditional procedures of appointment. Postmaster General Burleson presented a strong case for following the usual procedure of congressional recommendation, suggesting that those nominations with shortcomings in qualifications could be returned to the appropriate congressman for a new nomination. Otherwise, he counseled, a new procedure could do more to tear apart the fabric of the party than to reform it.

Inundated by the sheer volume of appointments to be made, Wilson eventually did retreat to more traditional practices, putting greatest reliance upon the recommendations of department heads and such political professionals as Thomas J. Pence of the Democratic National Committee and his own secretary, Joe Tumulty. As a consequence, many personal followers, progressives, and supporters of the Wilson program lost out to local organizational and factional considerations. Wilson's staff led the president into a strategy of making concessions that improved the prospect of immediate cooperation within the party at some cost to the long-run reorientation of the party's leadership and policies.[6]

Wilson also failed to pursue his concept of vigorous presidential party leadership in connection with the winter 1912–1913 elections of United States senators by state legislatures. Many states offered excellent opportunities for Democratic-Progressive alliances, and the implications for party composition of the next Congress were many, particularly since this was the last time that senators would be chosen by state legislatures. Wilson did nothing that might strengthen the forces of his adherents in Congress.

Despite his own election as a minority president, Wilson swept a large Democratic majority into the House of Representatives along with enough Democratic senators to make a majority in the upper chamber. In control of the two elective branches of government, Democrats were predisposed to follow the vigorous president's experiments in government.

For a time Wilson contemplated promoting an alliance with congressional Progressives elected in the sweep of Roosevelt's third party campaign. This again revealed Wilson's greater interest in his programs than in party organizational unity. However, he soon found that regular Democrats were surprisingly responsive to ordinary party pressures and to presidential patronage. One consequence was that Wilson was able to hold the Sixty-third Congress in special session for an unprecedented period of a year and a half.

With Burleson's help, Wilson was also able to convert the party caucus in the House of Representatives into an effective instrument for promoting the presidential program about which Wilson kept up a barrage of messages and personal pressure. For example, Wilson gave the revived Democratic House caucus the ordinarily impossible task of legislating a basic revision of the tariff. Working through the caucus, where a two-thirds rule applied, Wilson could more readily prepare for the full House a bill that would pass by an overwhelming majority without encountering the usual revisionist tactics. Then, from a vantage point in the President's Room just off the Senate chamber, Wilson maneuvered Senate Democrats into conducting a caucus of their own on the bill. This rare conclave subsequently declared the tariff bill to be a party measure, and the bill was passed in the Senate.

Democratic cohesion thus demonstrated, there followed a series of major legislative actions. Banking and monetary reforms were adopted in the Owen-Glass Federal Reserve Act of 1913, despite the strenuous objection of the banking industry. Growing malpractices among industrial monopolies were dealt with in the Clayton Anti-Trust Act of 1914, which specifically exempted labor and farmer organizations from its requirements. The Federal Trade Commission was created to look after the provisions of the Clayton Act. The Newlands Act improved the arbitration process in railway labor disputes. Federal farm loan banks were created to improve credit extended to farmers.

Wilson's progressive domestic program was, for the most part, adopted during the first year-and-a-half of his administration. The success of his reform legislation reinforced Wilson's impression that strong presidential leadership could indeed give the country a parliamentary form and style of politics. As the session ended in October 1914, however, World War I was beginning in Europe. Not until confronted by the problem of reelection in 1916 did Wilson again give as much attention to the passage of his domestic program. When he did, it was primarily to maintain his progressive support.

A meeting of the Democratic National Committee was held the day after Wilson's inauguration. National Chairman McCombs emphasized the necessity for broadening and regularizing the work of the committee.

I do not believe that, after an election, whether it results in victory or defeat, a committee should be dormant until a few months before another election. We should be in thorough cooperation all the time. . . . In order to assure a continuation of what we have accomplished, we must continue an organized army. . . . Two years from now, when we meet strong opposition, we can maintain ourselves in Congress and reorganize for the presidential battle of 1916.[7]

To implement McCombs's recommendation, the national committee approved a continuing headquarters in New York and opened a Washington office under the supervision of Thomas J. Pence. Plans were discussed for national committee cooperation with the congressional campaign committee in the 1914 campaign. These discussions led to the establishment of a novel joint campaign committee two months later.[8] Democrats once again were in agreement that their search for the national consensus required new approaches to organization.

The Democratic National Committee assumed a large role in the 1914 congressional elections. The manager of the Washington headquarters, Thomas J. Pence, issued a campaign pamphlet enumerating the achievements of the Wilson administration. The strategy was to link the congressional races to Wilson's great popularity. During the summer, the president expressed his desire to make a far-flung speaking tour on behalf of Democratic congressional candidates. In order to sound out local political conditions and prepare an itinerary for the president, National Chairman McCombs began a tour of the West late in July.

In August 1914, the first Mrs. Wilson died. The blow was a shattering one for Wilson and was offered as the explanation for his reluctance to stump the country in the congressional campaigns that fall. Another factor was the deepening crisis in the international field and the eventual outbreak of world war. As international tensions mounted, Wilson's popularity at home also increased, and this popularity was the "coattail" to which the national committee called attention. The president, however, limited his efforts to extensive letter-writing on behalf of congressional candidacies.

As has been true since the early days of the Republic, midterm congressional elections usually result in the loss of seats in the House of Representatives for the party controlling the presidency. The Democrats in 1914 lost 58 seats but maintained a majority of 19 votes. Republicans and anti-Wilson Democrats alike began reading the results as a rejection of the president. Furthermore, as supporters of William Howard Taft and Theodore Roosevelt began to make moves toward reconciliation on the Republican side, the Democratic party was reminded that Wilson had been elected by a minority of the popular vote in 1912. Renominating and reelecting Wilson in 1916 were by no means foregone conclusions, despite the usual advantages of an incumbent. It had not been clear how many Roosevelt Progressives might have otherwise been Wilson votes in

1912 or would become Wilson supporters in 1916. If Roosevelt and Taft were to become reconciled, said many Democratic leaders, there would be serious question whether Wilson could be reelected in 1916. These doubts kept other doubts alive, important among them the question of which party leaders would control the national party agencies in the event of defeat.

Nonpartisan for War but Partisan for Peace

By 1916, President Wilson was thoroughly absorbed in the problems of American foreign policy. The country was divided over its relations with the contending powers in Europe, but, for some time, benefited from trade with both sides. Wilson and the nation trod a difficult path between reports of German atrocities on the one hand and the irritations of an illegal British blockade on the other. Economics, common culture, and Allied propaganda, however, maintained the American drift toward the Triple Entente (Great Britian, France, and Russia). As this drift toward American involvement gathered momentum, Secretary of State William Jennings Bryan, the strongest pacifist voice in the administration, became increasingly frustrated in his efforts to bring the war to a negotiated conclusion. Doubting President Wilson's commitment to neutrality, Bryan resigned on June 9, 1915, rather than sign the second United States note of protest to Germany over the sinking of the *Lusitania*.

There was, in the final analysis, no question that the 1916 national convention in St. Louis would renominate Wilson. Wilson's influence was felt in the preparation of the platform, many planks of which he either drafted personally or explicitly had his approval. One sentence congratulated the president for his diplomatic victories and for having "kept us out of war." The phrase made the president uneasy, even more so when the keynote speaker, Governor Martin H. Glynn of New York, alluded to it. The convention responded so enthusiastically that, contrary to Wilson's intentions, the pacifism issue was projected directly into the campaign.[9]

On the Republican side, the 1914 midterm elections had proved disastrous to its progressive wing. In the first round of direct popular elections of U.S. senators, conservative Republicans won most of the major races. While some Republican progressives such as Harold Ickes strongly favored a continuation of a third party that would renominate Theodore Roosevelt, others pressed for a reconciliation

141

of Republican factions and a search for a national ticket acceptable to all. Supreme Court Justice Charles E. Hughes seemed to meet the requirements of both Taft's conservatives and pro-Roosevelt progressives, and he became the Republican nominee. Roosevelt, meanwhile, declined renomination by the Progressive party. With the news of these Republican and Progressive developments, Colonel House, now President Wilson's personal adviser, urged that the election campaign be taken as an opportunity to swing former Roosevelt Progressive voters into the Democratic column.

It was a relatively unexciting contest. The president made few speeches. His assistant secretary of the navy, Franklin D. Roosevelt, on the other hand, made many. So did the Republican Roosevelt, whose criticism of Wilson was at times expressed so extremely as to *gain* votes for the president! From the very first the Wilson campaign was short of money. Although some 170,000 persons contributed, relatively few did so in substantial amounts. Special endorsements were obtained from Henry Ford, Thomas Edison, and John Burroughs, Ford supplementing his endorsement with a special (and expensive) series of newspaper advertisements.

The outcome was close. For a time, as late California returns drifted in, it seemed that Hughes had won. In the final count, however, Wilson carried California by a few thousand votes, and the electoral college by 277 to 254. For a second time Wilson was a minority president, having received only 49 percent of the popular vote.

The United States declared war against the Central Powers on April 6, 1917. Although eager for a demonstration of national consensus, Wilson resisted suggestions that a "war cabinet," based upon a coalition between the major parties, be established. On the other hand, he appointed an impressive roster of Republicans to important positions in his war administration, including General Pershing, General Robert E. Wood, Admiral Mark Bristol, Admiral W. S. Sims, Harry Garfield of Williams College, Julius Rosenwald, Robert S. Brookings, Robert S. Lovett, William H. Taft, Edward Stettinius, Charles Schwab, Herbert Hoover, and others.

As the end of the war approached, Wilson evoked growing hostility not only to his demands for near-absolute wartime executive powers but also to the manner in which he requested and executed these powers. Congressional opinion was, by 1918, beginning to rise to its institutional defense, as in Jackson's and Lincoln's administrations. When some legislators proposed a congressional committee to supervise war expenditures, Wilson referred to it as an "espionage committee" and would have none of it. Legislative-executive relations deteriorated. By fall 1918, Republicans were looking forward to the possibility of winning control of Congress and putting an end to Wilson's style of presidential leadership.

Possibly the strongest denunciation of Wilson on personal as well as political grounds came from the Republican faction headed by former President Roosevelt and Senator Henry Cabot Lodge of Massachusetts. In August 1918, Lodge was elected Republican floor leader in the Senate. In the next few years, the personal vendetta between Lodge and Wilson became a prime influence in the international relations of the United States. Not only was Lodge his party's floor leader but also the ranking Republican on the Senate Foreign Relations Committee, in line to become its chairman should the Republicans succeed at the midterm elections. Anticipating just this prospect was enough provocation to send President Wilson "to the people" in a historic campaign effort aimed at forestalling the election of a Republican Congress in 1918.

By October 1918, the end of the war seemed imminent. On October 24, President Wilson, despite the bipartisanship of his appointments, launched an attack upon the Republican party, and especially its members in Congress. In his memoir of the war period, Herbert Hoover refers to the 1918 congressional campaign as "an unhappy interlude." Wilson's principal argument:

If you [the American People] have approved of my leadership and wish me to continue to be your unembarrassed spokesman in affairs at home and abroad, I earnestly beg that you will express yourselves unmistakably to that effect by returning a Democratic majority to both the Senate and the House of Representatives. . . . The return of a Republican majority to either house of the Congress would . . . certainly be interpreted on the other side of the water as a repudiation of my leadership.

The president thus staked his personal reputation and leadership upon an election in which he had no official part and probably with the knowledge that the party holding the presidency invariably loses seats in off-year congressional returns.

Herbert Hoover refers to this statement as a "mystery" and attributes it mainly to "politicians who pushed Mr. Wilson into an action so entirely foreign to his nature and his previous nonpartisan conduct of war affairs." The Wilson campaign was opposed by Secretary of State Lansing, Secretary of Agriculture Houston, Secretary

143

of the Interior Lane, and Attorney General Gregory. Apparently, the major proponents were Presidential Secretary Tumulty and Postmaster General Burleson. On grounds that "the President's hand in the treaty negotiations would be greatly weakened if the election went against him," Hoover himself addressed a public letter to fellow-Republican Frederic Coudert of New York on November 2 supporting the Wilson appeal for a Democrat Congress. Republican National Chairman Willcox denounced Hoover, and this letter became the basis for subsequent charges at Republican national conventions that Hoover was really a Democrat.[10]

Upon closer analysis, Wilson's midterm campaign statement of 1918 was perhaps not so "foreign" to his nature as Hoover believed. Wilson's most characteristic political reaction to a rising opposition to himself or his policies was to "go to the people." Philosophically, of course, the midterm message was consistent with Wilson's parliamentary conception of the presidency. In their psychological analysis of Wilson, the Georges explain his use of this procedure as follows:

> What Wilson needed for peace of mind, when political deadlocks with his opponents developed, was a practical device which would enable him to "test" his contention that he better represented the will of the people than did Congress (or, in other situations, the Princeton Board of Trustees, the New Jersey Legislature, the Allied negotiators in Paris), a device which, therefore, would serve as a psychological and political safety valve against any autocratic tendencies within him. The device which he most often used for this purpose was the "appeal to the people."
> That "public opinion" could be made the immediate arbiter in his power conflicts with his opponents was indeed a comforting thesis. It served to relieve Wilson of the responsibility to compromise when deadlock was reached. He could seek to impose his will in such situations, without meeting the need for compromise inherent in our system of divided and shared power, by self-righteously relying upon public opinion to uphold him—or, by defeating him, to save him from being guilty of autocratic behavior. The eagerness with which he turned to the device of an appeal to the people, and the poor judgment and unrealism he often displayed in so doing, testified to the highly personal function of the device in his hands.[11]

The new and aggressive Republican national chairman, Will Hays, led a prompt, vigorous, and personal counterattack against Wilson's statement. "President Wilson has questioned the motives and fidelity of your representatives in Congress. He has thereby impugned their loyalty and denied their patriotism." Hays was also able to obtain a joint statement from Roosevelt and Taft urging the election of a Republican Congress. The outcome was a Republican majority of two in the Senate and forty-five in the House. The principal loser was the peace negotiation scheduled to begin on January 12, 1919, in Paris.

Together, Lodge and Theodore Roosevelt, old political friends, launched a political and personal campaign against Wilson that harassed the president all through the Paris Peace Conference of 1919 and, for that matter, to the end of his term. Wilson returned from Europe on July 8 and shortly thereafter presented the peace treaty with its Covenant for a League of Nations to the Senate for ratification. The treaty was referred to the Senate Foreign Relations Committee, whose chairman now was Henry Cabot Lodge.

Senator Lodge favored American entry into a League of Nations only if the Covenant could be so revised as to protect certain basic interests of the United States. Lodge's strategy was to assume a revisionist posture in order to delay and, if possible, defeat the League proposal. His objectives were several, but fairly clear: to humiliate Wilson personally and politically, to protect American sovereignty, to reassert legislative ascendancy over the executive, and to create *the* issue for the next presidential contest in 1920.

On March 7, 1919, Republican National Chairman Will Hays in effect launched the 1920 presidential campaign on the theme of nationalism versus the League. On March 12, Democratic Chairman Homer S. Cummings asserted that the projected League of Nations was "too great a question to become partisan." At its May 28 meeting, on the other hand, the Democratic National Committee passed a resolution proclaiming that the League of Nations was the paramount issue before the country. The resolution urged prompt approval of the peace treaty and the League Covenant. Chairman Cummings explained the resolution by saying: "While I do not consider the League of Nations Covenant a party issue at this time, I do say that it would strengthen the pressure on the President to run again if it should be defeated in the Senate."

This was the first public intimation by a responsible party leader that Wilson might be available for an unprecedented third term. The prospect of a third term was of particular interest to congressional Democrats who might otherwise be disinclined to follow a lame-duck president. Sixty percent of the Democrats in the House were from safe districts in the Solid South, 55 percent in the

Senate. Some viewed the third-term talk as a tactic to maintain Wilson's influence in Congress.

The treaty in the Senate was slowed by requests for information, proposals for reservations, and pressures to amend. Wilson insisted that the treaty be ratified "exactly as it stood." In August 1919, the treaty was still in the Foreign Relations Committee. Wilson once again decided to try "going to the people." On September 3, he embarked upon an extended and passionate tour of the country in defense of the treaty and the League. On September 28, he showed signs of suffering from physical exhaustion. Four days later he was overcome by a stroke that paralyzed the left side of his body.

Wilson refused to allow his second wife or his physician to divulge the seriousness of his condition. During the height of the debate over the League in October, the President was literally incommunicado. He continued, however, to insist that he would accept no compromises or reservations, even the mild ones now being proposed by Lodge. The treaty failed in the Senate, 53 to 38.

When Congress reassembled in December, a spirit of compromise was not in evidence. On December 14, a White House statement indicated that the President was not considering a "concession of any kind." In a letter dated January 8, 1920, to be read to the Jackson Day Dinner in Washington by Chairman Cummings, Wilson made a typical proposal—that the League issue be taken to the people. "If there is any doubt as to what the people of the country think on this vital matter, the clear and single way out is to submit it for determination at the next election to the voters of the Nation, to give the next election the form of a great and solemn referendum." Speculation now grew regarding the president's interest in a third term. William Jennings Bryan came into the picture, opposing the president and urging ratification with reservations. The party seemed headed for a split convention. The importance of the two-thirds rule was widely discussed among Democratic leaders.[12] The third term became an integral part of Wilson's fight for the League Covenant, particularly when, again in March 1920, the peace treaty was rejected by the Senate.

The president's illness complicated pre-convention maneuvers, but candidate activity persisted nonetheless. Bryan's followers revived the Bryan Leagues. Bryan made much of the fact that he was the party's principal spokesman on Prohibition, which was going into effect in 1920. Wilson's former secretary of the treasury and son-in-law (married to Wilson's daughter Eleanor), William G. McAdoo, was among those most prominently mentioned. McAdoo, however, was handicapped by the "Crown Prince" tag and became a target for the more overt anti-Wilson sentiment.[13] Attorney General A. Mitchell Palmer, whose anti-Red campaign led to the arrest of thousands of suspects, kept himself in the headlines. Others named frequently were John W. Davis, ambassador to England, National Chairman Cummings, and the three-time governor of Ohio, James M. Cox.

During spring of 1920, Governor Cox invited Ohio National Committeeman Edmund H. Moore to manage his pre-convention campaign and George White, a financier and former congressman from Ohio, to assist. The many candidacies assured a divided convention in which the front-runners would have difficulty obtaining the necessary two-thirds vote, a circumstance for choosing second-preference compromise candidates. Cox had a combination of attributes ideal for the role of compromise candidate. Cox was a "winner," having been elected in a predominantly Republican state. He was a "wet" who, as governor, had strictly enforced the state prohibition laws. Edmund H. Moore was a "manager's manager," having close associations with Charles Murphy of Tammany, Roger Sullivan and George Brennan of Illinois, James Nugent of New Jersey, and Tom Taggart of Indiana. George White, formerly a student of Wilson's at Princeton, was a friend of the president, a "dry," and a member of the House of Representatives for three terms.

Other factors worked in Cox's favor. Governor Alfred E. Smith was the favorite-son candidate of New York, but he and the Tammany leaders were really interested in finding a second-choice candidate who was "wet," had a good labor record, and was not too closely associated with the Wilson administration. Cox met these qualifications. The Republican nomination of Warren Harding of Ohio also favored Cox. Ohio at that time was considered to be a pivotal state, its electorate a "weathervane" for the nation.

During the week following the Republican convention, newspaperman Louis Seibold was invited to spend a few days at the White House. Seibold's account of the president's activities and apparent state of health won for him a Pulitzer prize, his article testifying to Wilson's general good health and vigor of decision in the course of a day's work. The timing of the invitation to Seibold and the publication of his report, almost on the eve of the Democratic National Convention, were taken as evidence of Wilson's active interest in a third nomination.

The 1920 national convention met under the poorest of factional circumstances. "Wets" opposed "drys"; populists opposed conservatives; state bosses opposed Wilsonians. Each issue coincided factionally with the others. Complicating it all was the president's silence regarding his health, his interest in renomination, and his preference, if any, for a successor. Wilson clearly evoked the enthusiasm of the delegates. When his picture was unfurled at the opening of the convention, the demonstration was prolonged and warm. Only the New York delegation kept its seats, with two or three important exceptions; Franklin D. Roosevelt engaged in some vigorous pushing-and-pulling in order to carry off the New York standard for the Wilson parade.

Twenty-four candidates received votes on the first ballot. Of these, ten received between 20 and 42 votes each; only four received more than 100: McAdoo, 266; Palmer, 256; Cox, 134; and Smith, 109. The field was reduced to eight names by the sixteenth ballot; 729 votes were needed for the nomination. Cox reached a peak of 454½ votes on the fifteenth ballot, leading McAdoo by more than 100. The race reduced itself to a two-man match on the thirty-ninth ballot, and Cox received the nomination on the forty-fourth.

At various critical junctures in the convention's proceedings, there was renewed talk of turning to President Wilson as a candidate upon whom the party could unite. As the convention opened, National Chairman Cummings had remarked that "there will be no attempt to dictate from the White House." Wilson resisted many requests for public comment.

During the deadlock, Secretary of State Bainbridge Colby wired the president that at the first appropriate moment he would request suspension of the convention's rules in order to place the president's name in nomination. Before sending the telegram, Colby talked with Mrs. Wilson, who told him that the president was willing to have his name presented if the move was generally approved by the administration leaders present in San Francisco. Colby called a conference for Sunday morning, July 4, attended by National Chairman Cummings, Senator Joseph T. Robinson, and those cabinet members attending the convention, with the exception of Attorney General Palmer. Many felt that nomination of Wilson would not resolve the convention's problem, and would possibly expose the president to a humiliation. The group advised against carrying out Colby's suggestion, and the third-term movement ended with this conference.[14]

In the opinion of one student of this episode, "Colby was not working in the dark regarding the President's real desires." Woodrow Wilson's third-term position has been summarized by David Lawrence as follows:

My impression is that Wilson wanted the nomination primarily as a vindication of League of Nations policy. I am sure he realized that he was not well enough to serve another term in the Presidency. But with Wilson the nomination in itself would have been a vote of confidence by his own political party. He had . . . an ingrained feeling that confidence by a party should be shown periodically, just as it is in Britain. The fact that Bainbridge Colby was prepared to nominate Wilson fits with my theory that the whole thing had to do with vindication of his League of Nations policy. I believe he would have declined to run if he had been nominated.[15]

Since Cox's nomination was interpreted as a defeat for the administration, the vice-presidential place was offered to an administration man. Franklin D. Roosevelt was an anti-Tammany Wilsonian who was nonetheless a good friend of Governor Smith. He was nominated by acclamation after several others withdrew.

One campaign problem was the manner in which the League of Nations issue should be handled. Moore and the big-city leaders preferred to keep the League issue in second place to the more ambiguous issue of "progressivism." The Covenant had been twice voted down by the Senate, and the handling of treaty ratification was generally considered the greatest failure of the Wilson administration.

Cox and Roosevelt, however, held other views. Contrary to Moore's advice, Cox went to Washington shortly after the convention to visit with President Wilson. Roosevelt was present at the meeting. In Cox's words:

As the nominee of our party, the leadership of the campaign passed from [Wilson] to me. . . . There was some doubt at this time as to whether Mr. Wilson would live long. I would have reproached myself everlastingly if he had passed on without my going to him as an earnest of fealty to the cause which he had led.[16]

Wilson was confined to a wheelchair during the meeting. His poor health was reported by Roosevelt to have made a deep impression upon Cox. Both Wilson and Cox issued statements of unity and optimism to the press. Wilson's indicated that he would do all he could to help the campaign, and Cox's statement indicated that the League of Nations would be *the* issue.

149

The big-city Democratic organizations cut themselves loose from the Cox campaign as soon as it became a League crusade. Tammany leaders were rarely, if ever, seen at national headquarters in New York. The New York City Board of Elections, under Tammany influence, ordered separate ballots to be printed for presidential electors. President Wilson's main campaign effort, in the end, was his $500 contribution to the national committee for an educational fund on behalf of the League of Nations issue. The contribution was the beginning of a "Match-the-President" fund to raise sorely needed campaign money.

It was a losing campaign from the start. Division among Democrats and unity among Republicans (Theodore Roosevelt had died a year earlier) would have been sufficient to bring defeat to the party. In addition, 1920 was the first presidential year experiencing women's suffrage. The first women to go to the polls, as should have been expected, were those who were in higher educational and economic groups, that is, normally Republicans. The Harding landslide also gave the Republicans a 59–37 margin in the Senate and 296–135 majority in the House. With it began twelve years of Republican control of the White House.

The closing of the Wilson era was perceptively evaluated in *World's Work,* one of the leading news magazines of the day:

> Only two men have dominated the Democratic Party to the same extent as Mr. Wilson; these were Thomas Jefferson and Andrew Jackson. The influence of both extended to their periods of retirement. Ceasing to be President, Jefferson and Jackson became "sages"; the party leaders constantly consulted them on party policies and their approval was a powerful auxiliary in political campaigns. Dominant as Mr. Wilson has been for eight years, it seems inevitable that the role of "sage" will be denied him. The two Presidents who immediately succeeded Jefferson were his political disciples; Jackson's successor was his own selection; the party policies in both cases represented merely a continuation of the policies of the "master." But in San Francisco the forces in the Democratic Party which are most antagonistic to Mr. Wilson emerged triumphant.
>
> Probably the most important aspect of the Convention was the decisive influence exercised by such practical political leaders as Charles F. Murphy of New York, James R. Nugent of New Jersey, George E. Brennan of Illinois, and Thomas Taggart of Indiana.[17]

The Irreconcilables: Bosses versus Klansmen

During Wilson's first term, a new generation of young Democrats emerged, devoted to the president and to his brand of progressivism. Chief among these were Franklin D. Roosevelt and William Gibbs McAdoo of New York, Josephus Daniels of North Carolina, Carter Glass of Virginia, Vance McCormick of Pennsylvania, Thomas J. Walsh of Montana, to mention a few. These young Wilsonians were frequently on the opposite side of party issues from Charles Murphy of Tammany, Roger Sullivan and George Brennan of Illinois, James Nugent of New Jersey, Thomas Taggart of Indiana, and Edmund H. Moore of Ohio. The latter were an older generation of professionals—"bosses" to the Wilsonians—whose state machines were basically conservative.

Another source of political discomfort for the Wilsonians was the southern wing. Although the southern states were solidly Democratic, the Democratic parties within them were far from united. There were the more conservative and moderate congressional elements, represented by men like Underwood. There were also the fiery populist remnants of the Bryan era, which, like Bryan himself, were bringing religious fundamentalism into politics, including the prohibition of the sale and use of alcoholic beverages. Outside the Democratic party, but inescapably an influence upon it, was the Ku Klux Klan.

The Klan was a product of the Reconstruction era. It was organized then as a secret society expounding white supremacy and a nativist brand of Americanism. Its organizational life was revived around 1915 in reaction to the flood of immigrants coming into the United States, the patriotic fervor generated by the World War, and renewed fears of Negro advancement in southern communities. Within a few years, the Klan's membership spread into every state of the Union, achieving a membership of several million. By 1923, in some states, its leaders either controlled or significantly influenced the decisions of one or the other major party. During the 1920s the Klan aided in electing sixteen senators (nine Republicans and seven Democrats), eleven governors (six Republicans and five Democrats), and an undetermined number of congressmen.[18]

The nation, deeply wounded by its first involvement in a major international war, turned to isolationism. The plight of the debt-ridden farmers was never sufficiently resolved, but prosperity flourished among other economic groups in the country. Prohibition, put into the Constitution in 1919, was circumvented in practice by a high-living nation, a "reform" from which organized crime reaped the largest harvest. Traditional American toleration was in retreat as the Ku Klux Klan and other nativist groups infiltrated the political parties and resisted the Americanization of the recently arrived millions from overseas.

The Harding administration came to power with a host of problems confronting it and attempted a number of reforms. The business boom of 1919–1920 was followed in 1920–1921 by a depression, a decline in agricultural prices, over two million unemployed (a very high proportion of the labor force in that day), and a number of violent strikes. In addition there were the League and peace treaty issues. On the reform side, the Budget Bureau and the Veterans' Bureau were established. The state of war with Germany and Austria was formally ended. Harding endorsed American participation in a World Court and the Washington Disarmament Conference.

Another kind of political issue was disclosed by Senator Thomas J. Walsh, whose investigations broke the Teapot Dome oil scandal. Early in 1923 the public had its first intimation of the corruption surrounding the president. The head of the new Veterans' Bureau resigned in anticipation of the exposure of graft in his agency. Three weeks later his closest assistant committed suicide. Two months later a notorious associate of Attorney General Daugherty also committed suicide. Coming to the surface was Teapot Dome. Secretary of the Navy Denby had been persuaded to get the president to sign an executive order transferring control of the Naval Petroleum Reserves to the Department of Interior. There, through Secretary of Interior Fall's administrative decisions and several devious arrangements, leases were signed for the private exploitation of the oil reserve lands. Secretary of Interior Fall received a payoff for his efforts. Attorney General Daugherty was involved in these and still other connivances. President Harding's death on August 2, 1923, apparently did not spare him from knowledge of the misdeeds of his old friends; he must have been aware of them long before the Senate investigators.

Harding's death and President Calvin Coolidge's subsequent legislative defeats at the hands of a Republican cabal in the Senate seemed to set the stage for a Democratic revival in 1924. The void in Democratic presidential party leadership following Cox's defeat and Wilson's retirement, however, brought in a decade of aggravated factional controversy. Among the main actors in the heated and drawn-out drama were William Gibbs McAdoo, Alfred E. Smith, the southern leadership in Congress, and Franklin D. Roosevelt.

Complicating the struggle, and possibly delaying its resolution, were changes in the presidential electorate occurring during the period 1916 to 1932. According to one student of presidential elections,

152

"The election of 1920 was unlike the three that preceded it and the three that were to follow it. In this important particular—it did not present the familiar American alignment."[19] The "normal" Republican vote that had gone to the Progressive party in 1912 and in part to the Democrats in 1916 was not what was recovered by Republicans in 1920. There continued to be enough Progressives outside of the two major parties to encourage the La Follette candidacy in 1924. This Progressive movement kept the unsettled electorate stirred up. The nomination of Al Smith, a Catholic, by the Democrats in 1928 again prevented a return to the previous alignments of voters. All during the 1920s the number of women voters was increasing slowly, but their influence on the outcomes remained poorly understood. The final jolt was the Great Depression which provoked an enduring rejection of Hoover and Republicanism.

Preparations for the 1924 nominating battle began early. McAdoo, in a last-chance bid for the presidency (he would be sixty-one in 1924), tried to avoid a fight with the New York organization by establishing residence in California. His candidacy was informally supported by various elements in the Ku Klux Klan and the Anti-Saloon League. Cordell Hull, in his unwieldy job as national committee chairman, guided the party in the 1922 election to mid-term successes, which Democratic leaders applauded, and the Tennessee legislature recommended him for the presidential nomination. Henry Ford, the automobile genius of Detroit, also stood high among candidate names. In June 1923, Ford ranked second only to McAdoo in a *Literary Digest* poll of two thousand Democratic party leaders. Underwood, the favorite of the congressional wing, launched his own candidacy with a forthright campaign against the influence of the Ku Klux Klan in presidential politics, essentially an anti-McAdoo tactic. Tammany's Murphy proposed Governor Smith again, and after he conferred with Brennan of Illinois and Guffey of Pennsylvania, a stop-McAdoo combination was born that controlled four hundred votes at the 1924 national convention, that is, more than the third needed to veto a nomination.

Meanwhile, at former President Wilson's request, National Chairman Cordell Hull called upon him once or twice a month until the latter's death in February 1924.[20] Hull frequently gave Wilson written reports on his organizational efforts, and Wilson gave advice freely. Wilson commented on the various issues of the 1922 campaign. During the spring of that year, when the former president heard of proposals for a midterm national party conference, he wrote to Hull: "Such a conference would lead to nothing but talk and outside rumors about it which would be misleading and hurtful to the Party." Hull also had breakfasts every two or three weeks with another former titular leader, William Jennings Bryan, who he regarded as "a magnificent orator" but whose jugment he found lacking at times.[21]

The scandals of the Harding administration, the president's death, the elevation of the colorless "Silent Cal" Coolidge to the White House, and the congressional victories of 1922 raised Democratic hopes about prospects for victory in 1924. Most hopeful was McAdoo, whose excellent organization carried him to a resounding victory over Henry Ford in the South Dakota Democratic county meetings of late November 1923. On December 18, Ford, until this time considered a Democrat, announced that he would not run for president because he felt "perfectly safe with Coolidge." The way now seemed clear for McAdoo.

McAdoo was not without opposition from several significant quarters, including some of his former colleagues in Wilson's cabinet. Woodrow Wilson died on February 3, 1924, leaving no clear impression whom he might have favored. His secretary of state, Robert Lansing, and secretary of war, Newton D. Baker, leaned strongly toward a favorite son from West Virginia, John W. Davis, who had been solicitor general and ambassador to England under Wilson. Cox was opposed to McAdoo because he had "gone cold on the issue of the League of Nations for which his father-in-law, President Woodrow Wilson, had died. Besides, he remained silent at the sponsorship of his cause by the Ku Klux Klan."[22] There was also the big-city combine that controlled the convention votes of New York, Illinois, Indiana, Pennsylvania, Ohio, and several other states. McAdoo managers recognized their problem but could do little to get the two-thirds nominating rule repealed.

Two issues began to acquire particular importance in the late stages of the pre-convention campaign. Underwood announced in January that he would propose to the national convention a plank condemning the Ku Klux Klan as an agency of intolerance in American life. The Klan had reached into every state in the Union. In Texas it dominated the Democratic organization, in Indiana the Republican. During the 1924 primary elections, the Klan fought for and won control of several other state party organizations. The McAdoo victory over Underwood in Georgia's March primary was considered a major step in the Klan's march toward political power. The fundamentalist Protestantism of the Klan was particularly offensive in the multireligion regions of the country, that is, the Northeast, the West, and the urban centers. Underwood's stand against the Klan made him more than a regional candidate. The contest between the Klan and the urban centers was real and profound.

The second issue acquiring special importance was Prohibition. McAdoo was a pronounced dry, and the Anti-Saloon League mobilized its far-flung membership in his behalf. When Smith resoundingly defeated McAdoo in the April 1 Wisconsin primary, the result was widely interpreted as a wet-dry vote although neither candidate had campaigned extensively in that state.

By the end of April, Franklin D. Roosevelt agreed to serve as Smith's pre-convention campaign manager. After the defeat of 1920, Roosevelt had returned to business and the practice of law in New York. Roosevelt's battle against infantile paralysis began on August 10, 1921. Not until fall of 1922 was he recovered sufficiently to contemplate a return to politics. Throughout this period of personal crisis his wife, Eleanor, and his political adviser, Louis McHenry Howe, were constant sources of moral support. Howe took up residence in the Roosevelt household. Eleanor Roosevelt became active in New York Democratic party affairs. Management of the Smith campaign was Roosevelt's first major step back onto the national scene. The prestige of the former vice-presidential nominee made Smith McAdoo's principal opponent in 1924.

Bryan, now resident in Florida, campaigned against Underwood in Alabama and Florida. The Florida primary pledged Bryan's personal convention vote to McAdoo. Elsewhere, the Underwood campaign was faltering under the opposition of the Klan. Cox allowed the Ohio organization to use his name in their campaign to elect an anti-McAdoo delegation which won in the April primary by a five-to-three majority. Favorite sons and dark horses were being suggested in growing number.

As Underwood had promised, a platform plank condemning the Klan was introduced and became the first test of prospective alliances. The McAdoo managers countered with the suggestion that the nomination be made before the platform was adopted to head off bitterness over particular planks. They sought a recess during the nominating speeches so that balloting for the nomination could begin before the platform was reported. The anti-McAdoo forces supported a motion to adjourn rather than recess and won, 559–513. The platform committee's majority offered a general plank upholding religious freedom; a minority proposed a plank specifically condemning the Klan for its efforts to arouse religious and racial dissension. The minority plank was defeated by 543 $\frac{3}{20}$ to 542 $\frac{7}{20}$, a margin of four-fifths of a vote. Such a split in the party greatly devalued the worth of its nomination.

The first presidential ballot gave McAdoo 431½, Smith 241, Cox 59, Patrick Harrison 43½, Underwood 42½, Davis 31, and scattered votes for over a dozen other candidates. On the sixty-ninth ballot, McAdoo reached his greatest strength: 530 votes. By this time, it was clear that the votes for Smith, Underwood, Davis, and Baker would never shift to McAdoo. Tom Taggart proposed a conference of all leaders after the seventy-sixth ballot, but the conference failed to reach any conclusion.

On the ninety-third ballot Franklin Roosevelt announced that Smith would withdraw his name immediately upon the withdrawal of McAdoo. The two front-runners met for a three-hour conference but McAdoo insisted upon remaining in the race until the end of the ninety-ninth ballot.

Earlier, several leaders had asked James M. Cox to come to New York to use his influence as titular leader to help bring the proceedings to an end. Cox, who had withdrawn his name in favor of Baker on an earlier ballot, performed yeoman service upon his arrival. It was Cox's judgment that the most likely way out of the McAdoo-Smith deadlock was the the nomination of Carter Glass or John W. Davis. According to the Cox strategy, the delegates would be urged to try out Davis first and then Glass. The one-hundred-third ballot was to be the one for implementing the plan; it gave the nomination to Davis. Charles Bryan's nomination for the second spot was designed to appease the midwestern progressives lest they be driven to the new La Follette party.

Any chance of uniting the Democratic party against Coolidge was completely destroyed in the protracted convention. The new medium of radio, for the first time reporting a national party convention, gave the public a direct and vivid portrayal of the intransigence among the party's leaders. One leader's qualities were noted by the *New York Evening World:* "Franklin D. Roosevelt stands out as the real hero of the Democratic Convention of 1924." The *New York Herald Tribune* observed:

While the results of the futile ballots were droned from the platform in the Garden yesterday, there sat in the exact center of the great hall the one man whose name would stampede the convention were he put in nomination. He is the only man to whom the contending factions could turn and at the same time save their faces and keep square with the folks at home. . . . From the time Roosevelt made his speech in nomination of Smith, which was the one great speech of the convention, he has been easily the foremost figure on floor or platform.[23]

Davis suffered a crushing defeat at the hands of President Coolidge on election day. Almost immediately, McAdoo and Smith supporters began to posture themselves for the next round in 1928. Roosevelt exchanged a series of letters with Senator Thomas J. Walsh, who had been permanent chairman of the 1924 convention, concerning national organizational problems faced by the party.[24] Roosevelt was the only party leader with enough friends to raise so controversial a topic.

Roosevelt: Changing Party Organization and Electorate Behavior

During the early 1920s, Theodore Roosevelt's and Woodrow Wilson's progressivism nurtured some of the bitter fruit of agricultural discontent, emerging in different corners as La Follette Progressives or Farmer-Laborites proclaiming many of the policies that later matured under the New Deal. Agrarian and labor disaffection was voiced by progressives within each of the major parties in Congress. Progressive bills sought to alleviate unemployment, outlaw child labor, introduce old-age pensions, promote slum clearance, and, through the McNary-Haugen Bill, stabilize farm prices and reduce agricultural surpluses through the program of federal purchases.

As La Follette's candidacy gained momentum in 1924, it was generally anticipated that the Progressives would carry enough of the western states to prevent a majority in the electoral college, thereby throwing the election into the House of Representatives. Writing from Warm Springs in October 1924, Franklin Roosevelt observed:

I have a hunch that Davis' strength is really improving, but I still think the election will go into the house. Anyway, I am philosophic enough to think that even if Coolidge is elected, we shall be so darned sick of conservatism of the old-money controlled crowd in four years that we [will] get a real progressive landslide in 1928.[25]

To mobilize the party for a "progressive landslide" following the defeat of 1924, Roosevelt wrote the letters to Senator Walsh noted earlier, in which he reported his efforts to revitalize what he called the party's "archaic and outgrown" machinery.

In December 1924, deciding to bypass the national leaders, Roosevelt appealed directly to local leaders, particularly those who had been delegates to the national convention. In a letter that went out to three thousand Democratic leaders, he invited their advice on improving the party organization. Roosevelt indicated in the letter some of his own thoughts on the subject. The national organization should be more active and should work more closely with the state organizations. Publicity should be improved. Party leaders should meet more often.

In his letters to Senator Walsh, Roosevelt summarized the general feeling of the several hundred replies he received to his earlier letter to the leaders. Leaders "overwhelmingly agreed" that the Democratic party must stand for progress and liberal thought. Further, they saw a need for a clearer distinction between national issues and "those matters of momentary or temporary nature which are principally of local interest." The party also needed a respite from discussion of presidential candidates. Specific suggestions for immediate organizational reform included: national committee machinery should function "every day in every year"; the national committee should be brought into closer touch with state organizations; permanent headquarters should be put on a "business-like financial basis"; party information and publicity efforts should be greatly expanded; and party leaders from all sections should meet more frequently to plan for united action.

Finally, a very large number of the delegates who have written to me offer the suggestion that a conference of representative Democrats from every State be called by the Chairman of the Democratic National Committee at some central point this Spring, and that the primary purpose of this conference shall be to make recommendations to the National Committee, which, under the party rules, is the governing body between elections.[26]

Support for the midterm conference proposal was quick in coming, particularly from Senator Walsh, James M. Cox, John W. Davis, Cordell Hull, and Jonathan Daniels. The need for consensus-building machinery seemed urgent and self-evident. The reaction of most Democratic leaders in Congress was, however, at best, lukewarm. Some contended that even if the proposed conference confined itself to reorganization of the administration of the national party, mainly financing a continuous functioning of party machinery, it probably would be impossible to prevent discussion of factional differences over public policy. Other critics were concerned with procedures for selecting participants for the conference.[27]

The Roosevelt-Walsh proposal very shortly became a bone of contention within the party. William Jennings Bryan expressed the view that it was "too early" for a meeting of leaders. The 1925 Jefferson Day Dinner in Washington was called off because of suspicion that it would be converted into a midterm conference, and because Bryan, Roosevelt, Daniels, and others would not address it.

Roosevelt kept up his campaign for a reorganization conference throughout 1925. To avoid the impression that the conference was a pro-Smith or pro-Roosevelt maneuver, it would have been necessary for National Chairman Clem Shaver to issue the call. Despite pressures from Roosevelt, Shaver refused to act. The national chairman was obviously following the line of the Democratic leaders in Congress, many of whom were southerners with long tenure and seniority. In a midterm conference, these leaders would run the risk of having to share their policy prerogatives with noncongressional Democrats. By the end of 1925, the Roosevelt-Walsh proposal had, for all practical purposes, been "postponed out of existence."[28]

The nation, meanwhile, was getting a large dose of Coolidge policies, many of which were having deflationary consequences. Unemployment, child labor, old-age pensions, and slum clearance were deemed by Coolidge to be matters for local, not federal, agencies. Coolidge stood for economy, tax reduction, observation of the spirit of the Prohibition laws, and participation in the World Court. When Secretary of the Treasury Andrew W. Mellon suggested in 1924 that the federal treasury could afford tax reductions amounting to $300 million, Congress reduced tax rates considerably. The national debt at the end of 1926 stood at $19.3 billion, some $7 billion less than in 1919. Industrial profits were at all-time highs.

On a darker side, under the eyes of the "Puritan in Babylon," as William Allen White called President Coolidge, the nation was experiencing an orgy of gambling and law-breaking. Farm surpluses were multiplying as farm prices and income dropped. An agrarian rebellion was in the making, aggravated by Coolidge's stand against the McNary-Haugen Bill under which the federal government could purchase farm surpluses and stabilize farm prices. Franklin D. Roosevelt seemed right about expecting a "real progressive landslide in 1928."

Between 1925 and 1927 the Smith wing gradually built its

159

strength in preparation for the convention of 1928. In the 1925 mayoralty fight in New York City, Governor Smith engineered the replacement of Mayor John Hylan by State Senator James J. Walker, thereby demonstrating his own complete ascendency in New York Democratic affairs. In Connecticut, Homer S. Cummings, who had supported McAdoo, resigned as national committeeman after long years in that position, to be replaced by a pro-Smith man. "Wet" factions came into control of Democratic state organizations along the eastern seaboard: Massachusetts, New Jersey, Pennsylvania, and even states further south. The cause of the "drys" was on the wane throughout the nation and so was enthusiasm for another McAdoo candidacy.

A critical source of McAdoo strength lay in the Democratic organizations of the South. Governor Smith, as early as 1926, sent dapper and charming Mayor "Jimmy" Walker on a tour to cultivate that garden. During 1927, the Smith people spoke frequently of making a strong fight to abolish the two-thirds rule but retreated on this point as southern leaders became increasingly friendly. A final step in the Smith strategy to win over the South was to advocate that the national convention be held below the Mason-Dixon line. By late summer 1927, McAdoo saw the handwriting on the wall and in September announced that he was no longer a candidate for the nomination. With McAdoo's withdrawal went nearly a score of favorite son and dark horse candidacies that had thrived on the assumption of another deadlocked convention.

As the nominating situation on the Democratic side closed down, the one on the Republican side opened up. In an announcement on August 2, 1927, that surprised even his closest political associates, President Coolidge declared: "I do not choose to run for President in nineteen twenty eight." Secretary of Commerce Herbert Hoover became the Republican front-runner, having been mentioned as a presidential prospect since 1920.

The 1928 Democratic National Convention was an Al Smith rally, with southern overtones. Smith votes on the national committee put the convention in Houston, Texas. There was no mention of the two-thirds rule. On the wet-dry issue, the party platform simply pledged itself to "an honest effort to enforce the Eighteenth Amendment." Franklin D. Roosevelt, who had announced his support of Smith's nomination earlier in the year, made another impressive nominating speech on behalf of the "Happy Warrior." The *New York Times* characterized it as "a gentleman speaking to gentlemen."

There were approximately twenty seconding speeches. After Smith's nomination, the delegates balanced the ticket by selecting Senator Joseph T. Robinson of Arkansas as vice-presidential nominee. Robinson was a "dry" Protestant from a rural state, the first politician from the South to appear on the national ticket since the end of the Civil War.

Governor Smith, the first Catholic to win nomination for the presidency of the United States, promptly turned to the organization of his campaign. His first choice for the national chairmanship was Franklin D. Roosevelt, who, in commenting on the matter in a letter to his mother, noted: "I declined the National Chairmanship, and will decline the nomination for Governor." Roosevelt felt committed to spend as much time as possible at Warm Springs, continuing his recuperation.[29] Despite an intense draft-Roosevelt movement, Roosevelt refused to yield to subsequent pressure that he run for governor. By October 1, Smith asked him to accept the nomination as a personal favor, for Smith felt that only a strong gubernatorial candidate could help carry New York. The state convention nominated Roosevelt by acclamation, and he acquiesced.

The national chairmanship went to a prominent businessman, John J. Raskob of General Motors Corporation and long Smith's personal friend. With Andrew Mellon leading much of the business community in support of Herbert Hoover, Smith hoped to counter with Raskob. But Raskob was also a wet, a Catholic, and politically inexperienced. His selection proved to be costly in a campaign that was certain to have religious overtones. The Protestant South, rural and dry, could hardly accept a combination of Smith and Raskob.

To absorb some of the anti-Raskob feeling, Smith created a special advisory committee to the national chairman. But the forces stirred by Smith's candidacy were not that easily calmed. In Pennsylvania, former National Chairman Vance McCormick bolted the ticket on the Prohibition issue. Factional difficulties in Connecticut compelled National Committeeman Spellacy to resign. Anti-Catholic sentiment flared in the South. Wrote Walter Lippmann:

There are passions at work this year which are capable of dissolving the political habits of very large numbers of people. These passions are most fiercely at work precisely in the States which have hitherto been most invincibly partisan. Both the Democrats and the Republicans are threatened in their own stronghold. If North Carolina is doubtful, so is Massachusetts; if Florida is doubtful, so is Rhode Island. The catalytic agent in this process of dissolution is, of course, Governor Smith.[30]

Voter turnout is normally low in years of economic prosperity, but the election of 1928 brought out the highest increase in popular vote over an immediately preceding election since 1856, with the exception of 1920 when woman suffrage went into effect. The vote for Smith pulled the Democratic party's percentage of the total popular vote up from 29 percent in 1924 to 41 percent in 1928. The Democratic Solid South, on the other hand, was broken, with Florida, Texas, and states in the upper South going to Hoover. In the states where the Progressives had been strongest in 1924, Smith more than doubled the Democratic vote. In large urban states he brought large segments of the immigrant and working population, many of them voting for the first time, into the Democratic column.

Opinions can differ on whether or not the Smith nomination was a good thing for the Democratic Party, but it would be difficult to argue that any other possible candidate could have increased the Party vote so much in 1928, and especially in states where the Party was so much in need of an increase if it was again to become competitive. The contrast is especially striking against the record of Smith's two immediate predecessors, Cox and Davis.[31]

For Smith this was ostensibly his last race for office: "I certainly do not expect ever to run for public office again. I have had all I can stand of it. . . . As far as running for office again is concerned—that's finished."[32] In his own state of New York, Smith was defeated by about 103,000 votes. Franklin D. Roosevelt, on the other hand, was elected governor by 25,000 votes, a handful in the total of 4 million. Roosevelt's feat and Smith's retirement immediately raised the expectation that the new governor would be the Democratic presidential candidate in 1932. To letters of congratulations from across the nation, Roosevelt responded with appreciation and with "deep disappointment" over the defeat of Governor Smith. In one letter he included the following:

I am of course convinced that had we kept our national organization going between elections we should have done better and I hope that steps will be taken to have this carried out during the next three years. This is no time to discuss candidates but it is time for putting into effect a permanent working organization. I hope you will write me your views.[33]

Meanwhile, anti-Smith elements in the party announced their intention to eliminate "Raskobism" from the national chairmanship. Raskob, on the other hand, announced that he would not return to his former position as chairman of the finance committee of the General Motors Corporation but would serve out what he referred to as the "four-year term" for which he had been elected, transacting party affairs from the permanent headquarters in Washington.[34] Early in December, Raskob announced the call of a conference of party leaders after the Christmas holiday for a discussion of plans to strengthen the party and liquidate the $1.5 million deficit. Southern leaders referred to the proposed conference as a maneuver to put Smith at the head of the party again in 1932.[35]

In anticipation of his own conversations with ex-Governor Smith and National Chairman Raskob in mid-January, Governor Roosevelt issued a report on the survey he had been conducting among more than three thousand Democratic leaders throughout the nation. It was similar to the survey he conducted in 1924–1925. A preponderant number of the leaders, said Roosevelt, felt that the Republicans had "cheated" in the campaign against Smith. Most, however, had a genuine optimism about the party's prospects in the next elections. Roosevelt further reported:

One of the structural faults of our national Democratic organization in the past, which has resulted from our previous practice of laying the national committee carefully away in cotton wool after each election, to be taken out and dusted off just before the next Presidential election, has been the lack of any central clearinghouse for exchange of ideas among the leaders, great and small, of our party. . . .

One unanimous opinion . . . is that the crying need is publicity—publicity—publicity; that Democratic papers must be encouraged and increased in number; that the independent press of the country must be furnished with information and arguments as to the attitude of the Democratic Party on questions which are rightfully party questions.[36]

Smith endorsed the concept of a full-time national organization a few days later. The great support given the Democratic party, he said on a special radio broadcast, should "not be lost by failure to maintain an organization." This would require a national committee with "suitable and well-equipped offices" to provide a live point of contact for party members. He also called for effective publicity and information services.[37]

Shortly after, Raskob conductd a series of unpublicized conferences with the party's leadership in the Senate and the House of Representatives. Then he called together some sixty newspaper correspondents to announce:

I have succeeded in reducing the Party deficit from over $1,550,000 to about $800,000 with every indication of a further reduction to under

$500,000 within the next fortnight. . . . I have appointed today Mr. Jouett Shouse of Kansas City to be chairman of the Executive Committee, and he will immediately assume charge of the Washington Office.

Shouse, a former assistant secretary of the treasury under Wilson and a long-time McAdoo supporter, was to have a "permanent and adequate headquarters" designed to "work 365 days in the year." Raskob expected Shouse to acquire a competent staff for organization, publicity, and research. The research bureau would not only furnish materials to the publicity bureau at national headquarters but also information to the members of Congress. Raskob expressed the opinion that perhaps "the Senatorial and Congressional Committees would finally be brought into one organization."[38]

Shouse began at once to look around for a competent staff. For director of publicity he sought out the chief of the *New York World's* Washington Bureau, Charles Michelson. Many Democratic leaders were later to credit Michelson's vigorous anti-Hoover campaign for most of the Democratic successes that followed.

In 1928, as in other years, politicians linked the tariff by some obscure causal chain to most other economic woes. Thus, the American Farm Bureau Federation and the midwestern progressives led by Senator Borah blamed the chronic agricultural depression of the 1920s on the lack of adequate protection against foreign competition. Manufacturers complained to their representatives in Congress that costs of production at home and abroad needed to be "equalized" and that a higher tariff would accomplish this. Labor leaders, interested in maintaining employment, accepted the manufacturers' recommendations. During the 1928 campaign both candidates promised early action on the tariff problem. Hoover went so far as to promise a special session of Congress.

A special session met in April 1929. Congress sweltered over tariff revision from April to November 1929, and adjourned without passing a bill. It reconvened in December and struggled on through June 1930. The final product was the protectionist Hawley-Smoot Tariff Bill, passed by a 49-to-47 vote. Around the world this tariff act was seen as a retreat to isolationism at a time of grave international economic stress.

Factional attacks on Raskob continued throughout 1929 and 1930. During the Virginia gubernatorial primary, Bishop Cannon, who headed the anti-Smith movement in the South during the campaign of 1928, led anti-Smith Democrats into a coalition with the Republicans, making "Raskobism" the main issue of the state campaign. From Alabama, Senator Thomas Heflin raised the pitch of his opposition to the Smith influence. Anti-Catholics were joined by Drys, particularly Senator Furnfold Simmons of North Carolina.[39] The assault of the drys reached its height in Senate speeches by Simmons and Brookhart of Iowa on April 7, 1930. Appearing before the Senate lobby investigating committee the following day, Josephus Daniels, former secretary of the navy and Franklin Roosevelt's old boss, reiterated the charges set forth in his Raleigh *News and Observer* that the anti-Prohibition activities of Raskob constituted a peril to the Democratic party. Daniels's editorial suggested that Raskob resign as national chairman. Several weeks later, returning from a trip abroad, Raskob denied that he was about to resign, reiterated that it was time for action to modify the Eighteenth Amendment on Prohibition, and reported that there was growing disfavor abroad toward the nation's high tariff policy.[40]

When Franklin D. Roosevelt won his second gubernatorial campaign in 1930 with a 725,000 plurality, an Albany crowd of more than five thousand persons hailed him as "the next president." Support of Roosevelt's candidacy was not universal. Raskob and Shouse did what they could to take the limelight from Roosevelt. One device was an open letter to President Hoover, pledging that the Democrats in Congress would not cause difficulty for the ailing business community by pressing for tariff revision at the coming session and promising cooperation with the administration in the interests of business recovery. The letter, published the day after the 1930 elections, was signed by former presidential candidates Cox, Davis, and Smith, National Chairman Raskob, Democratic headquarters director Shouse, Senate leader Joseph T. Robinson, and John N. Garner, leader in the House. Roosevelt supporters became suspicious and openly hostile to Raskob's leadership of the national committee.

Raskob's efforts were by now admittedly intended to preserve a national rostrum for Al Smith. The agrarian South saw the working-class Smith and the capitalist Raskob as an evil alliance against the farmer. Southerners in Congress turned for leadership to one of their most experienced national politicians, Cordell Hull, who had just become United States senator from Tennessee. In Hull's words: "In the years following 1928, I strove hard but without particular publicity to organize members of the Democratic National Committee and important Democratic leaders generally, against control of the Democratic Party by Governor Smith and his associates in 1932."[41]

Hull particularly resisted Smith-Raskob plans to have the national committee prepare a midterm party platform. According to Hull, the Democratic National Committee "has no authority, expressed or implied, to prescribe issues for the Democratic rank and file of the nation," an attitude which came to be the standard posture of congressional Democrats. Governor Roosevelt, in a "Dear Al" letter to Smith, took the opportunity to align himself with the Hull forces. "Historically," Roosevelt observed, "the National Committee has always recognized that in between conventions, the spokesmen on policy matters are, primarily, the Democratic Members of the Senate and House of Representatives, together with individuals high in the Party Councils, who, however, speak as individuals."[42]

When Raskob, on February 11, 1931, issued a call for a meeting of the national committee, Roosevelt supporters saw an opportunity to challenge the Smith-Raskob leadership. Meanwhile, Senator Hull was lining up powerful supporters for what he called "the showdown": Senators Byrd and Swanson of Virginia, Robinson of Arkansas, and Cohen of Georgia. On March 3, two days before the meeting, Hull received a long-distance telephone call from Roosevelt: "I just called to say that I want to get in and help you make that fight down there. The two national committee members from New York will support you, and I will send Jim Farley along with them to cooperate in every way." Farley sat next to Hull throughout the national committee meeting, leaving little doubt on which side Roosevelt stood.

Raskob opened the meeting with a long statement on party policy. He proposed that the states be allowed to control the manufacture, transportation, and sale of intoxicating liquors. He urged that business and trade be relieved of "unnecessary and unreasonable governmental restriction, interference, and manipulation." He repeated his plan for a tariff commission. Whereupon the Democratic leader in the Senate, Robinson of Arkansas, rose to deliver a blistering rebuttal on the Prohibition issue. Coming to Raskob's support, Al Smith chided those at any Democratic gathering who would "drag" and "kick around the lot" anyone expressing his own opinion. But by this point, according to Hull's account, Raskob was convinced that he ought not create a test of strength in the committee. Raskob refrained from offering his resignation and from insisting upon an interim statement of party principles. The main business of the meeting reduced itself to approval of a proposal to allow a commercial concern to raise funds for the 1932 campaign. The outcome of the meeting was a setback for Smith and Raskob and an improvement of Roosevelt's standing among the southern leaders.[43]

For the first time since 1919, Democrats won a House majority in 1930 and elected John N. Garner of Texas as Speaker. The balance was nonetheless close, and Fiorello H. LaGuardia of New York assumed the leadership of a small group of Republican insurgents seeking to establish themselves as the swing votes between the two major parties in the House. In the Senate, a 48–48 tie immobilized that body, although Republicans were permitted to organize the leadership positions. Republican progressives in both houses spoke often of another third-party movement, but most Republicans conceded that none could offer President Hoover a serious challenge in the Republican presidential primaries. His renomination was assured.

Republican politicians were reluctant to come to Hoover's support in 1932. The depression brought a 45 percent unemployment rate among factory workers, an 86 percent decline in residential building since 1929, and a 75 percent drop in steel production over the same period. In May 1932, the Bonus Expeditionary Force arrived in Washington to insist upon increased veterans' benefits; some 700,000–800,000 veterans and their dependents were among the most economically destitute citizens in the country. On July 28, President Hoover authorized Secretary of War Hurley to disperse the bonus marchers. General Douglas MacArthur led several tanks and cavalry against the unhappy demonstration, and among his junior officers were Dwight D. Eisenhower and George B. Patton. It was also the year of the Samuel Insull and Ivar Krueger scandals which destroyed popular confidence in American business leadership and in the Hoover administration. Renomination of the Hoover-Curtis ticket sent many Republican progressives onto the Democratic campaign train.

Roosevelt's 1930 gubernatorial campaign collected around him a group of men who became the talented and well-integrated campaign team during his campaign for president. Louis M. Howe was ever present. James A. Farley was promoted, at Roosevelt's suggestion, from secretary to the chairmanship of the New York Democratic State Committee. Farley and Howe made weekly trips to Albany to go over political strategy. Frank C. Walker, an associate of Senator Thomas J. Walsh of Montana, also became very active at this time. Another member of the inner group was Samuel I. Rosenman, a state legislator who had been recommended to Roosevelt in

1928 by Governor Smith as particularly qualified in the preparation of policy statements and speeches on legislative issues.[44] Led by Farley, the team pursued its mission of lining up votes for Roosevelt's nomination.

On January 22, 1932, Roosevelt formally declared himself a candidate for the presidential nomination. On February 8, Smith let it be known, contrary to his earlier statements, that he was willing to be a candidate. With Roosevelt clearly the front-runner, the Smith strategy was directed at trying to achieve a veto power under the two-thirds rule. It was to this possibility that a group of Democratic senators addressed themselves at a Washington dinner on February 11 honoring Homer S. Cummings, the former national chairman.

Cummings agreed to serve as informal liaison between the Farley-Howe operation in New York and the Democratic congressional leaders. Cummings subsequently also undertook to serve as contact man with the various favorite-son movements that were anticipating a convention deadlock. One favorite son who immediately withdrew in favor of Roosevelt was Senator Hull. Cummings was especially diligent in his talks with Senator Connally of Texas concerning the favorite-son status of Speaker John Nance Garner.

The 1932 Democratic National Convention turned into a fight between two old friends: Roosevelt and Smith. The third candidate was Garner, favorite son of the Texas and California delegations. Heading the California delegation was William Gibbs McAdoo, who rose during the fourth ballot to settle old accounts with Smith by announcing that the decisive Garner votes would shift to Roosevelt. More than a decade had been required to clear away the intransigence that had beset the Democratic party in 1920.

Although the depression was worldwide, the voters blamed Hoover and the Republicans and turned them out by a margin of seven million votes. Roosevelt reassured his countrymen in his inaugural address with such phrases as "the only thing we have to fear is fear itself." Congress was called into special session. The New Deal was in progress.

The economic crisis, the reunion of Democratic forces, and the New Deal landslide apparently obliterated all recollection of the distant days in May 1832 when Democratic-Republicans held their nominating convention in Baltimore and formally converted the Jacksonian movement into a national political party. The centennial of the Democratic party in 1932 went almost unnoticed. The party had urgent public business.

8

New Deal,
Fair Deal,
Loyal Opposition

FRANKLIN D. ROOSEVELT'S New Deal
gave the Democratic party an auspicious and historic start into its
second century. The New Deal–Fair Deal era marked a watershed in
world, national, and party development during which the United
States became a world power, the federal government grew many
times over in functions and size, and Democrats became the nation's majority party. The New Deal coalition returned FDR to the
White House an unprecedented four times, kept Harry Truman's
Fair Deal in office for seven years, and made possible some cohesion as a loyal opposition during the Eisenhower interregnum.[1]

Building the New Deal Coalition

Of the thirty-nine million votes cast in 1932, Roosevelt won
seven million more than Hoover. Socialist Norman Thomas drew
off nearly a million votes. Other statistics were relevant to the Roosevelt landslide. In a labor force of about fifty million, between
twelve and seventeen million Americans were unemployed. More
than a third of the nation's banks failed during 1932–1933. Farm
foreclosures were rampant and harvests lay rotting. Relief funds for
the destitute, mainly from local and philanthropic sources, were
exhausted. Nations, even the scrupulous British, with World War I
debts to the United States, defaulted in their payments. Roosevelt
and the Democratic party faced the onerous responsibility of salvag-
ing the nation's economic system and, in the view of some, the
political system as well.

Roosevelt's "coattail" pulled in a Congress in which two-thirds of the seats were occupied by Democrats. Consensus among Democrats enabled Roosevelt to enjoy "one hundred days" of almost complete congressional support for his emergency measures. The legislative achievements of the first New Deal Congress marked new and enduring pathways in national policy. No session of Congress had ever worked so hard.

In all the legislative hubbub, it was almost impossible for 60 Democratic senators and 310 Democratic representatives to keep in touch with each other, let alone exercise concerted political action on behalf of the Roosevelt program. To cope with the coordination problem, the House Democratic caucus modified its whip system by dividing the nation into fifteen geographical districts, the Democratic congressmen from each electing an assistant whip. The new channels of communication enabled congressional Democrats to enjoy a rare degree of cohesion.

New Deal measures poured into the congressional hopper, many of them poorly drafted and hastily enacted in an atmosphere of emergency and near revolution. The Agricultural Adjustment Act (AAA) introduced price supports and crop reduction procedures for farm products. An emergency farm mortage financing plan sought to halt foreclosures. A securities exchange bill restored confidence in the stock market. The National Industrial Recovery Act (NIRA) provided for organized labor's right of collective bargaining, over $3 billion in public works, and the development of codes of fair competition aimed at reviving stagnated industrial enterprises.

The Civilian Conservation Corps (CCC) took hundreds of thousands of young men off the bread lines and put them onto long-neglected projects for conserving the nation's natural resources. Because starvation and destitution would not wait, the Federal Emergency Relief Administration (FERA), under Harry L. Hopkins, the Iowa-born social worker who had run New York State's emergency relief program under Governor Roosevelt, began dispensing $500 million in direct relief through state and local agencies. Hopkins soon found himself running a patronage machine comparable to Postmaster General Farley's, whose more than seventy-five thousand presidential appointments were themselves hardly a small political resource. Hopkins also found himself colliding with former Progressive Harold L. Ickes, public works administrator (PWA), who had other billions to spend for jobs.

An Emergency Banking Act led to arrangements for safeguarding bank deposits and improving the currency supply. Anticipating the repeal of Prohibition, an amendment to the Volstead Act permitted the sale of light beer and wine. The Muscle Shoals and Tennessee Valley Development Act created the Tennessee Valley Authority and launched a great and successful experiment in regional planning.

As Hopkins distributed FERA emergency relief funds during summer and fall of 1933, he repeatedly warned that money would run out during the dreary winter months ahead. Ickes's Public Works Administration, because of the extensive project planning it required, would be unable to meet this pressing need. Hopkins was able to convince the president that a work relief program that could employ four million persons within thirty days was necessary. This gave rise to the Civil Works Administration (CWA), also under Hopkins's supervision. In less than four months, CWA launched 180,000 work projects and spent over $933 million. A Hopkins-Ickes rivalry resulted that colored the internal politics of the Roosevelt administration for many years.

Perhaps before he fully realized it, Hopkins found FERA becoming a political machine parallel to Farley's, with cash resources that no political party manager had dreamed of before. The highly political character of FERA was nowhere better illustrated than in Hopkins's dealings with the federal unemployment director for Missouri, Judge Harry Truman. A presiding county judge since 1922, Truman had a statewide reputation for honesty and efficiency in the handling of public funds. The reputation was based upon Truman's achievements in building county roads and other public improvements during a period in which the Tom Pendergast machine was holding sway in Kansas City. A friend of Pendergast's brother, Mike, Truman was known in Missouri as a politician friendly to, but independent of, the Pendergast organization. Hopkins's search for a loyal but honest Democrat to administer relief in that state led to Truman, and the two men struck up a warm friendship. Both men were undoubtedly drawn to each other by their common origin in the Midwest, their reputations for honesty and efficiency, their talent for translating broad social objectives into meticulously administered programs, their scrappy postures in political battles, and their intense concern for the social and economic crisis that arose from mass unemployment. In 1934, Truman became United States senator from Missouri, with the support of *both* Pendergast and Hopkins.

The performance of Hopkins, as the biggest and fasted spender in Washington, was a matter of particular political concern to Roosevelt. Roosevelt asked Frank Walker to keep an eye on Hopkins's activities, particularly after CWA was inaugurated. The opportunities for waste and corruption in this program were enormous. After a thorough personal investigation of CWA activities in the field, Walker assured Roosevelt that criticism of Hopkins and CWA was entirely unfounded. "It is amazing when you consider that within the short time since CWA was established four million idle have been put to work. During Christmas week many of them were standing in a payroll line for the first time in eighteen months."[2] Largely as a consequence of Walker's reports, Roosevelt came to consider Hopkins one of his most trustworthy associates. In 1934, even as the Republican National Committee denounced Hopkins and CWA for waste and corruption, the president sent Hopkins to Congress for additional funds.

The midterm congressional election of 1934 was the first in American history in which the party of an incumbent administration gained rather than lost seats in Congress. The number of Democrats in the Senate rose to 69, in the House to 319. Perhaps an even more significant consequence of this unusual election was the realization by many southern Democrats that they were now a minority in the party they had so recently dominated.

From 1918 to 1930, the southern Democratic contingent was large and stable, as Table 4 indicates. Southern representatives in these seven Congresses constituted an average of 62 percent of the Democratic strength in the House. In the Senate, the same average prevailed. With Bryan and Wilson on the national scene, each with substantial southern followings, it was not surprising for southerners to insist upon exercising their preponderant weight in national party affairs. Not until 1932, when the New Deal swept a substantial nonsouthern Democratic majority into both houses, did southern Democrats again become a minority within the party's congressional wing. Democratic leaders, sensitive to the method of numbers for achieving representative collective action, promptly responsed to the new voting balance. The South's weakened status was confirmed at the very next Democratic National Convention when the two-thirds nominating rule was repealed.

By 1935, reaction to the momentum of the New Deal began to set in. Although unemployment and poverty were still very much in evidence, conservatives were increasingly resistant to the man-

TABLE 4
Southern Democratic Strength, in Percentages,
among Congressional Democrats, 1918–1936

Year	House of Representatives	Senate
1918	59.7	55.3
1920	81.7	70.3
1922	55.8	60.5
1924	62.8	66.7
1926	59.5	56.5
1928	63.2	66.7
1930	53.2	55.3
1932	37.4	43.3
1934	36.7	37.7
1936	35.0	34.2

Source: Compiled by author.

ner in which the Roosevelt administration seemed to be altering the traditional attitudes and values of American society. The right to work, the right to receive emergency relief, the right to bargain collectively in industrial relations, governmental encouragement of industrial "collusion" under the NRA, the payment of subsidies to discourage farm overproduction—these and other policies seemed to be turning the American value structure upside down. With Stalin, Hitler, and Mussolini rushing to power, the strong thrust of Roosevelt's leadership frightened some who believed it might carry with it the seeds of dictatorship. To mobilize this anti-Roosevelt sentiment, former Democratic National Chairman Raskob, with the endorsement of former nominees John W. Davis and Alfred E. Smith, inaugurated the American Liberty League. Jouett Shouse was appointed as the League's director, and Smith made a hard-hitting speech to launch the League's operations.

A few days later, Senator Joseph T. Robinson of Arkansas made a nationwide radio address replying to Smith's charges. Jim Farley turned the artillery of national committee headquarters against the League, with additional instructions to his staff that they "ignore the Republican party." The public was soon made aware that the League was a millionaires' club and that Smith's speeches had over-tones of personal bitterness. Roosevelt referred to the League as symbolic of the opposition of the wealthy to his programs. Almost to the day of his death in April 1936, Louis Howe worried about the possibility that the League's activities might influence the work of the platform committee at the 1936 national convention. He need not have been concerned. The draft that went before the platform committee was prepared by Sam Rosenman, under the president's supervision, with the collaboration of William Bullitt, Donald Richberg, and Harry Hopkins. In the last analysis, the League had little impact upon the party's fortunes in 1936.

Southern fears about becoming a minority appeared justified when the fundamental step was taken at the 1936 Democratic National Convention to change the two-thirds nominating rule to a simple majority arrangement. The South, which for generations had been able to veto unacceptable presidential candidates, could no longer do so. This rule, permitting a minority to veto an otherwise popular nomination, had created all too many costly factional contests. Serious discussion regarding abrogation of the rule began soon after the 103-ballot disaster of 1924. In the interest of harmony, the Smith forces set aside the discussion in 1928. A resolution at the 1932 convention, however, recommended to the succeeding convention that it consider the issue and make a change to majority rule. When the 1936 convention took up the matter, southerners objected, but to no avail. As a gesture to the southerners, the convention instructed the national committee to develop a plan of delegate apportionment that would take into account party strength and reward it by a bonus vote arrangement. The elimination of the hundred-year-old rule proved in later years to be a major step in the moderation of the character of southern politics as well as presidential politics generally.

There was little else for the Democratic convention of 1936 to decide. Despite the country's continuing economic problems, most of the opposition to Roosevelt was Republican. Within the party, Roosevelt, Garner, and Farley were about as popular as the leadership of a party could be. Roosevelt and Garner were renominated, and Farley continued as national chairman.

Between 1934 and 1936, Roosevelt nailed together the electoral coalition that, in various revivals and resurrections, remained the basis of Democratic victories for the next forty years. The ethnic and nationality minorities, a substantial number of whom were recent immigrants drawn into the electoral process by Al Smith's candidacy in 1928, were thoroughly mobilized by Farley and most of the big-city machines. Catholics, Jews, and northern blacks became the staunchest of Democrats, the latter voting 76 percent Democratic in 1936.

Encouraged by the collective bargaining provisions (Section 7A) of the NIRA, trade union organizing activity and membership increased by leaps and bounds, and the American Federation of Labor began a career of helping its political friends, mainly Democrats. Dr. Francis E. Townsend's program for old-age pensions brought out millions of neglected elderly citizens, to whom Roosevelt and Congress responded with the social security system. The poor were also being organized successfully by Socialist Norman Thomas, Father Charles E. Coughlin, whose radio audiences were the largest and most loyal of that period, and Senator Huey Long of Louisiana, whose Share Our Wealth Society claimed 7.5 million members. Among the poorest in the nation were millions of farmers and rural citizens who began to leave Republican ranks for the New Deal. Finally, turning to the universities for advice and personnel, Roosevelt brought the intellectual community into government to an unprecedented degree. In 1936, therefore, according to most analysts of that election, the domination of American national politics by rural interests ended and its leadership was assumed by urban forces: unions, ethnic minorities, city machines, intellectuals, consumer-oriented business enterprise, with assistance from poor farmers and the elderly—in short, the New Deal coalition.

The 1936 campaign produced strains among old political friends. The president asked Eleanor Roosevelt to "look in" on the campaign's management and report to him. National Chairman Farley interpreted this as lack of confidence. Southern leaders, many of them still rankling over the loss of the two-thirds rule, wondered when an opportunity would arise to demonstrate their importance to the party. Harry Hopkins, a social-worker-turned politician, replaced the deceased Louis Howe as Roosevelt's principal confidant, and this, too, evoked the enmity of Farley and the southerners.

Despite instructions from Roosevelt following the 1934 campaign to cut the cost of national headquarters, Farley maintained much more than the usual skeleton crew. From the beginning of 1936, the headquarters staff was occupied updating contacts with state, county, and local organizations and with the campaign against the Liberty League. Farley made several trips around the country to pep up the organization and to identify local problems. It was during one of these trips that he referred to "Alf" Landon, the Republican nominee, as governor of "a typical prairie state." Roosevelt was quick to admonish Farley, sending a memorandum on the same day of the speech to say that "the word 'typical' coming from any New Yorker is meat for the opposition." The Republicans nevertheless picked up the phrase and made much of it.[3]

In his memoirs, Farley referred to the 1936 campaign as the beginning of a "drifting apart" between Roosevelt and himself. During October, "they"—presumably the president and his other advisers—suggested that Farley not appear with the president on the platform of the campaign train. Farley's personal popularity apparently distracted too much attention from Roosevelt.

Looking back through the years, I find it hard to put the finger of memory on the beginning of the drift, so gradual was the process. Almost before I knew it, I was no longer called to the White House for morning bedside conferences. My phone no longer brought the familiar voice in mellifluous tones. Months dragged between White House luncheon conferences. Soon I found I was no longer being consulted on appointments, even in my own state. Then, too, I found I was as much in the dark about the President's political plans as the Chairman of the Republican National Committee. White House confidence on politics and policies went to a small band of zealots, who mocked at party loyalty and knew no devotion except unswerving obedience to their leader. . . . What few people realize is that relationship between Roosevelt and me had been basically political and seldom social. Strange as it may seem, the President never took me into the bosom of the family, although everyone agreed I was more responsible than any other single man for his being in the White House.[4]

On the other hand, there were those who were happy with Roosevelt. Joseph P. Kennedy of Massachusetts published a businessman's appreciation of the New Deal in a volume called *I Am for Roosevelt*. The voters were also appreciative and, in November, gave Roosevelt every state in the Union except Maine and Vermont.

In his second inaugural address, the president expressed his fervent hope that the work of the New Deal would continue, for he still saw "one-third of a nation ill-housed, ill-clad, ill-nourished." But a hostile Supreme Court had been invalidating a number of key New Deal measures. Heartened by the overwhelming electoral support he received in 1936, Roosevelt, in his annual message of 1937, expressed concern over the impasse between the executive and judicial branches. Then, in February, without seriously consulting Democratic leaders in Congress, he sent to the Senate a series of recommendations for a general reorganization of the judiciary from the Supreme Court down to the district courts. A central part of his proposal was a provision to add an additional judge to any federal court in which a sitting judge, having reached the retirement age of seventy, did not avail himself of the opportunity to retire on a pension. With six of the nine members of the Supreme Court over seventy, it was obvious that the proposal was a "court-packing" plan. Looking back over the years, one of Roosevelt's closest advisers, Judge Sam Rosenman, referred to the plan as "the most controversial proposal Roosevelt ever made during his twelve years as President," and one that "cost him much in prestige, particularly in party prestige."[5]

Others saw the Supreme Court proposal as a test of party control. The Republican strategy, directed by Senator Borah, was to let Democrats fight for and against the proposal among themselves. The non–New Dealers in the party, particularly those from the South, quickly saw an opportunity to remind a popular president that there were three branches in the national government and a southern interest to be taken into account in the Democratic party. It was also a time when the full consequences of the 1910 revolt against Speaker Cannon were being felt. The Speaker's powers under Cannon, for example, agenda-setting and committee assignments, had by now been assumed by a collective leadership of standing committee chairmen safely entrenched by their one-party constituencies and the seniority system. Most of this collective leadership consisted of conservative Republicans and Southern Democrats. The court-packing proposal offered a favorable opportunity to test this alliance and to challenge presidential power. Ironically, because of their seniority, Majority Leader Joseph T. Robinson of Arkansas, Pat Harrison of Mississippi, and James F. Byrne of South Carolina—all southerners—became responsible for carrying the legislative ball for the president's court plan. Opponents adopted a strategy of delay in order to permit events, some quite unexpected, to unfold and public opinion to manifest itself.

As though responding to the pressures of the court plan, Supreme Court decisions, actually concluded many months earlier, began to come forth favoring New Deal legislation. Justice Van Devanter, a persistent anti–New Dealer, announced his retirement in June, enabling Roosevelt to replace him with New Dealer Hugo Black. The most shocking development was the sudden death of Majority Leader Robinson on July 14, removing the president's most skillful arbiter in a very difficult battle.

The leadership fight that followed Robinson's death also revealed the deep split in the Senate's Democratic majority. The two candidates to succeed Robinson were Pat Harrison of Mississippi and Alben Barkley of Kentucky. The contest was close and the outcome decided only when the president indirectly endorsed Barkley in a famous "Dear Alben" note. The leadership fight, however, cost Roosevelt his court plan, which was rejected shortly thereafter. It was his first major legislative defeat.

Winning a Third Term and a World War

Possibly one of the principal incitements to division within the party was Roosevelt's statement of March 4, 1937, delivered at a Democratic victory dinner, that he longed to turn over his office to a successor on January 20, 1941, "whoever he may be," with the assurance that he was turning over to him a nation that was at peace, prosperous, and ambitious to meet the needs of humanity. While talk of a third term for Roosevelt had begun almost immediately after his reelection, his March 4 comments, which did not have the finality of a complete withdrawal, were thought to have come unusually and suspiciously early in the second term. Jockeying unabashedly among the presidential "availables" were Vice President John N. Garner, Speaker William B. Bankhead, Secretary of State Cordell Hull, Postmaster General and National Chairman James A. Farley, Senator James F. Byrnes of South Carolina, Jesse Jones, and Harry Hopkins. Of these, Farley was by far the most popular among the Democratic rank-and-file and in many ways the most available.

The opposition of many major Democratic leaders to his Supreme Court plan in spring of 1937, the split in the fight for the Senate leadership succession, and the defeat of his wages-and-hours and administrative-reorganization bills during the fall left Roosevelt with a keen concern about the effectiveness of his leadership. By the end of the year the problem of reasserting that leadership seemed paramount to him. Roosevelt was also aware that the resources of the presidency for disciplining recalcitrant Democrats were extremely limited, especially in what would normally be a lame-duck term. The usual presidential patronage was by and large disposed of. The leverage afforded by emergency programs had diminished. His March statement had emphasized his lame-duck status.

One instrument of influence never before used, however, was presidential endorsement or opposition in party primaries. One of the unwritten and unbreakable rules of American politics had always been that, in a federal system, national leaders should never intervene in state and local contests between fellow-partisans. At least, such intervention should never be overt. Indirect pressures, however, were assumed to be inevitable, and Roosevelt had not previously been reluctant to use these pressures.

During the 1938 session of Congress, Roosevelt considered a plan to intervene in certain Democratic primary elections to give support to liberals wherever they stood out clearly against conservatives. Hopkins, Ickes, and Corcoran strongly urged this course. Farley took the position that such a procedure would be unwise in the interest of party unity and, further, that, as national chairman, he personally would be technically prohibited from interfering in local fights. Farley had to and wanted to be neutral. When Roosevelt decided to embark upon the plan to endorse liberal Democrats, Corcoran was assigned management of that campaign. Hopkins, whose wife had recently died of cancer and who himself was recovering from surgery, took a back seat during his convalescence.

In a radio "fireside chat" on June 24, 1938, Roosevelt discussed the accomplishments and failures of the Seventy-fifth Congress. He closed with the following declaration:

As the head of the Democratic Party, however, charged with the responsibility of carrying out the definitely liberal declaration of principles set forth in the 1936 Democratic platform, I feel that I have every right to speak in those few instances where there may be a clear issue between candidates for a Democratic nomination involving these principles, or involving a clear misuse of my own name.[6]

During the summer and fall, Roosevelt urged the nomination of Lawrence Camp over Senator Walter George in the Georgia primaries, David J. Lewis over Senator Millard Tydings in Maryland, James H. Fay over Representative John J. O'Connor in New York. Roosevelt won only in the case of O'Connor. The Republicans gained eighty-two seats in the House and eight seats in the Senate. The "purge," as his opponents called it, was basically a failure, although it set an important precedent.

The returns seemed to confirm the positions taken by Garner and Farley, namely, that the New Deal needed to move to the right and that a reconciliation with conservatives in Congress was necessary. Farley wrote to party leaders throughout the country, inviting their evaluation of the returns and explanations for the defeats. The replies, which Farley passed on to the president, were a catalog of conservative complaints: criticism of the spending program; complaints about Congress of Industrial Organizations (CIO) influence in the administration; depressed farm prices; dissatisfaction with the WPA program; business protests about bureaucratic regimentation; and the unfriendliness of the press. Roosevelt thanked Farley for the letters in a memorandum dated December 2, 1938, and suggested that "you ought to start a special division of the National Committee to begin giving the (newly elected Republican Governors) 'the works' as soon as they take office." The suggested bureau was never established. Elsewhere, polls were showing Farley and Hull among the prospects most favored for the succession upon Roosevelt's retirement.[7]

The Congresses of Roosevelt's second term, although increasingly reluctant to endorse his programs, did establish the Farm Security Administration, which provided loans to tenant farmers; the United States Housing Authority, to extend financial aid to local governmental housing agencies; a minimum-wage law; and a plan for soil conservation payments to farmers who agreed to restrict production of specific crops. As the recession of 1938 mounted, Congress also found itself again putting millions into public works appropriations. One other kind of appropriation began to assume significant proportions at this time: defense spending. A war was brewing in Europe.

International politics worsened after 1937. Having conquered Manchuria in 1931, the Japanese once again invaded China in 1937. In Europe, during 1938, Hitler annexed Austria and the Sudetenland region of Czechoslovakia. This was followed in 1939 by Germany's annexation of all Czechoslovakia and the conclusion of a nonaggression pact between Germany and Russia. Within days, Germany invaded Poland. Great Britian and France declared war on Germany, and World War II began.

The disenchantments of World War I had left Americans isolationist and antiwar. President Roosevelt, long before Pearl Habor, anticipating the worst, proposed that the United States lease or sell essential war supplies to Britain as a gesture of friendship and as a measure of defense of American security. The lend-lease debate in Congress was a searching one and proved to be an indispensable precursor of subsequent defense legislation and repeal of the Neutrality Act.

In presidential politics the great question was whether or not, in view of the world crisis, Roosevelt would seek an unprecedented third term. If he did not, whom would he choose as a successor? James Farley and Cordell Hull were frequently mentioned, but never by New Dealers. Late in 1938, Roosevelt promoted Harry Hopkins from federal relief administrator to secretary of commerce, a move widely interpreted as a buildup for the succession. Confirmation was vigorously debated in the Senate. The following June, however, Hopkins began advocating a third term for Roosevelt. The intensification of the war in Europe made this a growing possibility. Vice President Garner and Postmaster General Farley openly declared their opposition to a third term and announced their own availability.

Hopkins became the kingpin of the 1940 national convention. According to Hopkins's reports to Sam Rosenman, the president wanted as his running mate Cordell Hull, James Byrnes, or Henry Wallace, in that order. Hull steadfastly resisted presidential pressure in order to continue as secretary of state "in the troublous days ahead." Senator Byrnes also resisted. "In my opinion," he later wrote in his memoirs, "the third-term fight would be a close one, and if Mr. Roosevelt should be defeated many would attribute his failure not to the real cause but to the fact that a South Carolinian had been selected as his running mate. It would then be many years before a national convention would again nominate a southerner for either office."[8]

The president's choice for vice president settled upon Wallace, whose record as secretary of agriculture and whose strong New Deal positions on domestic and international matters appealed to Roosevelt. Despite Farley's view that "the people look on him as a wild-eyed fellow," it was Roosevelt's opinion that Wallace would help the campaign in the farm states as well as the cities where he had the strong endorsement of the CIO.

The national convention moved to its duties with a strong undercurrent of tension. Roosevelt had a committed majority of the votes, but Hopkins was eager to have the nomination made by acclamation. But Garner and Farley refused to withdraw. The vote: Roosevelt, 946½; Farley, 72½; Garner, 61; Tydings, 9; and Hull, 5. His protest against the third term thus recorded, Farley moved to suspend the rules and make the nomination unanimous.

Trouble also arose during the vice-presidential selection. The anti–New Deal wing pressed for recognition by offering as candidates Jesse Jones, Speaker Bankhead, and Paul McNutt. The president told Rosenman, as they waited upon reports from Chicago: "I'm going to tell them that I won't run with either of those men [Jones or Bankhead] or with any other reactionary." Roosevelt reaffirmed his preference for Wallace at least three times in telephone conversations with Hopkins. Wallace was nominated, but 329 of the convention's 1,100 votes went to Speaker Bankhead and another 144 to others. Wallace's nomination established a precedent: the naming of a vice-presidential nominee from the same wing of the party as the presidential nominee.[9]

The convention established another precedent as a consequence of proposals initiated at the 1936 convention. A bonus vote of two delegates-at-large was henceforth to be given to those states going Democratic in presidential elections, a concession to the South.

Farley declined the management of Roosevelt's campaign, a departure made difficult by the unusual esteem and affection in which Farley was held by the party rank-and-file. A new group of men moved into the president's political staff. Hopkins, resigning as secretary of commerce because of ill health, worked with Rosenman and playwright Robert E. Sherwood as a three-man speech-writing team. Ed Flynn took over the national chairmanship after Joseph P. Kennedy declined. On election day, Roosevelt defeated Wendell Willkie by a five-million-vote margin and later enjoyed referring to the outcome as "close."

The election over, the war against the Axis consumed Roosevelt's full attention. By May 1941, he declared an unlimited national emergency. In August, he and Prime Minister Winston Churchill enunciated the Atlantic Charter. On December 7, 1941, the Japanese attacked Pearl Harbor, and the United States declared war against the Axis. On the battlefields, Douglas MacArthur and his American-Philippine troops made their classic stand at Corregidor. American supply lines began to stretch around the Arctic Ocean to the Soviet Union, across the South Atlantic to the British in North Africa, and more directly to the British Isles, where General Dwight D. Eisenhower would eventually train an allied force for an invasion of the Continent.

Although Congress was willing to support its wartime leader in most respects, some members with a long sense of history looked back over the nation's experience in previous wars and forward to some future accounting of Democratic party performance in this war. One of these was Senator Harry Truman of Missouri. In the Mexican War, the Civil War, the Spanish-American War, and World War I, Truman recalled, sudden and large increases in federal spending for military and related equipment and services had placed the handling of public funds and resources at the mercy of the inefficient, the dishonest, and the greedy. Truman also recalled Lincoln's bitter experience with the Radical Republican Committee on the Conduct of the War. It was inherently difficult for a congressional investigating committee, even one of the president's own party, to serve as a "friendly watch-dog" over defense spending. Nevertheless, in February 1941, Truman recommended the creation of such a committee, of which he became chairman.

With an initial fund of only $15,000 and an earnest intention of flushing out waste and corruption without embarrassing the Roosevelt war leadership, the Truman Committee set about its task. Its investigations produced masses of information about slovenly administration, incompetence, and dishonesty in defense expenditures. Without fanfare, the committee poked around in factories and through military installations. In the several years of its operation, the Truman Committee was credited conservatively with saving the federal government some $15 billion. Senator Truman's fiscal accomplishment and his political tact earned him the gratitude of Democrats and Republicans alike, but in particular the appreciation of President Roosevelt.

World War II set United States governmental funds and resources in motion at a rate never before experienced by any nation. Upward of $400 billion were spent for the war effort. Armaments were built and expended without stint. Where 1,100 combat planes were available before the war, the nation produced nearly 300,000 before the end of the war. Starting with only about 1,000 tanks, this force grew to over 80,000. During the first three years, some 45 million bombs were manufactured. The most dramatic of these was produced by the Manhattan Project, a scientific collaboration costing over $2 billion, successfully achieving nuclear fission, and ushering in the atomic era.

By 1944 the Allies were able to embark upon attacks against the German lines in Italy, a new offensive in Russia, and an invasion of France. In the Pacific, MacArthur began his return, as promised, to the Philippines.

The strain of the war effort took its toll upon Roosevelt, who, late in 1943, began to show signs of ill health. His renomination for a fourth term was nonetheless generally accepted within the party. Of greater concern to Democratic leaders was the vice-presidential nomination. Southerners were adamantly opposed to Vice President Wallace, whose radical New Dealism and statements on racial issues particularly offended them. Other candidates available were

183

Speaker Sam Rayburn, Senate Majority Leader Alben Barkley, Supreme Court Justice William O. Douglas, "Assistant President" James F. Byrnes, and Senator Harry Truman, whose investigations had by now given him national prominence.

Roosevelt decided to placate the southerners by letting Wallace defend his own candidacy. The other most active candidate was Byrnes, but his strong southern views on race soon eliminated him. The only name without substantial political liabilities was Truman's. With the president's encouragement, the convention eventually turned to Truman.

The 1944 Roosevelt campaign was possibly the least effective of his career. Even while the national convention was in process, the president was on his way to Pearl Harbor and Alaska for conferences with military leaders about the forthcoming Pacific campaign. He indicated that he might be too busy to make many campaign speeches, and those that he made in the opening weeks were strikingly poor in content and delivery. The Republicans hit hard on the theme that "the Old Man is finished." The CIO Political Action Committee, under Sidney Hillman's leadership, put tremendous effort into the Roosevelt-Truman campaign, which became the basis of Republican charges that the Democratic party was now dominated by Hillman and the Communist element in the CIO.

In addition to labor, another element in the New Deal coalition began to receive special attention in the 1944 campaign, namely, the black vote. Mechanization of southern agriculture and the labor shortage in northern war plants started an internal migration during the war years that placed over a million southern blacks into northern communities. Democratic urban organizations, such as Kelly's in Chicago, enlisted the newly resident voters and offered them a role in the nation's decisions, something blacks had been deprived of for generations. When the war ended, additional millions of blacks returning from the armed forces settled in the North. Thus, a black "swing vote" developed in large pivotal urban states and became an irrepressible force in national politics, the numerical basis for a new struggle for civil rights. Democratic National Chairman Robert Hannegan went to great lengths to mobilize state and local party leaders in 1944 to register blacks, war workers, and migratory workers. Hannegan also promoted simplification of ballot laws to enable persons on military duty to vote absentee.

Roosevelt finally began to turn his attention to the campaign. Before a Teamsters Union convention, he delivered his famous

"Fala speech" in which he berated the Republicans for libelous statements about his dog, Fala. This single speech gave the entire party and campaign a lift in morale. On October 5, from the White House, Roosevelt answered numerous Republican charges, particularly their references to communism in the Democratic party. Even as Republican nominee Thomas E. Dewey was criticizing the administration for its handling of the war, General MacArthur was leading the landing of American troops in the Philippines. On election day, the voters decided to return their commander-in-chief to the task he seemed about to bring to successful completion.

During 1944, there began an indirect conversation between Franklin D. Roosevelt and Wendell Willkie concerning the question of a realignment of the national parties of the United States. Sam Rosenman was the principal intermediary and reported the details in his memoirs.

During the last week in June, Roosevelt told Rosenman of a conversation with Governor Pinchot. Willkie had suggested to Pinchot that the time seemed right for a new line-up of the nation's parties. Beaten by the conservatives in his own party, Willkie was ready to encourage a coalition of liberals in both parties, leaving the conservatives in each party to join together if they wished. According to Rosenman, Roosevelt concurred: "I agree with him one hundred percent and the time is now—right after election. We ought to have two real parties—one liberal and the other conservative." Roosevelt's hope was that work begun immediately would make it possible for Willkie and himself to bring together a liberal party in time for 1948.

Since the unfortunate "purge" of 1938, Roosevelt had frequently discussed the necessity for a new alignment of political parties in the United States. In Willkie, he thought he had, for the first time, a Republican qualified to work with him on this extremely difficult undertaking. The president delegated Rosenman to arrange a secret meeting with Willkie in New York City. Such a meeting between Willkie and Rosenman did take place on July 5, 1944. Willkie expressed great satisfaction and looked forward to meeting with Roosevelt after election day. The project never got off the ground. By election day Willkie was dead, and five months later so was Roosevelt. Concluding his account, Rosenman observes:

The project was never even discussed between them directly. It was a Herculean task that these two political leaders had thought of undertaking. No combination other than Roosevelt and Willkie could have done it. And 1948 would have been the most opportune time to do it. . . . Had Roosevelt and Willkie lived, their political alliance might have been so firmly cemented by 1948 that the great schism and realignment might have taken place that year.[10]

A Fair Deal and More Party Discipline under Truman

In the eighty-two days during which he served as vice president, Truman's principal political assignment from Roosevelt was to see that Henry Wallace's nomination as secretary of commerce went safely to confirmation in the Senate. As presiding officer of that body, Truman had to break two ties to get Wallace confirmed. Meanwhile, Roosevelt was out of the city most of the time, at Yalta or at Warm Springs, leaving Truman as an unofficial "acting president."

Roosevelt's death came on April 12, 1945. It fell to the former senator from Missouri, usually described in the press as "just an average American," to carry the country to the victorious conclusion of a global war, to build the foundation of a world organization capable of guaranteeing the peace, to direct the reconversion of the nation from a highly controlled wartime economy to a free but stable peacetime one, and to accustom the people of his country to a new brand of political leadership in the wake of a dozen years under the cultured and charismatic patrician of Hyde Park.

The Germans surrendered, unconditionally, a month after Truman assumed the presidency. On July 16, Truman, Churchill, and Stalin met at Potsdam to coordinate Pacific strategy and lay the groundwork for peace negotiations. Even as the conference proceeded, a British national election resulted in a Labor government; Clement Attlee took Winston Churchill's place at the Potsdam conference table. During the conference, Truman received news of the first successful detonation of an atom bomb by American scientists at the Manhattan Project. Truman made the decision to bomb Hiroshima, which took place on August 6. Two days later the Soviet Union, belatedly, declared war against Japan. Nagasaki was bombed on August 9. On August 14, the Japanese surrendered unconditionally, signing the surrender document on the U.S.S. *Missouri* on September 2.

The last gun had barely ceased firing when Truman's domestic political troubles began and continued at a pace that might have caused even a Franklin D. Roosevelt misgivings. The nation remained the most powerful in the world, the most unscathed, and the most affluent. Old and new social and political interests were scrambling to understand and make the most of a time of kaleidoscopic change. These many interests were, as usual, represented in Congress, where their competing claims were juggled gingerly by legislators suddenly released from years of constraint under the Roosevelt "presence" and the demands of a world war. Farmers, workers, businessmen, and others sought to protect their New Deal and wartime gains. President Truman fell into wrangles with one after the other as he tried to hold the line against "quick killings" and special advantage. Thus, Truman's brief honeymoon with the Congress, the interest groups, and the country generally ended with his message of September 6, 1945, reaffirming Roosevelt's 1944 economic bill of rights. This message launched the Fair Deal.

But the economic goals of the Fair Deal were not easy to pursue. Labor, particularly the miners and the railroad brotherhoods, went on strike to break the wage ceilings that had been imposed during the war. The president countered with a plan to "draft labor" which brought the labor movement down upon his head. When the strikes ended, the draft-labor proposal was dropped. Election of the Republican Eightieth Congress brought with it the Taft-Hartley Act, whose provisions were viewed by labor as harshly punitive. The mood of Congress was angry and even Truman's veto of Taft-Hartley was overriden. On the other hand, the president's vigorous support of the Full Employment Act of 1946 was successful. For the first time in the history of the American free enterprise system the act made it the explicit responsibility of the federal government to guard the nation against economic depressions and mass unemployment. This legislation endeared Truman to labor.

In December 1946, Truman appointed a Committee on Civil Rights to investigate the deepening problems in that field. Senators Richard Russell of Georgia and Tom Connally of Texas, usually calm politicians, became extremely agitated and vocal in opposition to the committee. Its inevitably controversial report was rendered in October 1947. Three months later the president sent a bill to Congress implementing many of the committee's recommendations. The civil rights battle became a distinguishing feature of the Truman administration.

In response to the President's civil rights bill, a conference of southern governors sent a delegation, headed by Governor J. Strom Thurmond of South Carolina, to present their demands in Washington. In a public manifesto, over fifty southern Democrats in the House condemned the Truman civil rights program. Several southern governors revealed plans to deprive the president of their states' electoral college vote should he become the party's nominee. Southern Democrats were moving to reassert their old ascendancy in the party. Thus, Truman's positions on civil rights and labor provided the domestic setting of presidential politics in 1948.

While domestic difficuties kept Truman's popularity rating fluctuating, his moves in the foreign policy field resulted in relatively firm and stable popular support. His appointment of General George C. Marshall to succeed Byrnes as secretary of state brought to the administration some of the universal esteem in which the general was held. As relations with the Soviet Union deteriorated, American firmness in negotiations with the Communists hardened. The policy of containment of communism began to take form and came forth in March 1947 as the Truman Doctrine of aid to Greece and Turkey. In June, the Marshall Plan for emergency economic and technical assistance to less-developed countries and to countries threatened by communism was proclaimed.

However, these moves were not without challenge. The Soviet Union held Eastern Europe tightly under the control of its occupation forces. The Chinese Communists were driving the Chiang Kai-shek Nationalists off the mainland and onto Formosa. The external threat of Communist expansion and evidence of Communist spying within the United States led the president to ask for $29 million for the administration of loyalty checks of federal employees, setting the stage for the Communists-in-government witch hunt of the subsequent McCarthy era.

Thus, Truman began to lead the nation in one of the most painful about-faces in its history. The nation had been a habitual disarmer after each of its wars. This pattern appeared as usual immediately after cessation of World War II. Fair Deal leaders, however, soon read a new handwriting on the walls of international politics: a nuclear power cannot disarm. Nations such as the Soviet Union and Communist China, with programs for producing the millennium tomorrow, do not relax in victory. Former allies, devastated by war, cannot cope with the fires of economic and social discontent without a helping hand. In the wake of wartime devastation, Communist parties were making substantial gains in many countries, often with overt help from the Soviet Union. Perhaps the most unsettling aspect of American postwar foreign policy was its possession of an unprecedented weapon, the atom bomb. The bomb could hardly be used in ordinary military operations, yet it was considered the major deterrent to Soviet aggression and a symbol of American military responsibilities around the world. Finally, the infant United Nations needed American protection more than vice versa. In response to all this, Truman launched a vast program of American rearmament and remobilization.

As spring 1948 approached, southerners, liberals, and big-city Democratic leaders began to express disenchantment with Truman, and the question of his nomination for a full term in his own right began to be debated. Upon the resignation of General Dwight D. Eisenhower as army chief of staff in February 1948 to become president of Columbia University, Senator Russell of Georgia suggested that the hero of World War II be given the 1948 presidential nomination. Liberal and organization Democrats were also eager to find a winner for 1948, particularly in view of the Palestine crisis and the heat of the civil rights controversy, with their implications for Jewish and black votes. Much to Russell's surprise, Jacob R. Arvey, chairman of the Cook County (Chicago) organization, Mayor William O'Dwyer of New York, Leon Henderson of Americans for Democratic Action, a new anti-Communist liberal organization, and Representative James Roosevelt of California picked up and ran with the "dump-Truman" movement.

Truman was less upset about the Eisenhower movement than were his advisers. In Truman's memoirs, he later reported that he had personal assurances from Eisenhower that the general would stand by a letter released in January setting forth reasons for *not* running. Truman observed:

In 1948, I was in a position to control the nomination. When I had made up my mind to run, those in the party who turned against me could do nothing to prevent it. For this reason, Thurmond and Wallace had to bolt the Democratic Party and stir up their own following. If Eisenhower had gone after the Democratic nomination, there would have been a four-way split in the party, but otherwise, the situation would have remained unchanged. Presidential control of the convention is a political principle which has not been violated in political history.[11]

While the Eisenhower movement failed to achieve much momentum, other movements did. "Dixiecrat" forces began to take resolute steps in several southern states. Laws were changed in Virginia, Mississippi, Louisiana, South Carolina, and Alabama so that neither Truman's name nor the national party's regular symbol could appear on their respective state ballots in the usual manner. On May 10, a conference of southerners met in Jackson, Mississippi, and resolved to hold a separate national convention if Truman were nominated. In other quarters, the strategy of southern "regulars" was to unite behind Senator Russell as a sectional favorite son at the 1948 national convention.

Another defection was also under way. During 1946, Secretary of Commerce Henry Wallace began to enunciate foreign policy statements urging friendship with the Soviet Union. These speeches not only embarrassed Secretary of State Byrnes's peace treaty negotiations but also raised doubts about the seriousness of Truman's policies to "contain" Soviet expansionism. In September 1946, Truman dismissed Wallace.

New Deal liberals floundered in confusion over these developments; Wallace was a hero of that wing of the party. Meanwhile, the Progressive Citizens of America (PCA) was organized as a first step in a movement to create a Progressive party and nominate Wallace for president on a third-party ticket. As the extreme leftist character of the PCA leadership became evident, more moderate New Deal liberals decided to clear the political atmosphere by establishing a separate organization, Americans for Democratic Action (ADA). ADA leaders quickly readied themselves for battle against southerners in the national convention and against the Progressives in the election.

As factions mobilized on the eve of the national convention, international politics also heated up in Berlin where the United States, Great Britain, France, and the Soviet Union shared occupation responsibilities. The Western powers held West Berlin. The Russians occupied the eastern part of the city and all of the territory around Berlin. In late June, the Russians sealed off highway, rail, and river traffic in and out of Berlin in a bold attempt to force the Allies out of the city. Truman countered with the "Berlin airlift," using all forms of air transport to fly supplies and personnel into West Berlin. The dramatic and expensive airlift was symbolic of Western resistance to Soviet encroachments. It eventually led to the reopening of normal routes into the city. Americans "rallied round the flag" in support of Truman's actions, and the polls showed the president, just back from a cross-country speaking tour on the theme of the "do-nothing Eightieth Congress," more popular than ever.

At the national convention, Senator Barkley's keynote speech expanded upon the "do-nothing [Republican] Eightieth Congress" theme that President Truman had developed in June. It became the basic theme of Truman's later election campaign.

Incorporated in the credentials of the Mississippi delegation was a provision forbidding its delegates to bind the Mississippi party to the support of any nominee favoring Truman's civil rights program. Northern liberals, following a strategy developed by the leaders of ADA, adopted a minority report in the credentials committee, demanding that the Mississippi delegation be denied its seats. The liberals argued that no national party could afford such dubious loyalty. Although the minority report lost in a voice vote, several delegations asked the chair to put them on record in favor of the minority report. In this way, as many as 503 votes were registered, with 618 constituting a convention majority.

The southerners, a minority in the rules committee, took satisfaction over the deep division in the convention. Hopeful of denying the nomination to Truman, they proposed reinstatement of the two-thirds nominating rule. The time seemed right, they thought, for revival of southern influence in the presidential party. The proposal, however, was rejected by voice vote.

The next test came in connection with the civil rights plank. The platform committee's majority had written a relatively moderate plank. Southerners on the committee prepared three separate minority reports, each designed in some way to water down the plank. From the convention floor, however, northern liberals, led by Mayor Hubert H. Humphrey of Minneapolis and former Representative Andrew J. Biemiller of Wisconsin, offered an even stronger civil rights plank than the platform committee's in that it unqualifiedly endorsed the Truman program. Humphrey's dramatic speech and skillful handling of floor tactics also assured him a lasting place in the national party leadership. The Humphrey-Biemiller plank passed, 651½ to 582½, evidence of a Truman majority in the convention. The Alabama delegation withdrew, and the Mississippi delegation refused to vote on the nomination. Truman was nominated with 926 votes to Russell's 266.

The presidential campaign train, which eventually covered 31,700 miles, was managed by several fellow-Missourians: William Boyle at the central headquarters in Washington, Clark Clifford directing operations on the train itself, and Donald S. Dawson handling community relations along the route. By his own count, President Truman delivered 356 prepared speeches and 200 extemporaneous ones. Because of his astute selection of issues and localities to be visited, Boyle won a reputation as an outstanding campaign strategist.

In many ways, the situation was ideal for a Truman treatment. The president was accustomed to the underdog role. He was thoroughly familiar with the mosaic of group politics that had been complicating his administration. He, therefore, decided to address his principal appeals to four audiences: labor, farmers, blacks, and consumers. The Red issue—"Socialist" experiments with the economy, "softness" toward Communists—was pinned onto the Wallace Progressives, freeing organized labor to pay attention to the challenge of the Taft-Hartley legislation. In doing so, the AF of L and the CIO fervently supported Truman. If blacks had been skeptical about Truman's civil rights attitudes, doubt disappeared with the national convention's actions and the Dixiecrat bolt. The president, having wrestled with the "do-nothing Eightieth Congress" over support of farm prices and ceilings on the rising cost-of-living, was able convincingly to blame the Republican Congress for inaction on these issues. Farmers were particularly angered by declining farm prices. Perhaps most important of all was the effect of Truman's hard-hitting campaign style upon party workers. Win or lose, Harry was making "the good fight" and "giving 'em hell!"

Probably the greatest hurdle facing the Truman campaign was reports by public opinion polls indicating that Governor Thomas E. Dewey, the Republican nominee, had approximately a 49–44 percent lead in the electorate. Democratic party workers across the nation went about their duties with nervous fatalism. Meanwhile, the Dewey campaign was calm and ambiguous, designed to alienate none of the support the governor seemed to have "in the bag." But, despite Dixiecrat and Progressive defections and the persistently discouraging forecasts of the opinion polls, Truman came in two million votes ahead of Dewey.

In evaluating the election and the Truman period, Samuel Lubell has succinctly and interestingly summarized several tendencies characterizing 1945–1952 as a period of realignment of voter behavior. Political transformations were taking place among urban minorities, the new middle class, migrating blacks, the South in economic revolution, isolationists, farmers and their way of life, and organized labor. Whereas Dewey's response to such shifts was noncommittal, Truman's was "hectic, even furious, activity." Lubell's evaluation of Truman's seven years of leadership is as follows:

192

All his more important policies reduce themselves to one thing—to buying time for the future. Far from seeking decision, he has sought to put off any possible showdown, to perpetuate rather than break the prevailing stalemate.

This faculty for turning two bold steps into a halfway measure—no mean trick—is Truman's political hallmark. If it applied solely to our relations with the Soviets one might conclude that it was the only shrewd course left between an inability to make peace and an unwillingness to go to war. But the same middle touch can be seen in Truman's handling of domestic political and economic problems. When he takes vigorous action in one direction it is axiomatic that he will contrive soon afterward to move in the conflicting direction. In the end he manages to work himself back close to the center spot of indecision from which he started.[12]

After achieving his own electoral mandate, President Truman turned his attention to problems of national party organization in characteristic fashion. His double-edged search for a middle ground in disciplining the southerners was symbolized by the "hard line" taken by National Chairman Howard McGrath and the "soft line" of McGrath's successor, William M. Boyle, Jr. Shortly after inauguration day McGrath announced that he had proposed to the president a policy of awarding patronage positions only on the basis of "the appointee's record and an estimate of his future value to the Party." McGrath took pains to point out that there could be no "future value" to the party for a Democrat who did not go along with the party's nominees or platform. It followed, therefore, that the Dixiecrats would have no future in the party. McGrath's comment came in explanation of a press conference statement by the president, who had observed that Democrats are those people who support the Democratic platform, a document to be regarded as the law of the Democratic party. Asked whether he would consider congressional voting on repeal of the Taft-Hartley law as one of the tests of party loyalty, the president replied that he certainly would.

Several months later, Truman carried the issue of party loyalty a step further with his nomination of Leland Olds for a third term as federal power commissioner. A substantial number of Democratic senators opposed the Olds nomination. The president was determined to push it as a "party matter." It was apparently Truman's opinion that an impending political decision becomes a "party matter" at the president's fiat at some moment in advance of the decision. As party leader, the president could exercise this prerogative unilaterally and whenever he chose. Having thus identified a "party issue," the president could expect that, as a matter of party discipline, all members of his party in Congress would support his position. This was probably the strongest and clearest affirmation of presidential prerogative a party leader ever made.[13]

In August, after the president nominated McGrath to be attorney general, the national chairman called the national committee together to choose a successor. The press noted two "unusual" features of McGrath's call: first, he overtly recommended a specific successor, William Boyle; and secondly, he pointedly did *not* invite "members of the national committee of record in the states of Mississippi or Louisiana, because in my judgment, by their several actions at the convention and subsequently in the campaign they have left the Democratic Party." This was the Truman-McGrath "hard line" for disciplining the defecting Dixiecrats. McGrath anticipated a hard credentials fight at the national committee meeting.

The credentials contests materialized. Trumanite Democrats designated by "loyal" state conventions in 1948 laid claim to the vacant Mississippi and Louisiana seats. A more complex contest emerged from South Carolina where the Truman people argued that the same state party body that had instructed the 1948 presidential electors to vote against Truman had just chosen that state's new national committeeman, Senator Burton H. Maybank, an election without legitimacy. The South Carolina Trumanites thus wished to carry the test of party loyalty beyond the acts of national committee members into the acts of the state party agency selecting them. A Texas contest was strictly a factional fight involving no technical issue of party loyalty.

An old political friend of the president, National Committeeman Frank McHale of Indiana, was given the difficult job of chairing the credentials committee. McHale's committee turned for guidance to the *Democratic Manual*, an unofficial compilation of rules of the national convention prepared by Clarence Cannon, and found in Section 11 the power they needed. Based upon national committee actions taken in 1896, when it expunged from its rolls the names of two members who bolted Bryan and attended another national convention, the rule empowered the national committee "to expel members for cause." On this basis, the credentials committee recommended, and the national committee approved, expunging the names of five of the Dixiecrat committeemen.

Having boldly asserted a "hard line" in disciplining the Dixiecrats, President Truman immediately set out upon a characteristic swing toward an opposite action. On the evening of the expulsion ruling, the president dined with members of the national committee. In his address he invited the States' Righters and other dissidents to return to the party "as loyal Democrats." This "soft line" would be up to William Boyle to implement. Truman further declared that the Democratic party was "a national party and not a sectional party any more."

American political leaders were now becoming increasingly absorbed by the nation's confrontation with world communism. The Soviet Union had sealed off occupied Berlin; the United States had responded, in the midst of a presidential year, with the Berlin airlift. The United States and eleven European nations established the North Atlantic Treaty Organization (NATO), with the American taxpayer carrying the main fiscal burden. In Asia, Mao Tse-tung's Chinese Communists were chasing the Chiang Kai-shek regime across the Straits of Formosa, leading to Republican charges that the Truman administration had "lost China." In the fall of 1949, the Soviet Union detonated its first atom bomb, and the nuclear arms race became a party issue. Things seemed to be going poorly for the United States, and some Americans gained the impression that Communists were closing in from every side. As a consequence, the Truman administration and its Congresses anxiously reinstated defense appropriations, signed mutual defense treaties, and extended foreign economic and military aid. The Truman Doctrine, giving $400 million in aid to Greece and Turkey, set a precedent. The Marshall Plan inaugurated a program of aid to Europe which, within a decade, reached upward of $33 billion, admittedly a fraction of the cost of wars to save Europe. Congress also provided funds for the Point Four program of technical assistance to new nations and, in 1949, put a billion dollars on the line to build a stronger North Atlantic Treaty Organization.

The Cold War had a debilitating effect on American domestic politics. Evidence of active Communist espionage in the United States prompted Truman's federal loyalty investigation program, a move that soon led, ironically, to an era of Republican witch-hunting in government. Senator Joseph McCarthy, a Wisconsin Republican, set the tone of the 1950 congressional elections and inaugurated an era that bears his name with his flamboyant and irresponsible crusade against "Communist spies" inside the State Department and other federal agencies.

The Judith Coplin and Alger Hiss espionage cases filled the

headlines. Coplin had been an employee of the Department of Justice and Hiss a former official of the Department of State. The Coplin case dragged on until 1967, when charges were dropped. Hiss was found guilty of committing perjury in connection with the espionage charges against him. This conviction in January 1950 paved the way for pronouncements by McCarthy the following month that the federal bureaucracy was peppered with espionage agents. Democratic leaders running the government, he declared, must be either dupes or co-conspirators.

Republicans tacitly endorsed McCarthy's bargain-basement anti-communism, which they later credited with aiding their impressive gains in congressional seats in 1950. Republicans kept the domestic anti-Communist crusade rolling in campaigns throughout the ensuing decade, even after McCarthy himself was censured by his colleagues in the Senate.

The Korean crisis further fueled the McCarthy attack on the Democratic party. In 1950, that republic was a little over a year old. American troops, stationed there alongside Soviet troops since the end of World War II, began to withdraw. Suddenly, in June of 1950, North Korean Communists invaded the Republic of South Korea. President Truman ordered American military aid for a United Nations' "police action" that quickly became a large-scale and costly war. The frustrations of the Korean War agitated popular opinion in the United States well into the 1952 presidential campaign.

Stevenson's "Loyal Opposition"

Although the new Twenty-second Amendment making the presidency a two-term office did not technically prevent Truman from running again, the president eventually decided he would not. His search for a successor took him to Governor Adlai E. Stevenson of Illinois, grandson of Cleveland's vice president, successful governor of a pivotal state, moderate liberal, and a distinguished representative of the United States at the United Nations in 1947–1948. Stevenson shied from the honor, saying "No, but . . . " in what seemed an infinite variety of ways.

Stevenson's ambivalence was quite real. His chance for reelection as governor of Illinois was excellent; the chance for any Democrat's election to the presidency was, at best, fifty-fifty against a military hero of "Ike" Eisenhower's stature. The personal record of

Stevenson, a designer of his own programs in Illinois, could show better in a state race; but in presidential politics, it would be another man's record—President Truman's—that he would inevitably have to defend.

Even before Truman's withdrawal, the fissures in the Democratic party were plainly visible. Southern Democrats were preparing to unite behind Georgia's Senator Richard Russell. Senator Estes Kefauver of Tennessee had attracted national attention for his investigation into organized crime. As his investigation took him to the doorsteps of numerous organization Democrats at the state and local levels, Kefauver emerged as the candidate of many Democratic liberals. When he entered the early New Hampshire presidential primary in 1952 and won more votes than Truman, an incumbent president, this upset was credited with the president's subsequent retirement. Throughout the pre-convention campaign, Kefauver traveled the presidential primary route aggressively and with consummate skill. His primary successes made him a serious candidate for the nomination. In later years, the presidential primary route was emulated by many, most successfully by John F. Kennedy and James Earl (Jimmy) Carter.

Adlai Stevenson fully appreciated the difficulties that would confront the Democratic national convention. The Russell and Kefauver forces were bound to stalemate each other. The candidacy of the elderly Alben Barkley, beloved though he was, had the earmarks of a mere caretakership. Northern liberals, again led by ADA, had been working for a "loyalty pledge" to be imposed by the convention in order to prevent the seating of Dixiecrats who had been disloyal in 1948 or might again be in 1952. With the Democratic house so divided, Stevenson realized that he was the only man close enough to the center to reunite it. At the very last minute, he agreed to allow his name to go into nomination, which he received on the third ballot.[14] The convention also adopted a strong civil rights plank and a strong loyalty pledge requirement of all convention delegates.

Not since the Taft nomination in 1908 had a titular leader in the White House presented such complication for the campaign strategy of his successor. Wilson was ill during the Cox campaign in 1920, leaving Cox to run his own show. Taciturn Coolidge said little for Hoover in 1928. In 1952, however, how could nominee Stevenson give the party a "new look" without affronting Truman, an incumbent and highly activist president?

Stevenson's first decision was to replace National Chairman Frank McKinney, a Truman appointee and a professional politician, with Stephen A. Mitchell, a "clean amateur." This caused endless wrangling over the organization of the campaign. Stevenson's second decision, one rooted in his deep intellectual commitment to the educational function of American campaigning, was to present to the people his own extensive reformulation of the "basic issues of our times."

While the Eisenhower and Taft forces were coming together on the Republican side, Democrats were running their separate ways. Stevenson set up personal headquarters in Illinois and left national headquarters in Washington to Chairman Mitchell. President Truman set out on his own whistle-stop tour, one that inevitably blurred the candidate image of Stevenson. Certain southern Democratic leaders, feeling far more comfortable with the Eisenhower-Nixon ticket, were slow to endorse the Stevenson-Sparkman ticket. In the election, Virginia, Texas, and Florida went Republican, and Eisenhower became president.

Despite the Eisenhower landslide, Republicans in Congress took control by a bare one-vote margin in the Senate and by less than a dozen seats in the House. Senator Russell was quick to comment that Adlai Stevenson's "titular leadership" of the Democratic out-party meant "title without authority." Democratic policy, he asserted, would be determined in Congress over the ensuing four years, under the leadership of an unusual team of Texans: Senator Lyndon B. Johnson and House Minority Leader Sam Rayburn. In February 1953, Stevenson, retired from the duties of the Illinois governorship, took a vacation in the British West Indies. At this time, according to his biographer, "he resolved, there in the golden sunlight, to play out the role assigned to him with more planned consistency than most, if any, of his predecessors in that role had done."[15] Stevenson himself wrote in the published collection of his campaign speeches:

In our country this role is a very ambiguous one. . . . The titular head has no clear and defined authority within his party. He has no party office, no staff, no funds, nor is there any system of consultation whereby he may be advised of party policy and through which he may help to shape that policy. There are no devices such as the British have developed through which he can communicate directly and responsibly with the leaders of the party in power. Yet he is generally deemed the leading spokesman of his party. And he has—or so it seemed to me—an obligation to help wipe

198

out the inevitable deficit accumulated by his party during a losing campaign, and also to do what he can to revise, reorganize, and rebuild the party.[16]

Elsewhere, Stevenson acknowledged "that opposition leadership rests in the Congress, except that it is assumed by individuals for the most part ambitious to be heard."[17]

The period was a time of particular frustration for the presidential wing of the party. There were the structural difficulties of out-party leadership: a defeated presidential nominee holding no public office (Stevenson); a former president, retired but still outspoken (Truman); a congressional leadership, after 1954 in control of both houses, protective of its constitutional prerogatives (Rayburn and Johnson); and no legitimate rostrum from which a titular leader could speak.

Stevenson and Chairman Mitchell turned to fund-raising to pay off 1952 campaign debts and to prepare for the upcoming midterm election. National Committeeman Paul M. Butler of Indiana proposed a midterm national convention to help in the 1954 campaign and to perfect the party machinery for the 1956 contest. The midterm convention proposal was set aside, and instead plans for a series of regional conferences of party leaders were inaugurated. Meanwhile, Stevenson addressed Democratic dinners and similar gatherings. He also consulted at various intervals with what came to be known as the "Finletter Group," an ad hoc seminar of economists, lawyers, and other Democratic public policy specialists, under the chairmanship of former Secretary of the Air Force Thomas K. Finletter. When the Johnson-Rayburn leadership, as a consequence of Democratic victories in 1954, assumed control on Capitol Hill, Chairman Mitchell retired to his law practice. A knock-down national committee contest elevated National Committeeman Butler to the chairmanship.

Lyndon Johnson, a product of the New Deal era, was a Rayburn protégé and a tireless legislator. The 1954 election elevated Rayburn to Speaker and Johnson to Majority Leader. After 1954, the country witnessed a popular Republican president cooperating with a Congress under the leadership of a powerful Democratic team. The Rayburn-Johnson legislative strategy became known as "responsibility in opposition." With the Eisenhower administration practicing a "politics of postponement," there was, of course, relatively little for congressional Democrats to oppose.

Stevenson and his new national chairman, Paul Butler, persisted nonetheless in advocating the development of distinctive Democratic policy positions. They were eager to formalize the Finletter Group as a vehicle for broad communication within the party. Johnson and Rayburn, however, were reluctant to share the stage. An "information gap" developed between the Democratic titular leader and the party's congressional leaders. A typical situation arose during the Chinese Communist threat to the islands of Quemoy and Matsu in 1955. With the cooperation of Speaker Rayburn and Majority Leader Johnson, President Eisenhower requested and received from Congress advance authorization to do whatever in his judgment was necessary in the event of a full-scale Communist attack against these islands lying between Formosa and the Chinese mainland. Stevenson was at no time consulted during this crisis.

Stevenson's philosophy regarding the role of an opposition was stated in the collection of his addresses:

It should not surprise anyone to discover that this is primarily a book of criticism. If "the duty of a loyal opposition is to oppose," I cannot see how one can offer effective opposition without giving reasons for it and these reasons are, of course, criticisms.

Yet I very well know that in many minds political "criticism" has today become an ugly word. It has become almost *lèse-majesté*. And it conjures up pictures of insidious rascals hacking away at the very foundations of the American way of life. It suggests nonconformity and nonconformity suggests disloyalty and disloyalty suggests treason, and before we know where we are, this process has all but identified the critic with the saboteur and turned political criticism into an un-American activity instead of democracy's greatest safeguard.

The irony of this position—so often held by people who would regard themselves as most respectably conservative—is that it is nowhere more ardently embraced than in Moscow or Peiping. There the critic really is a conspirator and criticism is genuinely an un-Russian or un-Chinese activity.

In fact, if I were asked to choose a single principle which underlines more than any other the difference between the Communist and the free philosophy of government, I would be inclined to single out this issue of criticism, which we in the West not only tolerate but esteem. . . .

For, paradoxical though it may seem, free criticism can flourish only in a society where mutual trust is strong. The spirit of criticism shrivels when the citizens distrust their neighbors and the give and take of confidence gives place to the silence of suspicion. The neighborliness, the charity, the very goodness of a society, can best be measured by the freedom with which men may honestly speak their minds. Criticism is therefore not only an instrument of free society. It is its symbol and hallmark as well.[18]

In July 1955, Senator Johnson suffered a heart attack. His name, frequently mentioned for the 1956 presidential nomination, fell from that roster. Stevenson paid a visit to the Johnson ranch in Texas during the Senator's convalescence. Speaker Rayburn also attended. Shortly thereafter, Stevenson gathered his staff for an announcement of his candidacy. As he did, President Eisenhower suffered a heart attack. The "market value" of the Democratic nomination rose sharply, and Stevenson found himself suddenly sharing the candidate limelight with Senator Estes Kefauver, Governor Averell Harriman of New York, Governor G. Mennen Williams of Michigan, and Senator Hubert H. Humphrey. Stevenson now had to campaign hard for a nomination that he expected to be his by default.

President Eisenhower's subsequent recovery, renomination, and continued popularity reversed the situation and added an ironic twist to Stevenson's cause. The nomination that Stevenson had begun to fight so hard to win could now again be his by default. Once renominated by an overwhelming majority at the 1956 national convention, Stevenson threw the vice-presidential choice to the open convention, over the objections of Rayburn, Johnson, and Butler. A spontaneous and many-sided contest resulted, which included Senator Kefauver, Tennessee's other senator, Albert Gore, Hubert H. Humphrey of Minnesota, and John F. Kennedy of Massachusetts.

Kefauver, Humphrey, and Kennedy were well known to the delegates. Kefauver had caused the party regulars no small aggravation with his hard-hitting and impressive pre-convention campaigns of 1952 and 1956. Humphrey was an established leader of the liberal wing in the Senate and, together with former Governor Battle of Virginia, had been responsible for the skillful handling of the party's loyalty pledge problems. Kennedy, coming out of one of Massachusetts' best-known political families, was conspicuous not only for his dramatic career but also, in this convention, for placing Stevenson in nomination and narrating a moving documentary film viewed by the delegates.

The vice-presidential balloting, probably the most exciting in national convention history, was filled with surprises. The greatest surprise was the distribution of Kennedy's support: Georgia, Louisiana, and Virginia joined Massachusetts to support a Catholic

Democrat. Southern support was widely credited to Senator Johnson's efforts in Kennedy's behalf.

The second ballot was a horse race. With 686½ votes needed to nominate, Kennedy reached 618 and Kefauver 551½. Speaker Rayburn, as permanent chairman of the convention, began to recognize delegations wishing to shift their votes. With all the skill acquired in years of leadership of the House of Representatives, Rayburn recognized delegations in a sequence that gave the prize to Kefauver, with Kennedy very close behind. The unexpected strength of Johnson's candidate was not soon forgotten. It was later speculated that Rayburn and Johnson were clearing the decks for the advancement of a fresh young leadership in the party during the inevitable second Eisenhower term.

With election odds running against him, Stevenson decided once again to try to educate the electorate on the issues of the day. His most striking effort was his call for an end to nuclear weapon testing by the major powers. This pronouncement broke a fundamental custom of American politics: "Never introduce an entirely new issue into a campaign." In Stevenson's view, however, the hazards of nuclear fallout for world health were as urgent as the military necessity of keeping pace with Soviet nuclear development; the testing issue simply had to be brought to national attention.

On election day, Stevenson, like William Jennings Bryan before him, became a twice-defeated Democratic presidential nominee. Nonetheless, he persisted in his concern for maintaining a "loyal opposition." Within the month, Chairman Butler brought forth plans for creating a coordinating committee designed to keep party leaders from the Senate, the House, state houses, city halls, state organizations, national headquarters, and private life in consultation with each other.

Senator Humphrey, reflecting his estimate rather than his preference, predicted that the party leadership would probably be "essentially congressional." Majority Leader Johnson pointedly observed that "Mr. Stevenson can speak for himself." Johnson also anticipated continuation of the Rayburn-Johnson "responsible opposition" strategy. "We are a good and reasonable group of men working for the good of the country without parties, labels, or cliques." When questioned about the need to develop a distinctive Democratic party program, Johnson added: "No, we'll wait for the President. We'll support him when he's right and oppose him when he's wrong."

On Chairman Butler's recommendation, however, the executive committee of the national committee authorized him to appoint a board of not more than seventeen senior Democrats who would "advance efforts in behalf of Democratic programs and principles." Butler invited about twenty leaders, including Stevenson, Truman, Mrs. Roosevelt, Speaker Rayburn, and Senator Johnson. There were eight acceptances in hand at the time he announced the invitations: Truman, Stevenson, Governor Harriman, Governor Williams, Senator Kefauver, Senator Humphrey, Mayor Tucker, and Congresswoman Edith Green. The official congressional leaders took longer to respond.

On December 9, 1956, Speaker Rayburn wired Butler from Texas that he had consulted with House leaders McCormack, Albert, and Kirwan. He had concluded that it would be "a mistake" to take a place on a noncongressional policy-making body. The Speaker felt that the 233 party members in the House would probably resent their four leaders developing legislative policies on any committee outside the House. Majority Leader Johnson also declined a few days later, noting that "legislative processes are already very difficult, and the necessity of dealing with an additional committee not created by Federal law before taking action would only cause delays and confusion." Both Rayburn and Johnson expressed their willingness to consult informally with the new Advisory Council.

Liberal Democrats from the Northeast, upper Midwest, and the Far West were quick to disengage themselves from the Rayburn-Johnson response. Led by Senators Humphrey of Minnesota and Paul Douglas of Illinois, this minority developed plans for carving out a specific Democratic program, particularly in the civil rights field. As a necessary step in achieving civil rights legislation, for example, these legislative liberals announced a full-scale assault upon the filibuster rule. When the press interpreted this as part of a plan to remove Johnson from the leadership, Senators Kennedy and Humphrey issued emphatic denials, hailing Johnson as the only man skillful enough to lead the party in the Senate.

The Advisory Council thereafter went it alone as an organ of the national committee. It chose a five-man steering committee, of which Stevenson was chairman. It selected a staff and established task force committees in several public policy fields. Before the end of 1957, the Advisory Council issued some twenty-three statements on national policy. In February 1958, as members of Congress gathered for the new session, the Democratic Advisory Council issued its own "State of the Union Message," setting a precedent in opposition technique.

During 1957, there was mounting criticism of Eisenhower's failure to reciprocate the Truman policy of occasional consultation with the titular leader of the out-party. The president eventually invited Stevenson to serve as consultant for the administration's North Atlantic Treaty Organization plans. Stevenson would study the new NATO program and comment freely on it. Stevenson referred to his arrangement as a step toward "nonpartisanship" rather than "bipartisanship." He conferred with the Democratic party leadership before accepting in November 1957. The overseas implications were more significant than the domestic.

Stevenson's influence abroad is probably greater than it is at home. Here he's still the twice-defeated Democratic candidate, and there he's the Leader of the Opposition. Here he's the titular head of the Democratic Party, and not more than that; there—because European constitutional systems are so different from ours—he's billed in the popular mind as the official spokesman for the party of Roosevelt and Truman, the party that has traditionally had the more sympathetic approach to foreign affairs and America's relationship to Europe. Here he is a respected figure whose political future is at best highly precarious; there he's a powerful representative of a major segment of public opinion.[19]

The economic recession and midterm election of 1958 produced oversized Democratic majorities in both houses. In the Senate, Democratic presidential aspirants promptly began to warm up. As keeper of the Senate's timetable, Majority Leader Johnson cooperated in making available to certain colleagues valuable opportunities for demonstrating their capacity for leadership. Senator Humphrey made the liberal case against the filibuster rule as part of a strategy to pass civil rights legislation. When the issue was joined, the filibuster rule remained but, under Johnson's direction, a compromise was reached that brought out of Congress the first civil rights legislation in eighty-five years.

When Senator Kennedy initiated a minimum wage bill and legislation designed to eliminate racketeering in certain labor unions, which had been uncovered during his Senate investigations, antilabor amendments were tagged onto the Kennedy-Ervin bill, which then passed by the close margin of forty-seven to forty-six. Again Johnson stepped in to arrange compromises watering down the punitive character of some of the amendments. Senator Kennedy came out of the fracas having assured labor leaders that, although he was an investigator of unions and the son of one of the nation's wealthiest men, he was fundamentally and safely on the side of labor.

Still another presidential candidate was Senator Stuart Symington of Missouri, an established authority on military policy. In view of the fact that another expert on military policy was resident in the White House, Symington's criticisms of Eisenhower military budget requests carried special weight. Johnson aided Symington's every opportunity to make his points. The inquiries by the Rayburn-Johnson Congress into the nation's defense posture were spurred by excited world response to Sputniks I and II during the closing months of 1957. The Soviet Union, so often described as a backward peasant people, had beaten the most highly industrialized nation in the world by placing in orbit around the earth the first man-made satellite.

As Humphrey, Kennedy, and Symington put on able legislative performances, Johnson always appeared in time to take bows with each. Stevenson, however, was never entirely out of sight, even though congressional leaders rarely took public notice of him. In public opinion polls throughout 1958 and 1959, Stevenson ran neck-and-neck with Kennedy as the preference of Democratic voters; Johnson consistently came in third.

A period of American self-examination followed Sputnik, as did a reversal of the Eisenhower program of economy in defense spending. The Democratic Congress initiated research and development appropriations that carried the United States from the Atomic Era to the Space Age. The space industry moved up alongside public works and the manufacture of military weapons as a principal area of public spending. In a few short years, a Democratic president (Kennedy) would request the resources necessary to land the first man on the moon. Space, literally and figuratively, began to give American politics a new dimension.

As 1960 approached, Democratic senators—Johnson, Kennedy, Humphrey, Symington—were in the forefront of the candidate stable with the Gallup Poll now showing Kennedy consistently in the lead. Majority Leader Johnson, on January 7, 1959, just prior to President Eisenhower's annual message to Congress, delivered his own State of the Union address, in which he cast broadsides against "the burden of laggard government." The undeclared truce between the Republican president and the Democratic Congress came to an end as all hands prepared for the political seas of 1960.

Despite the encouragement of Mrs. Roosevelt and other party notables, Stevenson refused to become an active candidate. Kennedy, because of his youth and religion had the most difficult tests to meet, and approached these with one of the most aggressive and successful pre-convention campaigns in party history. Although Kennedy carried the Wisconsin primary against Humphrey, that contest had overtones of a Catholic-Protestant split. In the West Virginia primary, on the other hand, Kennedy set the religious issue to rest, and carrying the predominantly Protestant state, brought decisive commitments from big-city Democratic leaders in the East and Midwest. As convention time arrived, Kennedy and Johnson forces were firing heavily at each other, but making no mention of Stevenson.

At the convention, however, a Stevenson headquarters operated with as much energy and resourcefulness as its counterparts. If Kennedy, 160 votes short of the nomination, could be stopped, the prize might, on the third or fourth ballot, pass either to Stevenson or Johnson. For the Kennedy people, it was a first ballot nomination or bust; and first ballot nomination it was. In a move as logical as it was traditional, Kennedy offered second place on the ticket to his former mentor and current adversary, Lyndon Johnson. The North-South ticket turned to a popular westerner, Senator Henry M. Jackson of Washington, to serve as national chairman. The campaign, however, was managed by Robert F. Kennedy, the Senator's brother, and Lawrence F. O'Brien, a Massachusetts public relations man long associated with the Kennedys.

The 1960 presidential campaign strikingly demonstrated the nationalizing influences of various technological changes. The jet airplane brought the most distant corners of the nation within a few hours and was frequently used by the candidates, particularly during their final drives. The four televised debates between Kennedy and Nixon were without precedent and were subsequently credited to be a decisive factor in what turned out to be the closest presidential election in American history. Kennedy strategists had available the projections of Simulmatics Corporation, a group of social scientists who had developed a mathematical model of the United States electorate, using six million pieces of information about American voting behavior drawn from the findings of sixty-six nationwide public opinion surveys conducted since 1952.[20]

Speaker Rayburn and Senate Majority Leader Johnson, with substantial majorities in their respective houses, had arranged for a special session in advance of the conventions. Vice President Nixon, as presiding officer of the Senate, was compelled thereby to play an exposed but passive role in legislative activity. With the legislative agenda tightly in Johnson's hands, Kennedy led the fight for legislation on minimum wages, care for the aged, public housing, and other measures. The press and public witnessed a confrontation of the presidential nominees even more significant than the televised debates.

Kennedy won the election by 100,000 votes in more than 68 million cast. It was one of the closest outcomes in presidential history and one of the most evenly contested in each of the fifty states. Significantly, Nixon did as well or better than Eisenhower in six southern states. In many areas Kennedy ran behind the Democratic congressional ticket. The returns had an important bearing upon Kennedy's subsequent relations with Congress.

Between election day and the inauguration, President-elect Kennedy organized a number of policy task forces to prepare general policy guidelines for the new administration. Most of the personnel of these task forces were drawn from the membership of the Democratic Advisory Council's working committees. When the time arrived for appointments to the new administration, about thirty-two of the first seventy-eight appointees came from these task forces. The Democratic Advisory Council itself was dissolved in March 1961.

The party's experience with the Council left much for future leaders to ponder. The sheer technicality of national policy problems made it an important device for bringing together expertise in the out-party. The council provided a means of leadership consultation that was otherwise lacking. The task forces enabled policy specialists to come forward and to establish their party credentials. The council kept alive the fact that the presidential out-party has a continuing and vital interest in national affairs regardless of the party's status in the Congress. In short, in the presidency or out, Stevenson and the Democratic Advisory Council sought to maintain the party's essential role in developing and achieving the national policy consensus.

9

Reincarnations of the New Deal Coalition

IN one respect or another, John F. Kennedy's New Frontier and Lyndon B. Johnson's Great Society were the children of—perhaps reincarnations of—the New Deal coalition of organized labor, blacks, nationality minorities, Catholics, Jews, intellectuals, and, to a much lesser degree, poor farmers. In somewhat changing proportions, these were the electoral pillars upon which Kennedy and Johnson rested their bids for office and their domestic policies. Even in the election of James Earl (Jimmy) Carter in 1976, the old and enfeebled coalition revived long enough to help liquidate the Vietnam and Watergate eras.

The Brothers Kennedy

Joseph P. and Rose Kennedy raised a political family devoted to the service of their country and to the goals of the Democratic party. As congressman and senator from Massachusetts during the 1950s, John F. (Jack) Kennedy became the focus of the family's efforts to broaden the Kennedy influence in national affairs. Robert F. Kennedy, Jack's younger brother, assumed a crucial role as Jack's aide, confidant, and manager. Wives, husbands, and children of the Kennedys were also inescapably drawn into the vortex of the family's dramatic public life.

However, even as Kennedy became the first Roman Catholic to be elected to the presidency, other Catholics were changing their political preferences: the Irish, partly in response to the appeal of Senator Joseph McCarthy but more so as a consequence of growing affluence, were shifting to the Republican party; the Italians, many of whom were replacing the Irish in the leadership of urban machines, were also "soft" Democrats. Other demographic changes were occurring. Blacks were filling the urban ghettos and becoming the new urban majority. The suburbs of metropolitan areas were growing rapidly and becoming Republican strongholds. The Solid South was less and less solid, as greater numbers of Democrats became "presidential Republicans" voting for Hoover, Eisenhower, and Nixon and as greater numbers of disfranchised blacks registered under the new voting rights laws. The proportion of over-sixty-five "senior citizens" was also increasing and becoming a new source of political activism. Rural America continued to diminish in numbers of farms and farmers but not in productivity as new technology and new corporate agribusinesses took over. For the Kennedy administration, however, perhaps the dominant demographic characteristic was the youthfulness of its leader and the generation of party leaders that he brought to office with him.

As president-elect, Kennedy promptly assumed the initiative in preparing for the next session of Congress, in which Democrats had a slightly reduced House majority. Kennedy took a hand in the promotion of Senators Mike Mansfield to majority leader and Hubert Humphrey to Democratic whip. Using consultants and task forces, the president-elect pulled together bills, messages, and a State of the Union address. The first great legislative test for the new administration, however, came not in the choice of leaders or the presentation of programs but rather in the composition of the House Rules Committee, the keeper of the legislative agenda.

The Rules Committee was headed by Howard W. Smith of Virginia, abetted by a coalition of Republicans and southern Democrats. Only Speaker Sam Rayburn was reputedly a more seasoned political infighter than Smith, and it was a coup for Kennedy when "Mr. Sam" assumed leadership of a move to "pack" the Rules Committee with three additional members, of whom two would be Democrats friendlier to the president's program. The battle over the powers of the Rules Committee chairman was billed as comparable to the 1910 revolt against Speaker Cannon, a comparison that was somewhat overdrawn. Rayburn, Kennedy, Johnson, members of the cabinet, and the White House staff worked long and diligently to gather the votes. Even at that, the change was adopted by the narrow margin of 217 to 212. The battle tested the mettle of the young president and his success removed a substantial obstacle to his program.

That program during the first half year had approximately three hundred items, of which sixteen were given special priority. The president's congressional associates worked with small margins, particularly in the House. Legislation was slow, but it did eventually come forth: the Peace Corps, designed to give American youth an opportunity to help the people of less developed nations; the Alliance for Progress, a ten-year program aimed at raising Latin American living standards; unemployment compensation; minimum-wage legislation.

The nation and the Democratic party lost one of their strongest and steadiest hands with the passing of Speaker Rayburn in late 1961. "Mr. Sam" had been either Speaker or minority leader since 1940, two decades of service and political craftsmanship with few equals in American history. John McCormack, long a competitor of the Kennedys in Massachusetts politics, succeeded to the speakership.

The nation's youngest president and his youthful entourage had hardly taken their places on the "New Frontier" before one international crisis after the other began to break. As violence erupted in the Congo, Kennedy sent American support to help the United Nations end the secessionist movement there. As Communists poised for a take-over in Laos, Kennedy intervened with a fourteen-nation conference that brought that country to establish a coalition cabinet and an uneasy truce among its factions. Somewhat hesitantly, Kennedy endorsed long-standing plans for American support of a Cuban invasion by anti-Castro exiles, only to see this enterprise end in the Bay of Pigs debacle, a major blemish on his administration's record. In Berlin, the Kennedy administration watched as the Communists erected the Berlin wall, and then the president, in a compelling address delivered at the wall itself, used it as a symbol of the fundamental difference between freedom and totalitarianism.

Defeated by Castro Communists in Cuba, challenged in Berlin by Soviet leader Khrushchev's Berlin wall and threats to cut off Western access to the city, and confronted by Communist pressures in Laos, Kennedy was particularly sensitive to developments in Vietnam where Communist-led opposition to the American-supported regime of Ngo Dinh Diem was mounting. For some two thousand years Indochina had been the object of foreign invasions, particularly by the Chinese from the north, and the arena of endless warfare among its many peoples. During the seventeenth century, French Catholics set up missions and Dutch and English merchants established trading posts in the northern part of the country. France came into full possession of all of Vietnam in 1885 under the Treaty of Tientsin and governed through an Indochina council. By the end of World War I, various nationalist movements were active in different parts of Vietnam. In the north, these movements tended to be Communist, the principal of them led by Ho Chi Minh. In the south, the nationalists were predominantly religious organizations, principally the Cao Dai, a faith combining Catholic, Buddhist, Taoist, and Confucian principles.

As the end of World War II approached, French influence had practically disintegrated. The Japanese, hoping to win allies among the nationalists, helped them defeat the French and establish an independent state of Vietnam under Emperor Bao Dai. However, the emperor soon was compelled to abdicate in favor of Ho Chi Minh, leader of the Viet Minh nationalist forces. In 1950, after complex negotiations among the French, the Viet Minh, the Cao Dai, and others had established a provisional government under Emperor Bao Dai, the United States recognized the new state of Vietnam.

The Viet Minh continued to oppose the French and the following year joined forces with Communist-led opposition groups in Cambodia and Laos, receiving military aid from the new People's Republic of China under Mao Tse-tung. Presidents Truman and Eisenhower viewed these developments in Southeast Asia as diversionary tactics in the war in Korea and began a program of American aid to the French forces in Vietnam.

In 1954, the Viet Minh succeeded in defeating the French decisively at Dien Bien Phu. A Geneva conference led to the withdrawal of the Viet Minh to the north and the French to the south of latitude 17 degrees (the 17th parallel), recognition of north and south as separate administrative entities, and the anticipation that future elections would be conducted to reunify Vietnam. The United States began to send economic aid to South Vietnam, where, in 1956, Ngo Dinh Diem became the first president of a new Republic of [South] Vietnam.

Diem, however, was no democrat. Using repressive measures and American-trained police, Diem outlawed the religious and nationalist organizations, ended elected village government, and persecuted opposition leaders. Ho Chi Minh's Democratic Republic of Vietnam had by now become a serious threat to the military security of South Vietnam, with China and the Soviet Union sending growing quantities of military and economic aid to the North Vietnamese.

By 1960, most groups opposing Diem, including a number of former Viet Minh, went underground, conferred, and issued a manifesto calling for the overthrow of the Diem regime. This was followed by the formation of the National Liberation Front (NLF) in December 1960, on the eve of Kennedy's inauguration. The NLF established the Viet Cong as its military arm. A month later, the North Vietnamese announced their full support of the NLF and the Viet Cong.

Thus, in the very first days of his administration, Kennedy had to make a momentous choice between the NLF insurgents or the U.S.-supported but authoritarian Diem regime. Following the recommendations of General Maxwell D. Taylor, chairman of the Joint Chiefs of Staff, Kennedy chose to increase American military support to Diem, sending military advisers in excess of the number permitted in the 1954 Geneva Accords. He also began to send additional military equipment. Such were the apparently modest beginnings of a decade of American engagement in a war that was never declared, that cost fifty thousand American lives, and that bitterly divided the nation.

If the decision to send aid to Vietnam seemed minor and ambiguous at the time, the response to the Soviet challenge in the Cuban missile crisis of 1962 was perceived as momentous and clear. The test came in October 1962 at the height of the midterm election campaign. Although it had been known for some time that the Soviet Union was increasing its supply of weapons and military advisers to Fidel Castro, it was not expected that nuclear missiles would be included. Such weaponry, universally classified as "offensive," placed at the borders of the United States, represented a challenge that could not be ignored. President Kennedy proclaimed a naval "quarantine" of Cuba and demanded that the Soviet Union withdraw the missiles at once. The Soviet Union eventually did just this, and Soviet-American relations improved appreciably thereafter.

The American quarantine of Cuban waters at the end of October had predictable consequences for the election: all incumbents, Democratic and Republican alike, were beneficiaries of a surge of patriotism. Only in 1934, the height of the New Deal era, had an incumbent administration done as well in holding or gaining seats in Congress. Four additional seats were won by the Democrats in the Senate, and the party returned with almost exactly its previous majority in the House.

The Kennedys gave special attention to the implementation of

212

civil rights legislation. At the head of the Justice Department, Robert Kennedy stepped up legal actions in cases of infringement of voting rights. Before 1961 had ended, the Justice Department filed fourteen new cases charging racial discrimination by specific county registrars in five states of the Deep South and carried forward investigations in sixty-one other counties.

On the registration side, with Kennedy encouragement, civil rights organizations were brought together into a Voter Education Project, under the general supervision of the Southern Regional Council and funds from a number of private foundations. Southern blacks had been exasperatingly slow in registering and voting after the civil rights legislation of 1957; generations of disfranchisement and fear were not readily dissipated. Robert Kennedy also announced his intention to seek legislation that would eliminate the poll tax and literacy tests as prerequisites for voting.

These efforts notwithstanding, black leaders took the opportunity of a friendly administration to press hard for other changes: a permanent fair employment practices committee, legislation on school desegregation, more power for the attorney general in the voting rights field, an end to segregation in federally aided housing, etc. The Kennedys, however, insisted that the registration drive be given top priority not only to help black citizens exercise their rights but also, more indirectly, to change the composition and attitudes of southern Democratic leadership. With such encouragement, black politics entered a period of ferment.

The year 1963 opened with President Kennedy's proposals for a $13.6 billion tax cut, greater aid to education, and hospital insurance for the aged through social security. Racial tension accompanied the admission of James H. Meredith, a black, to the University of Mississippi. Meredith's admission to "Ole Miss" led the new segregationist governor of Alabama, George C. Wallace, to have himself photographed at the doorway of the University of Alabama to symbolize his resistance to racial integration. Racial crisis burst forth again in May 1963, when dogs and firehoses were used to disperse blacks in Birmingham, Alabama, during civil rights demonstrations. This was followed by a summer of blacks rioting, bombings, arrests, and federal troop movements. President Kennedy requested of Congress more extensive civil rights legislation, particularly in the areas of equal rights in employment and voting prerogative, but an ambivalent Congress seemed unable to bring its two houses to concerted action.

During the summer of 1963, a Harris Poll found Jack Kennedy more popular than ever, ten to eighteen percentage points ahead of any of his prospective Republican opponents: George Romney, Barry Goldwater, Nelson Rockefeller, or William Scranton. Kennedy's biggest gains were among blacks and young males, with steady and solid support from Jews, Poles, and unskilled labor. Catholics were another important stronghold, but Kennedy was becoming vulnerable among Italians and, surprisingly, the Irish. Two-thirds or more of the voters approved of Kennedy's efforts to maintain military security, his Berlin stand, the Peace Corps, his programs of aid to education and space research, and his handling of Khrushchev. On the other hand, voters split in their attitudes on his economic policies, handling of Castro, and his civil rights policies. Most felt negatively about his handling of farm problems and federal spending programs.[1]

Appreciating how disruptive civil rights issues had become within the Democratic party and eager to mend factional fences in preparation for 1964, Kennedy set out on a tour of sensitive southern political communities. During a motorcade through Dallas, Texas, on November 22, 1963, the president was assassinated. The nation was traumatized. Through the medium of television, the world was witness to a series of events—from bizarre to funereal—that took place over the next several days. Who was responsible for Kennedy's assassination continues to be a controverted question.

Paralyzed by shock and mourning, Congress, within the week, felt the guidance of a familiar hand. Lyndon B. Johnson, in his first week as president, made clear his full endorsement of the Kennedy legislative program. A master of the legislative process, President Johnson once again demonstrated that skill in the early months of his administration. He was able to bring an $11 billion tax-cut bill out of a reluctant Senate committee chaired by Harry Byrd of Virginia by demonstrating a willingness to economize, that is, by trimming approximately $5 billion off the Kennedy budget. He further appeased the economy-minded Virginian by consulting with him about the budget message before it was sent and by thanking him later for his cooperation during a national TV speech in which he announced the tax cut. He worked a similar coup by getting through Congress antipoverty legislation calling for over $900 million for programs designed to inaugurate an attack upon the "pockets of poverty" that still could be found in the world's most affluent nation.

Probably the most controversial and politically significant piece of legislation in 1964, a presidential year, was the Civil Rights Bill. Involved during every stage of the bill's movement through Congress, Johnson nevertheless gave the chief negotiating role to his longtime associate and sometimes opponent, Majority Whip Hubert Humphrey. Southern filibusterers were conceded a seventy-five-day opportunity to debate and show their constituents how stubbornly they could fight. Humphrey, on the other hand, made clear how stubborn the nearly two-thirds Senate majority would be. Republican Minority Leader Dirksen and Republican Whip Kuchel managed to detach a few vital Republican votes from the long-standing Republican-southern coalition; the Johnson-Humphrey team performed similar feats on the Democratic side. The bill passed only a few weeks before the Democratic national convention and made Humphrey again a hero of that body.

With Johnson's nomination a foregone conclusion, party and public interest centered on Johnson's choice for vice president. According to the public opinion polls, Hubert Humphrey was the leading choice among Democratic voters and among party officials. Humphrey was a northern liberal who had won the respect and trust of many southern leaders. Humphrey also had a substantial following among the party rank-and-file, gathered during his presidential attempts in 1956 and 1960. Liberal and minority groups in major urban centers invariably warmed to Humphrey's speeches.

Running close behind Humphrey was Attorney General Robert F. Kennedy. Kennedy's political claims could not easily be disregarded. The Kennedy family name represented large achievements in national politics. It also evoked the nation's sympathy for that family's—and the nation's—recent loss. The attorney general's handling of the many civil rights crises in the South, including the violence and murders arising that very summer out of the black voter registration drives in Mississippi, brought him support from all segments of the civil rights movement.

The logic of a Johnson-Kennedy ticket seemed compelling, but strain between Johnson and the Kennedys was a poorly concealed fact of the Washington political scene. The president settled the matter by issuing a statement that members of his cabinet, whom he hoped would remain "above politics," would not be among those to be considered for the vice-presidential nomination. Shortly thereafter, Kennedy resigned, took up residence in New York (brother Ted was now senator from Massachusetts), and ran for the

United States Senate against a popular Republican, Kenneth Keating. Kennedy won the seat in November 1964. It was generally assumed that he would before long make the race for president.

Although the slowly escalating war in Vietnam and the hardnosed policies of De Gaulle in Europe brought the Johnson administration great difficulties, the nation, by and large, remained absorbed in domestic politics in 1964. In a tense national convention, the Republicans took a surprising turn to the right and nominated Senator Barry Goldwater and National Chairman William Miller. Goldwater's subsequent behavior managed to alienate much of the eastern and some of the midwestern leadership in that party. Regardless of developments in the Republican party, however, President Johnson's popularity in the electorate, as reported in the public opinion polls, remained better than 60 percent against *any* prospective Republican nominee.

What little excitement there was at the 1964 Democratic National Convention arose from seating contests in the Mississippi, Alabama, and Georgia delegations. The Alabama contest gave further national exposure to that state's Governor George C. Wallace. Factions in these states were eager to walk out of the Johnson convention in protest over the civil rights disturbances in the South. Although the national committee sat these delegations apart from each other and from other southern delegations in the convention hall in an attempt to minimize their contact and visibility, the issues themselves were important politically and in terms of the party's capacity for self-governance. Johnson asked Humphrey to try to work out a compromise, and the senator from Minnesota worked long hours to do so.

The 1960 national convention had affirmed three party-loyalty requirements: (1) State parties would certify only bona fide Democrats as delegates to the convention. (2) National committee members from each state were to declare affirmatively for the convention's nominees. (3) Delegates must assure the voters in their respective states an opportunity on the ballot to vote for the convention's slate. In Mississippi eight electoral votes were given to Byrd rather than Kennedy in 1960, and the Democratic national committeeman refused to declare for the 1960 slate. The questions raised were: What is a bona fide Democrat? What is a bona fide state Democratic party? What action can be taken against a national committeeman who fails to fulfill his pledge? Matters were complicated politically by Johnson's elimination of Kennedy as a vice-presidential prospect, an action that embittered northern liberals and later, to a large degree, led to the candidacy of Senator Eugene McCarthy of Minnesota as the left-liberal antiwar spokesman.

To negotiate a compromise, the convention appointed a Special Equal Rights Committee, with Humphrey working behind the scenes. The committee recommended and the convention accepted the following arrangements: (1) The challenging delegation from Mississippi was seated because of the racial barriers that had been imposed during the selection of the regular delegation. (2) Both the regular and the challenging delegations from Georgia were seated, with delegate votes divided between them. (3) Alabama and the other disputed delegations were required to subscribe to a pledge not publicly to support the nominees of any other party in the election, a less-than-affirmative pledge, to say the least.

The convention also prepared the groundwork for future changes in rules and practices that would have profound consequences for the party: broader participation in delegate selection, more timely selection of delegates prior to the convention, elimination of racial bias in delegate selection, and abolition of the unit rule. The platform recommended reforms in campaign finance laws, voter registration, the conduct of presidential primaries, and the electoral college.

Johnson tried to maintain some suspense in the vice-presidential selection by giving unusual attention to Senators Dodd of Connecticut, McCarthy, and Humphrey. In his acceptance speech, he asked the delegates to choose his "trusted colleague," Hubert Humphrey, whom they did. Having completed its major tasks, the convention delegates turned to pay their respects to the deceased John F. Kennedy. A commemorative film was introduced by Robert Kennedy, who received a prolonged ovation.

Goldwater never recovered his lost Republican colleagues during the campaign. His "southern strategy," however, did push the South further along the road toward a two-party competitive politics. In addition to his own state of Arizona, Goldwater carried five southern states. But the Johnson-Humphrey landslide was comparable to the Roosevelt achievement in 1936. The electoral college outcome was 486–52.

With the landslide came Democratic majorities in both houses of Congress, also reminiscent of the early days of the New Deal coalition. Table 5 makes the comparison and also reveals that, in the seventeen Congresses from 1932 to 1964, Democrats held majorities in both houses in fifteen. Democrats were indeed the majority party as Johnson began his own presidential term.

TABLE 5
Democratic Congressional Majorities, in Percentages, 1932–1964

Election Year	House of Representatives	Senate
1932	71.3	62.5
1934	73.3	71.9
1936	76.1	79.2
1938	60.0	71.9
1940	61.7	68.8
1942	50.1	60.4
1944	55.6	58.3
1946	43.2	46.9
1948	60.4	56.3
1950	53.8	51.0
1952	48.5	49.0
1954	53.3	50.0
1956	53.6	51.0
1958*	64.8	65.0
1960	60.2	64.0
1962	59.3	68.0
1964	67.8	68.0

*Alaska and Hawaii admitted to Union. Senate membership rose from 96 to 100. House membership became 437 temporarily for 1959 and 1961 sessions, then returned to 435.
Source: Compiled by author.

The Great Society and the Johnson Anomaly

President Johnson campaigned on a unity theme, expressing the need for a "broad national consensus" and promising programs that would enable the United States to become a "Great Society." Yet, although he sought progressive programs that would bring national unity, Johnson's administration experienced unusually large-scale domestic strife. For example, although landmark civil rights legislation was enacted, racial tension and rioting ran high. Never before had an administration initiated so much in specific policy areas, yet encountered such frustration and disappointment in these same areas. Most frustrating was the war in Vietnam. Could greater American military pressure bring the North Vietnamese to the negotiating table? The Johnson administration had more than its share of political anomalies.

Johnson turned to the development of his own program, encouraged by his impressive popular mandate in 1964. As the Eighty-ninth Congress began its work, he urged the large Democratic majority in the House to modify its procedures so as to strengthen party discipline vis-à-vis seniority, thereby hoping to avoid having his Great Society program bottlenecked by archaic congressional procedures and practices. As an act of party discipline, the Democratic caucus censured John Bell Williams of Mississippi and Albert W. Watson of South Carolina for having endorsed Goldwater, also terminating their seniority.

A program of health insurance for the elderly—Medicare—was enacted and inaugurated in 1966. Former President Harry Truman, the man who "started it," was on hand for the bill-signing. A landmark Elementary and Secondary Education Act directed massive infusions of federal funds into special school programs for low-income neighborhoods, the development of high quality curriculum materials, educational research, aid to rural schools, and other aids to local school systems. Programs for the disadvantaged included: job training for the unskilled; economic aid for Appalachia and other economically depressed regions; low-cost housing for minorities; antipoverty programs of various kinds; increased social security benefits. Black participation in the electoral process was facilitated by the 1965 Voting Rights Act, which suspended literacy tests in low-turnout districts and allowed the attorney general to appoint registration examiners. Other support for black aspirations was forthcoming, ranging from assignment of federal troops to protect the Reverend Dr. Martin Luther King's civil rights march from Selma to Montgomery, Alabama, in March 1965, to appointment of Thurgood Marshall as a justice of the Supreme Court in 1967. In November of that same year, Carl B. Stokes of Cleveland and Richard G. Hatcher of Gary, Indiana, both Democrats, became the first black mayors to be elected in major American cities.

Such progress notwithstanding, blacks rioted in the Watts area of Los Angeles during August 1965 causing the death of thirty-five persons and some $200 million in property damage. Two years later there was another summer of racial rioting, looting, and burning in Newark, Detroit, and other cities. Dozens died, hundreds were injured, and thousands were left homeless. On July 27, 1967, President Johnson appointed a National Advisory Commission on Civil Disorders—the Kerner Commission—whose monumental report was published the following year.

The commission noted that 91 percent of American blacks lived in the Old South in 1910, but by 1966 one-third lived in the nation's twelve largest cities. The report dealt with discriminatory job hiring, housing, schools, police procedures, newspaper practices, and community attitudes; in short, a full range of social and political factors that motivated the violence. The commission's report was eloquent but not more so than Johnson's comment in an address to the nation on July 27, 1967:

The only genuine, long-range solution for what has happened lies in an attack—mounted at every level—upon the conditions that breed despair and violence. All of us know what those conditions are: ignorance, discrimination, slums, poverty, disease, not enough jobs. We should attack these conditions—not because we are frightened by conflict, but because we are fired by conscience. We should attack them because there is simply no other way to achieve a decent and orderly society in America.[2]

But the plague of violence remained. The Reverend Martin Luther King, Jr., was assassinated on April 4, 1968, in Memphis. Riots broke out in Washington, D.C., and 125 other cities in twenty-nine states. During April, students paralyzed Columbia University for two weeks to protest the university's plans to build a gymnasium in Morningside Park, a black neighborhood, and to oppose university ties with the Institute for Defense Analysis, a military research organization.

Foreign policy, never Johnson's strong suit, began to plague him almost immediately after his inauguration. On April 28, 1965, he reacted to an incipient Castro-style revolt in the Dominican Republic by sending United States troops to bolster the incumbent regime. He was promptly described as "trigger-happy" and "imperialistic" by New Left spokesmen, although, a month later, the Organization of American States established a peace-keeping force to maintain order on the island.

The war in Vietnam proved to be Johnson's "Achilles heel." What began as a side issue in the Korean War grew, almost imperceptibly at first, to become a cancer in the American body politic. Kennedy's decision in 1961 breached the 1954 Geneva Accords by sending a few hundred more military advisers to help the Diem regime cope with the escalation of North Vietnamese and National Liberation Front military actions. This was followed, in 1962, by the dispatch of helicopter pilots, along with more advisers. In November 1963, a military coup, with American acquiescence if not collusion, brought Diem's death and an end to his dictatorial regime. A series of coups ensued: one in January 1964, another in December 1964, a third in January 1965.

The successes of the NLF and North Vietnamese and the instability of the South Vietnamese government led Johnson, despite his campaign promise to keep American involvement limited, to send the first substantial number of United States ground combat forces to South Vietnam in March 1965. He also authorized the aerial bombardment of North Vietnam. These actions were taken without a declaration of war by Congress but presumably in fulfillment of the United States' treaty obligations to the Southeast Asian Treaty Organization (SEATO). Further escalation became inevitable as China and the Soviet Union began to pour aid into North Vietnam. By late 1966, there were over 380,000 American troops in South Vietnam, along with many thousands of other SEATO troops: Australians, New Zealanders, and Koreans. The question now was where and when would escalation cease.

By 1966, too, the war was beginning to reach deep into the American conscience. American casualties began to touch a growing number of families. The military budget requests were beginning to pinch. The remote battles, with all their blood and horror, began to appear regularly on family television screens. The American left, sympathetic to Ho Chi Minh's revolution, began to challenge the basic assumptions and goals of American involvement. Liberal senators, including Robert Kennedy, Eugene McCarthy, and George McGovern, began to demand reconsideration of Vietnam policy. The political scene was further agitated by civil rights marches into the South, rioting in black ghettos, a growing white backlash whose principal spokesman was Governor Wallace of Alabama, and student disquiet on many of the nation's major university campuses. Johnson's achievements in domestic policy were forgotten as he became the hate-object of antiwar groups. During 1966, Gallup polls began to show that less than 50 percent of the adult population approved Johnson's handling of the war in Vietnam.

Nothing Johnson said or did seemed to quell suspicions about his intentions in Vietnam. In his own words, " . . . we had three principal goals: to insure that aggression did not succeed; to make it possible for the South Vietnamese to build their country and their future in their own way; and to convince Hanoi that working out a peaceful settlement was to the advantage of all concerned."[3] These were familiar United States policy postures: halt aggression, national self-determination, and negotiated settlement of conflicts.

Despite the fact that American ground forces remained south of the 17th parallel, Johnson's critics charged that the aerial bombardment of North Vietnam represented nothing less than an undeclared war-to-the-death against a sovereign state. Even Johnson's December 1965 "peace offensive," during which he declared a thirty-seven-day halt to the bombing, was received with skepticism. Ho Chi Minh denounced the effort and insisted that all American troops be withdrawn from Vietnam. The North Vietnamese also used the bombing respite to move large numbers of troops and supplies southward.

The war in Vietnam had by now become a matter of confusion, misinformation, and profound division among Americans. To some it appeared that the world's mightiest nation was intent upon destroying a Socialist regime in the North in order to maintain a dictatorial one in the South. Others saw it as American support for an ally defending its territory against subversion within and aggression from the North, whose suppliers were Communist China and the Soviet Union. It was a kind of war with which few Americans were familiar: a war without a specific front; a military effort that did not call for all-out victory or destruction of the enemy's regime; a chronicle of wartime violence that daily appeared on home television. The extreme right in the United States called for a final "nuclear solution" and the extreme left insisted that the United States depart from Southeast Asia. By mid-1966 the profound split in the Democratic party was reminiscent of the war and peace factionalism of the Civil War.

The president became as disenchanted with many of his colleagues in Congress as they with his war policies. He took little part in the midterm congressional campaign. In contrast, on the Republican side, Richard Nixon led the party's attack on the "rubber-stamp" Democratic Congress. Democrats lost forty-seven seats in the House, three in the Senate, and eight governorships. A meeting of Democratic governors in December 1966 interpreted the election results as "anti-Johnson."

The anomaly of Johnson's leadership is in part explained by David Broder, a distinguished political reporter. Johnson's conception of national leadership, Broder notes, originated in the one-party state of Texas where political organization was personal rather than partisan and where notions of party program or party loyalty hardly existed. "His decimation of his own national party organization in 1966 was not accidental; it was the expression not only of his

Texas background but also his belief that partisanship is the enemy, not the servant, of responsible government."[4] Broder is referring to Johnson's abandonment of the Kennedy voter registration drive, particularly in the South, his 50 percent cut in the Democratic National Committee staff, and his failure to maintain contact with state party chairmen. After the election, AFL-CIO President George Meany warned the president that, without reconstruction of the party's grass-roots machinery, there were likely to be insurmountable problems in the 1968 campaign.

Johnson, however, believed in "consensus politics," writes Broder, in which support comes from a widely diverse constituency, each of whose elements must be provided with economic rewards. A carry-over from his congressional experience, Johnson's political technique was highly personal, placing tremendous demands on his personal energies. Further, he was accustomed to dealing with group leaders rather than with the general public. Finally, Johnson preferred to achieve policy decisions by private negotiation rather than public debate, and this, concludes Broder, called for the kind of secrecy that undermined his relations with the press. By the end of 1967, only 28 percent of Gallup's national sample approved of Johnson's handling of the Vietnam War.

Events overseas continued to go poorly and seemed beyond the president's influence. France withdrew from the North Atlantic Treaty Organization (NATO), whose creation had been considered a special achievement of the United States. The six-day war between Israel and the Arabs in 1967 reignited the chronic tensions of the Middle East. On January 30, 1968, the North Vietnamese launched a Tet offensive against South Vietnam, which, although defeated, demonstrated the vitality and the tenacity of the Communist war effort.

Divided by the war, led by a president whose popularity was in rapid decline, disturbed by violence in urban communities, the New Deal–Fair Deal coalition began to unravel visibly during 1968. Governor George Wallace prepared to lead southern and blue-collar Democrats, who were unhappy with growing racial tensions in the South and the cities, into a third-party movement. By December 1967, anticipating trouble from the Wallaceites, loyal Democrats in Alabama began forming a new organization that would assure that the regular nominee of the Democratic National Convention would have a place on the state ballot.

Elsewhere, Senator Eugene McCarthy of Minnesota, Vice President Humphrey's home state, announced his intention to challenge President Johnson's renomination; McCarthy placed himself at the head of the antiwar groups within the party, winning twenty of the twenty-four delegate seats in the New Hampshire primary early in March. In New York State, Senator Robert F. Kennedy was preoccupied with the difficult task of reuniting the party's contentious factions there. During 1967, polls showed Kennedy ahead of Johnson as the presidential preference of the public. As rumors spread regarding President Johnson's renomination plans, Kennedy found himself caught between an unwillingness to challenge an incumbent president and the unpleasant fact that many of his own supporters were forming ranks behind McCarthy. On March 17, Kennedy finally announced that he would seek the Democratic nomination.

Two weeks later, on March 31, in a televised broadcast to the nation, President Johnson declared a cessation of the bombing of North Vietnam as a gesture intended to bring the Communists to the negotiating table. As he concluded his address, Johnson added the following unannounced statement: "I shall not seek, and I will not accept, the nomination of my party for another term as your president."

Vice President Humphrey was Johnson's preferred successor and continued to be widely esteemed among most of the older leaders in the party and popular among the rank-and-file. However, like so many candidates before him, Humphrey found it necessary to defend an administration of which he was part but not the leader. In June, Gallup reported that 25 percent of the voters believed the United States was losing the war and another 47 percent that things were at a standstill. Asked whether Nixon or Humphrey could do a better job of dealing with the war, the survey revealed a dead heat: 41 percent for Nixon, 41 percent favoring Humphrey, and 18 percent undecided.

Younger antiwar Democrats were flocking to the McCarthy and Kennedy bandwagons intent upon breaking up the old coalition. Blacks' tempers flared with the assassination of Reverend Martin Luther King, Jr., in April, many turning to Kennedy. Wallace stirred the passions of his supporters not only against the old Democratic coalition but also the whole "Washington crowd." Humphrey found himself certain only of the help of party regulars, organized labor, and some elements in the civil rights movement.

Having lost the nomination once before to a Kennedy, Humphrey also anticipated that the senator from New York would be no ordinary opponent. Kennedy mounted an aggressive campaign in the presidential primary states while Humphrey rested his prospects on the commitments of party regulars in the convention states. By the end of May, just prior to the California and Oregon primaries, *Newsweek* estimated that Humphrey could depend on 1,279 votes at the convention, Kennedy 713, and McCarthy 280. This put Humphrey 33 votes short of the nomination with a Humphrey-Kennedy ticket in prospect. Kennedy's climactic primary victory was in California on June 5 when he beat McCarthy and an ostensibly unpledged slate of regulars who favored Humphrey.

But tragedy stood in the wings. Just after completing a victory statement at his Los Angeles headquarters, Kennedy was struck down by an assassin's bullet and died the following day. Once again, the nation and the party were deprived of one of their most beloved and talented young leaders. Confusion and despair reigned in the Democratic nominating process. Most of the Kennedy delegates held fast, tried unsuccessfully to enlist Robert's brother, Ted, and finally drafted Senator George McGovern of South Dakota, who had been an anti-Vietnam spokesman since 1963.

Outside the party, George Wallace's campaign had created the American Independent party whose candidate he would become. Wallace's following was strongest among southern whites, small businessmen, blue-collar workers, some recent immigrant groups, and others aggrieved by the demonstrations of the blacks and the young, in short, the constituents of what came to be known as the "white backlash." Wallace's departure from the Democratic party left Democratic conservatives—given the available alternatives— with no other choice than Humphrey.

Despair carried into the Democratic National Convention at Chicago in late August. As the vice president, whose nomination was by now assured, tried to pull together the embittered factions inside the convention hall, some ten to fifteen thousand antiwar demonstrators and the Chicago police tore into each other in unrestrained violence on the streets outside. On TV and in the other media the battle came across as a titanic confrontation of ideologies and heroes: the antiwar left versus the law-and-order right; pacifists versus patriots; "Uncle" Ho versus "Boss" Daley. This image became the albatross of the Humphrey-Muskie ticket.

With a new generation of Democrats intent upon winning control, old procedures and practices as well as old leaders were under heavy fire at the 1968 convention. The way was paved for the reform convention that came four years later in 1972. Although few state delegations still exercised it, the ancient unit rule whereby a delegation's majority determined how the state's entire convention vote would be cast on the nominations was abolished in 1968. A resolution was passed requiring state party organizations to adopt procedures so that delegates would be selected in the same calendar year as the national convention, thus presumably assuring that delegates would be attuned to current voter opinion. (Over six hundred of the delegates to the 1968 convention, for example, had been selected by procedures that provided for no means of voter participation subsequent to 1966.) The convention also authorized the creation of one reform commission on delegate selection, to which Senator George McGovern of South Dakota was subsequently appointed chairman, and another on convention rules, later placed under the direction of Congressman James G. O'Hara of Michigan.

The election campaign was arduous. The regular party organization was in a shambles. A new campaign organization had to be put together immediately, and Humphrey called upon Lawrence O'Brien, a member of the original Kennedy team, to serve as Democratic national chairman. September opinion polls showed Humphrey some fifteen percentage points behind Nixon. Wallace, who had taken his walk, appeared likely to capture about one-fifth of the votes. On September 30, Humphrey made a speech in which he sought to disassociate himself from the Johnson position on the bombing of North Vietnam, but it won him few converts among the antiwar people, who saw him as a man of the past. President Johnson himself remained as much in the background as possible, although a few days before the election he announced a new halt in the bombing of North Vietnam.

It seemed impossible to reconstitute the New Deal coalition. Union people were split, with a substantial portion of the blue-collar workers turning to Wallace. The ethnic minorities and the civil rights movement were split, most vocally between older civil rights leaders and younger black nationalists. The South was split, much of it ready to follow either the Nixon-Agnew slate or Governor Wallace. Liberal intellectuals were split between following the proven Humphrey, yet adamantly antiwar and smitten by the loss of another Kennedy.

Despite these divisions and handicaps, Humphrey came within 500,000 votes of Nixon in the final count. Some 72 million votes were cast, of which 13.5 percent were drawn off by Wallace, who carried five southern states. Nixon carried five other southern states. But Congress remained safely in Democratic hands, 58–42 in the Senate and 243–192 in the House. Had the great and durable New Deal coalition at long last come apart? Were a new Democratic party-in-the-electorate and a new Democratic leadership seeking each other out?

Organizational Reform and Factional Insurgency

Without a Senate seat or the presidency, Hubert Humphrey was nonetheless a titular leader with substantial political resources. His personal exuberance, his two decades of national party leadership, his status as vice president, and his near-victory over Richard Nixon despite the deep wounds in the Democratic coalition made it reasonable for him to try to exercise leadership of the out-party, anticipate reelection from Minnesota to the United States Senate, and expect serious consideration for a second presidential nomination in 1972.

Humphrey and National Chairman Fred Harris started up the work toward internal reform of the party's organization and procedures with the appointment of Senator George McGovern's Committee on Delegate Selection and Party Structure and Congressman James O'Hara's Commission on Rules in preparation for the 1972 national convention. Ironically, these steps were to lead to the undoing of Humphrey's presidential hopes, but they were also an essential and characteristic part of the party's search for consensus. There were changes going on in the party's constituency, the New Deal coalition, and the composition of the leadership. These changes evoked much analysis, discussion, and uncertainty for the next eight years.

For one, the trade union movement had reached a plateau in its growth and was having problems. The older generation of labor leaders and the younger leaders with an affinity for the New Left began to voice serious differences over public policies—Vietnam, race relations, welfare, etc.—and candidate preferences. Blue-collar and many skilled workers were following George Wallace rather than George Meany. Change and disagreement were occurring elsewhere. More affluent northern blacks were becoming increasingly interested in the Republican party. Black nationalism of the Malcolm X and Eldridge Cleaver types was seeking to convert the civil rights movement to religious or revolutionary ways. With the exception of Mayor Richard Daley's Chicago organization, urban machines had ground to a halt, one of several forms of urban decay and crisis. Women's liberation was gaining momentum. The young were pushing for the right-to-vote for eighteen-year-olds. Civil-rights and anti-Vietnam activists who had worked for Robert Kennedy, Eugene McCarthy, or George McGovern were looking more seriously to the Democratic party as an avenue for careers in politics. Wallace's South was getting to be as electorally competitive as Muskie's Maine. Learning from the black nationalists, other nationality groups—the Italians, the Irish, the Poles, etc.—embarked upon organized ethnocentrism and vociferous political demands. The Democratic party caught most of this heat and noise.

In the White House, Richard Nixon began to design an orderly image for the Republican party to stand in contrast with that of the fractious Democrats. Reorganization of the federal government was one of his early priorities, for better control of central policy planning and financial management. He tried to consolidate cabinet departments but failed to win congressional approval. He initiated legislative proposals in the fields of environmental protection, control of population growth, and welfare reform. The Post Office Department was cut loose to become a public corporation. He proposed a new system of federal revenue-sharing with state and local governments to replace the grants-in-aid programs that had been in operation since New Deal days and earlier.

Nixon gave his most visible if not most effective attention to the three problems that he had discussed most in his campaign: crime, inflation, and Vietnam. Federal aid to local law enforcement agencies was increased. Inflation became the target of frequent bulletins, price controls, and Federal Reserve Board actions. "Vietnamization" became the keyword for Nixon policy on the war. After so many years of hostility and distrust of "Tricky Dick," many Democrats found themselves frequently in uncomfortable collaboration with the president.

It was in the more dramatic fields of foreign policy and national security that Nixon chose to put on his biggest performances. For this, he recruited as his national security adviser a Harvard political science professor, Henry Kissinger, who had long been associated with Nelson Rockefeller.

[Nixon's] problem [in Vietnam] was to arrange the withdrawal at a pace fast enough to satisfy domestic public opinion but deliberate enough to avoid the impression of a rout and to protect, as far as possible, the survival chances of a non-Communist government in Saigon. The instrument of this "wriggle-out" policy was the Vietnamization program—a staged American withdrawal linked to intensified training and equipping of the South Vietnamese army.[5]

A third element in the Vietnamization strategy was to revive the peace negotiations with the North Vietnamese in Paris that Lyndon Johnson had succeeded in getting started on May 13, 1968.

All three elements ran into trouble. The South Vietnamese were difficult to train. The peace negotiations remained stalled. U.S. troop withdrawal moved very slowly. Meanwhile, the North Vietnamese military buildup, with the help of Chinese and Soviet equipment and advisers, and aid to the National Liberation Front went on apace. Although the New Left and antiwar Democrats kept up a tirade against Nixon and Kissinger, their demands lost bite because the Vietnamization program, except for pace and quantity, did seem to meet their demands. In April 1969 there were 543,000 American troops in Vietnam; by the end of 1971 there were 139,000.

In their statement of a "Nixon Doctrine," Nixon and Kissinger also sought to redefine the United States' role in world affairs. The United States would help allies defend themselves but could no longer be the sole "policeman of the world." The bipolar world of the two superpowers, the United States and the Soviet Union, had become multipolar with the emergence of Japan, China, and Europe as major global actors. The Cold War had to be replaced by "an era of negotiations," as exemplified by the conclusion of the Nuclear Nonproliferation Treaty (NPT) and the initiation of the Conference on Mutual and Balanced Force Reduction (MBFR) between NATO and the Warsaw Pact nations.

During all this, Democrats were taking a back seat and licking their wounds. Johnson had retired to his ranch in Texas and to preparation of his memoirs. Humphrey went back to teaching political science in Minnesota and preparing his campaign for a return to the Senate. The McGovern and O'Hara commissions were working hard. In the Gallup Poll issued in early March 1969, four out of five respondents in the national sample expected Ted Kennedy to be the next Democratic nominee for president and it looked as though a Kennedy might once again reunite the party.

Then, on July 19, 1969, a young woman named Mary Jo Kopechne was being driven home from a party by Ted Kennedy when their car swerved into the bay at Chappaquiddick. They were alone. Kopechne was killed. Kennedy swam away from the scene of the accident. The circumstances were ambiguous and the public discussion damaging enough to remove Kennedy as a prospective national candidate. Democrats turned again to Hubert Humphrey and Edmund Muskie as their most likely presidential possibilities for 1972.

Still $8 million in debt from the 1968 campaign and facing a midterm election in 1970, party leaders gave serious thought to the management of the Democratic National Committee. Humphrey was able to convince Lawrence O'Brien to take the national chairmanship, but even this much-esteemed "pro" ran into flak from southerners, McCarthy followers, and supporters of the late Robert Kennedy. After an impasse that reflected the divisions in the presidential wing, O'Brien accepted a unanimous invitation reached in a manner that made clear that he was not Humphrey's appointee.

The 1970 congressional election returns were only somewhat encouraging. Democrats lost two seats in the Senate but retained their safe majority. Nine additional seats—fewer than the average for the out-party—were won in the House. A significant long-term trend within the party-in-the-House, however, now became evident. For more than a quarter of a century, an increasing number of nonsouthern Democrats, that is, representatives from thirty-nine states, were being elected to the House. In 1970, there were 176 Democrats and 153 Republicans returned from nonsouthern states. Many of the Democrats were liberals who replaced conservative Republicans. In addition, the growing competitiveness of southern congressional races—only two Republicans from the South in 1946 but twenty-seven in 1970—was tending to liberalize representation from that section. Thus, the House of Representatives, previously the more conservative part of the legislative branch, was becoming more liberal.[6] This brought not only opportunities for liberal policies but also the election of a moderate liberal, Carl Albert, to the speakership in 1970, followed by efforts to liberalize the rules of the Democratic caucus, to be described elsewhere.[7]

By September 1969, the McGovern commission's reform proposals were ready for the Democratic National Committee. They were adopted unanimously on February 19, 1971. State delegations that failed to comply with the new rules could expect to be challenged at the convention. State delegations were called upon to take "affirmative" steps to encourage "minority"—blacks, women, youth, Chicanos—participation in the delegate selection process and their "reasonable representation" on the delegation. "Reasonable" meant relative to the groups' presence in the state's population. Older minorities called it a "quota" requirement. Few observers noticed at first that the prospective newcomers would come from the McCarthy, Kennedy, and antiwar ranks and would form new ranks behind George McGovern enroute to the national convention and the party's leadership.

Yet another liberalizing influence upon the party were the gubernatorial victories of Democrats in the 1970 elections. Twenty-nine Democratic governors occupied state houses during the 1971 reapportionments of congressional and state legislative districts following the decennial census, and these governors were likely to be more sensitive to liberal interests than their usually more conservative state legislative colleagues.

Perhaps the greatest—and most ill-founded—expectations of liberalization were raised by the extension of the suffrage to eighteen-year-olds. Responding to the youth activism of the late 1960s, a Democratic Congress passed the Voting Rights Act of 1970 which allowed eighteen-year-olds to vote in federal elections. In December of the same year, the Supreme Court upheld the requirements of the act, which also prohibited literacy tests as a qualification for voting. However, the federal eighteen-year-old requirement did not apply to state and local elections and the consequent confusion was expected to impair the electoral process. On March 31, 1971, Congress, with only one hour of debate, passed and sent to the states for ratification the Twenty-sixth Amendment to the Constitution giving the vote in all elections to all citizens reaching the age of eighteen. In a little over two months, the amendment was ratified, and eleven million persons between the ages of eighteen and twenty-one were thereby added to the 1972 electorate. Another fourteen million between twenty-one and twenty-five would also be eligible in 1972 to vote for a president for the first time.

The total of twenty-five million new voters terrified some politicians and captured the imagination of others. Frederick Dutton, a McGovern adviser, went so far as to predict that 70–75 percent of the registered new voters woud support McGovern. When McGovern announced his candidacy, his staff focused a large part of its efforts upon registering young first-voters. Dutton's prediction, however, flew in the face of well-established knowledge about first voters (twenty-one-to-twenty-five-year-olds in the recent past). This knowledge suggested that less than half (12–13 million in 1972) of the new voters were likely to go to the polls and that, despite the highly publicized campus activism of that period, overall, young voters tend to split the same way their elders do, that is, about 50–50, with a slight edge in favor of the Democrats. Regardless of the facts, the new youth vote as well as the new youth leadership were very much on the minds of established party leaders as 1972 approached.

Democrats, with the exception of Wallace supporters, tended to feel at ease about the influx of the young into party affairs. Unemployment was on the rise, and the young were among its most serious victims. The Vietnam War was still in progress, in fact, extended to Cambodia and Laos, where North Vietnamese, South Vietnamese, and Americans maneuvered freely to maintain or destroy Communist supply routes. Young activists, particularly on campuses, were the ones who led some of the largest mass demonstrations in history to protest the Cambodia foray, culminating in the tragic death of several students at Kent State and Jackson State universities in May 1970 and, a year later, the arrest of some seven thousand antiwar demonstrators in Washington, D.C.

The party once again in 1971 began to turn its attention to presidential politics. Humphrey was elected as Minnesota's senator, *junior* senator, that is. He and Muskie were still the front-runners in presidential preferences of Democratic voters, but Ted Kennedy's name persisted among the top three. In January 1971, long before others, Senator McGovern announced his candidacy for the presidency, turning over his reform commission duties to Congressman Donald Fraser of Minnesota. Few took the South Dakotan's candidacy seriously and there was some skepticism about the earliness of his announcement. In time, however, it became evident that McGovern was attracting the young in large numbers as well as successfully raising campaign funds through a massive mail solicitation. Further, McGovern planned to travel the primary election route, as did earlier insurgents Kefauver, Kennedy, and McCarthy.

The route soon became a very crowded highway as Muskie, Humphrey, McCarthy, Senator Henry Jackson of Washington, Senator Vance Hartke of Indiana, Representative Wilbur Mills, Representative Shirley Chisholm, New York's Mayor John Lindsay, Los Angeles Mayor Samuel Yorty, and Governor George Wallace entered the race. Muskie was the front-runner. As his fortunes fell, Humphrey's rose. Polls rarely gave McGovern more than two or three percentage points in popular support. When Wallace announced that he would enter the Florida primary, this was, by implication, an announcement of his return to the Democratic party, possibly as the southern candidate at the convention and a potential bolter afterward.

In the New Hampshire primary results in March, McGovern was a surprisingly close second to Muskie. In Florida, Wallace was the clear victor and Muskie a poor fourth. The April primary in Wisconsin, however, was won by McGovern. Soon after, Muskie left the race. Wallace came in second in Wisconsin and demonstrated his appeal outside the South. In a few weeks, the battle became a Humphrey-McGovern contest, with Wallace continuing to show surprising strength as a national candidate. In May, the day before the Michigan and Maryland primaries, Wallace was shot by a would-be assassin while campaigning in a Maryland shopping center. Alive but paralyzed from the waist down, Wallace was removed from the nomination race but remained a factor in political calculations.

McGovern now won primary after primary. In California, McGovern debated Humphrey, turned out a massive canvass of the voters run by young volunteers, and spent his largest campaign budget. He won the state's entire bloc of 271 votes as a consequence of a 44–39 percent Democratic primary vote victory over Humphrey. Wallace received about 15 percent of the California vote.

The implementation of the McGovern-Fraser commission rules brought a very different kind of delegate to the 1972 Democratic National Convention, raising some profound issues about the nature of representation within the party.[8] There were more women: about 36 percent of the delegates, up 22 points from 1968. The delegates were younger, 23 percent under thirty compared to only 2 percent four years earlier. There were more blacks: 6 percent in 1968, 14 percent in 1972.[9] Elected officials, older party regulars, labor leaders, and other stalwarts were in the galleries, lobbies, and hotel rooms, much of their participation reduced to watching the news over television.

As predicted, the number of credentials contests was overwhelming: twenty-three from fifteen states. The critical test was the seating of the California delegation with its 271 votes. California law prescribed a winner-take-all primary according to which all 271 Democratic delegate votes went to McGovern. Humphrey argued, however, that this was contrary to the McGovern-Fraser commission guidelines which prohibited a unit rule at any stage of delegate selection. Under this interpretation, McGovern's 44 percent of the popular vote should have earned him only 120 California delegate votes, with 106 going to Humphrey, and 45 to others. The credentials committee favored the Humphrey interpretation, but the convention majority voted to keep McGovern's California votes intact. To add salt to the wounds, the convention unseated Mayor Daley's Chicago delegation of 59 regulars, including the mayor himself, in favor of challengers led by Jesse Jackson.

After McGovern won the nomination, he could not be sure what its value was. Some of the oldest and staunchest leaders of the Democratic party had been bruised by the young McGovern enthusiasts. This was evident from the number of declinations McGovern received as he put out inquiries about prospective running mates for his ticket. He finally settled upon Senator Thomas Eagleton of Missouri. Even before the fall campaign could be organized, it was discovered that Eagleton had suffered a series of nervous breakdowns that put his qualifications in grave doubt. Eagleton finally withdrew from the ticket and was replaced by Sargent Shriver, a brother-in-law to the Kennedys and former director of the Peace Corps.

The Eagleton affair consumed precious campaign time and left the impression that McGovern lacked judgment and skill as a decision-maker. Nor did he successfully conciliate the convention's wounded. George Meany and the AFL-CIO withheld their usual endorsement of the Democrat slate. Mayor Daley concentrated on local races. Wallace's silence freed most of his following to continue their rightward shift to Nixon. Perhaps the most disappointing factor was the voting behavior of the first voters. Only 44 percent of the magic twenty-five million eighteen-to-twenty-five-year-olds actually voted. Of this eleven million, 50 percent voted for McGovern, 48 percent for Nixon, 2 percent for others.

Watergate Entry, Vietnam Exit

President Nixon preferred to play out his campaign effort on the world stage. From early in his administration, it was evident that he was taking his principal foreign policy advice from Henry Kissinger. From Kissinger's perspective, the United States' principal attention needed to be given to the other superpower, the Soviet Union. In an increasingly multipolar world, on the other hand, an emerging new adversary would also have to be acknowledged: Mao Tse-tung's People's Republic of China. The voice of Nixon, as a young congressman, had been the one that most often accused the

Democrats of having "lost China." As president, he embraced the Kissinger strategy for an opening to Communist China.

Signals went out to Peking through a variety of public and private channels, resulting in a Chinese invitation in 1971 for the United States to send its best ping-pong players to engage in a friendly match. This somewhat bizarre beginning was followed by secret conversations and preparations between Kissinger and the Chinese for a presidential visit to China in February 1972. During these preparations, Mao's China displaced Chiang Kai-shek's as the official Chinese delegation seated at the United Nations; the United States for the first time refrained from exercising its usual veto on this question. After the February visit to Peking, Nixon visited Moscow in May. The press coverage and the diplomatic coups at both capitals were, for all practical purposes, Nixon's election campaign. He spent most of the fall campaign season ostensibly and ostentatiously doing his job at his White House desk. Kissinger's October 26 pronouncement that "peace is at hand" in Vietnam sent a special pre-election thrill through the nation.

With these grand and carefully orchestrated events holding the attention of the press and the public, an awkward crime received little notice and some skeptical comment. On June 17, the Watergate Office Building headquarters of the Democratic National Committee was illegally entered at night. Five men carrying electronic eavesdropping equipment were apprehended, among them, James McCord, director of security of Nixon's Committee to Re-elect the President. CRP's director John Mitchell, Nixon's former attorney general and close friend, promptly fired McCord as well as CRP counsel G. Gordon Liddy, the latter for refusing to answer FBI questions about Liddy's connections with the bugging team. Shortly after, Mitchell himself resigned from CRP on the pretext that his wife, Martha, insisted that she would leave him if he did not get out of politics. Meanwhile, Democratic National Chairman O'Brien initiated a suit against CRP for $1 million. Most of the press and nearly all of the voters cynically dismissed the incident as just another typical last-minute election campaign fuss designed to make headlines and win votes.

The Nixon-Agnew ticket swept in with 61 percent of the popular vote to McGovern's 38 percent. This translated into a vote of 520–17 in the electoral college. Only Franklin Roosevelt and Lyndon Johnson had bigger electoral college landslides in this century. Nearly three-fourths of the Wallace voters of 1968, mostly blue-collar, cast their ballots for Nixon. But, overall, it was a reluctant electorate; only 54.7 percent turned out, the lowest participation since 1948. Some observers explained McGovern's defeat by citing Harris Poll findings that two out of every three voters described McGovern as having "too extreme liberal views." "What [the voters] resist is change that takes place in a non-traditional manner." The new McGovernite politicians, as demonstrated in the primaries and the raucous national convention, were not only insurgent factionalists, "they also had qualities generally associated with extremism: they were ideological, moralistic, and evangelistic." These are characteristics that undermine a coalition party.[10]

In Congress, Democrats fared well once again. The party's majority in the Senate was now 57–43, in the House 245–190. Mississippi and Louisiana, on the other hand, elected their first Republican congressmen since Reconstruction. Blacks were sent from Texas and Georgia for the first time in almost a century. Five more women were added to the nine already in the House.

Kissinger's statement notwithstanding, peace in Vietnam was not "at hand." The conditions that Kissinger had worked out with North Vietnam's Le Duc Tho in secret sessions in Paris were denounced as a "sellout" by South Vietnam's President Thieu. Further secret negotiations in Paris broke down. In December, Nixon resumed bombings north of the 20th parallel. New anti-aircraft missiles provided by the Soviet Union, however, enabled the North Vietnamese to take a deadly toll of U.S. bombers and pilots. An angry House Democrat caucus on January 2 voted 154–75 in favor of a policy barring further funds for U.S. military combat activities in or over Indochina. Two days later, Senate Democrats, 36 to 12, voted in their own conference for a similar resolution.

Finally, in Paris on January 27, 1973, North Vietnam, South Vietnam, the Viet Cong, and the United States signed an agreement to establish a cease-fire supervised by an International Commission of Control and Supervision, maintain the 17th parallel as a provisional demarcation line until elections could be held to reunify the country, withdraw foreign troops, and return American prisoners held by North Vietnam. Violations of the cease-fire began almost immediately. The United States and other foreign troops were withdrawn but, in October 1973, Hanoi charged the U.S. with having left 20,000 troops in "civilian guise." American observers in turn charged that 70,000 North Vietnamese troops had infiltrated to the South, bringing along 400 tanks and 200 artillery pieces. An average of nearly 200 Vietnamese—North and South—were killed daily in military actions during the first year of the so-called cease-fire.

There was no factional cease-fire among Democrats, either. When the Democratic National Committee convened in December 1972, National Chairwoman Jean Westwood, McGovern's appointee, was replaced by Robert Strauss, former national committee treasurer. A moderate conservative, a Texan with ties to labor, the urban organizations, and wealthy Democrats, Strauss bravely assumed the seemingly impossible task of pulling together the embittered factions. While McGovern's personal influence was diminished, many of his followers were firmly installed in the party's machinery at all levels. George Wallace, still struggling to recover from the assassination attempt, remained vocal. George Meany's executive assistant, Penn Kemble, was putting together a new Coalition for a Democratic Majority (CDM) made up primarily of COPE (AFL-CIO's Committee on Political Education), Humphrey, and Jackson supporters. The senior Democrats in public office, Senate Majority Leader Mike Mansfield and Speaker Carl Albert, were disinclined to assert themselves as party spokesmen. Faction-ridden and leaderless, the Democratic party seemed headed for its own internal "Vietnam."

Then, as he had so often before, Richard Nixon helped reunite the Democratic party. Distrust and loathing for Nixon had, after more than two decades, become second nature for most Democrats. Thus, when two young *Washington Post* reporters, Carl Bernstein and Robert Woodward, began to publish stories linking the June 17 Watergate break-in with the president himself, the Democratic Congress began to take notice. On January 30, 1973, McCord and Liddy were convicted on all charges against them. The other five Watergate burglars pleaded guilty. On February 7, the Senate set up a Select Committee to Investigate the 1972 Campaign, that is, the Watergate Committee, under the chairmanship of Sam Ervin of North Carolina.

The president had in August 1972 denied any White House connection with the break-in and refused to cooperate with the investigation. On April 17, 1973, following testimony by McCord before the Watergate Committee, Nixon announced his own investigation into the affair. With this, the Nixon administration began to unravel. Attorney General Richard Kleindienst dissociated himself from the investigation because of his friendship with many of the persons involved. Acting FBI Director Patrick Gray III resigned, following the disclosure that he had destroyed records at the behest of White House Counsel John Dean. On April 30, White House Chief of Staff H. R. Haldeman, Special Presidential Assistant John Ehrlichman, Counsel John Dean, and Attorney General Kliendienst resigned. On May 17, Sam Ervin's Watergate Committee began its public hearings. Under the glare of television and vigorous cross-examination, witnesses who had high positions in the Committee to Re-elect the President and the Nixon administration held the nation spellbound by their testimony.

Revelation followed revelation: a $200,000 illegal contribution to CRP by financier Robert Vesco; an illegal burglary of the office of the psychiatrist of Daniel Ellsberg, one of the defendants in the Pentagon Papers case; and, most damaging of all, on July 16, testimony by a former White House aide, Alexander Butterfield, that all of the president's office and telephone conversations had been secretly tape-recorded since early 1971. A battle for the tapes ensued, involving the White House, the Watergate Committee, Judge John Sirica of the U.S. District Court for Washington, D.C., and Special Prosecutor Archibald Cox investigating the Watergate affair under the direction of the new attorney general, Elliot Richardson.

As though this were not enough, on August 2, U.S. Attorney George Beall of Baltimore informed Vice President Spiro Agnew that he was being investigated in connection with accusations of extortion, bribery, and income tax violations. Agnew, as had Nixon, had earned the enmity of the press, intellectuals, and Democrats for his excessive attacks upon them in his campaign speeches. The charges against Agnew originated in his term as governor of Maryland but included acts performed during his current incumbency as vice president. On October 10, Agnew resigned from office and pleaded no contest to the felony of failing to report income on his 1967 tax return. A U.S. district court judge in Baltimore fined him $10,000 and placed him on three years' probation.

Two days later, under the provisions of the Twenty-fifth Amendment, President Nixon announced that his choice to fill the vice-presidential vacancy was Congressman Gerald R. Ford, Republican minority leader of the House of Representatives. By this time, there was also active consideration by the House Judiciary Committee of possible impeachment proceedings against Nixon himself.

At first elated over the troubles of Nixon and Agnew, Democrtic leaders began to have some trepidation about the impact of Watergate on the nation, particularly among its youth and its allies overseas.[11] The youthful disenchantment of the 1960s began to reappear. Opinion surveys were showing a dramatic decline in popular trust-in-government and in political leaders. George Wallace revived his now-familiar charge that "the Washington crowd" needed to be replaced. As Democratic leaders well realized, popular distrust and discontent could be a double-edged sword. The 1974 midterm election would probably tell which way it would cut.

With the United States thoroughly distracted by its internal scandals, foreign adversaries were encouraged to pursue their objectives. Communist military activity in Vietnam, Cambodia, and Laos escalated during the summer months. With most of his time and thought consumed by Watergate, Nixon virtually turned over the conduct of foreign affairs to Henry Kissinger, whom he appointed secretary of state in August.

On October 6, war broke out in the Middle East between Israel and the Arabs. The United States airlifted supplies to Israel; the Soviet Union airlifted equipment to its Arab allies. An oil embargo by the Arab-dominated Organization of Petroleum Exporting Countries (OPEC) was felt at every American gas station as automobiles lined up during the national fuel crisis. Kissinger flew to Moscow in October to dampen down the escalating conflict, but a few days later President Nixon authorized a global alert of all United States military forces in response to a Soviet intention to send combat troops to the Middle East. During November, Kissinger carried on "shuttle diplomacy" among the warring parties and succeeded in arranging a cease-fire. The Middle East situation strained the NATO alliance because the global alert had been called without consulting its members. Congress, nervous about another "Vietnam" in the Middle East, passed a veto-proof limitation on presidential war powers on November 7, requiring the president to report to Congress within forty-eight hours after committing forces to a foreign conflict or enlarging the number of troops equipped for combat in a foreign country.

With an eye to 1974 and 1976, Democrats began to face up to the difficult repairs to be made in their own party and in the reform of the election campaign process. The 1972 national convention had issued a call for a midterm national convention, the first of its kind, to be held December 6–8, 1974, at which party rules, particularly those growing out of the efforts of the McGovern-Fraser and O'Hara commissions, would be codified into a party charter. The site chosen was Kansas City; 2,035 delegates from every state and territory participated.

Under Chairman Strauss's guidance, the national committee devised rules that would minimize acrimony and unnecessary debate. "Issues seminars" were organized to permit free-flowing discussion of the more controversial public policy issues and party rules, for example, the meaning of "affirmative action" to encourage minority representation; the replacement of the winner-take-all primary with a system of proportional representation; disregard of nonbinding presidential primary preference vote results—so-called "beauty contests"—in the selection of state delegations.

In Congress, Democrats made a first attempt in November and December 1973 at enacting a campaign finance reform bill. Watergate findings were the immediate stimulus. More than $50 million had been spent for the Nixon campaign in 1972, most of it from large contributors and a substantial part from illegal contributions by large corporations. According to the reform bill passed by the Senate, 57 to 34, federal matching funds of up to $7 million would be provided to presidential primary candidates who raised at least $100,000 in private contributions. In the general election, presidential nominees would receive a maximum of $21 million in public funds, but private contributions would be prohibited. The measure was seen as correcting the financial balance between Republicans accustomed to large contributions and big-budget campaigns and Democratic dependence upon small contributors and shoestring campaigns. A filibuster by Republican senators and a few southern Democrats, backed by the threat of a Nixon veto, returned the bill to committee.

On February 6, 1974, the House of Representatives almost unanimously granted to its Judiciary Committee authority to pursue an inquiry regarding the possible impeachment of the president. The Senate Watergate Committee promised its full cooperation. As Nixon's taped conversations became public, the president became more and more incriminated. Even Republicans like Senate-leader Hugh Scott, who had staunchly stood by the president, were dismayed after reading or hearing the contents of the tapes. In nationally televised hearings from July 24 to 30, the House Judiciary Committee voted to recommend to the full House three articles of impeachment against Nixon. On August 9, Nixon resigned, the first president to do so, and was succeeded by Gerald Ford, the first president not chosen in a national election. On August 20, Ford named Nelson Rockefeller as his choice for vice president. On September 8, Ford granted the former president an unconditional pardon for criminal acts alleged or potentially alleged.

The 1974 midterm elections were a disaster for the Republican party. Over 60 percent of the votes cast in the races for House of Representatives were Democratic. Democrats gained 46 seats in the House, for a majority of 291; 5 seats in the Senate, for a majority of 62. Four more governorships were added to the Democratic ranks for a total of 36, a number that, together with Watergate, carried implications of particular consequence for the Democratic presidential choice in 1976, according to some analysts.

While a governor may be the focal point of his state's politics, not many state capitals are at the hub of a national communications network as Washington is. . . . Governors are far less dispensable [from their state duties] and geographically mobile than senators. . . . But the governors' inevitable separation from Washington politics may, under special circumstances, redound to their benefit. The moral squalor of Watergate and the horror of Vietnam, for example, cannot be held against them in 1976. Almost any Washington-based politician—no matter how energetically he seeks to avoid association with both—is vulnerable to the charge that he either supported, went along with, or was ignorant of these disasters.[12]

The Census Bureau also had significant observations. Noting the recent decline in voter turnout in both off-year and presidential year elections, the Census Bureau indicated that only in the South had there been improvement in voter participation: from 26.1 percent of the voting-age population in 1962 to 30.2 percent in 1970. The 1970 figure still, of course, left the South below the national norm of 43.8 percent for that off-year election.[13] Among the southerners turning out in increasing numbers were blacks who had begun registering to vote during the 1960s.

A New Spirit

At Kansas City on December 6, 1974, Democrats gathered for their unprecedented midterm national convention, and most were on their best behavior, greeting each other warmly, offering hospitality. But the presence of McGovernites, Wallaceites, the Coalition for a Democratic Majority (CDM), Mayor Daley, blacks, women, young new leaders, and others was bound to stir events to near-boiling temperatures. National Chairman Strauss and the CDM had, during the preparatory meetings of the charter-drafting commission headed by Terry Sanford, endeavored to clarify and soften some of the guidelines of the McGovern-Fraser commission; blacks and reformers walked out of that commission's meetings. At particular issue were the quota implications of such phrases as "reasonable representation" of minorities in the population and the kind of evidence that could demonstrate that "affirmative action" had been taken by a state party to assure minority participation. At another extreme were those Democrats who wished to restore the unit rule and "winner-take-all" primaries. As the principal manager of the convention, National Chairman Strauss had his hands full. "The clash that existed between those who stressed representative democracy and those who insisted on participatory democracy was a basic schism that seemed insoluble."[14]

Reconciliation and the party prospects for 1976, however, prevailed. Strauss negotiated several compromises: the phrase "reasonable representation" was removed; quotas were banned; state parties were required to adopt and implement "an approved and monitored affirmative action program." The charter would go into effect in 1980. Strauss, however, could not prevent some of the oratorical fireworks, particularly between the AFL-CIO's CDM and the new politics labor leaders and their associated groups. The lid had been kept on, but the boiling occurred nonetheless. Democrats were now up against one of their trickiest problems in consensus-seeking: Is participation the same as representation? Is representation the same as representativeness? Who best links the party consensus to the national consensus?[15]

The convention's public policy statements were not much less difficult to compose. There were the Nixon-Ford policies to criticize, and this helped. In futile efforts to thwart the "galloping inflation" that had beset the nation, Nixon had adopted an on-again, off-again program of price controls. On this matter, the Democratic program adopted at the convention called for an across-the-board system of economic controls. Unemployment had been skyrocketing; the Democrats called for a job program. The Arab boycott had been followed by shortages and sharp rises in fuel costs; the Democrats called for a mandatory energy development and conservation policy. It was easiest to agree about Watergate and Ford's pardon of Nixon.

The midterm convention was, of course, a propitious occasion for presidential candidacies to emerge. George Wallace still paralyzed but now actively performing his gubernatorial duties, was off and running. His resources were formidable: the 10 million voters who had supported him in the 1968 election; the nearly 4 million primary voters who favored him in 1972; more than $2 million in campaign contributions raised in 1974 from over 300,000 hard-core followers. On the other hand, Ted Kennedy, the front-runner in everyone's opinion, in a statement that was "firm, final and unconditional," removed himself from the race in September 1974 for obvious family reasons; he was, in effect, the head of the ill-starred Kennedy household, his own and those of his brothers. Hubert Humphrey, now a two-time loser (the election in 1968 and the nomination in 1972), seemed always available but, at this time, uncharacteristically silent. His protégé, Senator Walter F. Mondale of Minnesota, took a brief flyer by announcing his candidacy and then withdrawing in November before the midterm convention. Representative Morris K. Udall, with a longstanding liberal record, made an early entry in November.

Another early entrant was the governor of Georgia, Jimmy Carter. A few days after the midterm convention had concluded its business, Carter announced that he would seek the presidency, enter all state primaries, and seek delegates in nonprimary states. To follow the presidential primary route strategy adopted in the past by Kefauver, Kennedy, and McGovern sounded like an ambitious attempt. Carter was an "outsider" to Washington politics, a reform governor of a southern state, a former naval officer, and a well-to-do peanut farmer in his home town in Plains, Georgia. Few knew him. When the editors of *Democratic Review*, a party-affiliated magazine, during spring of 1975, asked 146 "experienced political observers" to evaluate nineteen announced or potential Democratic and Republican presidential candidates according to the "active-passive" and "positive-negative" scales made popular by Professor James David Barber, the greatest number of "Don't knows"—44 percent—were recorded for Carter.[16]

As 1975 progressed, others joined the fray. Fred Harris announced himself as the "new populist" candidate. Senator Henry ("Scoop") Jackson, generally perceived as organized labor's candidate, came along shortly thereafter, as did Lloyd Bentsen, a Texas insurance millionaire. Terry Sanford presented himself as the liberal southern candidate who would test George Wallace's candidacy in the South. Sargent Shriver, considered by many to be a "stalking horse" for a Kennedy candidacy, announced in September. Pennsylvania's Governor Milton Shapp, the first Jew to become a serious candidate, also threw in his hat. The following month Senator Birch Bayh entered. Frank Church of Idaho and Governor Edmund G. (Jerry) Brown, Jr., of California came in much later. A free-for-all seemed in the making, with several candidates hoping to play either a darkhorse role or become a member of a new Democratic coalition. There were those who were certain that Hubert Humphrey would be the only one who could again stitch together the coalition, but he behaved like the darkest horse of them all—the leading unannounced candidate in the race.

While the midterm convention was going on in Kansas City, other party news was being made in the House of Representatives, where the Democratic caucus was pressing forward major reforms in the system of committee assignments. One ostensive motivation for the changes was the conduct of Ways and Mean Committee Chairman Wilbur D. Mills in his relationship with a Washington striptease dancer. Ways and Means was then the committee that made the principal committee assignments and hence was the source of Mills's great power. A second motivation was the eagerness with which some seventy-five freshman congressmen wished to assert their influence and the skill with which Congressman Phillip Burton of California guided most of them in doing so. The caucus, in one reform, turned committee assignment powers over to the Steering and Policy Committee and also established the policy of barring chairmen of major committees from serving simultaneously as chairmen of other major committees.

The reform mood carried over into the Senate. Three months later, after a two-week filibuster, the Senate modified the filibuster rule. Henceforth, three-fifths of the entire Senate membership (sixty of the one hundred senators) would be sufficient to invoke cloture of debate, rather than the previous two-thirds of those present and voting (a potential maximum of sixty-seven votes) needed.

Meanwhile, President Ford was trying to cope with the affairs of the nation and the aftermath of the Nixon resignation. He saw as his main tasks the binding of political wounds and the reestablishment of the authority of the presidency. In this, his objectives and his performance were compared to Calvin Coolidge's first years in office following the Teapot Dome scandals. Coolidge's rectitude and conservatism—and, as it turned out, Ford's—were the best antidote the nation could have for its recently poisoned public life.

On the other hand, there were events and policies that Ford could not handle, and these became political concerns for the Democratic opposition. By May 1975, the national unemployment rate reached as high as 9.2 percent: economists considered 4 or 5 percent as the level required for "full employment." The annual inflation rate hovered around 10 percent instead of the more usual and manageable 5 percent. Ford met with Soviet leader Brezhnev at Vladivostok to develop guidelines for the SALT II arms control negotiators, but a SALT II agreement failed to be achieved before the end of his term.

In March 1975, North Vietnamese troops began a major attack against South Vietnamese forces in the Central Highlands. The attack became a South Vietnamese rout as troops raced civilians south to safety. On March 29, President Ford ordered U.S. naval vessels to Da Nang to help evacuate refugees. As the North Vietnamese approached Saigon, U.S. planes airlifted medical and military supplies into that city. On April 10, Ford asked Congress for nearly $1 billion in emergency aid for South Vietnam, but the request was turned down. Eleven days later, President Thieu resigned. A week later, Ford ordered the evacuation of all Americans and as many Vietnamese (over 100,000) who had worked closely with Americans as could be carried by U.S. helicopters and navy ships. In nearby Cambodia and Laos, Communist forces also swept to victory. In a feeble gesture to lift American morale, President Ford, on May 14, ordered a dramatic rescue of thirty-nine crewmen of the U.S. container ship *Mayaguez*. Ford's popularity rose sharply but dropped again when it was reported that thirty-eight American servicemen lost their lives in the rescue operation.

Despite these misfortunes, Ford announced on July 8 that he would run for a full term as president, thereby easing Vice President Rockefeller out of the Republican race and contesting the candidacy of former California governor Ronald Reagan. Rockefeller had for many years been one of the few liberal Republicans who could attract Democratic voters, but the Ford-Reagan contest assured that the Republicans would be nominating a conservative to head their 1976 ticket.

A mood of domestic forgiveness and reconciliation began to appear in interesting ways. President Ford inaugurated an amnesty program for Vietnam-era draft evaders and military deserters who applied for clemency by a given deadline. Congress approved a resolution restoring citizenship to General Robert E. Lee, commander of the Confederate Army of Virginia during the Civil War, 110 years after Lee petitioned for the restoration and signed the oath of allegiance. Alger Hiss, whose conviction for perjury in 1950 had been a major steppingstone for Richard Nixon's advancement to the vice-presidential nomination, now seventy years of age, was .

readmitted to the Massachusetts bar by the supreme court of that state. Black Panther leader Eldridge Cleaver, after seven years of self-exile from the United States to avoid murder and parole violation charges, returned, submitted to arrest voluntarily, and expressed his "confidence in the American system of justice."

The 1975–76 presidential "season" evolved against a backdrop of significant global and national events, most of which became, in one fashion or another, grist for the presidential political mill. In Africa, civil war raged in Angola after the Portuguese departed. Soviet and Cuban aid to one side brought United States covert aid to the other, until the Senate, voting 54 to 22, terminated funds for this purpose. In China, Mao Tse-tung and Chou En-lai died, bringing uncertainty to a new era of Chinese-American relations. Perhaps to assure Americans that all would be well, the Chinese government invited the Nixons to make a personal visit to Peking, which they did in February, to the embarrassment of President Ford during the New Hampshire Republican primary.

At the United Nations General Assembly, an Arab-sponsored resolution called Zionism "a form of racism and racial discrimination," and the "infamous act" was denounced by U.S. Delegate Daniel P. Moynihan, a Democrat who later became United States senator from New York. In Spain, Generalissimo Francisco Franco, the longest-lived of the European dictators, died, and King Juan Carlos cautiously began to lead that country toward democratic institutions, legalizing political parties as one major first step. In France and Italy, the Communist party leadership—Eurocommunists, as they began to call themselves—proclaimed their support for democratic institutions and their autonomy from Moscow domination as part of a successful tactic in the Italian elections and in anticipation of the first direct popular election of representatives to the European Parliament in 1979. On Cyprus, the United States did what it could to ameliorate the conflict between the Greek and Turkish populations. In Vietnam, the Socialist Republic of Vietnam was proclaimed on July 2, uniting North and South Vietnam and ending two decades of war.

On the domestic scene, there continued such unpleasant conditions as inflation and unemployment. New York City declared itself on the verge of bankruptcy because of its inability to repay short-term debts and cope with its cash needs. President Ford initially refused to provide federal help on grounds of gross mismanagement, to which New York City's Democratic mayor, Abraham

Beame, took exception. As the price of municipal bonds began to reflect the crisis, the issue became a partisan one. In South Boston, problems of school integration re-ignited the flames of racial tension. In Washington, D.C., a United States Court of Appeals upheld the convictions of John D. Ehrlichman and G. Gordon Liddy for their part in the burglary of Daniel Ellsberg's psychiatrist's office, and memories of Watergate were revived. Congressman Wayne L. Hays, a powerful House leader, admitted having a "personal relationship" with a staff aide, Elizabeth Ray, and resigned from office. The Supreme Court upheld public financing for presidential election campaigns, as provided in the 1974 Federal Election Campaign Act, as well as limitations on contributions, but the Court struck down limitations on spending except when presidential candidates accept federal funds.

From the longer perspective of history, however, perhaps the two most important events of the presidential year were the following. On July 7, President Ford held a state dinner to welcome England's Queen Elizabeth II, who had come across the Atlantic Ocean to help celebrate the two hundredth birthday of its former colony. On July 20, Viking I, a robot craft that had taken eleven months to complete the one-billion-mile journey, landed on Mars and began transmitting photographs of that planet back to Earth.

The Bicentennial year opened with the familiar approach to national disagreement, namely, the presidential nominating races. There were hard-fought contests in both major parties. The confrontation between Reagan and Ford on the Republican side was close and suspenseful; it held press and popular attention more consistently than the Democratic contest. There were so many Democrats running that it was difficult to tell who was a "real" candidate and who was not, or who was ahead and in which states, or, for most of the electorate, to even recognize all of the names.

Despite these difficulties, Democrats sensed a year of victory ahead. The usual rule that incumbent presidents are not likely to be beaten seemed not to apply in Ford's case since he was the first president to be appointed rather than elected. Younger and less-known Democrats were encouraged by the handicaps of the older and more famous Democratic names: Humphrey (two-time loser); Kennedy (Chappaquiddick, a Sherman-type statement on his non-candidacy); Muskie (loser); McGovern (loser); and Wallace (crippled, a party bolter). While these men had the advantages of name-recognition among the voters as well as records of substantial party

247

and public service, they were somewhat worn and tarnished. Rarely had so many Democratic presidential candidates appeared at local party caucuses or run in the presidential primaries as in 1976. Nor had there ever been so many primary elections in which they could run; the number had grown to thirty.

The first surprise came in the year's first delegate-selection tests. In the January precinct caucuses in Iowa, a weathervane state, Jimmy Carter won a two-to-one victory over his nearest rival, Birch Bayh. The press commentators began to look more closely at Carter, particularly since his support in Iowa had come from such a diversity of groups: rural and urban Democrats, Protestants and Catholics, and blue-collar and white-collar workers. However, a few days later, in the Mississippi precinct caucuses, George Wallace beat Carter by a three-to-one margin, thus sharpening the questions which of the two would be the "southern candidate" and whether *any* southern candidate could be elected in a nation that had not elected a southerner to the presidency in more than a century-and-a-quarter. (Lyndon Johnson of Texas was, technically, a southwesterner.) After Iowa and Mississippi, candidates began to drop by the wayside; Terry Sanford and Lloyd Bentsen were the first to withdraw their candidacies.

In the highly publicized New Hampshire primary, Carter won fifteen of the seventeen delegate votes and the greatest number of preference votes. Thereafter, Carter did poorly in Massachusetts, won easily in Vermont, and won again in Florida, which had previously been Wallace territory. The Florida outcome was particularly important in that it indicated that, if there were to be a southern candidate, it would be Carter, not Wallace. If there was any doubt, it was removed when Carter beat Wallace again in Illinois and North Carolina later in March. At this juncture, Bayh, Shapp, and Shriver terminated their candidacies, Jackson's never fully recovered, and Frank Church began his. Although Carter came in third behind Jackson and Udall in the New York primary, he beat both men in Wisconsin and Pennsylvania.

By mid-May, Carter had more than a third of the 1,505 delegate votes needed for the nomination and was 350 votes ahead of runner-up Jackson. Udall and Wallace were in third and fourth places, respectively. Rumors circulated about "stop-Carter" maneuvers. Humphrey's was the most likely candidacy to accomplish this, and he had strong support in the remaining states where delegates were yet to be chosen by caucus or convention. Humphrey was also everyone's second choice. Meanwhile, a new candidate, California's Governor Jerry Brown, stepped into the race, entering and winning the Maryland and California primaries. Brown's last-minute performance was impressive. He received more than 15 percent of all votes cast for Democrats in twenty-seven of the thirty primaries and was runner-up to Carter's nearly 40 percent.

By convention time, however, the nomination was Carter's. Humphrey declined to become a candidate. Udall's 329 convention votes and Brown's 300 were well below the 2,238 received by Carter. After carefully interviewing seven possible vice-presidential candidates, Carter chose Humphrey's colleague, Walter F. Mondale, as his running mate. The Carter nomination culminated nearly two years of active campaigning in perhaps the most arduous pursuit of presidential primary delegate votes in nominating history. Could this southerner beat the incumbent president, who was nominated shortly thereafter by a divided Republican convention?

The evidence consistently pointed to an extremely close election campaign. During September and October, Ford and Carter engaged in a series of three nationally televised debates. The vice-presidential nominees, Robert Dole and Mondale, also had a TV debate that was lively and later thought to be critically helpful to the Carter-Mondale ticket. One major unknown was the Wallace vote. What would the southern and the blue-collar Wallaceites do? Carter's southern origin and Wallace's endorsement helped the Democratic ticket in the South. The AFL-CIO's enthusiastic endorsement and COPE campaign, with its mailing list of more than 12 million trade union members in forty-six states and its 120,000 volunteers in worker neighborhoods, helped bring back large numbers of blue-collar voters.

As election day approached, the Gallup Poll found Ford ahead by one percentage point, 47 to 46, and the Harris Poll found Carter ahead by one point, 46 to 45. Neither polling organization would forecast the outcome. A second major unknown in the contest was the voter turnout; most polling organizations, noting the post-Watergate disenchantment, expected a particularly low rate of participation; many potential voters were either disinterested or ambivalent.

The outcome was indeed close. Carter's 51 percent of the popular vote brought him 297 votes in the electoral college, where 270 were needed to elect. Texas and nearly every state east of the Mississippi River supported Carter; nearly every state west of the

Mississippi went for Ford. Significantly, Mayor Daley failed to deliver Illinois, although he expected to. With the exception of Virginia, every state that had been in the Confederacy voted for their fellow-southerner.

Organized labor was able to deliver a bulging 62 percent of its voting members to Carter; 59 percent of the blue-collar workers voted for the Democratic nominees. The Joint Center for Political Studies estimated that 6.6 million black voters, or 70 percent of those registered, turned out to vote, a turnout that was 12 percentage points higher than in 1972. Of these black voters, from 83 to 94 percent cast their ballots for Carter, the higher figures usually in the South.[17] Carter had apparently drawn the recently registered southern blacks into the electoral process just as Al Smith had the new immigrants in 1928. But overall voter participation for the nation was low, even lower than in 1972; only about 53.3 percent of the eligible voting population troubled to vote.

Ordinarily, in so close an election with so low a voter turnout, the Republicans are advantaged. President Ford obviously believed so when he later quipped, as he delivered his 1977 State of the Union message to Congress, that this was "his last message— *maybe.*" He sounded like a man who would test his voter appeal again in 1980. Much evidence supported his optimism. In about thirteen states with a total of 174 electoral votes, the difference between the two major candidates was 2 percent or less. Eugene McCarthy's third-party candidacy cost Carter four states with twenty-six electoral votes and underscored the Democratic party's vulnerability to third parties.

What Carter and the Democrats had succeeded in doing was to get out the "normal" Democratic voters—union members, blacks, certain ethnic groups, and liberals—in more than their usual number in certain places, that is, the industrial states of the Northeast and the rapidly industrializing and now electorally competitive states of the South and Southwest (Texas, specifically). An unusual number of Carter-Mondale voters cited Walter Mondale's presence on the ticket as a major factor in their decision; ordinarily, the second man on the ticket makes small difference. On the other hand, Carter received only 49 percent of the eighteen-to-twenty-one-year-old vote, a group that usually tends to vote Democratic. These new voters also turned out to vote in the least numbers, perhaps a consequence of the alienation they experienced during the Vietnam and Watergate years in which they were forming their political attitudes. Perhaps, too, as in the cases of women, new immigrants, and blacks before them, the youth vote has yet to be fully incorporated into the national consensus—a familiar challenge for the Democratic party.

Had the New Deal coalition been revived in 1976? Most analysts agreed that the major components had remained in or returned to the fold: organized labor, blacks, liberals, the South, Catholics, and Jews. But the proportions were quite different, for, over the years, the size and solidarity of each component had changed. Union membership had reached a relative plateau, and the more affluent workers were less loyal to the Democratic party. Farmers were fewer, better off, and, as they had been before the New Deal, more Republican. Blacks had increased in numbers, loyalty, and turnout, and this trend was likely to continue, particularly in the South. Liberals, Catholics, and Jews had become more volatile in their party preferences. The South was hardly the Solid South of the New Deal era, with racial demagoguery now disappearing, blacks participating, industry growing, unions organizing, and Republicans winning office. These shifts and changes left Democratic leaders pondering whether or not the time had come for a new examination of the structure of the party's and the nation's consensus and for a new Democratic coalition.

In his inaugural address, President Jimmy Carter sought to reestablish a relationship between the old and the new:

Two centuries ago our nation's birth was a milestone in the long quest for freedom, but the bold and brilliant dream which excited the founders of this nation still awaits its consummation. I have no new dream to set forth today, but rather urge a fresh faith in the old dream.

Ours was the first society openly to define itself in terms of both spirituality and of human liberty. It is that unique self-definition which has given us an exceptional appeal—but it also imposes on us a special obligation to take on these moral duties which, when assumed, seem invariably to be in our own best interests.

You have given me a great responsibility—to stay close to you, to be worthy of you, and to exemplify what you are. Let us create together a new national spirit of unity and trust. Your strength can compensate for my weakness, and your wisdom can help to minimize my mistakes.

Let us learn together and laugh together and work together and pray together, confident that in the end we will triumph together in the right.

10

The Party's Changing Architecture: At the Grass Roots

A POLITICAL organization may have structural traits that define its "basic personality." The traits acquired during infancy may remain as enduring components of "personality" into maturity. Change among trait components may be significant for vitality, adaptability, and success. Applying the psychological metaphor to the Democratic party, one finds that the vitality, adaptability, and success of the party have indeed been related to changes experienced among its many structural components: the types of voters, social groupings, and organized interest groups that have comprised the Democratic party-in-the-electorate; the party's grass-roots organizational units and their rank-and-file workers; the state, sectional, and factional coalitions bringing together the party-in-the-electorate; and the leadership in the party-in-Congress and the presidential party. These structural components make up the architecture of the Democratic party, through which the party has conducted its search for internal consensus and for a winning balance between its internal consensus and the national consensus.

The Party-in-the-Electorate: Voters, Interests, and Issues

According to the doctrine of popular sovereignty, government is an organization established by and conducted according to the will of the people rather than any special group or elite. This doctrine was first articulated in the eighteenth century. The Founding Fathers endorsed it somewhat cautiously; witness the invention of the electoral college as an indirect means for allowing the people of the United States to choose their president. The crucial questions have always been: Who are "the people"? How shall their "will" be measured? Political parties have been the major organizational response to these questions.

In his Federalist Paper Number 10, James Madison recognized that "the people" are hardly a faceless mass of individuals but rather a changing array of social groupings—citizens, farmers, laborers, merchants, co-religionists, etc.—with different social, economic, and political needs and objectives. These group interests, or "factions," as he called them, are politically organized in varying degrees, and their spokesmen or leaders are in constant search of allies to help them achieve their objectives. The allies may be leaders of other organized interests or politicians seeking election to public office. In short, "the people" are individuals in loose social groupings. These groupings become, to some degree, organized interests. Organized interests are groups whose leaders must know how to function in coalition politics.

In a democratic and constitutional society, elections are a principal means for measuring the "popular will." Thus, the design of the electoral system is a major influence upon how social groupings and organized interests will try to get what they want from society and the extent to which they may succeed. For example, a design that calls for majority rule will compel many disparate minority interests to negotiate with each other in order to pool their collective voting strength to achieve the requisite majority. This design rule will, in practice, promote a politics of coalitions and compromises. If the design also calls for freedom of speech and freedom of association, then the society will experience the continual emergence of new social groupings and new spokesmen responding to new conditions and issues. These spokesmen—new and old—are perhaps the principal vehicles of political change as they exercise their roles as discoverers of each new issue, makers of each new coalition, and measurers of each new consensus; the vitality of a democracy rests upon their skills.

The principal difference between an ideological-totalitarian political party and a liberal-democratic party is the capacity of the latter to allow political communication to flow influentially to and through its leadership. Such communication is usually about group needs, demands, and public issues. The needs are articulated by group spokesmen. The demands are usually supported by some evidence of electoral strength. The public issues are usually those demands that are given recognition and priority by office-seekers as they try to construct coalitions representative of the broadest possible consensus. A liberal-democratic party-in-the-electorate is, at any given time, the sum of the political groups and public issues that comprise its working coalition and its electoral support among the voters.

The ideological-totalitarian party, on the other hand, will have none of this. Its ideology requires orthodoxy that stifles the articulation of demands and prevents the framing of public issues in the language of compromise and moderation. A totalitarian party's procedures are exclusionist; only the most faithful, by some test, may belong and only force rather than consent is relied upon to bring "the people" along in the policy directions set by the leadership.

From this perspective, the political experience of the United States has been unique in the extent to which it has evolved its two major parties as distinctively liberal-democratic organizations engaged in an equally distinctive American form of coalition politics. Samuel Lubell's sun-moon analogy succinctly summarizes the experience of the two major parties-in-the-electorate:

> Thumbing back through history, we find relatively few periods when the major parties were closely competitive, with elections alternating between one and the other. The usual pattern has been that of a dominant majority party, which stayed in office as long as its elements held together, and a minority party which gained power only when the majority coalition split.
>
> Our political solar system, in short, has been characterized not by two equally competing suns, but by a sun and a moon. It is within the majority party that the issues of any particular period are fought out; while the minority party shines in reflected radiance of the heat thus generated.[1]

Lubell goes on to observe that the immediate strategy problem for a minority party is to determine which elements of the majority coalition can be split off most readily. In this connection, third parties have special significance because they "shed such penetrating light on the inner torments of the majority party." As one element leaves the majority coalition, another may join that coalition. Realignment goes on all the time. "Each time one majority sun sets and a new sun rises, the drama of American politics is transformed. Figuratively and literally a new political era begins."[2]

The early formative traits of the Democratic party-in-the-electorate may be found in colonial days. From the outset of colonial politics there was a basic clash between the mercantile-financial interests on the one hand and the independent farming interests on the other. As early as 1676 frontier farmers sought a lighter tax burden and greater military protection from the Indians. When the royal authorities in Virginia, for example, failed to respond, farmers supported Bacon's Rebellion. Nearly a century later, when merchants became angry over British commercial and tax regulations, they were, somewhat unexpectedly, joined by farmers long troubled by the same royal tax collectors. This coalition made the American Revolution.

Independence put an end to a period of economic prosperity. Deflation brought depression and a severe crisis for agrarian debtors. The currency of the Continental Congress became worthless. Banking, commercial, shipping, and fishing interests joined together with Federalist party leaders to produce programs for stabilizing the economy and the credit structure. Mortgaged to the hilt, farmers turned to the Jeffersonians for political help and to the frontier for a place to make a new beginning. In choosing the latter, migrating farmers soon ran into western land speculators—and further debt.

This coalitioning of interests prompted Madison to observe in his Federalist Paper Number 10 that "the most common and durable source of faction has been the various and unequal distribution of property. Those who hold and those who are without property have ever formed distinct interests in society." This was the economic situation when Alexander Hamilton proposed to the First Congress the new government's first financial program. The national debt, domestic and foreign, was about $75 million. Hamilton took a sound-money position: pay the debt at full face value and levy taxes that would cover the cost. In other words, establish the government's credit by taxing farmers to pay off securities held by bankers. The Jeffersonians argued for repayment of the debt at its much lower market value. In the end, security-holding creditors made about $40 million on this transaction, at the expense of farmers.

Thus, in the very first years of the Republic, independent farmers, particularly those at the frontiers, became a major component of the Jeffersonian Democratic party-in-the-electorate. When Andrew Jackson embarked upon a crusade against the Bank of the United States and on behalf of cheap credit, he was simply responding to the demands of "normal" Democratic constituencies: farmers, frontiersmen, and debtors.

Jackson also attracted another group in the electorate: urban workers. Changes in state suffrage laws during the 1820s redefined who were "the people" and removed many property requirements for eligibility to vote. This brought urban laboring people into the electoral process in unprecedented numbers. The Jacksonians were able to bring together the farmers of the western frontier and the South and the workers of the cities into a powerful new electoral coalition against the mercantile-financial interests of the Northeast. The persistence of the Jacksonian coalition until 1860, despite farmer defections and the North-South split over slavery, kept together not only the Democratic party but also the nation.

There was also a significant religious dimension in the Democratic party-in-the-electorate during the Jeffersonian and Jacksonian eras. From the beginning, Democratic-Republicans tended to affiliate with the dissident religions: Baptist, Presbyterian, Methodist, etc., all more or less hostile to the established Congregational Church. When Jackson arrived on the scene, his most intensely loyal campaigners and supporters were the Scotch-Irish Presbyterians. By the 1820s Tammany Hall in New York had become an overwhelmingly Irish organization and a pillar of Jacksonian strength. These cores of religious attachment to the early Democratic party later served as magnets that attracted to the party thousands and eventually millions of co-religionists as they immigrated into the American "melting pot."

The collapse of the Democratic coalition was manifest during the divisive national conventions of 1860 and throughout the Civil War. The Democratic leaders of the South, mostly plantation owners, had served as principal leaders in the Buchanan administration; they became, almost to a man, the leaders of the Confederacy. The rest of the party, on the other hand, suffered "the most disastrous loss of leadership ever sustained by a major American party" through the death of Stephen A. Douglas six weeks after the fall of Fort Sumter. As Wilfred Binkley wrote, "No man of Douglas' generation, excepting Lincoln, had been more resourceful in discovering or inventing the formulas that enabled vast aggregations of voters to rationalize divergent interests by means of a common pattern of thought."[3]

Douglas Democrats, led by August Belmont, fell in behind Lincoln's war effort. These were the War Democrats, found mainly in the Northeast and the Middle Atlantic states. Midwestern Democrats, on the other hand, were less enthusiastic about making war against their best customers in the South. These midwestern farmers organized themselves as Peace Democrats. The Peace Democrats found allies among eastern workers, particularly in New York, whose Mayor Fernando Wood was advocating that New York City also secede from the Union. Why, he argued, should workers, who were the principal conscripts for the army, leave their families destitute to go and fight a war to free slaves who would eventually compete for their jobs? With major components of the Democratic coalition—southern plantation owners, eastern workers, and midwestern farmers—no longer willing to give unqualified loyalty to the party, this left organizational leadership largely in the hands of New York bankers and lawyers.

Postwar depression led the agrarian Peace Democrats of the Midwest to become cheap-money Greenbackers. In the eastern financial and manufacturing centers former War Democrats became sound-money proponents favoring payment of all debts in gold specie. The Democratic party remained in this disarray until 1876 when the settlement of the disputed Hayes-Tilden election ended the Republican military occupation of the South and made possible a revival of Democratic organizations in that section. Racism, religious fundamentalism, and agrarian protest soon became dominant themes of southern Democratic discourse as the section's young leaders scrambled to win the support of unhappy farmers.

By the 1890s, the party of Lincoln had become a party of finance, corporations, stock-raisers, lumber interests, manufacturers, older workers, and prosperous farmers. The Democratic party, on the other hand, remained an awkward coalition of southern populists, urban workers, newly arrived immigrants, and, in growing numbers, lower-income, heavily mortgaged western farmers. The agricultural depression of the early 1890s and the panic of 1893 should have brought the usual components of the Democratic party-in-the-electorate running back into the fold. However, Grover Cleveland's policies proved a major deterrent to this homecoming. His demand that Congress reduce tariffs offended workers, manufacturers, and many farmers. His use of federal troops in the Chicago railway strike of 1894 further alienated workers. His sound-money posture, probably arising out of his associations as a corporation lawyer, infuriated the poor farmers of the West and the South, who turned to the Populist party. Mining interests in the silver-producing states also took up cudgels against the gold-standard policies of Cleveland.

William Jennings Bryan came along to appeal, unsuccessfully, to the old Jacksonian party-in-the-electorate, namely, the agrarian debt-ors who had taken temporary refuge in the Populist party, the city workers who were being organized by city machines, the new flood of immigrants from Europe, and the religious fundamentalists of the South and the West. Woodrow Wilson was the beneficiary of Bryan's preparatory efforts at coalition-building. Wilson provided stronger economic cement. The farmers of the South and West were assured a flexible currency through the creation of the Federal Reserve Banking System and the inauguration of rural credit programs. Labor, which had by now become significantly unionized, won employee compensation laws, a precedent-setting eight-hour day for railway train-men, labor dispute mediation machinery, and a statutory assurance, in the Clayton Act, that labor would not be considered an ordinary commodity subject to market price fluctuations. Middle-class consumers, a potentially new component for the Democratic party-in-the-electorate, enjoyed goods at lower prices as a consequence of Wilson's successful efforts to reduce tariffs. Possibly Wilson's most important contribution to the future of the Democratic party-in-the-electorate was his encouragement of labor organization.

The Wilson administration proved to be an interregnum for the Democratic party. It required a depression and the political talents of Franklin D. Roosevelt to put the pieces back together again. The New Deal coalition was a modern version of the ancient Democratic party-in-the-electorate. Poor farmers—shattered by years of agrarian depression and again mortgaged to the teeth—returned to the party of Jefferson. Labor, certain of a growing organizational future in the administration of a Jacksonian heir and a Wilson protégé, added its strength. The new immigrants, having cast their first ballots for Al Smith, stayed with the party. The South, exhausted by poverty and racism, was incapable of any other choice. These were the components of the reunited Democratic party-in-the-electorate that kept Roosevelt in office and made the Democrats the majority party for the next two generations.[4]

During the 1930s, public opinion polls made it possible to test with some exactitude which of the many social groupings were giving their votes to whom. Were the component parts of a coalition really delivering their electoral strength to the party's leadership? Who, for example, liked FDR during his first two terms? According to an analysis by the Gallup Poll, the answer was: 59 percent of the farmers, 61 percent of the white-collar workers, 67 percent of those in the middle-income bracket, 80 percent of those on relief, 68 percent among those under twenty-five years of age. The small number of blacks registered and actually voting in the 1930s shifted almost en bloc from the Republican to the Democratic party. The foreign-born, who started with Smith, stayed even more overwhelmingly with Roosevelt, according to the poll findings.[5]

Some of the group characteristics of the Democratic party-in-the-electorate from Truman to Carter are revealed in the degrees of group support for Democratic presidential candidates reported in Table 6.

Several generalizations may be drawn from these and other data elsewhere:

1. Men and women tended to have comparable party and candidate preferences. Women, however, liked Harry Truman and Hubert Humphrey particularly well in 1948 and 1968, respectively. (Could it have been Truman's respect for Bess—"the Boss"—and Humphrey's for Muriel?) Conversely, women were cool toward Stevenson in 1952 and 1956. (Could it have been Stevenson's recent divorce?)

2. After 1948, nonwhites, particularly blacks, were increasingly supportive of the Democratic nominees, reaching a 94 percent peak in 1964 but declining slowly thereafter. A similar tendency was observable among Spanish-speaking groups.

3. The less formal education the voter had, the more likely he or she would vote Democratic. This factor was associated with the tendency of the poor, blacks, and manual laborers to be Democrats.

4. Voters in the professions and business were Democrats to the extent of only about one-in-three but were attracted in more than usual numbers to Kennedy, Johnson, and Carter.

5. White-collar workers were weakly attached to the Democratic party and fluctuated widely in their support. Manual laborers, that is, blue-collar workers, have been more strongly Democratic than white-collar workers but also have fluctuated, particularly when they voted for Eisenhower in 1956, Wallace in 1968, and Nixon in 1972. Union membership makes a difference, and this is clearly indicated by the 66 percent for Kennedy in 1960, the 80 percent for Johnson in 1964, the 62 percent for Carter in 1976, and the contrasting 46 percent when the AFL-CIO declined to endorse McGovern in 1972.

6. Farmers have been one of the most fickle of Democratic support groups. When in trouble, as in 1932–1936 and 1948, farmers have tended to return to the Democratic party; otherwise, they prefer Republicans.

TABLE 6
Group Support for Democratic Presidential Tickets, in Percentages, 1948–1976

Group	1948	1952	1956	1960	1964	1968	1972	1976
Sex								
Male	53	47	45	52	60	41	37	52
Female	58	42	39	49	62	45	38	52
Race								
White	55	43	41	49	59	38	32	48
Non-white (mainly blacks)	64	79	61	68	94	85	87	83
Education								
College	30	34	31	39	52	37	37	42
High School	55	45	42	52	62	42	34	54
Grade School	65	52	50	55	66	52	49	58
Occupations								
Professional & Business	28	36	32	42	54	34	31	43
White Collar	47	40	37	48	57	41	36	51
Manual Labor	67	55	50	60	71	50	43	59
[Union Members]	74	61	57	65	73	56	46	62
Farmers	66	33	46	48	53	29	38	43
Religion								
Protestant	53	37	37	38	55	35	30	46
Catholic	64	56	53	82	75	61	48	55
Jewish	—	—	—	82	90	83	66	68
Age								
18–21	—	—	—	—	—	—	50	49
Under 30	62	51	43	54	64	47	44	56
30–49	54	47	45	54	63	44	33	51
50 and older	48	39	39	46	59	41	36	48
Income								
Under $2,000	63	55		Under $7,000			62	62
$2,000–2,999	66	46		$7,000–15,000			35	57
$3,000–3,999	52	47		Over $15,000			18	50
$4,000–4,999	47	49		Over $20,000			—	38
$5,000 up	32	34						
Nationalities								
Irish	—	47	—	—	55	—	47	—
Italian	—	60	—	67	75	50	42	—
Polish	—	50	—	68	74	—	—	—
German	—	40	—	—	50	—	—	—
Spanish-speaking	—	—	—	85	90	87	73	—

Sources: Compiled from numerous sources. Different survey organizations use difference socioeconomic categories when reporting their findings, and, often enough, the same organizations will change categories or introduce new categories as new social groupings gain political prominence. For example, the Spanish-speaking and eighteen-to-twenty-one-age categories have become important only in recent years.

Also, income categories, due to inflation and the redistribution of wealth, have changed over the years. For these reasons, a number of the figures in Table 6 are estimates extrapolated from available data in relevant socioeconomic categories. The sources include: Robert Reinhold report, *New York Times*, November 4, 1976; Mark R. Levy and Michael S. Kramer, *The Ethnic Factor* (New York: Simon & Schuster, 1973); Richard L. Rubin, *Party Dynamics* (New York: Oxford University Press, 1976); Gallup Poll report, *New York Times*, December 8, 1968, and December 14, 1972; Harris Poll, *Newsweek*, November 2, 1964; Hugh A. Bone, *American Politics and the Party System* (4th ed.; New York: McGraw-Hill, 1971).

7. There can be little doubt that Catholics and Jews have been overwhelmingly Democratic in the past, but this attachment has been weakening in recent years, mainly as a consequence of their growing affluence. Jews are also particularly sensitive to candidate policy positions regarding Israel's fortunes in the Middle East.

8. The youngest and the oldest voters have been among the least reliable Democrats, possibly because they have been the most likely stay-at-homes on election day.

9. As expected, the poor have tended to be Democrats, but they, too, as we shall see, have diminished in number and have tended to be the most frequent nonvoters.

10. The great loyalty of the Irish, Italian, and Spanish-speaking groups of earlier years appears to be melting away.

Another method of identifying the group components of the Democratic coalition has been developed by Professor Robert Axelrod. Combining size of group, rate of turnout of the group in relation to nationwide turnout, and party loyalty of the group in relation to degree of loyalty in the entire party-in-the-electorate, Axelrod has computed a measure of the actual magnitude of the "contribution" made by each group to the Democratic and Republican parties in each of the presidential elections from 1952 to 1976.

As compiled in Table 7, the evidence confirms much that is found in Table 6 and reveals other significant tendencies.

1. The contribution of the poor (P) to the Democratic coalition has dropped sharply, from 28 percent in 1952 to 7 percent in 1976. The decrease, according to Axelrod, is due almost entirely to the dwindling size of the group, that is, due to their gains in real income. (This finding points up one of the fundamental anomalies of Democratic policies aimed at redistributing more of the total national wealth to the poor, namely, that such policies, if successful, may diminish the electoral strength of the party.)

2. The contribution of blacks (B) has risen strongly, largely be-

TABLE 7
Group Contribution to Democratic Coalition, 1952–1976

Year	Percentage Contribution					
	P	B	U	C	S	CC
1952	28	7	38	41	20	21
1956	19	5	36	38	23	19
1960	16	7	31	47	27	19
1964	15	12	32	36	21	15
1968	12	19	28	40	24	14
1972	10	22	32	34	25	14
1976	7	16	33	35	36	11

P = poor (income $3,000/year).
B = black (and other nonwhite).
U = union member (or union member in family).
C = Catholic (and other non-Protestant).
S = South (including border states).
CC = central cities (of 12 largest metropolitan areas).

Source: Robert Axelrod, "Where the Votes Come From: An Analysis of Electoral Coalitions, 1952–1968," *American Political Science Review,* Vol. 66 (March 1972), No. 1 pp. 11–20. Also, ibid., Vol. 68 (June 1974), No. 2 p. 718, and Vol. 72 (June 1978), No. 2, p. 623. The size (s) of a group is the proportion of all adults of voting age who are members of that group. The turnout (t) of a group is the proportion that voted in a given election. The loyalty (l) of a group to a certain party is the proportion of the votes of that group which are cast for that party. The national turnout (T) is the proportion of all adults who vote. National loyalty (L) is the proportion of all votes that go to the given party. The contribution (C) of a group to the electoral coalition of a party equals the proportion of all the party's votes that come from members of that group. The formula: $C = stl/TL$.

cause black turnout has doubled since 1952, particularly during the Kennedy and Johnson years.

3. Labor (U) has always voted more Democratic than the national average, but the relative size of this group in the total voting-age population has been declining gradually. In 1968, the low percentage—28—reflects the large-scale defections to Wallace. While the fall-off in the contribution of union members to the Democratic coalition has been substantial—from 38 percent to 33 percent, labor's support continues to be a major factor in party success.

4. The Catholic (C) contribution has been relatively large, with 1960 exceptionally high because of Kennedy's nomination. The weakness of this source of support, however, is evident from its fluctuation and its drop to 34 percent in 1972.

5. Although the South (S) has tended to become more competitive and less solidly Democratic, the southern contribution has been

between one-fifth and one-fourth of all Democratic votes in part because of the increase in voting participation by southern blacks. The 1960 contribution was exceptionally high probably because of Johnson's presence on the national ticket and in 1976 because of Carter.

6. Significant for the future of urban party organization is the continued decline in central city voters' (CC) contribution to the Democratic coalition. It is in the central cities that the poor, the less educated, the less skilled, and those least likely to vote tend to live.

Axelrod describes the Republican coalition, on the basis of similar data, as follows:

The Republican coalition can be thought of as consisting of the overlapping majorities that are the precise complements of the minorities that describe the Democratic coalition. This makes the Republican coalition a combination of the nonpoor, whites, nonunion families, Protestants, northerners, and those outside the central cities.[6]

Several coalition problems for the Democratic leadership emerge from the information in Tables 6 and 7. Any Democratic coalition in the near future must rest heavily upon the sturdy foundation of organized labor and organized blacks. But what must the party do to better represent, hence be more attractive to, other groups, old and new? One *old* group has been the farmers. Perhaps this challenge will resolve itself as more farms become corporate agribusinesses and more farm workers become unionized. Perhaps the most difficult *new* challenge is the recruitment of the very young into the Democratic party-in-the-electorate. This may require innovative policies and organizing approaches. A similar observation may be made about the oldest voters. In the case of the poor, with the disappearance of urban machines and the continued redistribution of national wealth through welfare and other means, this group is likely to continue to decline as a source of Democratic electoral strength.

Much of what happens in the party-in-the-electorate depends upon the preferences and skills of group leaders as they develop coalitions within the parties. There is substantial evidence that in the last three or four decades the coalitions comprising the two major parties have come to represent persistently distinct points of view on most public issues. The more influential and the more active the members, that is, the respective sets of party leaders, the more dissimilar have they become in their policy views. The educated and the affluent of the citizenry are most likely to be among these leaders, and such people have become a large component of the electorate. Of the 140 million voting-age Americans in 1972, for example, about 35 million had attended college, of whom 12 million were Republicans, 11 million Democrats, and 12 million Independents. Significant differences in issue orientations existed among these college-educated party leaders and may be expected to sharpen future policy debates and tighten coalitional alignments.[7]

Within the party, liberal Democrats tend to see the tempo of social and political change speeding up. They, therefore, urge their fellow-partisans to design creative new programs of public policy capable of meeting new conditions. Conservative Democrats, on the other hand, tend to point to the traditional interests of the party's constituencies and argue that serving these interests also serves the party. How rapidly is the Democratic party-in-the-electorate, American society, and the world at large actually changing? Is it true, as Theodore Lowi suggests, that "the most important difference between liberals and conservatives is to be found in the interest groups they identify with"?[8] As the twenty-first century approaches, what new grass-roots electoral coalitions should the Democratic party represent, and with what policies?

Grass-Roots Organization

Until recent years, local organization—in the election precincts and wards of the cities and in the counties of rural areas—has been one of the distinguishing structural characteristics of the Democratic party. The principal drive for local organizing has been from local group or community leaders rather than from state or national leaders. The principal motivation of local leaders has been to mobilize a body of loyal and "deliverable" local votes with which to negotiate with higher echelons of party leadership at the state and national levels. The names assigned to these local organizations have varied over the decades: caucus clubs, committees of correspondence, Sons of Liberty, Tammany societies, democratic societies, city machines, county rings, etc. Their prevalence supports the view that Democrats are inveterate grass-rooters, a people-organizing party.

Immigration and Migration as Factors

Local Democratic organizations have had much people-organizing to do, given the migratory lives of so many of those citizens who have been principal sources of support for the party: the poor, the laborers, those belonging to dissident churches, the downtrodden, the immigrants, and, more recently, the blacks. This task has fallen most heavily upon party organizations in the cities, the city "machines." Rather than a single "melting pot," the United States may be more accurately characterized as a collection of urban "melting pots" where immigrants from abroad and migrants from within, particularly from the farms and the South, have, respectively, been Americanized and brought into the civic process of the nation. Local Democratic party organizations have been the chief civic educators and electoral mobilizers. The massive dimensions of this task may be better appreciated by examining the population and immigration data in Table 8.

TABLE 8
Population of and Immigration into the United States*

Period	Total Population	Immigration for Period
1776–1820	9,638,453	250,000 est.
1821–1830	12,866,020	143,439
1831–1840	17,069,453	599,125
1841–1850	23,191,876	1,713,251
1851–1860	31,443,321	2,598,214
1861–1870	39,818,449	2,314,824
1871–1880	50,189,209	2,812,191
1881–1890	62,979,766	5,246,613
1891–1900	84,371,985	3,687,564
1901–1910	102,370,018	8,795,386
1911–1920	118,107,150	5,735,811
1921–1930	138,439,069	4,107,209
1931–1940	150,621,231	528,431
1941–1950	154,233,234	1,035,039
1951–1960	179,323,175	2,515,479
1961–1970	204,765,770	3,321,477

*Population is for last year in each period.
Source: 1972 World Almanac, pp. 148–49, 289.

The land mass north of the Rio Grande on the North American continent has been a magnet for human settlement for more than thirty thousand years. Early Indians came to it over the land bridge from Northeast Asia to Alaska and, by the time of Columbus's discovery of the continent, they are estimated to have numbered ten million. The approximately four million non-native population of the United States at the time of the writing of the Constitution had, of course, descended from the early settlements of northern and western Europeans in Virginia and Massachusetts and from the importation of slaves. Most of the Europeans were English, German, Scotch, and Irish, of Protestant faiths. One of the great ironies of America's past is the fact that at the time of the signing of the Declaration of Independence, about 22 percent of the population in the new land of freedom consisted of enslaved blacks from Africa.

Immigration became a mass movement after the 1840s, consisting mainly of Irish escaping the potato famine in Ireland and Germans fleeing poverty and revolution in their homeland. The Irish crowded into the cities of the East Coast. The Germans continued on westward. Most of these new immigrants belonged to the Catholic Church. Democratic city machines were hard put to organize, provide services to, maintain order among, and Americanize in time for the next election these waves of humanity.

Another upsurge of immigration came between 1880 and 1920, mainly from southern and eastern Europe: Italy, the areas of the old Austro-Hungarian Empire, and Russia. This included Catholics and Jews. On the West Coast, the importation of Chinese laborers began to make a difference in that population's composition. It was during this period that the United States began to enact immigration quotas and exclusion laws. Yet, to this day, the United States is looked upon as a land of refuge, and immigrants still come to escape the pogroms of dictators, the devastation of war, or the poverty and famine of the land of their birth. A "brain drain" continues to bring persons of talent and training. More recently, the numbers of illegal and unrecorded Spanish-speaking immigrants, particularly from Mexico and other Latin American countries, has reached into the millions: over six million in 1976, according to official estimates. In sum, the United States has admitted more immigrants than any other nation, 45,154,053 since 1820 when immigration data was first included in the census. This has been a large number of people, and a high proportion became—although they did not always remain—Democrats through recruitment by the party's grass-roots organizations.

The immigration statistics do not cover the great waves of internal migration that also had great consequence for party organization at the local level. The westward movement filled the frontiers and still continues; California became the most populous state in the Union in 1964. Movement from the farm to the city has been inexorable. The United States began as a colonial nation; only six of its cities had more than 8,000 population. It is now a nation with twenty-six central cities, each with more than 500,000 and each central city at the heart of a larger metropolitan area. The farm population was 95 percent of the nation's people in 1800 but only 6 percent in the 1960s. From the end of World War II to the end of the 1960s, southern blacks moved by the millions to northern cities. Between 1950 and 1970, some thirty-four million whites moved from central cities to suburbs. In recent years, the migration of blue-collar workers to the South as it industrializes has increased dramatically, not to mention the movement of older citizens seeking the warmer climes of the "southern rim." All of these internal migrations have had substantial impact upon party politics and have kept local party leaders busy recruiting new neighbors into old organizations.

"Highly organized urban political parties are generally conceded to be one of America's distinctive contributions to mankind's repertory of political forms."[9] The federal structure of American parties has been characterized by weakness at the higher levels of organization and strength at the bottom levels. This local strength has been made possible, typically, by a disciplined local party hierarchy led by a single executive (the "boss") or a unified board of directors (the party's local central committee). This organization has effectively controlled nominations for public office and thereby has controlled local public officials. Very often the party leadership has no public or even party office, operating through a system of informal relationships. The "machine's" leaders, officials, and loyal voters were held together by the distribution of available material rewards (job patronage, contracts, financial contributions, food, personal services, etc.) and through a variety of psychic rewards (friendship, ethnic or personal recognition, recommendations, etc.). Only in recent decades has this "old style" of local organization given way to newer forms: Democratic clubs, union locals, ethnic organizations, or, most often, no organization at all.

A number of factors have promoted Democratic urban organization. The poor and the uneducated are always the least politically active, hence more needful of and more responsive to direct neighborly contact such as provided by the older-style city Democratic machines. Democrats are usually more numerous than Republicans. They are also less wealthy, making it more practical for

Democrats to concentrate on organizing "people-power" rather than soliciting "money-power." Unable to buy or rely upon the mass media to make their case, Democrats have preferred to communicate through organization. This emphasis upon grass-roots organization and localism has stimulated such typical Democratic policy postures as home rule and states' rights, which in turn have in the past provided philosophical justification for promoting party organizational strength at the local level.

Democratic Societies, Early Machines, and Tammany Hall

Local partisanship was in evidence in the colonies. The caucus clubs of the colonies became the patriotic societies and committees of correspondence of the Revolution. When the proposed Constitution for a Federal Union divided popular opinion in 1787 and 1788 between Federalists and Antifederalists, organized party-like coalitions at the state and local levels, as we have seen, were already a familiar part of the new nation's political life.

In the period 1789–1792 local party organization was uneven in the nation at large. But colonial and revolutionary electioneering experience brought relatively trained hands to the task of building parties capable of naming slates and delivering electoral majorities. In some places, notably New York and Pennsylvania, committees of correspondence continued to nominate and campaign. In other places, however, the absence of organization led to large numbers of candidates for any particular office. For example, in Boston in 1792 there were as many as twenty-seven candidates for only five positions as presidential electors. Sometimes political leaders were unable to make their ticket-building selections stick; candidates denied nomination simply ran on their own or ran as candidates of the opposition. To bring these election situations under control was an important objective of patriotic and Tammany societies between 1792 and 1800.

At first many of these societies were disinterested in nominating slates or managing election campaigns. Their initial motivation was to discuss the issues that deeply divided the new nation and, frequently, to express opposition to Federalist policies. The first such society to appear was organized by recent immigrants, German-Americans in Philadelphia: the German Republican Society. On April 13, 1793, the *National Gazette* announced this society's formation.[10]

Late in May 1793, a Norfolk and Portsmouth Republican Society appeared in Virginia. A third society, organized soon after, became one of the most influential; the Philadelphia Society, located at the seat of national government. This society enrolled many national leaders as members and aggressively urged the formation of similar societies in every section of the nation. In many ways, the Philadelphia Society was the Boston Caucus Club reincarnate.

Eleven other societies were organized during 1793, twenty-four during 1794, and three during 1795. These local organizations were numerous in states where the Democrats would later have their most active grass-roots organizations: Pennsylvania (nine societies), Virginia (five), South Carolina (five), New York (four), New Jersey (three), and Kentucky (three).

A more fraternal kind of organization—the Society of St. Tammany (after Tamanend, a chief of the Delaware Indians who was known for his love of liberty)—was also emerging during this period, particularly in New York, Virginia, Pennsylvania, Rhode Island, North Carolina, and one or two other states. By 1794, the Tammany Society in New York began to work beyond its original fraternal objectives, turning frequently to debates on current public issues and engaging in electioneering activities.

Certain characteristics of these post-revolutionary popular organizations were directly traceable to the revolutionary committees of correspondence and Sons of Liberty: the practice of associating together for public action; the extensive use of committee forms of organizational structure; the key role assigned to committes of correspondence. So effective were these American political action societies that the English began to imitate the organizing technique during the 1780s and, not long after, the French Jacobin clubs followed suit.[11]

The societies of Philadelphia were the first to argue that "political parties" were legal and essential instruments of equilibrium in the rough seas encountered in the pursuit of liberty. President Washington did not share this conception. In his message to the Third Congress on November 19, 1794, he—undoubtedly on Alexander Hamilton's advice—went out of his way to condemn the activities of "certain self-created societies," implying that these socieites had been responsible for the Pennsylvania Whiskey Insurrection.

In general, the societies were city or county political association. They usually held monthly meetings in courthouses and other public buildings. With the decline of the outdoor mass meeting as a nominating body, the societies more generally began to assume nominating functions. All had committees of correspondence which kept in touch with societies in other counties and states.

During most of this formative decade (1790–1800), the Democratic-Republican societies focused their electioneering efforts upon winning local and congressional offices. These efforts produced a nominal Democratic-Republican majority in the House of Representatives in 1793, but, as indicated earlier, party support of Madison was initially quite unreliable. By 1795, however, the Democratic-Republican majority became better disciplined, particularly as Democratic-Republican interest in capturing the presidency increased.

Organization in many localities took on a modern appearance. For example, Aaron Burr, a Tammany leader, introduced the device that came to symbolize modern organizing proficiency: the card index of voters' names. The closeness of the presidential vote in 1796 underscored the importance of grass-roots organization. Virginia, Pennsylvania, New York, New Jersey, and Maryland were then the principal states in the electoral college. In the 1796 election, 71 votes went to Adams, 68 to Jefferson, and 59 to Pinckney. A shift of less than 100 popular votes in Pennsylvania would have put Pinckney instead of Jefferson into the vice-presidency. Again in 1800, a change of 214 popular votes in New York City, where Tammany had been particularly effective in its campaign work, might have turned the election against Jefferson.

After Jefferson became president and as the Federalists began to disintegrate, local Democratic-Republican groups persisted in their grass-roots efforts. Systematic observation of party preferences among the local citizenry became part of their standard operating procedure. A letter from Alexander Wolcott, collector of the Port of Middletown (Connecticut), to fellow-partisan William Plumer described the technique.

Have each county leader appoint a manager for each town in his county, wrote Wolcott. Each town manager should appoint district managers who would list the names of all male freemen, taking pains to divide this list into "decided Republicans," "decided Federalists," "doubtful." These district managers, continued Wolcott, were to get all eligible freemen to take the necessary oath at registration time and furnish these freemen—particularly the friendly ones—with "votes" (the prepared paper ballots of that day). Each town manager was to be assigned dates for forwarding their estimates of voter preferences to county managers who, in turn, were to consolidate and forward them to the state manager. In addition, every manager was to be active in the circulation of campaign literature and, on election day, in reporting his own estimates of local election returns.[12]

Between 1800 and 1830 several factors profoundly influenced the shape of local party affairs. Despite the War of 1812, recurring depressions, and incessant frontier warfare, the country was, in general, experiencing an era of peace and prosperity. Population growth and migration to the West kept older eastern city and county party leaders preoccupied with the loss of loyal voters and the need to recruit new voters. Ohio's population multiplied eleven times, Mississippi's seven times, and Tennessee's three times, a consequence of the purchase of the Louisiana Territory from France. Western politicians could appreciate that all rifle-bearing men were equal before the hardships of the frontier. Hence, the new western states, as rapidly as they became organized, extended the vote—that great leveler—to all white men of legal age (twenty-one years, in the Anglo-Saxon tradition).

These egalitarian suffrage practices (although still excluding women and most of the black and native American population) soon filtered eastward where workingmen's groups and fraternal associations among the foreign-born—most of Democratic-Republican leaning—began to press for removal of property ownership and tax payment as suffrage requirements. By 1830 universal white manhood suffrage was radically altering the electoral environment in the older states. This was reinforced by the introduction of the penny newspaper (newspapers had been previously been expensive upper-class media), a resurgence of local Democratic-Republican organizations (many of which had become dormant during the Era of Good Feeling), and the appearance of the muddy-booted "mob" at the inaugural of General Andrew Jackson, the popular hero who was to transform the presidency into an agency of the mass electorate. Jackson, as we have seen, attracted the newly enfranchised voters into the Democratic party, giving older city and county party units another lease on life and the less experienced Democratic organizations at the frontiers large infusions of new blood.

To speak of city political "machines" and "bosses" is to conjure up images of Tammany and its grand sachems. Tammany Hall has been the most famous "machine" of all. Rare has been the reform candidate for city office who has failed to condemn his opponent as a "Tammany boss." Yet, after his long career of tilting at the machine-driven windmills of urban politics in the early years of this century, the great muckraking newspaperman Lincoln Steffens conceded that no political system functions without organization or leaders who can understand the special brokerage requirements of a democratic politics. On this basis, he was willing to concede that urban bosses and machines may merit general recognition as important contributors to American self-government.

The Tammany Society was initially a fraternal and benevolent association of enlisted veterans of the American Revolution. The Order of the Cincinnati, on the other hand, attracted officer veterans. In time, the Cincinnati tended to support the Federalist cause whereas Tammany became part of the Jeffersonian coalition. Aaron Burr, its first "boss," led Tammany to its first great political triumph in national politics when it carried New York for the Jefferson-Burr ticket in 1800, to the consternation of the dominant Hamilton organization.

Over the next five decades the Tammany organization grew, as did New York City and the nation. Tammany's alliance with Van Buren helped carry New York for Jackson in 1828. The society's bitter factional divisions during the 1840s and 1850s reflected the growing national schism between North and South. Nonetheless, as wave after wave of immigrants arrived from Europe, they found that the great American "melting pot" seemed to be located mainly in New York City, with Tammany grand sachems stirring together the foreign-born ingredients. In 1868, for example, "Boss" William Marcy Tweed had printed (by a company of which he was president) some 100,000 applications for citizenship and 69,000 certificates of naturalization. Tammany-appointed judges certified thousands of new citizens a day at times, nearly all "obligated" to Tammany Hall.

In the 1860s Tammany suffered the Tweed Ring. William Marcy Tweed and his henchmen captured control of the organization in 1863, and, through it, control of the New York City government. The Tweed Ring's graft and theft from the city treasury cost New York an estimated $75 million. Tweed's ostentatious expenditure of the loot added public insult to his skulduggery; for example, a reported $700,000 wedding for his daughter.[13] Within Tammany, however, John Kelley, Richard Croker, and the Scannell brothers fought a steady battle to free the organization and the community from Tweedism. By 1871–1872 they were joined by many eminent wealthy Democrats who had previously remained aloof, including Samuel J. Tilden and Abram Hewitt.

In the aftermath of Tweed, Tammany went through several years of diminished influence. But under the direction of "Honest John" Kelley and his successor, Croker, the organization reestablished its influence in the rapidly changing New York political environment. Croker's biographer, writing in 1901 of the achievements of his subject, was moved to declare: "Tammany Hall, as a 'machine,' is perfect."[14]

The "pyramid of Tammany power" at the close of the nineteenth century consisted of some 90,000 party workers and more than 220,000 voters in a total population, including children and noncitizens, of more than a million. There was a captain for each city block, another captain for each voting precinct, a leader for each of thirty-five assembly districts, a five-member finance committee selected by the leaders, and finally, the chairman of the finance committee, that is, the boss. This was the organizational structure that spread from Tammany Hall on Fourteenth Street, a million-dollar edifice, into thirty-five assembly district clubhouses, each valued at approximately $100,000. The expressive language of Croker's biographer describes some of Tammany's operations *circa* 1900:

To conduct a campaign Tammany Hall spends about three hundred thousand dollars. This money is given out the night before an election; each "leader" having his share. The wage and the number of election workers are fixed. There are to be ten men in each voting precinct to wear the badge and get the people to the polls. These receive five dollars each or fifty dollars to a precinct or over seventy thousand dollars for this one item alone covering the entire town. Then there are carriages to bring the lame, the halt, and the blind. There are halls to rent, and fireworks to purchase, and stands to put up, and trucks to hire for "orators" in the three or four weeks of a canvass. Told and counted, the over-all expense clambers to three hundred thousand dollars. This sum is not hard to get. Contributions come from every quarter; some of them secret and not caring to be known.

. . . . There are hundreds to whom a part of their subscriptions is returned as "too large," or "more than the organization needs."

Following an election, what money is left is generally given to a charity or to some cause of worth. Within the past four years there have in this manner gone, to the poor of this town, forty thousand dollars; to the cause of Cuba, forty thousand dollars; almost as much to the Galveston sufferers; almost the same sum to rear a monument to Parnell, and to pay the mortgage on the Parnell estates in Ireland and save them to the family of that dead liberator. Tammany keeps no books; there's no way of dis-

273

covering who gives or how much; the funds are banked in the name of a treasurer who acts as secretary to draw checks and aid the work of the finance committee.

This is the money, and in a sense, the military side of Tammany Hall. There is still another, and it is this latter which makes it well-nigh impregnable in local affairs. Tammany is a political organization one day in the year; it is a charitable, benevolent, fraternal organization three hundred and sixty-five.[15]

It is in the latter role that we see the boss in his function as a broker. In an era when employment agencies and union hiring halls were rare and the United States Employment Service nonexistent, unemployed laborers by the hundreds could be found applying for work every morning at the doorstep of their Tammany captain. The Tammany leadership was geared to refer these unemployed to builders, contractors, and nearly every other business enterprise in the city. Satisfaction was expected in the form of competent job performance from the Tammany referrals and regular contributions from the employers. Tammany could do other things for cooperating builders, contractors, and other business enterprises. Its influence in the city's administrative departments could facilitate petitions of one sort or another, favor a Tammany contractor's bid, allocate public funds and credit in a manner favorable to friendly interests, provide police protection, and so on.

Tammany also rendered service to countless persons facing minor penalties in the city's police courts. A Tammany representative was usually present to pay the small fine. In gratitude, the petty criminal, escaping imprisonment, would presumably "vote right" at the next election. Nor was this a haphazard procedure in which an obligated citizen might renege or forget to vote; the records of the city courts served as a reckoning book for keeping track of those who had become politically obligated.

When well-led, Tammany could also channel the expression and resolution of community dissatisfactions. The machine was always sensitive to the complaints of the disorganized, the underprivileged, the unemployed, and the newcomers. The boss who knew his business would always be out in the field ready to greet some newly organized community interest. If business leaders or the wealthier taxpayers registered serious dissatisfaction with the high cost of local government, an astute boss would either retrench or remind them of the even higher costs of riots, unemployment, vandalism, and public relief to the needy.

A Sampler of Bosses and Machines

The "honor roll" of Democratic bosses is filled with the names of men who were able to maintain and operate the governments of major urban communities during periods of otherwise unmanageable growth and change and in the absence of other strong leadership. There were: William Marcy Tweed, John Kelley, and Richard Croker of New York; Edward Flynn of the Bronx; James Michael Curley of Boston; Fred Ludin, William Hale Thompson (ostensibly a Republican), Anton J. Cermak, and Richard J. Daley of Chicago; Martin Behrman of New Orleans; George Cox of Cincinnati; Thomas Pendergast of Kansas City; Frank Hague of Jersey City; Abraham Ruef of San Francisco; Edward Crump of Memphis; and others. Bosses were "bad" when the civic costs of their operations became onerous. Machines were left unmolested when they charged a "fair price" for their services.

In the quaint language of Richard Croker's biographer, the cities and the nation derived great good from the much maligned machines of the nineteenth century.

It [the machine] is in perpetual arms political; and it acts as coastguard of American institutions. The "machine" makes captive the ignorant, the anarchistic, and the unrepublican, as he lands. It ties him hand and foot with its discipline and makes him harmless. As a suppressive influence, moving for public order and to the subjection of what else might be a mob spirit and rise to become those small first gusts of violence which unchecked conflate as riots, the "machine" is to be extolled.

In either the theory or the ethic of politics the "machine" cannot find defense; in the practice of politics, and peculiarly in cities, the "machine" cannot find dispense. That is because both theory and ethic deal with man as he should be, while practice deals with man as he is. And hence the "machine".[16]

In most respects, city machines of the twentieth century were very much the same as their nineteenth century antecedents. The following tells briefly about some of these.

Boston. Democratic politics here was for generations rooted in its ward leadership; a single city-wide boss never emerged. Until the late 1920s the two most powerful organizations were the Hendricks Club of the Eighth Ward, for forty years dominated by Martin Lomasney, and the Tammany Club, through which rose James Michael (Jim) Curley. Sometimes as allies, more often as competitors, and always in shifting coalitions with lesser ward organizations, these two wards gave Boston and Massachusetts Democrats whatever cohesion they could achieve until the 1940s. From these organizational roots came such party eminences as Maurice Tobin, the Fitzgeralds, their descendants the Kennedys, John McCormack, and others.

Memphis. Edward Crump rose to the top of Memphis politics as part of a reform movement in 1903 and remained there for more than half century. The pillars of Crump's winning coalition were the city's long-resident blacks and a small but cohesive community of affluent immigrants and their heirs. Unchallengable in Memphis where he was four times mayor, Crump was allied with a tough country machine—the Sheriff Birch Biggs's gun-slinging organization—in eastern Tennessee which enabled him to dominate that state's politics until the end of World War II.

Unions, reformers, and war veterans were bringing down one boss after the other during the 1950s. In the case of Tennessee, World War II brought back to that state a wave of politically conscious middle-class veterans as competent with guns as the infamous Biggs Machine. The New Deal and the Fair Deal also left a trail of local young liberals. For example, the emergence of Estes Kefauver as a presidential prospect in 1952, over Boss Crump's objection, was evidence of a new era. The Crump organization was forced to retreat to its home base in Memphis by the mid-1950s, where it remained until the death of the boss himself.

Jersey City. In 1897, a twenty-one-year-old lad named Frank Hague won his first election as constable of Jersey City. In a city rife with political gangs and rough election-day methods, Hague rose to be mayor by 1918, elected his first governor in 1919, and by 1925 had a 100,000-vote bloc in Hudson County with which he could frustrate all attempts to overthrow him. He held sway until his influence was ended by labor unions and a coalition of other New Jersey Democrats.

In the late 1940s, Hague ran into the rising influence of the New Jersey Congress of Industrial Organizations (CIO), one of the most successful of labor's vote-getting organizations. Hague was also confronted by an alliance of hostile county and regional leaders in New Jersey. At the same time he suffered a loss of allies in the national party, then under the leadership of President Truman. Hague's regime had become one of the most flamboyant in party history and, for the citizens of Jersey City, the most costly (on a per capita tax basis) in the country. New Jersey Democrats devoted the 1950s to the isolation and elimination of the Hague machine.

Chicago. During the 1920s, the "Windy City" was a scene crowded with gangsters (Al Capone), corrupt business magnates (Samuel Insull), and the purchasable machines led at different times by Republican Mayor William Hale Thompson and Democratic boss George E. Brennan. Brennan inherited the Cook County Democratic organization that had been built up by Roger C. Sullivan during the decades between 1890 and 1920. Relentless rivalry within the Democratic party, particularly after 1910, permitted the Republicans to win several local elections. During the 1920s, however, two Democratic leaders pulled together a winning coalition: the Kelly-Nash machine. Edward J. Kelly was chief engineer of the Chicago Sanitary District. Patrick A. Nash, long associated with Roger Sullivan and George Brennan, was in the sewer contracting business. Both men prospered from their contracts for the disposal of Chicago's wastes.

Before the end of the 1920s, a reform climate emerged in Chicago. The man who held the principal reins of the Democratic organization at this time was a Czech-American named Anton J. Cermak, who masterfully developed coalitions among the city's many nationality groups—Polish, German, Russian, Italian, Swedish, Irish, Czech, Austrian, Lithuanian, and Greek—which won him the mayor's office in 1931. Cermak was killed in an assassination attempt upon President-elect Franklin D. Roosevelt in 1933, leaving the city's Democratic leadership again entirely in the hands of Kelly and Nash. Kelly became mayor. Nash took the job of Cook County party chairman. The Democratic ward leaders in most of Chicago's fifty wards became aldermen. By the mid-1930s, some thirty thousand organization people were on the city and county payrolls.

Patrick Nash died in 1943. The aging Mayor Kelly promoted Colonel Jacob Arvey into the county chairmanship and Arvey began actively to direct party affairs. Eager to modernize the party's image, Arvey recruited a businessman, Martin Kennelley, to succeed Kelly as mayor in 1947. Arvey also sought out, nominated, and helped elect Adlai E. Stevenson and Paul H. Douglas as governor and United States senator, respectively, in 1948. As his director of the Illinois Department of Finance, Governor Stevenson appointed the former minority leader of the Illinois Senate, Richard J. Daley. A lawyer and Cook County leader since 1935, Daley succeeded Arvey as Democratic county chairman in 1953. Meanwhile, Mayor Kennelley's administration had acquired a reputation for purity and inaction.

Defeating Kennelley in both the primary and the general election in 1955, Daley, as mayor, began to give Chicago a unique combination of old-style machine politics and new-style reform.[17] A scandal in the police department, for example, was handled by appointing a University of California professor of criminology as superintendent of police. A decade's immigration of southern blacks, which put unprecedented strains upon the city's housing, educational, and employment facilities, was met with some $400 million in housing projects and $500 million for jobs in superhighway construction. Racial tensions were minimized by the party's assiduous attention to the large-scale population shifts. Republicans and Democrats alike regularly fell in line behind the Daley banner. In 1975, Daley, an anachronism by some standards, was elected to his sixth term in the mayor's office.

Daley's influence in Democratic presidential politics began to manifest itself during the 1950s when he was a sturdy supporter of Adlai Stevenson. It was in 1960, however, that Daley demonstrated his special mix of new- and old-style politics. Personally favoring Kennedy, Daley nonetheless wondered how the electorate, particularly Protestants, would take to the young Catholic from Massachusetts. Other city Democratic organizations, usually led by Irish or Italian Catholics, also speculated about the religious issue. The final test of this problem came in the West Virginia primary. When Kennedy beat Humphrey in this predominantly Protestant state, Daley promptly came out for Kennedy, and other city leaders quickly followed suit. But nomination was not enough in this close contest between Vice President Nixon and Senator Kennedy. In the electoral college count, the Illinois vote was decisive, carried by a few thousand votes in Chicago gathered in late and under dubious circumstances. The Republican National Committee considered but rejected a plan to call for a recount.

In contrast, later presidential election years were unfortunate for Daley. Humphrey's defeat in 1968 has been in large part attributed to the Chicago "police riot" against thousands of youthful antiwar demonstrators outside the Democratic national convention hall, witnessed by millions over television. In 1972, Jesse Jackson's challenging delegation was seated and Daley's ousted by the McGovern forces. In 1976, despite assurances to Carter, Daley was unable to deliver Illinois to the winning presidential ticket, nor was he able to elect most of the state Democratic ticket. It seemed as though this was "Boss" Daley's "last hurrah," and indeed it was. A few weeks later, at the age of seventy-four, the last of the city bosses died as he did the rounds of party and civic functions. With him went an American political genre.

New York. The Tammany Hall story, as we have seen, is the classic case. After a century-and-a-half of famous bosses—Aaron Burr, William Marcy Tweed, John Kelley, Richard Croker, Charles F. Murphy, George W. Olvany, and others—the Tammany organization was never again the same after a fusion ticket swept Fiorello LaGuardia into the mayoralty in 1933. A colorful Republican progressive while in the House of Representatives, LaGuardia gave New York City its most sweeping political reorganization in decades and, not surprisingly, formed a warm alliance with New Dealers in Washington while doing so.

Technically, Tammany Hall was the New York County (Manhattan) Democratic organization. So long as New York County remained the most populous and the richest of the city's five boroughs, Tammany was the kingpin of the city-wide Democratic machine. But as population surged into Brooklyn (Kings County) and the Bronx (Bronx County), the shifts produced challengers to Tammany's hegemony. During the New Deal–Fair Deal period, the most influential of these challengers were Frank V. Kelly of Brooklyn and Edward J. Flynn of the Bronx (national party chairman from 1940 to 1943).

One Tammany boss, Carmine S. DeSapio, merits examination as an example of the vicissitudes of party reform at the local level. A "new style" boss during the 1950s, DeSapio had risen through New York County Democratic politics during the 1940s, his ascendancy reflecting the emergence of Italian influence in a party organization that had long been considered an Irish preserve. Although frequently charged with having underworld connections, DeSapio, after assuming leadership in 1949, put together a thoroughly reformed Tammany. He cut down the number of committeemen, backed election reform legislation, attracted growing numbers of blacks and Puerto Ricans into leadership positions, set up rent-control clinics, and otherwise conducted an impressive public service operation. Most of these efforts helped DeSapio promote the candidacy of his choice for mayor, Robert Wagner, who was elected in 1953.

By 1958 DeSapio had achieved sufficient statewide influence to put forward what was predominantly his own slate of nominees for state office, including support for the incumbent Governor Averell

Harriman. The ticket, however, went down to defeat in November, and DeSapio's place in the party's leadership was an uneasy one thereafter. Three years later he was not able to mobilize enough support in his own district to win reelection as party committeeman. He suffered a similar fate when he made another race for committeeman in 1963. DeSapio's defeats, it should be added, were at the hands of a reform candidate of the new Democratic club movement. Modern political conditions in the cities, particularly those arising out of the New Deal, were finally catching up with party organizations at the local level, making their survival impossible in the old style that nurtured them or the new style that sought to modernize them.

The Last Hurrah

When the New Deal arrived, numerous city machines were thriving in various parts of the nation: Frank Hague in Jersey City, James Curley in Boston, Ed Crump in Memphis, Tom Pendergast in Kansas City, Ed Kelly and Pat Nash in Chicago. It was the New Deal, however, that created the very social and economic institutions that soon led to the demise of most of these local organizations. An expanded civil service system eliminated job patronage. Federal welfare services eliminated the need for local party charity. Organized labor began to operate the local registration and election efforts that had been the work of party ward organizations. Public education and a growing economy had created an urban middle class less easily organized or led than the uneducated and needy immigrants and laborers of old. The exodus of this middle class from the cities to the suburbs greatly complicated the matter. Underneath was the underworld; a generation of organized crime's involvement in local politics was finally exposed during the 1950s.

Organized Crime. In the United States more than in any other nation the apprehension of criminals is the responsibility of local governments. As a consequence, city machines were able to be at hand to bring the petty criminal under obligation to it by bailing him out, paying his fines, or providing legal counsel. Petty criminals, individually or in gangs, have always been an all too common urban phenomenon. Cities often are unable to provide adequate police protection, leaving nationality and other urban groups to arrange their own self-protection. Cities, crowded with unemployed and unskilled workers in need of money and other resources, tend to be the loci of the theft and other small-time illegal activities. Local politicians, as community managers, can hardly ignore such elements in their constituencies, particularly during eras when elections are themselves occasions for fraud and violence.

In the twentieth century, particularly during the Prohibition era, crime became highly organized. Statewide and national gangs emerged. Criminal syndicates took on the organizational character-istics of large corporate holding companies. Before long, local branches of syndicates, local parties, and local governments were thoroughly entangled with each other. Mayor Jimmy Walker of New York City, for example, symbolized the rapprochement. The dapper "Jim" represented the high life of the city during Prohibition and oversaw a complex coalition of Tammany politicians, city officials, and syndicate criminals. In many other communities, too, party grass roots were overgrown with criminal weeds. For example, in 1927, Al Capone contributed $250,000 to the campaign chest of Chi-cago's Bill Thompson, a Republican. In the 1940s, Frank Costello controlled and financed the activities of Tammany's central execu-tive committee. In return for such munificence, local public officials were expected to arrange for light or selective police enforcement of certain laws, mediate and moderate gang wars, and provide con-tract and other economic opportunities to criminal enterprises.

The repeal of the Eighteenth Amendment in 1933 put the un-derworld in search of other profitable activities. The largest oppor-tunities came in supplying such illegal services as gambling and such goods as narcotics. Lesser enterprises involved auto thefts, jewel thievery, kidnappings, murders, etc., not to mention the in-timidation of businesses by racketeers. During the prosperous 1950s, according to some estimates, as much as 10 percent of the national income was going to organized crime, most of whose ac-tivities required political protection.

Since law enforcement was primarily a local government func-tion, it was often difficult for even virtuous city machines to stay "clean." Responding to popular demands for action against orga-nized crime, Senator Estes Kefauver of Tennessee launched a Senate investigation that dramatically revealed underworld operations not only in major cities but also in the nation's small towns and middle-sized communities. According to the findings of the Kefauver Crime Committee, criminals entered local politics in the following typical ways: (1) by direct bribery of law-enforcement officials; (2) by enlisting, through campaign and election support, important political leaders willing to protect criminal activities or aid the advancement of gang interests; (3) by bringing law-enforcement and other public officials directly into the criminal business organization. The Kefauver Committee found organizational links between the Chicago syndicate of Tony Accardo, Jacob Guzik, and the Fischetti brothers and that of Frank Costello, Joe Adonis, and the Lansky brothers in New York; both were coordinated by the Mafia organization.

Local party organizations were thoroughly shaken by the investigation, even in those instances where city machine leaders were themselves fighting crime. The Kefauver Committee published its reports in 1950 and 1951 and by the late 1950s local crime commissions were established in scores of cities. The crime investigations subverted the efforts of numerous city machines to reform themselves and win public confidence. New-style "bosses" disappeared, as did the machines they tried to repair.

Patronage and Welfare. Job patronage and welfare services were long the life blood of local party organizations. New Deal programs and agencies eventually drained away this source of organizational nourishment. Federal relief administrators such as Harry Hopkins and national party leaders such as James Farley managed public job and welfare resources of unprecedented size and local impact. Local bosses could perhaps still wheel-and-deal with construction contracts, petty criminal cases, and some community development programs, but their long-time control over jobs and welfare was soon a lost treasure. As federal government agencies took over local welfare functions, civil service employment requirements for employment followed and job patronage became a thing of the past.

Organized Labor. The New Deal gave unprecedented encouragement to union organization. As a consequence, labor, like other organized interests, developed a sharpened concern for party politics and election outcomes. Wages and working conditions, labor leaders discovered, were inextricably related to the general costs of education, medical care, credit, food, housing, and so on. And these costs were profoundly influenced by public policies. Electing friendly policy-makers to the presidency, Congress, and local offices became a major preoccupation of organized labor.

Prior to the 1950s the basic labor approach to politics was nonpartisan: "Reward our friends, and punish our enemies," regardless of party. But as the number and strength of union locals grew in many communities and as aging party machines declined, union officials found that they could perform many of the activities—registering voters, helping candidates campaign, raising funds, getting voters to the polls—ordinarily carried on by the parties. Unions began to adopt one or another of the following political strategies, depending on local conditions: (1) aid the campaign of friendly candidates, with money, publicity, and volunteers; (2) where it could operate as a balance-of-power influence, throw its resources to the party or candidate that makes the best bid; (3) challenge the party regulars in the primaries; (4) engage in a year-round take-over of party positions and organs; (5) develop alliances with other groups in order to influence party decisions.[18] At times, in the absence of precinct and ward party organizations, union locals were the sole representatives of the Democratic party interest.

We have already noted to what extent Harry Truman owed his election in 1948 to the concerted campaign efforts of the trade unions. Labor's role continued to grow during the 1950s and was a particularly important source of support for Kennedy and Johnson in the early 1960s. However, during the latter decade it became evident that union leaders were able to deliver relatively fewer and fewer labor votes. By 1968, significant numbers of workers were following George Wallace into a third party. McGovern's presidential nomination in 1972, over labor opposition, was further evidence of labor's somewhat diminished influence within the national party.

At the 1974 Democratic midterm convention in Kansas City, one AFL-CIO spokesman warned that the party "will go down to division and ruin" if labor's interests continue to be ignored. However, it seemed no longer clear what and whose these interests were. Blue-collar workers, teamsters, and other union rank-and-file did not seem to be following the older leaders of labor. A younger leadership, usually in "activist" unions, was pushing to the forefront while older leaders held sway in long-established organs such as the Committee on Political Education (COPE) or the Coalition for a Democratic Majority (CDM).

Another significant recent development from the point of view of grass-roots political organization has been the emergence of public service employee unions as influential activist groups in local politics. An estimated thirteen-to-fourteen million public service employees work for local, county, and state governments in the United States. More than a million are members of the AFL-CIO's largest union, the American Federation of State, County, and Municipal Employees. Others are organized by police, firefighters, and teachers unions. Public employee unions have already assumed a major role in the politics of local and state governments, particularly on issues involving taxation and the financing of public agencies. A Coalition of American Public Employees (CAPE) was organized in 1972 to support the McGovern candidacy for president.

Club Movement. In the 1950s the Democratic club movement had many of the impulses and characteristics of turn-of-the-century reform movements. Both were constituted by citizens of somewhat better education and income and both were anti-machine. The clubs differed from the earlier movements, however, in their commitment to operate *within* the party organization rather than trying to influence party politics from outside. The contemporary Democratic clubs, once organized, sought official recognition within the formal structure of the Democratic party. While the clubs have felt free to endorse any candidate they wish for party nominations, they have remained committed to work for whichever Democratic nominee is chosen. Club members have characteristically given principal attention to ideological controversies, often discussing public policy issues longer and louder than most older party regulars could find bearable. Nevertheless, the party has given the clubs a regular place within the organization, in effect, legitimizing insurgency and reformism as party functions.

As National Chairman Stephen A. Mitchell pointed out in his book about the club movement, the concept of the neighborhood political club goes as far back as the early days of the Republic.[19] In California, by 1954, neighborhood clubs throughout the state joined to form the California Democratic Council, which endorsed state candidates, took stands on issues, and campaigned actively. By 1957 there was a Democratic Federation of Illinois. In New York, there was the Committee for Democratic Voters that defeated DeSapio in 1959. Other significant club movements emerged in Michigan, Kansas, Pennsylvania, and Colorado.

As the citizenry becomes increasingly educated and affluent, its interest in political participation also increases. These citizens often tend to deride the inclination of party regulars to compromise policy positions, avoid philosophical discussion, and concentrate on the less ideological chores of election administration. Clubs appear to thrive principally when recruiting new participants. Regulars, on the other hand, frequently thrive precisely because of a *lack* of popular participation. Mitchell described the situation in these words:

Put in its simplest form, if a county chairman can keep the number of active party members down to say, one hundred, he can probably distribute enough favors to keep these one hundred beholden to him and insure his re-election. If he expands the active membership to two hundred, his difficulties increase; he may run short of favors, discontent may grow, and factions of the disappointed may develop to challenge his leadership. The larger the organization, the greater the menace. Thus the temptation to keep active party membership low and controllable is very great. The aging process is accelerated by this exclusiveness, which brings a shrinkage of political participation.[20]

The Democratic club movement, then, has been a grass-roots attempt to develop new modes of participation for new kinds of participants, incorporating reformism directly into the party structure. The club movement may also prove to be a method for regularizing the development of an important form of subgroup within political parties, namely, factions. A systematically organized factionalism may well be for the vitality of party what systematically competitive parties have been to the vitality of the nation.

In general, the disappearance of the boss and the machine may be something less than a blessing. The widespread urban riots of summer 1967, for example, led President Johnson's National Commission on Civil Disorders to observe:

Specifically, the needs of ghetto residents for social welfare and other public services have swelled dramatically at a time when increased affluence has diminished the need for such services by the rest of the urban population. By reducing disproportionately the economic disability of other portions of the population, particularly other ethnic urban minorities, this affluence has left the urban Negro few potential local allies with whom to make common cause for shared objectives. The development of political alliances, essential to effective participation of minority groups in the political process, has been further impaired by the polarization of the races, which on both sides has transformed economic considerations into racial issues.

Finally, these developments have coincided with the demise of the historic urban political machines and the growth of the "city manager" concept of government. While this tendency has produced major benefits in terms of honest and efficient administration, it has eliminated an important political link between city government and low-income residents.[21]

Such recent developments in the cities and the growth of the cities generally seem to call for the invention of new kinds of city "machine" capable of reviving the local people-organizing functions of the Democratic party.

Chasing the Mobile Voters

The ailments of local and state party organizations have, as noted earlier, been aggravated by massive internal migration. About 20 percent of the American people currently move from one residence to another each year. In the mid-1970s this amounted to about 42 million persons, including children. Of these, some 6.8 million moved from one state to another, another 6.5 million moved from one county to another, and over 28 million moved within the same county, usually between precincts and wards. Of the 42 million movers, some 28 million were over-eighteen adults, that is, potential voters. It has been a major responsibility of local party organizations to keep track of these mobile citizens.

Local party leaders will testify to the organizational drain caused by keeping up with arrivals and departures of resident voters. Further, the reduced cost of travel from one part of the nation to another, the comprehensive coverage of events provided by the national media, and the willingness of citizens in one part of the country to help fellow citizens politically in other parts contribute to the growing impact of nonresident "outsiders" upon local politics. It is even becoming fashionable for party leaders in one part of the nation to take up residence and run for office in another.

One consequence of this increasing mobility is an end to local political isolation. Local politics in one place cannot remain untouched by the events of nearby or, for that matter, remote communities. What happens in Selma, Alabama, has consequences for party politics in New York, Chicago, and San Francisco, and vice versa.

Another consequence has been a less stable partisan complexion in the cities. "Democratic cities" are fewer. One of the great "silent" issues confronting managers of urban redevelopment, for example, is the impact their decisions may have upon the voting composition of the redeveloped areas. If redevelopment policy produces high-priced dwellings for high-income voters, Republican voters are likely to live where Democrats lived before. On the other hand, if racial and other minorities continue to flock into the cities, whole urban communities may, as so many did in the 1960s, become disaffected political ghettos.

Thus, mobile voters, a high proportion of whom are Democrats, have become an organizational problem for local leaders in a way that their nineteenth century counterparts rarely experienced. In the "old days," when immigrants or farm workers came to the city, the newcomers sought out urban relatives and friends, and they came to stay. Precinct captains could soon know who and where they were. Today, however, there are fewer precinct captains, more citizens on the move, and greater anonymity and disconnection all around. Not until voter registration becomes as simple as dropping a postcard into the mail or simply appearing and identifying oneself at the polling place will party workers be able to keep up with the heavy traffic of mobile voters.[22]

Nationalizing the Grass Roots

The urban machines were still enjoying their heyday when the New Deal arrived. The machine politicans, one after the other, have since uttered their last hurrahs, but it is not clear what or who shall take their place. The nationalization of party organization, the spread of primaries, and the residential mobility of voters have complicated the search for new forms of grass roots organization.

Structural change also goes on among the state party agencies, spurred by the demands of primary election systems, new requirements of national convention delegate selection and participation, new standards for legislative apportionment, and more closely contested general elections. Whence will come new shapes and vitality for the state organizations? How will the party manage its affairs in the state legislatures, the governors' offices, and the offices of United States senators? What future role will the state parties play in the ever-changing federal structure of the party and the nation?

From the point of view of political parties generally, local politics in the United States is in particular disarray. The reformers and progressives of the first half of the twentieth century succeeded in making local elections "nonpartisan" and city managers the chief executives of "clean" municipal administrations. Nonpartisan contests for local offices, however, all too often have led to low voter turnouts, and those who did vote were not much deceived about the partisan backgrounds and affiliations of the candidates for whom they voted. What was most affected and weakened was party organization.[23]

Weakened party organization at the local level has had a number of debilitating consequences for community life. The informal neighborly social network provided by earlier precinct and ward organizations has withered. Their place has only in part been taken by more formal, costly, and forbidding social agencies. It is now more difficult for a citizen to voice a grievance, seek help, or find political friends within walking distance of his or her residence. Civic duty, patriotism, and general civic education are no longer the tutoring responsibilities of a nearby precinct captain. Perhaps most serious is the absence of local party agencies capable of identifying, recruiting, and giving civic responsibilities to natural leaders in the community, a lack that has often been cited as a cause of ghetto riots, crime, and other urban maladies.

John and Robert Kennedy were particularly disturbed by the triple-headed problem of urban blight, nonparticipation by the poor in the electoral process, and disintegration of local party organization. Their responses were still in gestation when President Kennedy was assassinated. What did emerge as the Democratic response was President Johnson's "war on poverty," particularly the Community Action Program (CAP). CAP was designed to put federal funds into a wide range of projects in urban slum areas in an attempt to rehabilitate the areas, bring the poor into the political process, and provide opportunities for ghetto leadership to emerge. Without the guiding hand of party loyalty or accountability, however, CAP opportunities and resources were all too often exploited by street gangs (the Blackstone Nation in Chicago, for example), radicals not particularly interested in strengthening the two-party system or the American political process, and untrained program administrators.[24] Local party organization was hardly a beneficiary of the Community Action Program, as the report of the National Advisory Commission on Civil Disorders (Kerner Commission) testified. In fact, CAP was perceived by many local party leaders as a direct challenge to themselves and their friends in city hall, that is, in the phrase of Daniel P. Moynihan, "para-governments" with Washington connections.

Another response to local political disorganization has been the "Little City Halls" concept. Initially, but unsuccessfully, attempted in New York City. Little City Halls have since been established in more than a hundred municipalities across the nation, the largest of which has been Boston.[25] Essentially, a Little City Hall is a "miniature replica" of the mayor's office. It is located in trailers, offices, and storefronts in residential communities throughout the city. Boston's twenty-two wards, for example, are serviced by seventeen Little City Halls. From five to ten city staff are stationed in each Little City Hall to provide such services as consumer protection and rent control information, voter and Selective Service registration, property and auto excise tax collection, notarization and copies of official documents, translation and interpreting, visitations to nearby nursing homes and similar institutions, and whatever emergency help a local situation may require. Shades of the party clubhouse! Outlining the reasons for the success of Little City Halls in Boston, Mayor White warned:

> To be meaningful and to really fill the need for local representation, decentralization [by creating Little City Halls] must be *political* and it must conform to the existing power structure of a given government. It serves no purpose to provide an urban neighborhood with genuine legislative representation if ultimately the city legislature wields little innovative political power. Similarly, it does little good to set up Little City Halls if the mayor is powerless to satisfy local needs.[26]

A third approach to the problem of debilitated local politics has been revenue-sharing, those blocs of federal financial grants-in-aid to state and local governments. Within certain constraints, these revenues may be spent for purposes and according to procedures set by local government officials. Approximately thirty-eight thousand jurisdictions across the nation are eligible for the $30.2 billion to be distributed over a five-year period.

The consequences of revenue-sharing for local politics are not yet clear. It apparently has done little to provide resources for party organization except where party organization is already strong. There has been a tendency for incumbent officials to favor using the new source of funds as the basis for reducing local property taxes, which favors Republican-leaning middle- and higher-income property owners. Democrats have preferred to administer revenue-sharing through specific programs, particularly those favoring lower-income citizens, rather than through bloc grants. The basic anomaly of the revenue-sharing approach is that it has some of the appearance and consequences of political decentralization yet reinforces a relationship of dependency between local and federal governments.

A fourth response has been a renewed interest, particularly among Democrats, in returning to partisan local elections. As the heat of the anti-machine movement cools or is forgotten, the advantages of party slates on the local ballot are once again noticed: the availability of organized political friends at the neighborhood level; the prospect of greater interest and turnout in local elections; the opportunity to hold a party organization as well as particular candidates accountable for what happens in local government, and so forth. Further, "nonpartisanship" has not always been synonymous with "purity of politics." A return to partisan local elections, however, is likely to be long in coming and at an uneven pace. It will undoubtedly continue to be preferred by Democrats more than others and is likely to favor Democrats where it does occur.

A fifth possible approach to the rehabilitation of Democratic party organization at the local level would call upon the Democratic National Committee to develop stronger ties to and services for local party clubs, candidates, and associated groups, possibly through the new types of congressional district organization discussed above. Computer technology has already made possible the information management of such closer local-national relationship, and, in fact, has already been exploited by private campaign service organizations. Drawing upon telephone books, party registration lists, city directories, and other public informational sources, these campaign organizations have compiled on magnetic computer tapes the names, addresses, telephone numbers, and, often, party preference, age, religion, and certain political opinions of tens of millions of citizens. From these lists, it has been possible to print address labels, personalized letters, "walking-lists" for local vote canvassers, fund-raising appeals, and sample ballots for all voters. One observer was led to comment as follows about the 1974 election campaigns:

A machine possibly wrote you this past fall to request your vote. If it was well done, it looked like a personal letter from the candidate, with his signature at the bottom. And it focused so precisely on the particular issues that are important to you that you might have sworn the candidate had read your mind.[27]

Such services made available by the Democratic National Committee to local candidates nominated or endorsed by the Democratic organization would undoubtedly strengthen overall party influence. Such information could also be useful in reviving and serving precinct, ward, congressional district, and other types of local party clubs. It is estimated that eight or nine known facts about a citizen—party, stand on issues, place of residence, etc.—enable a candidate or a computer to write about three hundred different "personal" letters to that citizen. Rather than depersonalizing politics, however, the computer may enable party candidates and officials to know and appeal to voters in a much more personally relevant way.

Such ties between national and local party organizations are likely to take place long before the end of this century, with profound consequences for strengthening party organization at both levels, particularly as it becomes easier to communicate with candidates, party officials, and party workers as well as voting citizens. As mobilizers of the electorate, parties cannot help but find strength in knowing *each* of the grass roots—even those that get uprooted and moved around a bit.

A Decline in Party Loyalty?

In recent years, Democratic party fortunes have been increasingly subjected to a triple-threat voting tendency in the party-in-the-electorate: independence, nonvoting, and ticket-splitting. It has been a simple faith among Democrats that they are the party of the poor and the average person, of whom there are greater numbers than the rich and the elite. If this were the case, Democrats would win all the elections. This is obviously not the case. Under the Democratic label are many Independents who frequently cross party lines, many nonvoters, and many who split their tickets.

There are several ways of ascertaining the party preferences or leanings of voters. One is the voter's self-description at the time of registration to vote. Another is self-classification when asked by opinion pollsters. Another is by actual voting record ("For which party did you vote in the last election for such-and-such office?"). A fourth is by attitudes toward certain issues: Democrats are presumed to be favorable to an activist role for government in economic and social problems, more willing to expend public funds, and interventionist in foreign affairs while Republicans are presumed to be more passive, cautious, economy-minded, and nationalist. Of these methods, self-classification has been the one most regularly and reliably used by pollsters. The findings of one polling organization are presented in Table 9. The questions asked: "Generally speaking, do you usually think of yourself as a Republican, a Democrat, an Independent, or what? (If Republican or Democrat), would you call yourself a strong or not very strong (Republican/Democrat)? (If Independent), do you think of yourself as closer to the Republican or the Democratic party?"

The proportion of the electorate identifying itself as "Independent" has almost doubled, from 22 percent in 1952 to 41 percent in 1974. Of these, between 8 and 13 percent have been Independents who lean toward the Democratic party, a generally larger proportion than Republican-leaning Independents. At times, the rise of Inde-

TABLE 9
Party Identification by Self-Designation, in Percentages, 1952–1974

Survey Date	Democrats		Independents			Republicans		Don't Know	Size of Sample
	Strong	Weak	Dem.	Indep.	Rep.	Weak	Strong		
Oct. 1952	22	25	10	5	7	14	13	4	1,614
Oct. 1954	22	25	9	7	6	14	13	4	1,139
Oct. 1956	21	23	7	9	8	14	15	3	1,772
Oct. 1958	23	24	7	8	4	16	13	5	1,269
Oct. 1960	21	25	8	8	7	13	14	4	3,021
Nov. 1962	23	23	8	8	6	16	12	4	1,289
Oct. 1964	26	25	9	8	6	13	11	2	1,571
Nov. 1966	18	27	9	12	7	15	10	2	1,291
Nov. 1968	20	25	10	11	9	14	10	1	1,553
Nov. 1970	20	23	10	13	8	15	10	1	1,802
Nov. 1972	15	25	11	13	11	13	10	2	2,705
Nov. 1974	18	23	13	20	8	12	6	*	1,528

*Less than 1/2 of 1 percent.

Source: Based on Warren E. Miller and Teresa E. Levitin, *Leadership and Change: The New Politics and the American Electorate* (Cambridge, Mass.: Winthrop, 1976), Table 2–1, p. 36.

pendents seems to be at the expense of the Republican party, whose proportion of self-identifiers fluctuated between a high of 29 percent in 1956 and 1958, Eisenhower years, and a low of 18 percent in 1974, the Watergate period. The Democrats have held fairly steady, fluctuating between a high of 51 percent of the electorate in 1964, following the Kennedy assassination, to a low of 40 percent in 1972, the year of the McGovern insurgency.

Lest Democrats assume that they have a safe two-to-one margin of support in the electorate, two other facts need to be emphasized: (1) There are more Democratic-leaning than Republican-leaning Independents, as noted above, who are readier to swing back and forth between the parties. (2) The tendency to stay at home on election day is a more virulent civic disease among Democrats and Democratic-leaning Independents than among those identifying with other parties. How reliable is a self-declared Democratic voter who tends to switch parties on election day? What good is the vote of a self-declared Democrat who fails to get to the polls?

In registering to vote, an essential first step in electoral participation, fewer Democrats than Republicans get themselves registered. In 1974, the Gallup Poll found that, whereas 81 percent of those who identified themselves as Republicans had registered to

TABLE 10
Voter Registration, in Percentages, 1974

Party Identification	Registered	Not Registered	Don't Know
Republicans	81	18	1
Democrats	73	25	2
Independents	62	37	1
National	71*	27	2

*Cf. Census Bureau report of 77 percent registered eligible voters in 1968, 72 percent in 1972, and 67 percent in 1976. U.S. Bureau of the Census, *Current Population Reports*, Series P-20, No. 322.
Source: San Francisco Chronicle, November 28, 1974.

vote, only 73 percent of the Democrats had done so. Independents, the group with so many Democratic-leaning voters, registered an even smaller portion of their number: 62 percent. (See Table 10).

What do these precentages mean in numbers of people? An extrapolation to the 1976 electorate illustrates the problem. In 1976, according to the Census Bureau, there were 150 million Americans of voting age (eighteen and over). After deductions for aliens, convicted felons, and others ineligible to vote, the potential voting population remained at 146 million, of whom 67 percent registered to vote, that is, 97,820,000. Conversely, an awesome number of more than 48 million potentially eligible adult citizens were *not* registered to vote. By combining the 1974 party identification data in Table 9 and the registration data in Table 10, we find the distributions reported in Table 11.

Table 11 indicates that there were 78,840,000 potential Democrats among the eligible voting age population, that is, the sum of all who identified themselves as strong and weak Democrats and as Democratic-leaning Independents. Of these, an estimated 52,501,000 were registered to vote and 26,339,000 failed to register, the latter representing a loss of about 33 percent of the identifiable potential Democrats during the registration process. Surveys of unregistered potential voters usually find that about 30 percent fail to register out of choice, and the other 70 percent—some 18,437,000 of the unregistered Democrats in this illustrative case—are unable to register because of such administrative roadblocks as residence requirements, inconvenient location of registration places, etc. Little wonder that registration drives are the key to so many Democratic victories.

Closer examination of Table 11 points up another familiar char-

TABLE 11
Estimated Eligible, Registered, Not Registered, and Actual Voters, 1976 (in thousands)

Party Identification (Percent of Sample)*	Eligible Voter, 1976	Percent Registered in 1974, Gallup†	Adjusted Percent Registered 1976	Est. Registered Party Identifiers, 1976§	Est. Party Identifiers Not Registered||	Actual 1976 Presidential Vote
National (100%)	146,000	71	67‡	97,820	48,180	79,636
DEM-strong (18)	26,280	73	69	18,133	8,147	
DEM-weak (23)	33,580	73	69	23,170	10,410	
IND-Democratic (13)	18,980	62	59	11,198	7,782	
Total	78,840			52,501	26,339	40,276
IND-Independent (20)	29,200	62	59	17,228	11,972	827#
IND-Republican (8)	11,680	62	59	6,891	4,789	
REP-weak (12)	17,520	81	76	13,315	4,205	
REP-strong (6)	8,760	81	76	6,658	2,101	
Total	37,960			26,864	11,096	38,533

*See 1974 data, Table 9.

†See Table 10.

‡Census Bureau report of actual percentage national registration. Other percentages in this column are adjusted to be comparable with 1974 Gallup findings in Column 3. 1974 percent registered (Column 3) is divided by 71 percent (1974 national registration). Quotient is then multiplied by 67 percent (1976 national registration). All products rounded.

§Column 2 (Eligible Voters) multiplied by Column 4 (Adjusted Percent Registered, 1976). Column total does not agree with national total because of rounding.

|| Column 5 (Estimated Registered Party Identifiers) subtracted from Column 2 (Eligible Voters).

#McCarthy received 658,000 votes and Maddox, 169,000.

Source: Compiled by author.

acteristic of some Democratic voters, that is, the inclination to defect. Most of Carter's 40,276,000 votes undoubtedly came from the 52,501,000 registered Democratic identifiers, but this was a shortfall of about 12,225,000 potential Democratic votes. On the other hand, Ford's 38,533,000 votes represent an 11,669,000 excess over the 26,864,000 registered Republican identifiers. Clearly, Ford attracted a substantial number—almost equal to Carter's shortfall—of Democratic-leaning Independents and weak Democrats.

Nonvoting is a perennial problem in the American electoral process. While legal restrictions and administrative roadblocks have been in large part responsible for preventing higher voter participation, there are also many voters who fail to register or, if registered, fail to cast their ballots *as a matter of choice*. Thus, for many, nonvoting is a consciously chosen option motivated by reasons ranging from bad weather on election day to displeasure with both or all candidates.

For others, voting may be a novel political act to which they must slowly become accustomed. Table 12, for example, describes the proportion of eligible voting-age population (twenty-one years and older until 1972 when the eighteen-year-old vote began) that has participated in presidential elections since 1920, the first in which women had the suffrage. Only about 26 percent of the eligible women voted in that election, and this is reflected in the very

TABLE 12
Voting Age Population Actually Casting Ballots in
Presidential Elections, 1920–1976

Election	Percent Voting	Related Event
1920	44	Women's suffrage
1924	44	
1928	52	New immigrants
1932	53	
1936	57	Organized labor
1940	59	
1944	54	Servicemen overseas
1948	52	
1952	63	Women participation
1956	60	
1960	64	Catholic participation
1964	62	Black participation
1968	61	
1972	56	18-year-old vote
1976	53	Post-Watergate

Source: Compiled by author.

295

low turnout of 44 percent. By the 1950s, women were participating on a par with men. A similar process seems under way among the newly enfranchised eighteen-to-twenty-one-year-old voters, less than half of whom have got to the polls in the first two elections—1972 and 1976—in which they have been eligible to participate.

From Table 12 we may compute that between 36 and 56 percent of the voting age population have been nonvoters in the presidential elections of recent decades. Yet, presidential elections are the ones in which voter turnout is usually at its maximum in the United States. By comparison, the vote cast for congressmen is several percentage points lower in presidential years and in midterm years about half the presidential vote. Voting for state and local offices drops off in a similar fashion, as Table 13 demonstrates.

Of particular concern for Democrats, then, is the fact that the typical nonvoter has characteristics similar to those of typical Democrats: people with less income, less formal education, and less occupational skill; affiliation with low-status churches; disadvantaged ethnic or nationality background; city dwellers; and youth.[28] The more inclined a voter may be to stay at home on election day, the greater the likelihood he would have been a Democratic voter had he gone to the polls. It follows that the Democratic party is in particular need of efficient organization, attractive candidates, and acceptable policy positions if it is to get its reluctant party-in-the-electorate to the polls. But a programmatic dilemma also seems to follow. Will more income, more education, and greater occupational skill not only bring more potential Democrats out to the polls but also, as these qualities improve, encourage them to join the more affluent, the better educated, and more highly skilled who seem to prefer the Republican party?

Table 9 described the rise over the last two decades in numbers of voters who prefer to identify themselves as Independents rather than as partisans, from 22 percent in the early 1950s to about 35–40 percent in the 1970s. The table also revealed a large number of "leaners" toward one or the other major party among self-declared Independents; in 1974, for example, 13 percent of the voters labeled themselves Independents "close to" the Democratic party and another 8 percent were Independents "close to" the Republican party. It could well be that these "leaners" are simply weak partisans. The line between the two classifications is difficult to draw. Table 14 reports the shifting party preferences of "leaners" between 1940 and 1976.

TABLE 13

Who Did *Not* Vote: Characteristics of Nonvoters, in Percentages

Characteristic	1972 Presidential Election	1970 Midterm Congressional Election	Last Local Election
Party			
Republican	17	—	—
Democratic	27	—	—
Independent	28	—	—
Income			
15,000 and over	13	26	32
10,000–14,999	22	37	38
5,000–9,999	31	48	47
Under 5,000	41	42	51
Education			
College	17	37	39
High School	31	41	44
Grade School	35	33	43
Religion			
Jewish	14	20	30
Catholic (white)	25	36	40
Protestant (white)	24	36	41
Race			
White	25	37	41
Black	42	46	47
Residence			
Rural	26	33	38
Towns	24	36	46
Suburbs	24	38	41
Cities	31	45	43
Age			
50 and older	20	20	30
30–49	19	28	33
Under 30	46	76	69
Sex			
Male	26	39	41
Female	28	38	42

Source: Louis Harris Poll report in United States Senate Committee on Government Operations, 93d Congress, 1st Session, *Confidence and Concern: Citizens View of American Government* (Washington, D.C.: U.S. Government Printing Office, December 3, 1973), pp. 317–19.

TABLE 14
Party Voting Preferences of Independents in Presidential Elections, in Percentages, 1940–1976

Election	Democratic	Republican	Other	Related Event
1940	61	39		FDR third term (charismatic leader)
1944	62	38		World War II (crisis)
1948	57	43		Dixiecrats (party bolt)
1952	33	67		Eisenhower (charismatic
1956	27	73		leader)
1960	46	54		Close election
1964	66	34		Black registration; Kennedy assassination
1968	32	47	21	Wallace third party bolt
1972	33	65	2	Labor and regulars' nonsupport of McGovern
1976	48	52		Close election

Source: William H. Flanigan and Nancy H. Zingale, *Political Behavior of the American Electorate* (3d ed., Boston: Allyn and Bacon, 1975), p. 59; *New York Times,* November 4, 1976.

Studies of voting behavior prepared in the late 1940s and the 1950s concluded that Independent voters tended to be persons of less education, less income, less skill, less political information, and less interest in politics. More recent studies reveal that Independents today are a much more mixed bag: better education, particularly among the young; higher occupational skills, particularly in the professional-managerial category; higher income; plenty of political information; and substantial interest in politics.[29] Independents today simply do not *feel* an attachment between self and party and this has been variously interpreted as alienation, an end to the party system, "electoral disaggregation," etc. It may also be the case that political parties today are no longer the grass-roots organizations they once were. People then related to and communicated with other people, resulting in a strong sense of group attachment. Today, parties are more mass-mediated organizations in which the existence of party leaders and fellow-partisans must be *surmised* from evidence in the press or on television. "Independence" may be more a matter of experiential remoteness than voter alienation.[30]

Another partial explanation for the rise in numbers of Independents may be, as suggested earlier, the caution of new voters. Independence has been on the rise, for example, among the young and blacks, and these are precisely the groups with the most newcomers to the electoral process in recent years, particularly 1972 and 1976.

Yet another explanation for independence may be the psychological usefulness of this label for those voters seeking an electoral halfway house as they move from one party to the other. During the 1950s many southern Democrats were beginning a permanent move to the Republican party when they voted for Eisenhower. On the other hand, many New England and midwestern Republicans were moving into the Democratic ranks. Such disaffiliating voters may prefer to think of themselves as Independents during the years that they make the shift.

Another phenomenon related to independence is ticket-splitting wherein the individual votes for the candidates of more than one party in the same election, for example, a Republican for president, a Democrat for congressman, etc. The incidence of split-ticket voting has been on the rise since the beginning of the century, but most notably since the early 1960s.[31] For example, the percentage of congressional districts carried by presidential and congressional candidates of different parties in each election year has risen steadily from about 3 percent in 1920 to 43 percent in 1972. According to the Harris Poll, the percentage of voters who reported splitting their tickets for president and congressmen between 1960 and 1972 increased from 3 percent to 16 percent.[32] However, it remains to be demonstrated whether ticket-splitting is a consequence of declining party loyalty, separate voter judgments about the merits of different candidates on the ballot, improvements in the ballot and election administration, or some other factor.

Yet another kind of evidence is offered as indicative of a decline in party loyalty, namely, the assertion that voter concern with public policy issues has overtaken party identification as the primary influence in voter choice. Studies of voting behavior in the 1940s and 1950s generally concluded that only a very small part of the electorate—between 12 and 15 percent—were in any way interested in the policy issues raised by the parties. Most voters were then influenced instead by their attachment to specific groups, their feelings about the general state of affairs, their attraction to a particular candidate, or their customary partisanship. Since the 1960s, however, issues have presumably grown in importance as a factor in voter decisions. Voters generally have more information and are more opinionated about issues than previously. The Democratic clubs and the party reform movements were generally described as a response to this increased concern with issues. The explanation offered for the trend is straightforward enough: the electorate is better educated, more affluent, and more exposed to the mass media. Furthermore, the electorate is less constrained by personal obligation to party organization, as used to be the case in the days of city machines.

There has also been a growing inclination for pollsters and political leaders to use ideological categories such as "conservative," "middle-of-the-road," and "liberal" in describing voters' preferences on clusters of issues and voters' self-classifications when asked. As Table 15 reports, there were roughly equal proportions in the conservative and liberal categories during the 1960s (and, in fact, as far back as the 1940s). During the 1970s, with data now being collected on middle-of-the-roaders, conservatives outnumbered liberals by about three-to-one.[33]

The distribution of conservative-liberal identification *within* each of the major parties is at least equally as important as the distribution in the electorate at large, particularly with respect to the national nominating and legislative processes. At the national nominating conventions and in the Congress, if coalition politics is to work, leaders must constantly be in search of the middle-of-the-road, and this search is often phrased as a matter of ideological labels. As Table 16 reveals, the Republican ideological leanings have been decidedly conservative, usually more than half of that electorate classifying itself in this way. Democrats, on the other hand, distribute themselves more evenly along the ideological spectrum, usually reflecting, but slightly more liberal than, the overall national distribution. The Democratic tendency to polarize among themselves on ideological issues can be better understood by examining the near-equal proportions in the conservative and liberal columns of Table 16.

It is difficult to draw from the data of Tables 15 and 16 any firm conclusion that ideology has diminished party loyalty. One theory suggests how this consequence may follow not so much from ideological attachments but rather from the more general influence of crosscutting issues in the party realignment process. James Sundquist, in noting that parties undergo fundamental change from time to time, theorizes that such realignments are usually precipitated by one or a cluster of new political issues. The issue or cluster of issues must be one that cuts across the existing line of party cleavage. The

TABLE 15
Ideological Orientation of Voters, by Self-Classification, in Percentages, 1960s and 1970s (National Samples)

Poll	Conservative	Middle-of-Road	Liberal	Other, DK*
Gallup, 1961:	46	—	41	13
Gallup, 1963:	46	—	49	5
Gallup, 1964:	34	—	37	29
Gallup, 1970:	40	35	20	5
Gallup (Roper), 1971:	39 (41)	29 (27)	26 (24)	6 (6)
Gallup, 1972:	37	33	26	4
Roper, 1973:	41	28	25	6
Gallup (Harris), 1974:	38 (30)	36 (43)	26 (18)	— (12)
Roper, 1975:	39	28	27	5

*DK = don't know.
   Sources: Gallup data for 1961, 1963, and 1964 are from George H. Gallup, *The Gallup Poll: Public Opinion 1935–1971* (3 vols.; New York: Random House, 1972). Gallup data for 1970, 1971, and 1972 are from *Gallup Opinion Index*, Reports 65, 72, and 83, pp. 17, 15, and 10, respectively. Harris and Roper data are from press releases. Special thanks to Everett C. Ladd, Jr., and Diane L. Reed of the Social Science Data Center, University of Connecticut, for invaluable help in providing or locating much of the data for Table 15.

issue must be provocative enough to dominate political debate and polarize the community. The normal response of a coalition party is to straddle such a crosscutting issue. A realignment crisis occurs when a party's moderate centrists lose control to one or the other polarizing factions. Zeal and ideological labels and content usually characterize realignment crises. A third party may appear, depending upon a variety of circumstances internal or external to the party. Realignment ends with the emergence of a stable new coalition. With the passing of the generation of voters whose party loyalties were "forged in the passion of the great realigning issue," the electorate as a whole will show a lessening of the strength of party loyalty. The voters claiming to be Independents will increase and the stage set for some new crosscutting issue to generate realignment.

Another investigation of the ideological orientations of Democrats and Republicans, using a liberal-conservative index of voter responses about various issues, found evidence of ideological polarization particularly among party activists (those who contribute time and money to political campaigns). Since 1956, conservative Republican activists have outnumbered their liberal fellow-partisans by a two-to-one or three-to-one margin. On the other hand, Democratic

301

TABLE 16
Ideological Orientation of Republicans and Democrats, in Percentages

Year	Percent of Republicans who classify themselves as:				Percent of Democrats who classify themselves as:			
	Conservative	Middle-of-Road	Liberal	Other, DK	Conservative	Middle-of-Road	Liberal	Other, DK
1939	73	—	26	1	42	—	56	2
1970	57	30	10	3	32	38	26	4
1971	53	28	16	3	33	28	33	6
1972	54	27	16	3	29	34	33	4
1974	46	42	8	4	26	42	22	10
1976	55	36	9	1	36	39	23	2

Sources: George H. Gallup, *The Gallup Poll: Public Opinion 1935–1971* (3 vols.; New York: Random House, 1972), for 1939 data. *Gallup Opinion Index*, Reports 65, 72, and 83, pp. 17, 15, and 10, respectively, for 1970, 1971, and 1972 data. Survey data. American National Election Study, for 1974 data. Yankelovich Surveys for 1976 data. Research Center, Center for Political Studies, University of Connecticut, for invaluable help Special thanks to Everett C. Ladd, Jr., and Diane L. Reed, Social Science Data Center, University of Connecticut, for invaluable help in providing much of the data for Table 16.

activists, particularly after 1964, have leaned in the liberal direction by more than a three-to-one ratio. Activists, it was also found, tend to be more attached to issues and candidates and less committed to party as an organization. "Thus, what appears as a growing emphasis on candidates and issues rather than party among the public at large is even more strongly felt among the activists."[34]

Another familiar hypothesis revived at every national election states that the growing numbers of independent voters and dissatisfied nonvoters may be ready to follow certain leaders into an enduring new third party. A closer examination of the facts, however, should quickly convince proponents of such a new party that Independents and nonvoters are an unreliable basis for party formation. Independents are inclined to switch back and forth between parties (Table 14) and move in and out of active voting participation (Table 12). Nonvoters include many who doubt altogether the merits of the party system and the electoral process as a whole, and hence are the least likely to become excited by a new third party. Any who try to get them to the polls will find that these are the most costly votes to gather.

In conclusion, it seems that the party system is undergoing important transformations but is hardly at its end. There remains a hard core of committed partisans in each major party. Those who identify themselves as Independents reveal a strong tendency to "lean" toward one party or the other with some regularity. The nonvoters, as have all nonvoters in the past, seem to need to be got to the polls by reducing the administrative roadblocks and by putting together an organization that will practically carry them there as the city machines used to do. The nature of ticket-splitting is still debated among experts; it may simply reflect a disinterest in voting for candidates below the top of the ballot, a tendency that the city machines also knew how to handle. Finally, there are those analysts who point out that the evidence upon which conclusions about declining party loyalty are based is usually derived from surveys of presidential voting behavior. These analysts offer substantial evidence of their own that the voting patterns found in congressional and local elections in fact show great stability and tenacity in party loyalty.[35]

As for the Democratic party-in-the-electorate and its grass-roots organizations, it is evident that the essential structural traits of the party's early organizational "personality" for the most part remain. It continues to be the party of the less affluent, the less advantaged in education and skills, and the newcomers to the nation and the civic process. It is the party that Independents and those who are most reluctant to vote leave and return to most readily. The Democratic party's talents for searching out the national consensus seem to derive from the usual congruence of its structure with the changing political shape of the nation at large.

11

The Party's
Changing Architecture:
At the National Level

GEOGRAPHY has played a central role in the evolution of the political system of the United States. In some political systems, the basic unit of political representation—hence the share in collective decisions—has often been the social class, in others the organized group, in still others political party strength. In the United States the basic unit has usually been territorial: the single-member district. Despite the practice of gerrymandering and the decennial ordeals of legislative redistricting, the boundaries of territorial units—states, counties, congressional districts, cities, towns, election precincts, wards, etc.—have been relatively stable and have provided the political system with an often unappreciated element of predictability. The less predictable and often destabilizing changes in population composition, public opinion, party strength, group formation, and class interest have taken place *within* this framework of territorial units. This has had great consequence for the structure of the political parties, leading to federally organized parties, sectionalism, one-party districts, gerrymandering, decentralization of the power structure within parties, and similar phenomena.

The Founding Fathers set the basic pattern by acknowledging that the colonies were independent communities that could be brought together only as a federal system of sovereign states. In the Constitution the states were accorded equality under the law and in the United States Senate. The House of Representatives was created to bring the new national government closer to "the people"; its short two-year term and decennial post-census redistricting were designed to keep the representatives in the lower house responsive to shifts in popular opinion and popular residential patterns. The new federal government adopted what had already emerged in the mother country and the colonies: territorial units of representation, bicameral legislatures, and the expectation that changing combinations of popular interest and opinion would be organized for political action informally within the basic and relatively stable territorial units. Having thus dispersed the constitutional units of power, Americans turned to electioneering organizations and political parties to recombine these units into effective coalitions of influence at the various levels of public decision-making.

Party leaders responded by organizing themselves to accomplish the requisite numerical majorities. If nothing else, a party leader must know how to design voting systems and count votes. The organizational history of the Democratic party reflects these responses to the numerical requirements of the system. At first the state legislatures were the principal centers for coalition-building and party development for the purposes of selecting not only state officers but also United States senators and presidential electors. The congressional caucus arose to facilitate coalitioning for purposes of national legislation, promoting party organization in the congressional districts, and presidential selection. City machines grew out of the need to mobilize the new urban mass electorates. The Jacksonians built new agencies of national party in order to free the presidential selection process from congressional domination. Sectional coalitions arose among politicians representing profoundly different regional economic and social philosophies. Primary elections were invented as a response to the development of intraparty factionalism and a recognition of the importance of insurgency within the parties.

Some of these developments in party organizational structure are surveyed briefly in the pages that follow in order to identify some of their major attributes in the past for comparison with their tendencies in the present.

Stakes in the States

Scholarly and popular fascination with city machines and presidential politics has diverted attention from less visible centers of party politics, such as rural machines, state legislative parties, and the electoral college. Yet, the Republic began with a 95 percent rural population and with the belief that the farm was closer than the city to God and godliness. Many of the structural traits of the Democratic party, therefore, derive from the manner in which the party accommodated organizationally to the residential patterns of that rural electorate. Rural economic and social interests advanced their objectives by winning electoral majorities within districts in which supportive residential patterns were found. For example, we have seen how the Democratic city machines mobilized the votes of urban dwellers on a block-by-block, precinct-by-precinct basis. A single city block may contain enough voting population to constitute an election precinct. A rural "neighborhood," on the other hand, may consist of a population spread out over many miles. Economic interests also tend to differ according to population grouping; for example, propertyless laborers of many kinds live in city precincts but land-owning small farmers make up rural precincts. Just as city dwellers have been organized by ward bosses and "city-hall heelers," so rural voters have been organized by rural machines sometimes referred to unflatteringly as "county courthouse gangs." Just as city hall has been the focus of much of urban party politics, the county courthouse and the state legislature have been the centers of rural politics. Since the 1950s, as we shall see, a new dimension has been added with the phenomenal growth of metropolitan suburbs.

Rural Machines and Suburbia

A panoramic view of residential population trends in the United States can help point up and in part explain several changes in party politics at the state level. Although the nineteenth century city machines had always played a key role in the nation's party politics, party and electioneering organizations were primarily rural in character during the first century-and-a-quarter. In 1790, the nation had only 24 places with populations of more than 2,500 persons each. By 1970, there were 6,435 such places, with 69.5 percent of the population of the United States living in them. Six of these places had populations of more than one million persons each, 56 had more than 250,000 each, 396 had more than 50,000 each. During the decade from 1910 to 1920, the predominantly rural nation became a predominantly urban one as the proportion of urban dwellers rose from 45.6 percent in 1910 past the halfway mark to 51.2 percent in 1920.

Professor Arthur N. Holcombe, one of the earliest analysts to examine the proposition that economic and social interests can exert

the greatest influence in national politics if they can control the greatest number of states and congressional districts, made such an examination for the 1910–1920 period. Those interests, he hypothe-
sized, which are concentrated in particular localities or sections are
in a position to secure more political representation in proportion to
their economic strength than those which are distributed more
evenly throughout the nation. He demonstrated this by classifying
congressional districts into four urban-rural types on the basis of
1910 census data: *metropolitan* (cities of at least 200,000 inhabitants,
together with suburbs); *urban* (cities of 100,000–200,000); *semi-urban*
(cities of at least 50,000–100,000); and *rural* (districts containing no
city with as many as 50,000 inhabitants). Holcome then divided the
nation into five political sections: Northeast, Middle West, Upper
South, Lower South, and Far West. The distribution of urban and
rural congressional strength that he found at that time, just as the
nation was becoming predominantly urban, is reported in Table 17.[1]

TABLE 17
Urban-Rural Character of Congressional Districts, by Political Sections, in
Percentages, 1910–1920

Political Section	Metro- politan	Urban	Semi- Urban	Rural	Total
Northeast	60	14	18	31	123
Middle West	25*	6	20	74	125
Upper South	9	5	8	56	78
Lower South	3	5	9	57	74
Far West	8	2	3	20	33
Total	105	32	58	238	433

*Two Illinois congressmen elected at large not included.
Source: Arthur N. Holcombe, *The Political Parties of Today* (New York: Harper &
Brothers, 1924), p. 109.

Thus, during 1910–1920, 55 percent, that is, 238 of the total 433,
of the members of the House of Representatives were from rural
districts, mainly in the Middle West and South, and these districts
had strong agricultural interests. On the other hand, only 32 percent, that is, 137 of the 433, of the House membership came from
metropolitan and urban cities of 100,000 or more, mainly in the
Northeast, and these districts contained a wide variety of often
competing economic interests.

Beginning in the 1950s, a new, politically significant residential pattern began to emerge: suburbanization. As Table 18 indicates, the proportion of the total United States population living in cities of one million or more began to decline in the 1940s, from 12.1 percent in 1940 to 9.2 percent in 1970. On the other hand, the proportion of the total population living in "other urban places" and in communities of 10,000–100,000 rose dramatically, from 8.9 to 18.3 percent and from 18.8 to 27.5 percent, respectively. These increases reflected the movement of persons from large central cities to the outlying suburbs. About 55 million of the nation's 203 million inhabitants at the time of the 1970 census were suburban dwellers. One of the most significant demographic and political facts associated with this trend has been its racial composition. During the 1960s, central cities lost about 2.5 million whites and gained over 3 million blacks. Of the 55 million suburban dwellers in 1970, 94 percent were white and only 6 percent black.

TABLE 18

The Rise of the Suburban Population, in Percentages, Selected Years from 1910 to 1970

Places by Population	1910	1940	1950	1970
1,000,000 or more	9.2	12.1	11.5	9.2
500,000–1,000,000	3.3	4.9	6.1	6.4
100,000–500,000	9.6	11.8	11.8	12.1
10,000–100,000	14.9	18.8	19.6	27.5
Other urban places	8.7	8.9	15.0	18.3
Rural areas	54.3	43.5	36.0	26.5

Source: *Encyclopedia Americana* (Danbury, Conn.: Americana Corp., 1978), vol. XXVII, p. 535.

In sum, the United States began as a rural-agricultural community, became a predominantly urban nation early in the twentieth century, and took the shape of suburbia after the 1950s. There were consequences for party politics. Holcombe summarizes the earlier agrarian basis of party success succinctly.[2] The Federalist ascendancy of the Washington-Adams period rested particularly on a combination of the commercial interests of the North Atlantic coast section, the tobacco planters of Virginia, and the rice planters of South Carolina. Jeffersonians succeeded by organizing chiefly the back-country grain growers from Maine to Georgia. The Jacksonian Revolution was accomplished by adding to these grain growers—the most numerous single occupational group in the nation at that time–the newly enfranchised urban workers. Republican ascendancy came with the rise of the Radical Republicans, whose political strength rested primarily upon a politics of sectionalism, particularly military control of the South. Beginning with the New Deal, however, urbanization, immigration, union organization, black migration, and the decline of sectional politics began to have their cumulative effect, that is, the emergence of the contemporary Democratic majority.

The spectacular growth of the suburbs after World War II has, according to some observers, diluted the New Deal–Fair Deal Democratic majority. The evidence, however, has not been conclusive. There is, in fact, evidence that most of those who moved from central cities to the suburbs were Republicans before as well as after their moves. Nor have the middle-class life styles of suburbia significantly affected the Democratic party preference of the many trade unionists who also migrated from the central cities. If anything, racial attitudes, consumer consciousness, and home ownership have been the factors most influencing suburban voter behavior, and, at least in the presidential contests, Republican candidates have sought to capitalize on these special suburban factors. However, in congressional, state, and local elections, Democrats have won their full measure of the available Democratic vote in the suburbs.[3]

The Party Battle in the State Legislatures

The political spotlight in the United States tends to shine brightest on the local level where personal contact with politicians is often direct and tangible or at the national level where the press is most attentive. State capitals are notoriously out of sight; politicians there often beg for attention. Yet, national and sectional politics are significantly shaped by the competitive and other characteristics of party politics at the state level.

Where, then, is the hub of state politics? Historically, it has varied from state to state and time to time, but most conspicuously and most often the hub may be found in the state legislature, the governor's mansion, or the office of a United States senator.

In the early agrarian politics of the nation, two state "machines" based in two major state capitals won particular renown for their ability to extend their influence from their own state legislative politics to sectional and national politics: the "Richmond Junto" and the "Albany Regency." The Richmond Junto illustrates the manner of organizing legislative and electoral power in a one-party state of that period. The Albany Regency and its intense concern with factional coalitions reflect the way politics went in a highly competitive two-party state. Both were located in states—Virginia and New York—with great economic and political power during the first half-century of the Republic.

Richmond Junto. Most Americans remember Patrick Henry best for his great revolutionary phrase: "Give me liberty or give me death!" Most would undoubtedly be uncomfortable about including this patriot's name on a roster of American party bosses. Yet, state boss he was—leader of the potent organization called the Richmond Junto. The Junto had its roots in the Virginia Assembly, where Patrick Henry was the principal Antifederalist leader, so powerful that he was able to prevent James Madison's election to the Senate in the First Congress under the new Constitution. Madison instead went to the House of Representatives.

Over the years Henry and his successors at the head of the Junto developed strong working alliances with fellow-partisans in Kentucky, North Carolina, and Georgia, with connections into their several local rural organizations. These interstate alliances gave the Richmond Junto a major role in national politics for over half a century.

The Junto was particularly powerful during the years of "the Virginia Dynasty," that is, the presidencies of Jefferson, Madison, and Monroe, later taking second place to New York's Albany Regency during the Jacksonian era from 1824 to 1836. The Junto's influence was again felt in national affairs during the decade following the mid-1830s. Andrew Stevenson of Virginia chaired the Democratic National Convention of 1836 when John Tyler of Virginia ran against Van Buren's first choice for vice president. The Virginians also were responsible for placing Tyler on the winning Whig "Tippecanoe and Tyler, too" ticket in 1840. They later defeated Van Buren's efforts to gain a third nomination in 1844 by swinging against him on a critical test vote.

Albany Regency. Early state politics in New York was dominated by such eminent families as the Livingstons, the Schuylers, and the Clintons, who constructed alliances with other New York Jeffersonians, for example, Aaron Burr and Daniel D. Tompkins.

In April 1812, when Vice President George Clinton died, a Democratic-Republican convention in New York nominated DeWitt Clinton to oppose Madison for the presidency. Madison, however, now had the support of New York's Governor Tompkins as well as Tammany Hall. In 1816, when Monroe received the presidential nomination, Tompkins was elevated to second place on the successful ticket.

With Tompkins in Washington, leadership of the state anti-Clinton faction fell to Martin Van Buren, whose influence rested among the membership of the state legislature. Clinton was nonetheless elected governor despite the opposition of the Van Buren legislative faction. By 1818, Van Buren was able to name the Speaker of the Assembly and control the principal sources of patronage in the state. In 1821 Van Buren became New York's United States senator. The Albany Regency was now firmly established; it was essentially the Democratic-Republican caucus of the New York State legislature. It concentrated its operations entirely at the state capital, never organizing at the county or local levels. The Regency did, however, nurture allies in nearby state legislatures.

The Regency, by welding together an enduring coalition with Tammany and other anti-Clinton factions in the state, next created the "Bucktail" faction. For years, the Regency and the Bucktails ran New York, distributed offices, and directed the affairs of the state's Democratic party. Thurlow Weed, who created the opposition Whig-Republican equivalent of the Regency and who himself dominated much of New York politics from 1830 to 1860, spoke of the leadership of the Regency as "men of great ability, great industry, indomitable courage and strict personal integrity."[4] The national alliances generated by the Regency enabled Van Buren to become president in 1837.

For generations, therefore, the centers of party politics lay outside of the national capital in key state legislatures. This was in keeping with the anti-executive and decentralizing political patterns established by the colonists. It also reflected some of the basic governmental arrangements written into the Constitution. For example, the power to regulate elections and establish the qualifications of voters was assigned to the state legislatures. Presidential electors were to be named in any manner prescribed by state legislatures, and until the 1820s these bodies retained a substantial place for themselves in this process. Eligibility to vote for members of the lower house of the state legislature was the standard adopted in the Constitution for voting for representatives to Congress. Selection of United States senators was left entirely to the state legislatures, until, in 1913, the Seventeenth Amendment transferred that power to the electorate at large.

The growth of state party organization outside the state legislatures during and after Reconstruction produced governors and United States senators who became the bosses of powerful nonlegislative state machines. After Reconstruction, political transactions no longer were conducted mainly in the state legislative marketplace but instead began to depend upon the governor's or the senator's capacity to negotiate with his national party, with the president, and with allies in the United States Senate.

In recent decades, the Democratic party has maintained a solid role in state politics, as indicated by the data in Table 19. Democrats controlled more than half of the fifty state senates nearly all of the time during the 1954–1974 period, more than half of the lower houses in eight of the eleven election years described, and a majority of the governorships for all but two of the election years. On the average, during this twenty-year period, Democrats controlled twenty-nine states senates, twenty-nine state houses of representatives, and thirty governorships, a three-to-two margin over Republicans. More recently in the case of governorships, the 1976 margin of thirty-seven Democrats to twelve Republicans (with one Independent in Maine) dropped to 32–18 in 1978.

According to an Index of State Interparty Competition developed by Austin Ranney, the states in which the Democratic party

TABLE 19
Governorships and State Legislative Chambers Controlled by Democrats and Republicans, 1954–1974

Year	Upper Houses			Lower Houses			Governorships	
	Dem.	Rep.	Tie	Dem.	Rep.	Tie	Dem.	Rep.
1974	40	7	2	42	7	0	37	12*
1972	29	19	1	31	17	1	32	18
1970	26	21	1	22	25	1	29	21
1968	25	22	1	23	25	0	16	34
1966	29	18	1	25	22	1	24	26
1964	34	12	2	39	9	0	33	17
1962	28	20	0	27	29	1	33	17
1960	30	18	0	31	17	0	34	16
1958 (50 states)	31	17	0	29	9	1	35	15
1956	25	21	2	28	20	0	31	19
1954 (48 states)	20	25	1	26	20	0	27	21
1954–1974 average	29	18	—	29	18	—	30	20

*Maine elected an Independent governor in 1974.

Source: Thomas R. Dye, *Politics in States and Communities*, 3d ed. (Englewood Cliffs, N.J.: Prentice-Hall, 1977), p. 101.

held the strongest statewide sway during the period from 1946 to 1963 were those that, in Table 20, had an Index score greater than .70: South Carolina, Georgia, Louisiana, Mississippi, Texas, Alabama, Arkansas, Florida, Virginia, North Carolina, Tennessee, Oklahoma, Kentucky, Arizona, West Virginia, Maryland, and New Mexico. The Index of State Interparty Competition was computed from (a) the average percent of the popular vote won by the gubernatorial candidates of each party, (b) the average percent of the seats in the state senate and state assembly held by each party, and (c) the percent of all gubernatorial terms during which the same party controlled both houses of the legislature as well as the governor's office.

During the 1960s, changes in the makeup of state legislatures began to take place as a result of one-man-one-vote decisions of the Supreme Court in the reapportionment cases of *Baker* v. *Carr* (1962) and *Reynolds* v. *Sims* (1964). Thereafter, rural over-representation in state legislatures decreased. The suburbs acquired greater numbers of seats. There was also an increase in the number of competitive legislative districts. The recent state legislative reapportionments of the 1970s have tended to favor Democrats, at the same time making state legislative contests even more closely competitive.

The data presented in Tables 19 and 20 are reminders that state capitals continue to be important centers of party politics in the United States. The tables also indicate the degree and location of Democratic strength at the state level. However, it should also be made clear that state party politics is not highly organized. State party organization has been weakened by the spread of primary elections, excessive state regulation of party organizational structure and procedure, and stringent state controls over the campaign financing practices of the state parties.[5] While voters are willing to cast their ballots for the candidates of their state parties, state parties have come to be relatively weak and shifting coalitions of state legislative factions and/or the personal organizations of individual governors or United States senators.

What has been the situation in the governors' mansions? Governors did not come into their own as party leaders until after the Civil War. Thus, for example, neither party nominated an incumbent governor for president until 1876, at which time the Democrats chose Governor Samuel J. Tilden of New york and the Republicans nominated Governor Rutherford B. Hayes of Ohio. By 1956, about sixty governors had been in contention for their respective party's

TABLE 20
Indexes of State Interparty Competition in the Fifty States, 1946–1963

| (Most Democratic) | | | | | | | | (Most Republican) | |
1.00–.90	.89–.80	.79–.70	.69–.60	.59–.50	.49–.40	.39–.30	.29–.20	.19–.10	.09–.00
S.C.	Va.	Ky.	Alaska	Wash.	Hawaii	Calif.	Wis.	N.D.	
Ga.	N.C.	Ariz.	Mo.	Del.	Colo.	Neb.	N.H.	Vt.	
La.	Tenn.	W.Va.	R.I.	Nev.	Mont.	Ill.	Iowa		
Miss.	Okla.	Md.		Mass.	Minn.	Idaho	Kans.		
Tex.		N.M.			Utah	Mich.	Me.		
Ala.					Conn.	N.J.	S.D.		
Ark.					Pa.	Ind.			
Fla.						Ore.			
						Ohio			
						Wyo.			
						N.Y.			

Source: Austin Ranney, "Parties in State Politics," in *Politics in the American States,* ed. Herbert Jacob and Kenneth N. Vines (Boston: Little, Brown, 1965). p. 65.

presidential nomination and sixteen had received it, reflecting solid political footing in their home states. Another indication of a growing party leadership role for Democratic governors (Table 21) has been the rising proportion of Democratic governors who have served as delegates to the national nominating conventions, from none in 1848 to 74 percent in 1956.

TABLE 21
Democratic Governors Serving as Delegates to National Party Conventions, Selected Years

Year	Governors	Delegates	Percent
1848	20	0	0
1860	20	1	5
1872	12	1	8
1884	25	4	16
1896	17	5	29
1908	20	11	55
1920	21	11	52
1928	21	9	43
1932	27	18	67
1936	38	23	61
1940	30	18	60
1944	22	18	82
1948	24	15	63
1952	23	19	83
1956	27	20	74

Source: Paul T. David, Ralph M. Goldman, and Richard C. Bain. *The Politics of National Party Conventions* (Washington, D.C.: Brookings Institution, 1960), pp. 98, 148.

This trend notwithstanding, governors are by no means always powerful in state politics. In the mid-1960s, for example, the Advisory Commission on Intergovernmental Relations, using five factors as the components of a "power index," characterized the governors of only ten states as "very strong," twelve of "medium" strength, and eleven as "weak."[6]

Since popular election of United States senators was established in 1913, the senator has also been a principal competitor of the governor in state party affairs. Despite the contemporary disadvantages noted earlier, the senator generally has had certain advantages. For example, he is more likely, because of his location at the news center of Washington, to receive the publicity that is the lifeblood of politicians. Further, while the governor is struggling valiantly but never too successfully with growing state fiscal and policy problems, the senator is visibly and impressively among those in Congress and in Washington dispensing some of the major resources of the nation.

State Electorates in Presidential Politics

The party balance in state contests is often different from the balance that emerges from the presidential competition for state votes in the electoral college. This is in part due to some difference in the importance of the stakes. Governorships and state legislative seats are obviously less prized stakes than the presidency; they are also more subject to party-ticket voting wherein voters focus more on party than on candidate. The presidency, on the other hand, is not only the biggest prize but also a prize whose pursuit must take into account many non-state factors: larger voter turnout, ticket-splitting, special emphasis on candidate attributes, national interest-group coalitioning, more media coverage, etc. But the presidency can only be won by first winning state popular pluralities needed to capture state electoral college votes on the traditional winner-take-all basis and, then, winning popular pluralities in sufficient states to collect a majority of the votes in the electoral college, that is, 270 or more of the 538 electoral votes. Hence, the presidential voting habits of *state* electorates have always been a matter of prime concern to leaders of the presidential wing of the party.

Which have been the great state strongholds of the Democratic presidential party? Table 22 offers a summary overview for the party's first century, from 1824 to 1932, inclusive, and makes a comparison to the more recent 1936–1976 period. The table reports the number of presidential elections in which each state participated and the proportion of the state's electoral college votes that went to the Democratic presidential slate.

These aggregate figures do not reflect cyclical fluctuations in state support of Democratic nominees. They do reveal where the main sources of electoral strength for the presidential wing were during the party's first century. Twelve states went Democratic in two-thirds or more of the presidential elections in which they participated. Nineteen states were as often Republican. Only seventeen states appear, over the long run, to have been relatively competitive two-party states, and only three of these—New Jersey, New Mexico, and Arizona—in the close 50–50 category. The table also clearly suggests the basis for the pre–New Deal claims by southern Demo-

TABLE 22
State Electorates Supporting Democratic Presidential Tickets, 1824*–1932 and 1936–1976

State	Number of Elections in Which State Participated, 1824–1932	Percent Won by Democratic Ticket, 1824–1932	Percent Won by Democrats, 1936–1976
Texas	20	95.0	72.7
Alabama	27	92.6	63.6
Mississippi	26	92.3	54.5
Arkansas	24	91.7	81.8
Georgia	26	88.5	72.7
Virginia	26	88.5	45.4
Louisiana	26	84.6	54.5
South Carolina	17	82.4	63.6
North Carolina	27	77.8	81.8
Florida	20	75.0	54.5
Missouri	28	71.4	72.7
Oklahoma	7	71.4	45.4
Tennessee	26	65.4	54.5
Kentucky	28	60.7	63.6
New Jersey	28	50.0	45.4
New Mexico	6	50.0	54.5
Arizona	6	50.0	36.4
Delaware	26	46.2	54.5
Montana	11	45.4	45.4
Idaho	11	45.4	45.4
Illinois	28	42.9	54.5
Maryland	28	42.9	63.6
Indiana	28	42.9	18.2
Colorado	14	42.9	27.3
New York	27	40.7	63.6
Utah	10	40.0	45.4
West Virginia	18	38.9	81.8
Nevada	18	38.9	54.5
Wyoming	11	36.4	36.4
Nebraska	17	29.4	18.2
California	21	28.6	45.4
New Hampshire	28	28.6	36.4
Washington	11	27.3	54.5
North Dakota	11	27.3	18.2
Pennsylvania	28	25.0	63.6
Connecticut	28	25.0	54.5
Ohio	28	25.0	45.4
Wisconsin	22	22.7	45.4
Kansas	18	22.2	18.2
Maine	28	21.4	18.2
Michigan	25	20.0	45.4
South Dakota	11	18.2	18.2

TABLE 22 *(Continued)*

Rhode Island	28	17.9	72.7
Oregon	19	15.8	36.4
Iowa	22	13.6	27.3
Massachusetts	28	10.7	81.8
Minnesota	19	5.3	81.8
Vermont	27	0.0	9.1
Hawaii†	—	—	80.0
Alaska†	—	—	20.0
District of Columbia‡	—	—	100.0

*1824 or first participation after admission to Union.
†First presidential election after admission was in 1960.
‡Given vote in Electoral College from 1964 on.
Source: Compiled by author.

cratic politicians that the "heart" of the Democratic party lay in their section of the country. Who can contest that Arkansas, Alabama, Georgia, Mississippi, Texas, Virginia, South Carolina, North Carolina, Louisiana, Florida, Missouri, and Oklahoma have been more *consistently* Democratic in their presidential preferences than any other state? By comparison, Democratic successes in, say, New York and Illinois have been far less reliable. What better basis need there have been for southern demands for considerate treatment and significant influence in the presidential wing of the party?

National party attention must go to those larger and more closely contested states whose greater number of electoral college votes make them more sought-after prizes. Table 23 illustrates how the relative weight of selected states' electoral college strength has varied over the decades, altered by shifts in population and by the dispersal of total electoral college strength among increasing numbers of states as they entered the Union. In the Washington-Adams election of 1789, for example, Virginia was the unchallenged leader with 14.8 percent of the electoral college's strength. Massachusetts and Pennsylvania were tied for second place at 12.4 percent. Thus ranked, Virginia received the presidency, Massachusetts the vice presidency, and Pennsylvania the national capital. This tendency to go after big-state electoral votes would of course end if a constitutional amendment were to replace the electoral college with a single national constituency that elects its presidents by direct popular pluralities. One consequence of direct election of presidents is likely to be a weakening of state party organization.

319

TABLE 23
Percentages of Electoral College Votes of Original States, 1789–1800, 1824, and 1976

State	1789	1792	1796 1800	1824	1976
Connecticut	8.6	6.7	6.5	3.1	1.5
Delaware	3.7	2.2	2.2	1.2	0.6
Georgia	6.3	3.0	2.9	3.4	2.2
Kentucky	—	3.0	2.9	5.4	1.7
Maryland	9.9	7.4	7.2	4.2	1.9
Massachusetts	12.4	11.8	11.6	5.8	2.6
New Hampshire	6.2	4.4	4.4	3.1	0.7
New Jersey	7.4	5.2	5.1	3.1	3.2
New York	9.9	8.9	8.7	13.8	7.6†
North Carolina	—*	8.9	8.7	5.8	2.4
Pennsylvania	12.4	11.1	10.9	10.7	5.0
Rhode Island	—*	3.0	2.9	1.5	0.7
South Carolina	8.6	5.9	5.8	4.2	1.5
Tennessee	—	—	2.2	4.2	1.9
Vermont	—	3.0	2.9	2.7	0.6
Virginia	14.8	15.6	15.2	9.2	2.0
(Total Votes in Electoral College)	(81)	(135)	(138)	(261)	(538)

*North Carolina and Rhode Island did not ratify the Constitution in time to participate in the election of 1789.

†California surpassed New York in population in 1970 census and now has the largest bloc of electoral college votes: 45, or 8.4 percent of total.

Source: Compiled by author.

This process of shrinkage has also had consequences for sectional coalitions. In 1820, for example, the seven states of the Old South—Alabama, Georgia, Louisiana, Mississippi, North Carolina, South Carolina, and Virginia—together possessed 29 percent of the strength of the electoral college. By 1860, this proportion had dropped to 21 percent. For southerners in 1860 their problem had come to be a choice between political eclipse within the Union or survival outside it in a new confederacy. By 1932, in a Union of forty-eight states, the seven states of the Old South had diminished to merely fourteen percent of the electoral college's total strength, and as we have seen, New Deal and Fair Deal leaders sought to make the most of the shrinkage.

Patterns of state party politics began to change significantly under the impact of Roosevelt's New Deal and Truman's Fair Deal. Many states lost their one-party inclination and became more competitive in contests for both statewide offices and the state's electoral votes. This tendency is demonstrated by Paul T. David in a tabulation of the voting in presidential and gubernatorial elections from 1896 to 1956, shown in Table 24. David gave each state its percentage weight in the electoral college and found a decided disappearance of one-party states, both Democratic and Republican, in presidential voting. A decline in one-sideness of gubernatorial voting also occurred, chiefly among the Republican states.

TABLE 24
Rise in State Party Competitiveness, in Percentages, 1896–1956

Categories of States*	Period 1896 to 1927		Period 1928 to 1956	
	President	Governor†	President	Governor
One-party Republican	50.0	35.1	1.5	7.5
Two-party Leaning Republican	10.7	10.5	23.1	18.4
Two-party Uncertain	10.3	16.4	23.4	33.0
One-party Leaning Democratic	4.9	12.3	40.2	14.0
One-party Democratic	24.1	25.7	11.8	27.1

*States were classified as "one-party" when one party was victorious in 80 percent or more of the elections during the period, as "leaning" to one party when that party was victorious in 60 to 79.9 percent of the elections, and as "uncertain" when neither party won more than 60 percent of the time.
†Based on the period 1901–1927.
Source: Paul T. David, "The Changing Political Parties," in John R. Owens and P. J. Stadenraus, eds., *The American Party System* (New York: Macmillan, 1965), p. 438.

The post–New Deal changes in presidential support within state electorates may also be seen in Table 25, which summarizes the data in Table 22, comparing 1936–1976 with 1824–1832. The comparison shows that the number of competitive states in presidential elections has doubled from seventeen to thirty, states preponderantly Republican have declined from nineteen to ten, and the Democratic dozen, formerly all in the South, have dropped to eleven and are now found in different sections of the country.

Thus, the dissolution of the one-party states of the Democratic South has been accompanied by a decline in one-party Republican states as well. A Republican senator can be elected in South Carolina. A Democratic governor can be elected in Vermont. The formerly Republican Midwest is contested territory. Competition has increased in Georgia, South Carolina, Mississippi, Alabama, and Louisiana, where it is no longer uncommon for the state to vote for

TABLE 25
State Party Competitiveness in Presidential Elections; 1824–1932 and 1936–1976
Compared

Period	Democratic 2/3 of Times	Competitive	Republican 2/3 of Times
1824–1932 (48 states)	12	17	19
1936–1976 (50 states, and D.C.)	11	30	10

Source: Based on Table 22.

a Republican or third-party presidential nominee. Voters in the states are dividing more evenly and shifting more frequently between the major parties.

What future may be anticipated for the party at the state level? Future state electorates will undoubtedly be more evenly divided between the major parties. The competition for the support of these electorates will surely motivate the building of stronger and more formal party agencies at the state level. Where in the state political structure will this organizing effort probably take place? At the governor's mansion? Governors' constitutional powers may increase and this may have side effects for their influence over their party when in office. However, governors come and go, and state parties may not often be in control of the governor's office. Hence, the principal center of state party development is not likely to be around the governor's office. Around the party's United States senator or senators? Again there is the problem of turnover of incumbents and the additional probability that a senator's attention will remain focused on congressional and presidential politics in Washington. Publicity advantages and a role in the dispensation of federal resources may continue to give the senators major place in the politics of their home states but not on a sustained enough basis to have an enduring effect upon state party organization. The party leadership in the state legislature is another possible organizing center, and here the probabilities are higher.

The state legislature is a body with a corporate life separable from the political fortunes of particular individuals. The opportunities for revitalizing party agencies or creating new ones are therefore ever present and not contingent upon any particular party leader being in office. The need to organize will grow as the consequences of reapportionment take hold, as mastery of the primary election process improves, as state legislative districts become more competitive, and as transactions with the national party require greater state party representativeness and cohesion. In addition, the state legislature is a prime agency for recruiting, training, and testing new leadership talent.

For those who may be overly concerned about the future of the federal system in this country, the prospect of a more vigorously competitive state party politics offers much hope. "States' rights" may even become less a facade for local party oligarchies and more an aspect of state responsibility as stronger and more responsive state parties contribute to the vitality of each state and the nation as a whole.

Sectionalism: Then and Now

During its first hundred years, the Democratic party lived in a political environment crisscrossed by sectionalism. At first the sections were simply North and South. The "West"—which then lay east of the Mississippi—acquired a sectional consciousness during the 1820s and 1830s and became the "Midwest" during Reconstruction. The Mountain States of the Rockies and the Far West along the Pacific completed the collection of U.S. regions by the end of the nineteenth century.

American political sectionalism has been reinforced by economic, cultural, and partisan distinctions among the regions; for example, manufacturing, finance, and Republicanism in the North; cotton plantations, tenant farming, slavery, and Democrats in the South. During the New Deal era sectionalism, particularly the southern variety, began to decline as a decisive factor in party politics. When it was influential, sectionalism rested upon the local strength of particular state parties and coalitions among state parties, for example, the Richmond Junto and the Albany Regency.

Those first president-makers, Alexander Hamilton of New York and Thomas Jefferson of Virginia, dealt with sectional requirements when they proposed in their prolific correspondence how the national tickets should be composed. As we have seen, the first president, Washington, came from Virginia and his vice president, Adams, from Massachusetts. Later, Adams accepted Jefferson of Virginia as his vice president. The Virginia Dynasty—Jefferson, Madison, and Monroe—had vice presidents from New York (Burr and Clinton) and Massachusetts (Elbridge Gerry). The West came into the presidential sectional balance with Henry Clay of Kentucky and Andrew Jackson of Tennessee. In the twenty-five presidential and vice-presidential slates put together by the nominating conventions of the Democratic party from 1832 to 1928, inclusive, sectional combinations were consummated as follows (section of presidential nominee indicated first): eleven North-Midwest, four North-South, two each South-North, Midwest-South, Midwest-North, and Midwest-Midwest, one North-North, and one (1836) North with three vice-presidential nominees from different regions.

The role of sectionalism in American politics was given a classic exposition by the eminent historian Frederick Jackson Turner. Throughout the nineteenth century, according to Turner, rival societies, free and slave, existed in the North and the South. Emigrants from each of these societies marched side by side into the unoccupied lands of the frontier West, each attempting to dominate the back country. With the disappearance of the frontier, a more stable pattern of sectionalism developed, each territorial unit with its own political characteristics and interest.

The deliberations of Congress and national party conventions led to decisions which could be characterized as "treaties between sections" in the manner of treaties between nations. The national political parties were, in Turner's view, the most effective single political institution for the prevention of sectional disunion. Party ran across all sections and evoked intersectional or nonsectional loyalties. A dissenting minority within one section had an organic connection with party associates in other sections at the same time that the majority interests of a section received their proper political recognition. Thus, the voter could act continentally and the politicians were compelled to act on policies that transcended their particular sections.

Until the 1930s, as noted earlier, a major factor in sectional political behavior was the one-party character of nearly two-thirds of the states: twelve one-party Democratic states in the South and nineteen one-party Republican states mainly in New England and the Midwest. Sectionalism rested heavily upon the noncompetitive character of party politics within particular sets of states. The tendencies more recently, however, have been toward greater party competition in a greater number of states and are likely to have consequences for the future of sectionalism and the Democratic party.

One of the most visible changes is the disappearance of the Democratic "Solid South." This sectional bloc consisted of the eleven states that, between the end of Reconstruction (about 1876) and the end of the New Deal (mid-1940s), almost unanimously gave their vote to Democrats at all levels: presidents, governors, state legislators, United States senators and representatives, mayors and school board members. The Solid South arose as a reaction to the conditions of the Reconstruction era. Scarred by the battles of the Civil War, southerners sought postwar power through the secret armies of the Ku Klux Klan. Without economic resources to replace lost slave property and ravaged lands, the South sank into impoverishment, whose grim companions were ignorance and racism. Victims of the vengeful Reconstruction programs of the Radical Republicans, the South in turn ostracized blacks and Republicans, excluding both almost entirely from its precincts and ballots.

The racial reaction to Reconstruction focused the brunt of southern frustration and dissatisfaction upon an accessible scapegoat: the ex-slave. Many southern blacks, without group traditions to provide ego-strength and fearful of migrating from the land of their childhood, fatalistically accepted this treatment as part of the "natural order" of things. The natural order of southern politics had very specific political features that reinforced and perpetuated it. Among these:

1. Legislative numbers. Until the 1930s, nearly a fourth of all the seats in Congress were occupied by Democratic senators and representatives from the eleven southern states.

2. Two-thirds Democratic nominating rule. Prior to 1940, Democratic national conventions required a two-thirds majority to nominate. By maintaining unity among themselves and soliciting a few additional votes from border states or splinter factions, the southerners were able to veto any candidate who failed to lend a friendly ear to their demands.

3. Filibuster. The United States Senate has traditionally permitted unlimited debate. This assured that any protest or dissent worthy of at least one senator's—not to mention twenty-two—interest would be articulated and could even bring the legislative process to a standstill.

4. The white primary. Using poll taxes, special literacy requirements, grandfather clauses, and other election administration devices, for decades southern whites were able to exclude blacks almost entirely from the electoral process, leaving the selection of public officers and policies to local white rural machines.

5. Seniority. In Congress, a one-party district usually permitted incumbents long tenure, long tenure led to seniority, and seniority meant committee chairmanships and other powerful posts. A Democratic majority in either house of Congress—fairly normal in this century—repeatedly put a phalanx of long-termed and senior southerners into committee chairmanships, the major gateways of national legislation.

6. The race issue. When no other political clarion call worked, the southern politician could always use the race issue to bring pressure for unity. With blacks feared and excluded from the polls, a southern politician could be certain that his position on race was the ultimate aid to reelection.

In recent decades, much has happened to diminish these ancient pieces of southern political architecture.

1. Legislative numbers. New Deal landslides gave the Democrats nationwide congressional majorities far in excess of what they needed to produce legislative decisions. (See Tables 4 and 5.) Southern representatives in both houses were no longer so vital to the passage of legislation nor so capable of preventing it. To forestall this loss of power, southern Democrats forged a coalition with conservative Republicans in the late 1930s, but this tended to be a limited-purpose alliance. In 1957, liberal Democrats in Congress informally organized the "Democratic Study Group," an informational and voting bloc that successfully countered southern influence from time to time. The Great Society landslide in 1964 and the post-Watergate Democratic victories of 1974 have further weakened the southern legislative bloc.

2. Two-thirds nominating rule. The rule was abolished in 1936 and southerners were unable to have it reinstated during the "stop-Truman" maneuvers of 1948. One consequence has been the shift from a multifactional to a predominantly bifactional politics within the party. Bifactionalism tends to increase the use of ideological and policy distinctions, for example, liberal versus conservative, pacifist versus military interventionist. With the two-thirds rule gone, Democratic national conventions will probably less often experience such stalemates as those of 1920 (44 ballots) and 1924 (103 ballots), but they are more likely to be divided by stubborn and durable factions.

3. Filibuster. In 1917, the procedure for closing debate in the Senate was slightly modified so that only two-thirds of those present and voting rather than two-thirds of all members was required for

cloture. After 1949, Senate liberals engaged in repeated efforts to ease the cloture provisions. One approach has been to reduce the proportion of votes needed from two-thirds to three-fifths, that is, from 67 to 60 percent of those present and voting. Another has been to distinguish between procedural issues, for which two-thirds could be retained, and substantive issues, requiring three-fifths or less.

The philosophical issue is not a simple one and is likely to be troublesome for some time. Liberals as well as conservatives have used the filibuster and recognize it as a potent tool in the hands of a minority with intensely felt views. Minority rights continue to be valued in American politics, and, often enough, the filibuster is a minority's last nonviolent tactic. In March 1975, after prolonged debate, the Senate changed its cloture rule from two-thirds of those present and voting to three-fifths of the full membership (60 votes). Liberals tried but were unable to reduce this to a simple majority of those present and voting.

Between 1917 and 1975, under the two-thirds cloture rule, there were 103 cloture votes of which 24 were successful. Sixteen of the 24 occurred during the 1971–1975 period, indicating a decline in minority power in recent years. Only one bill—a 1974 proposal for a consumer protection agency—might have passed if the three-fifths rule had been in effect. If a simple majority could have voted cloture, another 24 of the 103 cloture votes would have succeeded. The 1975 three-fifths rule is not likely to open flood-gates of new legislation, but it is yet another step toward compelling senators to vote on substantive issues rather than on parliamentary procedures.[7]

4. The white primary. The exclusion of citizens from participation in party primaries on racial grounds came under attack in the courts during the 1920s. The *Classic* (1941), *Allwright* (1944), and other decisions by the Supreme Court placed fairly strict legal restrictions on these discriminatory practices. The Civil Rights acts of 1957, 1960, and 1964 further armed the attorney general with powers for combating racism at the ballot box. The Civil Rights Act of 1965 provided for direct federal intervention through the appointment of federal examiners who could register persons in counties and states falling below certain registration standards. The antipoll tax Twenty-fourth Amendment went into effect in 1964, eliminating the poll tax in the few states where it still was levied. As a consequence, black registration in the South rose from 12 percent of those of voting age in 1948 to more than 62 percent at the beginning of the 1970s, bringing the level of black registration to

within eight-to-ten percentage points of white registration. As anticipated, the exercise of the vote has radically changed the political life of the black citizen in the South as politicians of all parties and factions now vie for his or her support.

5. Seniority. The rule of seniority in Congress has been subject to attack for more than a generation and has been significantly diluted by the introduction of other criteria for committee chairmanship assignments. Party is an increasingly influential criterion, particularly through the use of the secret ballot in caucus decisions. Committee assignments now also take into account the legislator's geographical origin, special competence, and factional orientation. The "Johnson rule" of the Eighty-third Congress added another consideration, requiring that each new Democratic member of the Senate receive at least one major committee assignment.

The increase in party influence and the decline in numbers of safe one-party constituencies continue to diminish seniority as a southern "bargaining chip" in congressional brokering. More specifically, by the early 1970s, after both parties in the House of Representatives began employing criteria other than seniority for choosing committee chairmen, their respective caucuses also began to vote on acceptance or rejection of Committee on Committees recommendations for chairmen and ranking minority members. In 1973, House Democrats required caucus votes on each committee chairmanship to be accomplished by secret ballot if one-fifth of the members so desired. A similar rule was adopted by Senate Democrats in 1975. In 1975, too, the House Democratic caucus, as we shall see, used their new chairmanship selection procedure to replace three senior chairmen from the South with three younger northerners. The seniority rule, another substantial resource in sectional politics, is soon likely to be gone, its demise hastened since 1971 by retirements and deaths among aging southern leaders.

6. The race issue. Although race continues to seem the most intractable of southern issues, a new generation of southern politicians has seen the wisdom of setting it aside as a topic of campaign rhetoric. The growing size of the black vote has contributed to moderation in matters of race. Furthermore, blacks in growing numbers are being elected to state and local offices. Many younger southerners proudly claim that the South is handling its racial difficulties more skillfully and successfully than other sections of the nation.

A substantial part of the change must be credited to the opening of the ballot box and the emergence of a competitive party politics. A new era in southern political, economic, and social life has undoubtedly begun, and, with it, perhaps a new sectional politics. The increase of regional governors' conferences and regional meetings of party officials seems to assure many more decades of some type of sectionalism. Southerners, it must be conceded, are old hands in national politics and are not likely to remain isolated so long as sectionalism continues to be a factor in national politics. Southerners will undoubtedly find new grounds for political collaborations within the South and between the South and other sections. For example, such nonracial issues as land and resource conservation, housing and urban redevelopment, industrial growth, and similar problems may bring Pacific and Mountain States' Democrats of the West together into public policy alliances with the South in Congress and at the national conventions. Just as New York (the largest state in the Union after 1812) and the South put together the Jacksonian Revolution of the 1830s and 1840s, so may California (the largest state in the Union after 1964) and the South generate some yet-to-be-named political revolution of the 1980s and 1990s.

The Party-in-Congress

Within the three branches of the national government, partisanship emerged earliest and most naturally in the most numerous branch, the Congress, and, within Congress, in the more numerous house, the House of Representatives. This imitated the evolution of legislative parties in the British system, where the House of Commons was the site of the earliest partisan groupings. This historical comparison quickly weakens. In the British system, the king's prime minister and his cabinet are chosen from the membership of Parliament to administer the executive agencies of government. The choice of prime minister came to depend upon which party held a majority in the House of Commons. Thus, the prime minister and his governing cabinet are directly beholden to their parliamentary party and the membership as directly to the electorate. The American presidential system, on the other hand, has no such direct line of political accountability. Presidents, United States senators, and members of the House of Representatives respond to different selection procedures and electoral constituencies. Nor is there any simple and direct method, such as a vote of confidence or a ministerial resignation, by which presidents, senators, and representatives may conclusively influence each other. Even the presidential veto and the congressional override tend to be limited weapons of interbranch power. Congressional and presidential politicians, therefore, have had to improvise their own tools of influence, and most of these tools have been wielded through some form of party organization.

During the first century, the Democrats and their political predecessors made creative improvisations in the party-in-Congress, as described below. The Madisonians and the Jeffersonians organized the party caucus so well and it became so powerful that it soon earned the deprecating title "King Caucus." During the Reconstruction era, the Johnsonians inaugurated the congressional campaign committee system with which to do battle with the Radical Republicans. The positions of Speaker, party floor leader, and party whip grew steadily more powerful in the service of both major parties. These were some of the more significant organizational tools of the party-in-Congress for most of the century prior to the New Deal.

Congressional Caucus

Madison's Democratic-Republicans, contending with a Federalist administration, conducted the first congressional caucus on April 2, 1796, under conditions described earlier. Actually, this caucus simply formalized earlier consultations, the object being a stricter mobilization of fellow-partisans for what was expected to be an extremely close vote in the Senate on the Jay Treaty. The vote turned out to be 20–10, precisely the two-thirds needed to ratify. In the House action on appropriations for implementing the treaty, the favorable vote resulted from a tie broken by the chairman of the Committee of the Whole. The caucus invoked party loyalty and discipline for the first time in deciding a public policy issue. It was with respect to nominations for president and vice president, however, that the caucus gained greatest power and notoriety between 1800 and 1820.

Both Democratic-Republicans and Federalists in Congress held secret caucuses in 1800 to decide behind which of their respective candidates they would unite in the presidential and vice-presidential races. After the election, unhappy with this mechanism of party organization and unhappier with Jefferson's election, the Federalists never again used the congressional caucus for nominating purposes. The Jeffersonians, on the other hand, continued to use the caucus but with decreasing effectiveness. Secrecy was discontinued; participants began to respond to constituency rather than collegial pressures; caucus rules became more formal, although contending factions were not reluctant to use a fast parliamentary trick now and then. Factions were quick to form behind particular leaders. In 1812, when Madison was renominated, Clinton supporters bolted to make a separate nomination. By 1816, after western congressmen arrived for the first time to the halls of Congress, the caucus was being challenged as unrepresentative and dominated by an "old guard."

Apart from its more visible and controversial activities in the presidential nominating field, the Democratic-Republican caucus was a powerful instrument of national policy. Although Jefferson was indisputably the strongest president of the period, his achievements were possible mainly through his handling of the congressional caucus. In an anti-executive party and era, Jefferson maintained the appearances of a passive presidency. With the aid of the caucus, however, he dominated the selection of the Speaker of the House, the principal committee chairmen, and the principal policy actions. Whereas Washington thought of himself as a Whig king, Jefferson operated as a prime minister.

The caucus was at its best when demanding party loyalty under conditions of close party competition, as it did at its first meeting in 1796. However, in a one-party system, such as prevailed between 1816 and 1824, the caucus tended to be ineffective, the cockpit of competing factional ambitions and an object of public suspicion. King Caucus was put to rest by the Jacksonian machine in the mid-1820s, at least in matters of presidential nomination. Jackson was the first president to be nominated and elected without congressional involvement. His independence from Congress eventually stimulated the formation of the Whig party, a coalition of congressional leaders including Clay, Calhoun, Webster, and others seeking to reestablish legislative supremacy.

The influence of the Democratic caucus has waxed and waned over the decades. Its principal and most persistent role has been to serve as the vehicle for selecting the party's leadership in the House: the Speaker or Minority Floor Leader, the party whip, the chairmen of the Ways and Means committees, and the principal appointed staff. When a Speaker was strong, he tended to give the caucus little to do in the policy field. A strong president, on the other hand, would occasionally ask the caucus to make some particular issue or legislative vote a "party matter" in the hope of pulling extra votes on grounds of party loyalty. With the brief exception of a strong House caucus during Wilson's presidency, in the immediate decades prior to the New Deal, the Democratic caucus was little used. This changed somewhat under Franklin D. Roosevelt.

Congressional Campaign Committees

Another agency of party is the congressional campaign committee. Here again the Democratic-Republicans scored a first. At the conclusion of their tumultuous nominating caucus of June 1812, the Madisonian managers arranged for the appointment of a Committee of Correspondence to conduct the ensuing national campaign. This was the first congressional campaign committee and included one representative from twenty-five of the nation's twenty-seven state delegations to Congress.

Campaign committees called "committees of correspondence" were created from time to time over the next three decades. Headquartered in Washington, of varying composition, they usually had responsibilities for the presidential campaigns. In 1842, a more exclusively congressional campaign committee was created by the Democrats. In this midterm election, Democratic legislators from both houses and most states formed a campaign committee to publish a declaration of principles and to mount a unified attack upon the Whig administration of President Harrison.

The use of joint presidential-congressional campaign committees was revived by the new Republican party in 1860 (known as the Republican Executive Congressional Committee) and again in 1864 (this time called the Union Congressional Committee). Both committees issued scores of campaign pamphlets and undoubtedly prompted the formation of the pro-Johnson National Union Campaign Committee of 1866, the first of the modern congressional campaign committees.

When Andrew Johnson, a Democrat, became president upon Lincoln's assassination, he kept most of Lincoln's cabinet but inherited little of Lincoln's personal political following and no party machine responsive to his own direction. Radical Republicans in Congress were hostile to him personally, his Democratic background, his moderate program for Reconstruction, and any plans he may have had to seek reelection. Johnson's political friends, on the other hand, advised the president to build a party organization of his own and to use the presidential patronage freely to nourish it. Johnson's allies called a novel midterm National Union Convention for August 11, 1866, in Philadelphia, and hoped to attract both

Democratic and Republican moderates to it for the purpose of acclaiming Johnson and organizing a midterm campaign committee. Although leading Republicans attended and conspicuous "Copperhead" Democrats were denied seats, the Johnson leaders nonetheless had difficulty keeping the convention from becoming a purely Democratic rally.

The pro-Johnson convention established a National Union Executive Committee consisting of two congressional delegates from each state as well as delegates from territories and the District of Columbia. It also chose a nine-member Resident Committee to coordinate campaign efforts from Washington. Working with the Resident Committee, Johnson inaugurated another presidential tradition by taking his famous "swing around the circle," a grass-roots campaign tour of the country between August 28 and September 15 in support of pro-Johnson congressional candidates. Not to be outdone, the Radical Republicans organized their own midterm convention, congressional campaign committee, and grass-roots campaign. The Radicals were able to win a majority in both houses of Congress.

The congressional campaign committee was employed again in 1868 and acquired its modern functions, namely, gathering information about the electoral situation in the congressional districts, fund-raising (particularly on behalf of closely contested districts), and the distribution of press releases and party literature in the local races. Early Democratic congressional campaign committees often involved themselves in both presidential and congressional campaigns, tending for a time to do more on the presidential side. During the last quarter of the nineteenth century, the committees were made up of members from both houses. Senators, who tended to be wealthier than members of the lower house, sometimes served as chairmen and principal financial contributors. During the 1880s these committees began to do less and less in presidential campaigns and focused almost entirely on the election of members of the House of Representatives. With adoption of the Seventeenth Amendment in 1913 requiring direct popular election of senators, party members in the Senate established their own senatorial campaign committees.

Throughout the Reconstruction period from 1866 to 1880, the congressional campaign committee, as had the congressional caucus of the pre-Jacksonian era, served in large measure as an instrument of legislative influence over the executive branch. This was particularly evident in the victory of congressional Radical Republicans over President Johnson and in Radical influence over the Grant administrations. Similar congressional influence was often exercised among Democrats through the committees' large role in presidential campaigns, the unabashed fund-raising practice of collecting from federal officeholders a percentage of their salaries in the guise of "voluntary contributions," and the scarcity of winning Democratic presidential nominees.

M. Ostrogorski's description of congressional campaign committees, written in 1902, and paraphrased below, best summarizes the activities of the committees from the turn of the century to the New Deal. Each "congressional committee," as he called them, is a temporary agency that disappears with the expiration of the particular session of Congress. "Considerations of general policy are even more foreign to the congressional committee than to the national committee; it pays no heed to platform or programs and simply endeavors to ensure the success, at the congressional elections, of the candidates who bear the party label, whatever their complexion."

A congressional campaign committee, according to Ostrogorski, divides all the congressional districts into categories: "the good, the hopeless, and the doubtful." Almost entirely neglecting the first two groups, the committee directs most of its efforts toward the districts of the last category. Its methods include overt propaganda by party speakers and through political literature. There are also methods of a more secret kind, in which money fills "a not inconsiderable place."

The sinews of war are supplied to the congressional campaign committee by wealthy members of the party, but these donations, noted Ostrogorski, are usually much smaller than those made to the national committee. The "calculated generosity" of the donors is obviously reserved for the presidential campaign in which there is a greater stake. (Public funding of presidential campaigns has sharply curtailed this practice since 1974.)

The congressional campaign committee intervenes most actively in the midterm campaigns, reported Ostrogorski. At the request of the candidates, the committee sends them speakers, political literature, and sometimes money. The committee hardly remains inactive in the intervals between elections. At these times, it follows closely the fortunes of the party in the districts. It analyzes the vote at each succeeding election by counties and if it notes a decline in the votes polled by a party candidate, it makes inquiry into the causes. Perhaps the fault lies with party factions. The candidate may not be popular. The policies of the party may be creating discontent. The congressional campaign committee tries to rectify these difficulties. It is in constant touch with county committees, the latter making the congressional committee the confidant of their troubles. With the opening of presidential campaigns, the congressional campaign committee places all its resources at the disposal of the national committee and becomes its close ally, diminishing its own initiatives, for in the presidential year "all the elections follow the fortunes of the contest for the president."[8]

Recent Advances in Congressional Party Organization

Over the generations, the pendulum of power has swung back and forth between the legislative and executive branches. Much of the momentum of these swings has been derived from organizational changes that strengthen the influence of one or the other branch. Prior to Andrew Jackson, Congress, and particularly the House of Representatives, was the center of party and governmental politics at the national level. Presidents from Washington to John Quincy Adams acted *as though* the Constitution had created a parliamentary system similar to the one emerging in England. In the 1820s and 1830s, however, Jackson and Van Buren created presidential party agencies that converted the presidency into an independent power center in national politics. Then the Senate during the 1850s and the Radical Republicans in both houses during the 1860s and 1870s succeeded in reasserting legislative supremacy.

At the turn of the century, the presidency was once again swinging toward the pinnacle of party politics. The philosophical case for this shift was cogently made by Woodrow Wilson. His perception, like that of the first presidents, was that the parliamentary model should and could apply to the American system. Wilson argued tht it was the president, acting as a prime minister, who must be ascendant over Congress. The Budget Act of 1921 in effect gave presidents a basic tool of prime ministerial management, namely, a Bureau of the Budget devoted to the preparation of an executive budget.

Franklin Roosevelt avoided such institutional speculations. Instead, his New Deal programs created a political environment in which significant changes in the organization of the party-in-Congress became necessary and began to take place. All seven Congresses elected during Roosevelt's incumbency were Democratic in both houses, usually overwhelmingly so. The Democratic majorities were attributed largely to the "coattail effect" of Roosevelt's popularity. As we have seen, the size of the Democratic majorities reduced the influence of the southern bloc although it also stimulated the emergence of the congressional coalition of conservative Republicans and southern Democrats. The Democratic majorities also enabled an activist president to help develop the formal party organization in Congress that would permit his associates there to promote his programs more readily. One new legislative arrangement was the modified whip system described earlier, wherein the Democratic congressmen within fifteen regional groupings elected an assistant whip from each. Another consequence of Roosevelt's influence was the elevation of particularly astute and skilled men to positions of senior party leadership in both houses: William B. Bankhead of Alabama (1936–1940) and Sam Rayburn (1940–1961) in the House of Representatives, Joseph T. Robinson of Arkansas (1933–1937), and Alben Barkley (1937–1948) in the Senate.

In 1944 and 1945, Congress created a special committee, headed by Senator Robert M. La Follette, Jr., and Congressman Mike Monroney, to study its internal organization and operation. This self-study was timely in that the legislative consequences of the 1910 revolt against Speaker Cannon had become an obstacle to congressional-presidential party cooperation by the late 1930s. The report of this Joint Committee on the Organization of Congress led to passage of the Legislative Reorganization Act of 1946, a milestone in congressional development. The number of standing committees was reduced by more than half. Each committee was provided with a professional staff. A Legislative Budget was created to set overall appropriation and national debt ceilings. Lobbyists were required to make quarterly financial reports.

While these and other provisions followed the recommendations of the La Follette–Monroney Committee, several major practices, although challenged, were left untouched, particularly the seniority rule for selection of committee chairmen and the agenda-setting powers of the House Rules Committee. A provision to create policy committees for each major party in each house, potentially a threat to the authority of the Speaker and the Rules Committee, was deleted from the bill by the House of Representatives.

The policy-committee concept was resurrected the following year in the Senate and authorized for this body. Because of their minority status, Senate Republicans, then under the leadership of Robert A. Taft, built their Policy Committee into a useful coordinative agency and broadened its functions and staff considerably over the years. The Democrats, on the other hand, preferred to have their Senate leadership functions rest with the Majority Leader who also served as chairman of three principal party organs: the Democratic Policy Committee, which was used primarily to schedule Senate legislation; the Steering Commitee, which assigned party members to all standing committees; and the conference of all Democratic senators, which formally confirmed the selection of the party leadership.

Under Speaker Rayburn and Majority Leaders Barkley and Johnson, the House Democratic caucus and the Senate conference were rarely used. The three leaders were candid in their explanations. Policy discussion in caucuses divided the members sectionally and ideologically. This, they argued, produced only negative results: the exaggeration of differences, the opening of new conflicts, and the failure of every effort to reach consensus. It also inhibited their own leadership initiatives.

Recognizing the legitimacy and tenacity of such differences, approximately eighty liberal Democratic congressmen inaugurated ad hoc consultations among themselves in 1957. Five of the legislators initially contributed part of their respective clerk hire allowances for the appointment of two staff persons to serve the group. By 1959, the group formalized itself as the Democratic Study Group, conducted regular discussion sessions on policy and legislative strategy, created an efficient whip system of its own capable of bringing most of its now more than one hundred members to the floor within a few minutes, and became a voting coalition nearly as powerful as the Democratic southern bloc. With two such coalitions, little in the way of compromises could be expected to come out of the Democratic caucus.

The liberal coalition notwithstanding, the twelve-member Rules Committee remained the bastion of House conservatism. Two southern Democrats and four Republicans frequently voted together to deadlock the efforts of the other six Democrats to advance bills supported by the Democratic majority. In 1961, President Kennedy and Speaker Rayburn, in a special effort requiring every resource at their command, were able, by a House vote of 217 to 212, to enlarge the Rules Committee to fifteen. Two of the three additional members were Democratic "regulars" although they did not always vote on the liberal side.

In 1965, the large number of new Democratic congressmen carried into office by the Johnson landslide adopted a twenty-one-day rule which survived only that Eighty-ninth Congress. According to this rule, on the second and fourth Mondays of each month, the Speaker was empowered to recognize any member of a standing committee for the purpose of calling up any resolutin pending in the Rules Committee for more than twenty-one days. The rule thus provided the Democratic leadership with an important opportunity for circumventing the Rules Committee; seven of eight bills called up this way were enacted. The twenty-one-day rule was repealed by the Ninetieth Congress when there was an influx of new Republican members.

By 1975 Democrats were again in a numerical position to deal influentially with problems of party organization in Congress. Voter reaction in 1974 to Watergate and the Nixon resignation swept two-to-one Democratic majorities into both houses: 291 to 144 in the House of Representatives, 62 to 38 in the Senate. Seventy-five of the 291 House Democrats were freshmen of moderate-to-liberal orientation. With the cooperation of Speaker Carl Albert and other senior leaders, these freshmen became a critical factor in the organization of the Ninety-fourth Congress.

Preparation for substantial congressional reform had been going on for some time. In 1970, Common Cause, a citizen lobbying group, and the Democratic Study Group (DSG) worked closely to accomplish changes in Democratic caucus organization. In 1970, the caucus changed its rules so that election to each standing committee chairmanship could be voted upon separately and by secret ballot. In 1970 and 1972, the senior Democrat on each committee was, as usual, reelected, although liberals did test the new rule by unsuccessfully challenging the chairman of the House District of Columbia Committee, John McMillan of South Carolina.

Other rule changes in 1972–1973 had immediate consequences: creation of a Democratic Steering and Policy Committee in the House to recommend legislative priorities and policy to the caucus; open committee and subcommitee hearings; guarantee of one major committee and subcommittee assignment for every Democratic member regardless of seniority. The new Steering and Policy Committee consisted of twenty-four members: the Speaker, the Floor Leader, the caucus chairman, nine members chosen by the Speaker to represent such interests as the black caucus, congresswomen, and freshmen, and twelve chosen by the caucus to represent different geographical regions. Following a report by a committee under the chairmanship of Congressman Jonathan B. Bingham, the Democratic Study Group recommended still further changes intended to strengthen the caucus.

In 1974, Congressman Phillip Burton, who had been chairman of the Democratic Study Group, was on hand to welcome the seventy-five new Democrats just elected, help incorporate most of them into the DSG, and mobilize them as part of the organizational reform movement. Many of the newcomers appreciated the fact that the DSG had been an important factor in their electoral victories.

When the Ninety-fourth Congress and the Democratic Steering Committee convened, Majority Leader Thomas P. O'Neill routinely nominated for reelection the senior members of the House standing committees. The Steering Committee, voting by secret ballot, rejected two of the senior members—Wright Patman of Texas and Wayne Hays of Ohio—but approved the other eighteen. In the full Democratic caucus the next day, the caucus vote rejected the Steering Committee's recommendations and singled out two other senior members to be denied chairmanships: W. R. Poage of Texas and Edward Hebert of Louisiana. In later votes by the Steering Committee and the caucus, Patman, Poage, and Hebert were replaced by younger and more liberal represenatives but Hays was reinstated. A major challenge to the seniority rule had thus been successfully carried out by a party agency. Burton, who had been one of Congress's most outspoken liberals, was elected chairman of the newly energized House Democratic caucus.

Other caucus procedural changes were also made at this time. Responsibility for committee assignments was shifted from the Democratic members of the House Ways and Means Committee to the Democratic Steering and Policy Committee, a more liberal body now chaired by and under the influence of the Speaker. The Speaker was also given the power to select members of the powerful Rules Committee. In addition to a more influential role in the election of committee chairmen, the caucus gave itself authority to elect subcommittee chairmen for the powerful House Appropriations Committee. A system for making caucus votes public was devised. Discussion was begun regarding caucus power to bind Democrats on matters of legislative procedure but not on substantive issues; for example, to direct Democrats in committees to move particular bills to the floor but without the caucus declaring a party line on how to vote on the substance of the bills. This was intended to be another way of further diluting the power of the Rules Committee and of encouraging full-scale discussion of substantive issues.

In the Senate a somewhat less publicized series of reforms took place in 1975. Committee hearings were opened to the public, except when a committee majority, with a quorum present, votes to go into executive session. The Democratic conference could, after 1977, vote by secret ballot on each standing committee chairmanship. Incumbent chairmen failing to receive 80 percent of the conference vote would become subject to contest and another vote.

There was also a change in the Senate's rule governing cloture. Under the new rule, cloture could be accomplished by a three-fifths vote of the entire constitutional membership of the Senate, that is, sixty of the one hundred members, instead of two-thirds of those present and voting. The new three-fifths rule could cut off debate on substantive issues but *not* on procedural matters. Procedural issues would continue to be governed by the two-thirds-present-and-voting rule. The new procedure was considered a modest but significant victory against the filibuster.

Since Democratic caucus and House rules may be changed with each new Congress, some questioned whether specific 1975 House caucus changes would remain. A similar doubt may be expressed about the Democratic conference and Senate rules changes. What cannot be doubted is the long-term trend in both houses to strengthen the instruments of party consultation and discipline. For the Democrats, the party-in-Congress, whatever its current factional balance, has been successfully elevated to a new importance in legislative and policy leadership.

The Future Party-in-Congress: New Concepts of Caucus

For all practical purposes, Congress, particularly the House of Representatives, has been a Democratic body since the New Deal. Therefore, the direction and degree of the party's legislative organization have had important consequences for the organization of Congress itself. The Legislative Reform Act of 1946, the battles over the membership of the House Rules Committee, the pressures to eliminate the filibuster, the creation of the liberal Democratic Study Group, the changes affecting the selection of committee chairmen, and the strengthening of the Democratic caucus have all contributed to new and still-evolving forms of congressional and party organization.

Will such developments in the party-in-Congress continue and will the pace of change accelerate? The probabilities are good that the party-in-Congress will grow stronger. The electorate is likely to return substantial Democratic majorities long enough to keep alive these reform efforts. The Democratic House caucus and Senate conference will continue to develop—in steering, policy, and similar management committees—methods of collective leadership through which the factional balance may be kept current and moderate. Seniority will continue to give way to party, expertise, regional, and similar considerations in leadership assignments.

The pace of such developments is contingent upon the composition, experience, and ideological orientation of the Democratic members in any particular session. This, in turn, may become contingent upon the extent to which congressional districts become more universally competitive, turnover in office increases as a result of competitiveness, and candidates become more beholden to central party agencies such as the congressional campaign committee or the national committee for nomination and campaign resources.

More provocative and speculative questions about the future may be raised with respect to whether or not the party-in-Congress may or should ever become the chief center of power in the national party in the manner of parliamentary parties in Great Britain and other parliamentary systems. Could the party-in-Congress some day (a) coordinate itself in both houses sufficiently to provide a base for decisive influence at the national nominating conventions, (b) compose the national committee and the national chairmanship in such a way as to bring these agencies in line with the policies and strategies of the congressional party, and (c) devise a system for designating a "loyal opposition" spokesman in Congress for the party when it loses the presidential contest? Or, coming from the other direction, will the presidential wing or the national convention reform itself sufficiently to exercise a more comprehensive influence over the caucus and the party-in-Congress? These questions are not likely to be answered in the near future, but they are more likely than ever to be raised.

The questions are titillating and some recent proposed reforms could create political conditions conducive to the development of a more parliamentary form of party system. This appears to be inherent in several of the proposals of the O'Hara Commission. Congressmen Fraser and O'Hara explicitly advocated a more centralized party structure, with the hierarchy of organizational units beginning at the congressional district level.[9] This could conceivably be a highly significant first step toward coordination of congressional, senatorial, statewide, and presidential units of representation and campaign organization within the party. With the disappearance of the city machine and the decline of the anachronistic county organizations, the congressional district is probably the most politically vital unit upon which to build a new kind of grass-roots organization with strong links to the national agencies of the party. Congressional district committees, for example, could become meaningful representative bodies at the base of the party; congressional district staffs could serve combined electoral, legislative, and national party functions.

The proposal to organize at the congressional district level adds significance to the proposal to extend the term of representatives to four years, to be elected coterminously with the president. Such a constitutional amendment would have profound effects upon the electoral organization of the parties. It would reinforce the congressional district as the basic grass-roots unit. The national committee campaign on behalf of the presidential slate and the congressional campaign committee effort on behalf of the most closely contested districts would demand a high degree of coordination. Voter response to party behavior in Congress would come to have a greater impact on voter acceptance of the presidential nominee, and vice versa. This would lead to even greater congressional party leadership participation in the platforms and nominations at the national conventions.

The proposal for direct popular election of the president and vice president, ending the electoral college system, may also reinforce a trend toward parliamentarianization of the national party system. The need to compete in every state with equal energy for every popular vote would multiply the need for a highly organized national committee with direct lines to the grass roots. How large a grass-roots organization is the national committee likely to prefer under such circumstances? The more than 100,000 precincts, each with only a few hundred voters and a high turnover of precinct captains? The more than 3,000 counties whose electoral fortunes are usually quite divorced from those of the national leadership? Or the 435 congressional districts whose national leadership, particularly under conditions of close competition, is intimately concerned with the presidential "coattail" and control of Congress? A direct election system would favor closer ties between the national and congressional district organizations, similar to the ties that exist in parliamentary parties.

Other proposals, not requiring constitutional amendments, could move the party in a similar direction. The 1974 Democratic Charter, for example, has expanded the membership of the national committee to 350. Add another 85 members and develop new methods of selection and the national committee membership could be organizationally tied directly to the 435 congressional districts, where year-round party staffs could work, delegates to the national conventions would be selected, and the constituency's policy concerns could be more clearly channeled into party platforms and congressional legislation. Some observers might suggest that this would be a typically American way of backing into a parliamentary system.

Whatever the future direction of party organization in Congress, the congressional setting is likely to continue to be a network of constituency, committee, expert, and partisan relations in which persuasion and brokerage are the principal techniques for achieving consensus. As in the case of the evolving presidential party, the great challenge to the party-in-Congress over the next half century is likely to be how best congressional fellow-partisans may organize themselves for systematic communication in the process of achieving consensus.

The Presidential Party: Leaders and Organizations

The president's formal constitutional constituency is the 538 members of the electoral college. Each state's voters choose a number of presidential electors equal in size to their congressional delegation in both houses. Originally, the politics of selecting presidential electors took place mainly in the state legislature. (See Table 3.) Today, the plurality popular vote in a state for one or another presidential nominee elects a slate of his pre-designated supporting electors. Thus, unlike the parliamentary system, an American presidential candidate has his own distinct constituency and system of winning election. As a consequence, presidential politics has developed its own organizational components within the parties, frequently referred to as "the presidential party."

During the administrations of Washington and Adams, the presidential parties were essentially the personal coalitions built by Hamilton and Jefferson, whose personal correspondence was the main means for soliciting electoral college votes. From Jefferson's to the second Adams's election, the congressional caucus was the principal influence in the presidential party system. Then, Jackson's "Kitchen Cabinet" served as the chief agency of a presidential party for a brief interim between the demise of the caucus and the arrival of the national nominating convention. It was the national convention, established in 1832, that became the formal center of the modern presidential party.

The national conventions have nominated the party's presidential candidates and their vice-presidential running mates. The platforms written by Democratic conventions are presumably declarations representing the views and promises of all members of the party, but, in practice, platforms are interpreted as guidelines for the presidental nominee and his prospective administration.

Organizationally, the national convention is the supreme unit of the national party, yet it has little directive power over the party-in-Congress and, prior to the 1950s, even less influence over state parties. Until recently, when state parties were given selection powers, the national convention selected the national committee to function as the party's permanent agent between conventions. The national committee, in turn, elects the national chairman, who, in the post–New Deal era, has, among other activities, been responsible for the operation of a permanent headquarters in Washington.

Between national convention and election day, a presidential campaign organization comes into being, often an agency apart from the formal party structure. This campaign organization is likely to be run by the nominee's most trusted political colleague, who may or may not also be chosen as the national committee chairman. A major task of this short-lived campaign organization is to bring together the nominee's defeated opponents for the nomination, party regulars who may be less than enthusiastic about his candidacy, and his own loyal followers—in time for election day. Each nominee thus fashions his own presidential party: the coalition of national convention delegates who nominate him; the national committee that will support his campaign or administration; the national chairman of his own or friendly persuasion; the campaign manager with sufficient skill to reunite all Democrats and get them to the polls. Another component has recently been added: the political advisers that the president may appoint to his Executive Office staff. Although not a formal element of the party structure, these advisers have in fact become a major source of partisan advice and managerial help.

The party-in-Congress is a large group, most of whose members remain relatively anonymous. The presidential party, however, centers conspicuously around one, two, or a few persons: the winning or losing presidential nominee, the leaders of major factions in the national conventions, the national party chairman, and a few others. The names of defeated presidential nominees are readily forgotten by later generations. In their own day, however, presidential nominees are among the best known persons in the nation and their national chairmen are often the best known of the party's "regulars." A brief examination of some of the collective characteristics of these men may reveal something about leadership in the Democratic presidential wing during its first century.

The first Democratic national nominating convention took place in 1832. Between 1832 and 1932, inclusive, the party conducted twenty-six national conventions. These conventions conferred the Democratic presidential nomination upon twenty different men: Jackson, Van Buren, Polk, Cass, Pierce, Buchanan, Douglas, McClellan, Seymour, Greeley, Tilden, Hancock, Cleveland, Bryan, Parker, Wilson, Cox, Davis, Smith, and Roosevelt.

What have presidential nominees—Democratic, Whig, and Republican included—been like since 1831, and in what attributes have Democrats differed from the norm? One study permits generalizations for those nominated between 1831 and 1956, inclusive.[10] The nominees of all major parties for this period were men between the ages of fifty and fifty-four when first nominated, with Democrats younger and closer to fifty than the Republicans. More presidential nominees were born in New York and Ohio than any other state, the former tending to be the principal natal state of Democrats. Nominees were most often sons of professional persons, farmers, or public officials, the Democratic nominees departing only slightly from the norm for the entire group. The nominees were almost invariably professional persons, usually lawyers, and again the Democrats were like the entire group. (While most presidential nominees had read or otherwise studied law in preparation for the bar, they were not always holders of B.A. or LL.B. degrees.) Democrats nominated the only Ph.D. in the 1831–1956 period (Wilson); McGovern in 1972 was the second Ph.D. Most nominees were Presbyterians or Episcopalians, with a preponderance of Democrats belonging to the Presbyterian church. Democrats were also distinguished for having placed the first member of the Catholic faith (Smith) at the head of its ticket (and, later, for electing the first Catholic, Kennedy, to the presidency).

The average presidential nominee in either major party had governmental experience in at least two or three offices, usually at the state or federal levels of government. Democrats drew more frequently from United States senators and state governors and less frequently from the military than the Republicans. The nominees, without major differentiation between parties, also held executive positions at one or another level of the party organization. The Democratic party, in its first-time presidential nominations of recent decades, seemed to prefer the following type of man whenever available: " . . . able political leaders who are still in the prime of life, and who have come up through elective executive office in states where politics is vigorous and competitive, without necessarily having as yet taken on the characteristics of a 'father image.'"[11]

The presidential nominee, whether he wins or loses, is only a *titular* leader of his party, under "contract" for the general support of the party. In the literal sense of a contract, the national convention *offers* him the nomination, which he may or may not *accept*. The nominee holds no formal office in the party, although he has many degrees of informal influence.

If the presidential party does have a *formal* leader, it is the national party chairman. The Democrats were the first to create this office in 1848 and, between 1848 and 1932, placed twenty different men into that position. The twenty: Benjamin Hallett, Robert McLane, David Smalley, August Belmont, Augustus Schell, Abram Hewitt, William Barnum (who held the tenure record of twelve years and one month), Calvin Brice, William Harrity, James K. Jones, Thomas Taggart, Norman Mack, William McCombs, Vance McCormick, Homer Cummings, George White, Cordell Hull, Clement Shaver, John Raskob, and James Farley. In the generalizations that follow, covering the period from 1848 to 1959, additional chairmen include Edward J. Flynn, Frank Walker, Robert Hannegan, James McGrath, William M. Boyle, Jr., Frank McKinney, Stephen Mitchell, and Paul Butler.

Democratic and Republican national chairmen, as a single group, were usually in the forty-five-to-forty-nine-year-old age bracket at the time of first election, with the Democrats tending to be younger. Most chairmen were born in New York, Pennsylvania, or Indiana, with New York the major place of origin. Most chairmen were natives of their state of birth rather than transients from other states, reflecting the fact that they usually worked their way step by step through the local and state party hierarchy.

346

Most chairmen held either the LL.B. or a high school diploma, with Democrats tending to have slightly less formal schooling. Chairmen generally had occupations as professional persons or public officials. The fathers of Democratic chairmen tended to have less occupational training than the average for all chairmen. The religious affiliation among Democratic chairmen was most frequently the Catholic faith; Presbyterian among the Republicans. The governmental experience of the chairmen was mainly in state legislatures and appointive federal posts.

In general, the presidential nominees have tended to have personal attributes as broadly diverse and in many respects similar to those of the American electorate at large. The national chairmen, on the other hand, have been more closely representative of the rank-and-file party workers. The chairmen have been "organization men"—increasingly so in recent decades, and more so on the Democratic side—in that they have had many years of experience in party work and have gone up the organizational ladder steadily during their careers.

Roosevelt and Truman were Jacksonians in presidential style and attention to party organization. The Roosevelt-Truman period saw national party headquarters staff established and grow in size and function. In the more than two decades since, national headquarters has had an average of about 290 employees during presidential election years and 80 or more during interim years. In 1973, taxpayers were allowed to assign one dollar of their tax payments to a presidential campaign fund; such public funds may be expected to add to the resources and responsibilities of the national conventions and national committees. More generally, the several organizational components of the presidential party are likely to continue develping functionally and structurally, stimulated by the growth of the presidency, the pressures of intraparty and interparty competition, and the further public recognition of their significance in a democratic society.

Perhaps the weakest link in the system of presidential parties is in the "titular" status of the presidential nominees. The defeated nominee has no legal or traditional basis for continuing to serve as the leader of a "loyal opposition," a familiar position in the British and other parliamentary systems. In their substantial efforts to keep the party together or to serve as its out-party spokesman, Tilden, Bryan, and Stevenson sharpened popular awareness of the lack of *an* opposition leader in the national political structure. Their difficulties in exercising some of the functions of opposition leadership only demonstrated the problems in a federal system, with separated powers among the branches of national government, and with decentralized party organizations. Yet, party development over future years is likely to compel further attention to the titular nature of presidential leadership, particularly in the out-party. An increasingly competitive party system demanding top-to-bottom organizational coordination and factional reconciliation seems certain to keep alive concern about the role of presidential party leadership—in office or in opposition—in the overall affairs of the national party.[12]

The National Convention in Transition

Contemporary development of the Democratic National Convention as the party's principal governing body advanced substantially after the elimination of the two-thirds rule in 1936 and Truman's election in 1948. The party began to concern itself systematically with issues of organizational representativeness, self-governance, and party loyalty. The national convention of 1932, it will be recalled, recommended that the next convention consider the question of two-thirds rule. The convention of 1936 did so and abolished the southern wing's century-old veto power over the party's nominating process. In 1948, hoping to punish President Truman for carrying forward his civil rights program, southern delegations sought to reinstitute the two-thirds rule. Failing this, and unable to modify the civil rights plank of the 1948 platform, the Mississippi and most of the Alabama delegations withdrew from the convention in compliance with instructions from their respective state conventions to do so if a civil rights plank were adopted.

Subsequently, the anti-Truman southerners nominated a Thurmond-Wright States' Rights ticket, expecting to exercise their ultimate veto through the election process. The States' Rights ticket carried Alabama, Louisiana, Mississippi, and South Carolina, plus one elector in Tennessee, thirty-eight electoral votes in all. In Alabama, the national Truman-Barkley ticket was not even placed on the ballot; in the other three states, the national nominees were on the ballot but not as the candidates of the official state Democratic parties. The Dixiecrat strategy failed, and Truman won.

As 1952 approached, the Dixiecrats retained control of the state parties in Louisiana, Mississippi, and South Carolina, but a loyalist faction led by United States Senators Lister Hill and John J. Spark-man won control of the party machinery in Alabama. It had been customary in southern states for party officers and delegates to take an explicit pledge of loyalty to the state party. The Hill-Sparkman loyalists on the state committee were able to pass a rule requiring all candidates for national convention delegates to make a similar pledge of loyalty to nominees chosen by the national convention. In Georgia, Louisiana, Mississippi, Texas, South Carolina, and Vir-ginia, however, Dixiecrats were able to prevent adoption of such a pledge. In some cases, state parties reserved the right to put on the Democratic ballot whomever they wished. These states also sent delegations in 1952 with instructions to bolt or withhold commit-ment to the national ticket if circumstances required.

At convention time there were contesting loyalist delegations from Mississippi and Texas. The seating contests in these delega-tions set off a chain of events that led to the Moody (Senator Blair Moody of Michigan) amendment to the convention rules. The Moody resolution, adopted by voice vote, included the following requirement:

No delegate shall be seated unless he shall give assurance to the Creden-tials Committee that he will exert every honorable means available to him in any official capacity he may have, to provide that the nominees of this Convention for President and Vice President, through their names or those of electors pledged to them, appear on the election ballot under the heading, name or designation of the Democratic Party.

After further negotiations between southern and liberal fac-tional leaders, it was acknowledged that many of the delegations were already legally bound by commitments made under their state laws. It was therefore agreed that "for this convention only" the loyalty pledge assurances "shall not be in contravention of the exist-ing law of the state, nor of the instructions of the state Democratic governing bodies." Although the spirit of compromise prevailed, the Democratic National Convention had firmly and for the first time asserted a fundamental loyalty requirement for the representa-tives of state parties.[13] Thus began two decades in which Demo-cratic National Convention rules were studied, discussed, and changed so as to make the national convention a more representa-tive assembly, facilitate the conduct of its business, and strengthen the implementation of its decisions.

In preparing for the 1956 national convention, the Democratic

National Committee created a Special Advisory Committee on Rules, whose report was adopted by the national committee on November 17, 1955. The work of this advisory committee led to the adoption of twelve new rules by the 1956 convention.[14] Of these, Rule 1 stated the expectation that state Democratic parties would "undertake to assure that voters in the State will have the opportunity to cast their election ballots" for the convention's slate. Rule 2 asked that all state parties send only "bona fide Democrats" to the national convention. Rule 3 required all members of the national committee to declare publicly their support for the convention slate. Failing this, a committee member could have his or her seat declared vacant. Nine other rules dealt with procedures for polling delegations, filling vacancies on the ticket, speeding up the preparatory work of the convention's committees, and similar procedural matters.

The 1960 and 1964 Democratic conventions were, for the most part, unity rallies. In 1964, however, a loyalist and predominantly black delegation contested the credentials of the regular delegation from Mississippi. Investigation revealed gross racial discrimination on the part of the regular delegation; President Johnson assigned Senator Hubert Humphrey and union leader Walter Reuther the task of working out a compromise. The compromise, rejected by both Mississippi delegations, would have had the Mississippi regulars sign a loyalty oath, award the loyalists the two at-large delegate seats, have the next convention call include a provision that would assure the voters in each state the right to participate in party affairs "regardless of race, color, creed or national origin," and create a Special Equal Rights Committee of the national committee to help states implement the provision. As chairman of the committee, Governor Richard J. Hughes of New Jersey in 1967 reminded national committee members and state chairmen of the six criteria that would be applied in implementing the nondiscrimination policy during the review of credentials for seating delegates at the 1968 convention. Thus, the party took another step in the direction of making itself accessible to and representative of all the citizens of the nation. Groundwork was thus laid for later recommendations by the McGovern-Fraser Commission.

The 1968 convention in Chicago took place during a time of rancor: antiwar demonstrations; the assassinations of Martin Luther King, Jr., and Robert F. Kennedy; urban riots; campus protests; Senator Eugene McCarthy's challenge to the party establishment. McCarthy's supporters at the 1968 convention strenuously protested procedures that disadvantaged their cause. During their pre-convention campaign, McCarthy managers pointed out that state systems of delegate selection often allowed for no *recent* expression of voter preference but, in fact, settled the selections much earlier, in many cases, two years earlier. The McCarthy people protested the haste with which the platform was considered. The unit rule of state delegation voting was criticized as undemocratic. In the party's best tradition, McCarthy demanded more "open" and more representative convention proceedings.

The 1968 convention did succeed in abolishing the unit rule. It also resolved that state party organizations should do their best to select delegates to the 1972 convention under procedures open to voter participation during the calendar year of 1972. Two commissions and their chairmen were subsequently appointed by the Democratic national chairman, Senator Fred R. Harris, to carry out the reforms and devise new ones. The Commission on Party Structure and Delegate Selection was chaired by Senator George S. McGovern of South Dakota, and, subsequently, when McGovern became an active presidential candidate, by Representative Donald M. Fraser of Minnesota. This group dealt with activities of state and local parties that bore a relationship to delegate selection to the national convention. A second group was the Commission on Rules, headed by Representative James G. O'Hara of Michigan, whose mandate was to prepare the first full set of formal regulations ever written for Democratic national conventions. Both commissions were to report to the Democratic National Committee.

At the conclusion of its extensive research and hearings, the McGovern-Fraser Commission came forth in 1970 with its report, *Mandate for Reform*, in which it recommended eighteen guidelines for reorganization of national convention delegate selection. Among the guidelines were such requirements as: publication by the state parties of written rules for delegate selection; prohibition of the unit rule at all stages of delegate selection; adequate notice of all public meetings; prohibition of proxy voting; a quorum of 40 percent to be required of all party committees involved in the selection process; a limit of 10 percent in the number of members of a delegation chosen by state party committees; no *ex officio* seats on the delegation for public or party officials; in states using the convention system, selection of at least 75 percent of the delegation in congressional district or smaller constituencies.

The most difficult and controversial guidelines were those relating to the social attributes of delegates. The goal was to enable blacks, Chicanos, women, and the young to have access to a party institution that was largely populated by older white males. The McGovern-Fraser Commission recommended that state parties and presidential candidates take affirmative action to assure minority representation on their delegations "in reasonable relationship to the groups' presence in the population of the state." However, these distributions of representation were *not*, according to the commission, to be accomplished by mandatory quotas although some states inevitably did use quotas. As the McGovern candidacy later demonstrated in 1972, the opening of doors inevitably carries the risk of bringing in inexperienced and, in many ways, unrepresentative delegates and driving out many who, although older and possibly more conservative, had made honorable contributions to the party and had a legitimate vested interest in it. The guidelines proved significant, too, in the success of the McGovern candidacy which led to challenges in twenty-one of the 1972 convention delegations on grounds of noncompliance with the nondiscrimination requirements.

The O'Hara Commission on Rules brought forth in 1972 its recommendations, which dealt with the apportionment of representation among the states (later modified by the national committee), the election of the convention manager and arrangements committee, the designation of hotel facilities by lot, new procedures for filing delegation challenges, regional public hearings by the platform committee, proportional representation of the states on the convention's standing committees, advance publication of major committee reports, abolition of the motion to table (thereby requiring delegates to vote on the substance of an issue), restrictions on the offering of motions from the floor (to reduce the risk of unexpected and misunderstood motions), the elimination of favorite-son nominations, limits on nominating and seconding speeches, elimination of floor demonstrations, and other rules intended to speed up the convention's work. The commission also compiled a set of written rules for the conduct of Democratic national conventions, that is, a compendium of established practices along with the newly recommended changes. Most of the O'Hara commission work was endorsed by the national committee and implemented at the 1972 convention.

Organized labor and members of the House Democratic caucus were uneasy with many of the O'Hara recommendations, particularly those that promised to tighten the party's relatively loose organizational structure, that is, proposals for a party charter, formal memberships, an organizational structure based on committees at the congressional district level, regular midterm national policy conferences in even-numbered years between presidential elections, a national party executive committee to include the national chairman, Senate and House leaders, regional chairpersons, and state and local representatives, and an elected national chairman. These proposals to the national committee were put off for later consideration by the 1972 national convention.

The 1972 national convention came at the end of a generation of effort to improve the organization of the Democratic party, that is, improve its quality as a representative institution and its capacity for disciplined and responsible political decision-making. In such an effort, dislocation was inevitable, and the 1972 McGovern candidacy stirred up dislocations. A further irony was the extent to which the 1972 national convention became *un*representative of many of its most loyal constituencies as it strove to reach out and incorporate hitherto nonparticipating constituencies. On the one hand, the proportions of young (eighteen to twenty-nine), women, and black delegates were dramatically increased over previous conventions and more closely mirrored the proportions of these demographic types in the nation's total population. On the other hand, many characteristics were significantly absent or underrepresented: persons, other than students, who had annual incomes under $10,000; those with less than a high school education; nonprofessional occupations; businessmen; workers. Democrats who happened to be good enough politicians to be holding public office or running successful local party organizations (Mayor Daley's unseating was the most visible example) were explicitly excluded by the rules, the quotas, or the outcomes of the selection process.

Representativeness, as we noted early in this volume, should extend to opinions on salient policy issues of the day. The evidence of the Kirkpatrick study reveals how much more representative 1972 *Republican* convention delegates were of the policy views of Democratic party identifiers (see Table 9) than were the 1972 Democratic delegates. Table 26 summarizes part of this evidence. Policy questions were asked in such a way that the respondent could indicate his or her preference on a scale between two opposites. For example: "Some people believe that all able-bodied welfare recipients should be compelled to work. Others believe that the most impor-

TABLE 26
Policy Views of 1972 Party Identifiers and National Convention Delegates, in
Percentages

Issue Opposites	Democratic Delegates	Democratic Identifiers	Republican Delegates	Republican Identifiers
Welfare:				
Abolish poverty	57	22	10	13
Obligation to work	28	69	75	79
Busing:				
Bus to integrate	66	15	8	5
Keep children in neigh-				
borhood schools	25	82	84	93
Crime:				
Protect the accused	78	36	21	28
Stop crimes regardless				
of rights of				
accused	13	50	56	56

Source: Jeane J. Kirkpatrick, "Representation in National Political Conventions:
The Case of 1972," *British Journal of Political Science* (July 1975), pp. 265–322.

tant consideration is that no American family should live in poverty
whether they work or not."

According to Kirkpatrick, "Democratic rank-and-file and elite
remained essentially united on [such issues as] inflation, union
leaders and business interests [and this] reflects the persistence of
the 'new Deal consensus' on these questions but the sharp divisions among Democratic elite and rank-and-file on the 'new' cultural and social issues provides evidence on how the new issues cut
across the older alighments.[15] The dilemma is an old one. How can
a political party incorporate new participants and acknowledge new
issues without alienating old participants, ignoring old issues, and
losing the next election?

Maintaining its reformist momentum, the 1972 national convention directed the national chairman to appoint a successor to the
McGovern-Fraser Commission for the purpose of making "appropriate revisions" of the 1972 delegate selection guidelines in anticipation of the 1976 convention call. The new Commission on Delegate Selection and Party Structure had as its chairperson Barbara
Mikulski of Baltimore. Following the O'Hara Commission recommendations, the convention also directed the creation of a Charter
Commission to prepare a charter draft, the first of its kind, and to
help convene a Midterm Conference on Party Organization and
Policy, the first of its kind, in 1974 to consider the charter draft.

Former Governor Terry Sanford of North Carolina was appointed to head the commission.

In its resolution relevant to the 1976 national convention, the 1972 convention once again asserted claims to ascendancy over state party organizations and, significantly, state laws as well. The convention's actions in the Tennessee and Illinois (Daley) seating contests had in effect been assertions of national party ascendancy over state laws and state party rules. "The Call of the 1976 Democratic National Convention," the resolution declared, "shall require that the delegates to the Democratic National Convention be chosen in a manner which assures that no delegate is mandated by law or party rule to vote contrary to his or her expressed presidential choice. . . . Where state law controls, State Parties are required to make all feasible efforts to repeal, amend or modify such laws."

Later events in Connecticut illustrate the effect of this resolution. During spring 1975, the national committee began to negotiate with state parties, notably Connecticut's, to replace systems of delegate selection under existing state law with new systems in keeping with national party requirements. In the Connecticut case, for example, the Democratic state convention had in the past chosen national convention delegates, who invariably included a number of state party leaders *ex officio*. The new system negotiated in 1975 prohibits *ex officio* selections and calls for primaries to elect delegates to six congressional district conventions which in turn shall select national convention delegates according to proportional representation of the candidate preferences revealed in the primary and at the congressional district conventions. In this fashion, the nationalization of the party continues.

The issues and hostilities of the 1972 national convention were present, although in less agitated form, when the Midterm Conference on Democratic Party Organization and Policy convened in Kansas City on December 6, 1974. The 2,035 delegates, chosen at special party elections conducted mainly at the congressional district or lower level of organization, came to hear, debate, and approve the recommendations of the Sanford Charter Commission.[16]

The unprecedented "Charter of the Democratic Party of the United States" (see Appendix) brought together in one document most of the organizational and procedural practices developed by the party over the preceding two decades. The proceedings of the Kansas City convention also sketched, in broad outline, many elements of the party's probable future reorganization agenda. Many proposals *not* incorporated in the Kansas City charter were significant and are likely to be debated for years to come as the reorganization process continues.

The charter provisions on national convention delegate selection reiterated much that had been prescribed by the McGovern-Fraser Commission and the 1972 convention. The unit rule was eliminated at all levels of the selection process. Winner-take-all procedures in primaries and state conventions were to be replaced by systems of proportional representation. Delegates were to be chosen in the same calendar year as the national convention. Convention representation was to be apportioned on the basis of state population (50 percent of a delegation's strength) and previous Democratic presidential vote (50 percent). No party or public officials could be delegates *ex officio*.

The controversial affirmative action provisions were refined and broadened. The national and state parties were required to adopt and carry out affirmative action programs to encourge full participation in all party activities by all Democrats, particularly minority groups, native Americans, women, and youth. One measure of implementation of these affirmative action programs would be actual participation of these groups to the degree "indicated by their presence in the Democratic electorate." Mandatory quotas, however, were not to be imposed to accomplish these goals. While a state delegation could be challenged on the basis of its performance under an approved affirmative action program, those state parties that had adopted and implemented an approved and monitored affirmative action program would not be subject to challenge *solely* on delegation composition or presidential primary results. Thus, the charter assured that the party would not escape the dilemma of every representative institution, namely, how to achieve a fair sample of the population to be represented without imposing rigid apportionment quotas that might some day no longer reflect the composition of the population. Years of over-representation of the southern Democratic parties were reminders how difficult it could become to rearrange a system of *mal*apportionment.

The composition of the Democratic National Committee was broadened by the charter to include representatives of state party organizations, elected Democrats, and special constituencies, all to be chosen by timely and open election processes. The executive committee of the national committee was broadened in membership and functions, making it potentially the mechanism for eventually dealing with the thorny problem of coordinating the presidential and congressional party agencies. Regional caucuses were to select half of the membership of the executive committee. Three national councils were created to perform special party functions. An Education and Training Council would assist members and candidates in campaign organization, issue development, and voter registration. An Independent Finance Council would manage party finances and assist candidates with their problems in this area. A Judicial Council would arbitrate disputes on delegate selection and affirmative action plans.

The principal Kansas City proposals that were defeated or postponed for another day were those making midterm conferences mandatory and establishing a single elected four-year term for the national chairman. The preamble and seven of its twelve articles were to go into effect immediately; five articles would become operative in 1980. To the extent that it could, the Kansas City conference climaxed a generation of party effort to reconstruct its organizational architecture in a way that would centralize and modernize it as a representative institution and facilitate its search for party and national consensus. For some, the conference's charter seemed to be the end of a long journey; for others, only a beginning.

The Future Thrust of Presidential Parties and Factions

Examination of the future of the party at the national level brings up questions about not only the federal system but also the separation-of-powers aspects of the party's organization. In the party, as in government, leaders are caught in situations of institutionalized ambivalence. On the one hand, how shall they use their separate organizational bases in the presidency, Congress, and elsewhere as springboards of influence; on the other hand, how shall they overcome the institutional separations in order to achieve common electoral and policy objectives? The national party's needs and organizing thrust has an important but limited centripetal effect upon the organizational trends at the other levels. Well into the future, the national party will also continue to need to reorganize and centralize itself for the growing competition for votes in every corner of the nation, the coordination of congressional and presidential wings of the party, the replacement of local machines with something else, the revitalization of party leadership centers at the state level, and the requirements of transnational party development. Above all, the commitment to continue reorganization must

357

carry with it a commitment to maintain the party as a vital and viable representative institution, capable of finding and measuring the consensus it seeks.

Political parties, as the managers of government, cannot avoid reflecting in their own organization the structure of the governments they manage. As a consequence, in the United States, the major parties have been as federal as the nation and as divided at the national level as the national branches of government. James Mac-Gregor Burns has referred to this condition as "a four-party system," each of the two major national parties consisting of two distinct parties: the congressional and the presidential.[17] It has also been true that the national parties—in their respective legislative coalitions, nominating conventions, campaign collaborations, and informal channels of consultation—have served as vital "connectors," to use the term of Edmund Burke and Henry Jones Ford, among men of like mind in the various separated branches and levels of government.[18] The future of American politics may thrust these "men of like mind" closer together as they face the challenges of intensified competition, expanding organization, and complex public problems. Such trends are likely to place the congressional and presidential wings of the party under greater pressure to coordinate their agencies, resources, personnel, policies, and public images.

This coordination is not likely to be easy to design and implement. The independence of party leaders in the presidency, in the Senate, and in the House of Representatives has had important practical as well as constitutional implications. Dispersion of the centers of influence has allowed party leaders the flexibility needed to pull together new coalitions in response to changing times. The multiplicity of routes to party and public offices has afforded new leaders a variety of opportunities for being promoted in the system. The diverse interests of a complex society have tended to be better represented by a great many competing leaders who *must* listen to their constituencies rather than by a few safe-district leaders who need not listen. As a result, coordination of congressional and presidential leaderships is likely to continue as one of the more difficult organizational problems of the Democratic party.

Efforts at coordination have of course been tried. Members of Congress show up as delegates and leaders at the presidential nominating conventions, sometimes serving in vital arbitrating capacities among the warring factions. In recent years, Congress, particularly the Senate, has been a principal supplier of presidential timber: Truman, Kefauver, Symington, Russell, Humphrey, Kennedy, Johnson, McGovern, Jackson, and others. Presidents and presidential candidates have been increasingly available for duty as campaigners in midterm congressional elections; President Kennedy in 1962 actually provided the central impetus and coordinative mechanisms for that off-year campaign. The presidential wing, particularly during the Stevenson years, created the Democratic Advisory Council to serve, hopefully, as a policy-pronouncing and strategy-developing forum among Democratic leaders in and out of Congress, in or out of the presidency, and at all levels of party organization. Organizational inventions to accomplish this will undoubtedly again be attempted in the future; the national committee's Advisory Council of Elected Officials created in 1973 and its new executive committee established under the 1974 charter have been two recent moves along these lines.

The Advisory Council, following the precedent of the Stevenson era council, was composed of elected officeholders representing states, large cities, and Congress brought together by the Democratic National Committee in an attempt to bridge the gap between presidential and congressional wings. In keeping with its policy-charting responsibilities, the Advisory Council organized eight policy panels to report at the Kansas City midterm conference. The new executive committee, with at least half its membership to be chosen by regional caucuses of members of the Democratic National Committee, also holds great potential for bringing together, perhaps indirectly, the congressional and presidential wings as well as other interests within the party.

Efforts at congressional-presidential coordination continue to be complicated by Democratic preference for strong titular leaders. With Woodrow Wilson and Franklin Roosevelt as unforgettable models, Democrats have been committed to activist presidents and strong titular leadership but uncertain about party organization. The activism of a Truman, Kennedy, or Johnson stands in contrast, for example, to the passivity of an Eisenhower or the withdrawal of a Nixon. Truman did not mince words about his strong partisanship and gave substantial attention to the advancement of party organization. Adlai Stevenson, although defeated, devoted himself to the development of new conceptions of opposition party leadership. The Kennedys began to lend some of the organizing style of Boston ward politics to the presidential wing, but seemed reluctant to build up the formal party agencies. Johnson, a genius in the management of a one-party state like Texas and the brokering of the congressional "club," turned out to be particularly ill-suited for building the presidential party as an organization. Humphrey, defeated, recruited the talents of Lawrence O'Brien to carry on the difficult tasks of reorganization. McGovern's activities in the field of organization and procedure are credited with having led to the insurgent national convention of 1972 and the constitutionalizing midterm charter convention of 1974. Carter, another activist leader from a one-party state, encountered difficulties in presidential-congressional relations and party management almost from the outset of his administration.

The problem of congressional-presidential coordination, in the next half century, is likely to be complicated by yet another, somewhat less obvious tendency: the development of relatively cohesive and enduring factions within the party. "Faction politics," we are told, "is a reality; there is such a subuniverse of politics as *faction politics*, much as there is *party politics* or *interest group politics*, and faction politics merits our attention as such."[19] This book has, in effect, been a history of factional politics within the Democratic party, and the names of the different factions in different periods appear throughout this history: North-South, War and Peace Democrats, soft-money versus hard-money, gold-standard versus free-silver, liberal-conservative, etc. We may anticipate that this parade of factions will continue and perhaps become more institutionalized as intraparty units.

In the past, factions have been short-lived collaborations, often organized for a single candidacy, a single election, or a single issue, then disappearing. Such factions have lacked distinct and durable ideologies, heroes, and symbols. They have lacked clear organization and stable procedures. In the last two generations, particularly after the repeal of the two-thirds nominating rule at the national conventions and the decline of the southern wing, factional organization has shown signs of change. Component groups in the Democratic coalition sometimes acquire political stability, for example, the coterie of congressional Democratic liberals organized as the Democratic Study Group and the recent labor-oriented Coalition for a Democratic Majority. When intraparty factions acquire long-term organization, sustained membership, and cohesive issue orientations, they will also engage each other in conflicts on nominations, programs, procedures, and other matters as political occasion demands. Underpinning all this would be the Democratic party-in-the-electorate which, as we have seen in Table 16, has divided into fairly stable liberal-conservative groupings.

One of the most serious difficulties of factional politics arises from the question of whether a minority or losing faction in any particular intraparty contest is later willing to remain in the party to help in the battle against the opposition party or, in anger, decides to bolt to form a third party or simply stay at home on election day. In the past, this problem of factional reconciliation has usually been handled by balanced tickets on which the losing faction is given major but secondary recognition on the slate, in the legislative leadership, in the campaign organization, or in the new administration if the party wins. If factions become more formalized—acquire names, maintain headquarters, adopt programs, develop procedures, etc., the need for factional reconciliation may become more obvious and strategies for accomplishing reconciliation more explicit.

In general, the factional future of the Democratic party is difficult to forecast from an organizational point of view. Much depends upon accidents of personality, for example, George Wallace's ability to take so many Democrats with him into a third party, probably institutional changes such as direct popular election of the president and the growth of the primary election system, and the increasing importance of ideology for the voting behavior of large segments of the electorate. What can be expected is the formalization of factionalism within the party and the host of organizational problems that this will bring. This competitive factional politics will undoubtedly evolve within the framework of an increasingly competitive party system.

While interparty competition will at first be most visible and influential in presidential politics, its future in the United States is likely to prosper and evolve in constituencies at all levels: congressional, state, and local. In a society where competition is a familiar and valued condition of life, many consequences of the intensification of party competition may be anticipated.

1. Party policy positions and campaign appeals in general will become increasingly alike, despite increased voter interest in ideological issues. This reflects not only the broad consensus that exists on most basic issues but also the need for both parties to appeal to the same uncommitted voters if an election majority is to be won. On the other hand, new public issues will undoubtedly continue to make their way to the center of the political marketplace via new

minor parties or defections by minority factions within each of the major parties. These minorities will continue to obtain a hearing if they appear to be pivotal to the outcome of the major party races. How should the interests of factional minorities be safeguarded without destroying the moderate thrust of American politics? This question is likely to become more difficult to answer over the next decades.

2. A possible consequence of increased competition may be stalemate or indecision in some specific areas of public policy. An evenly divided political community can move ahead in policy areas where there is general agreement on fundamentals. But what if there should be intense disagreement on fundamental aspects of a particular public problem? What if the disagreement should coincide with other fundamental social differences, as in 1828, 1860, 1896, and 1932? These years climaxed long periods of stalemate and inertia in specific areas of public policy. If such circumstances occur again, what institutional and other safeguards may the party and the nation develop to prevent the political paralysis that accompanies such close and sustained divisions?

3. As competition tightens, campaigning will probably intensify. Not unlike many other American enterprises, the political parties, as producers and purveyors of public leaders and public policies, will be expending more and more resources delivering their "messages" about "products." The cost of campaigns will inevitably rise not only as a result of the expensiveness of newer communication technologies such as television but simply because there will be more and bigger campaigns. The time needed for campaign preparation and buildup will also become greater, as it already has; party campaigns may become election-to-election enterprises.

In view of the vital public service rendered by the parties, will public revenue resources—as in the 1974 federal campaign finance legislation—be allocated to help parties meet these high costs? How may the "equal time" principle be modified to furnish guidance in the distribution of such resources to the major parties and to other parties? What position should the Democratic party—usually short on money and long on organization—take on these matters?

4. Another consequence of intensified competition and more campaigning will be increased organization. As party operations become year-round, as growing numbers of competitive districts have to be coordinated, and as financial and other resources have to be regularized, it will become even more necessary to maintain

permanent party headquarters, full-time professional staffs, and stable lines of communication and political intelligence at all levels of party effort. Some observers have already noted an increase in the professionalism of state party staff.[20]

As the institutionalization of the presidential party proceeds at the national convention, in the national committee, in the national chairmanship and national headquarters, in congressional-presidential relations, in the titular leadership out as well as in office, in factional politics, and at all levels of party organization in the increasingly competitive years ahead, the party will continue to ponder, as it has in the past, what are the essential requirements of representativeness and reconciliation.

Beyond the Nation: A Democratic International?

Although unnoticed by most Americans, there is strong evidence that a transnational political party system is emergent and likely to become one of the world's principal political institutions.[21] Americans have some difficulty perceiving and participating in this significant institutional development for several reasons: an anti-party tradition, a doctrine of nonintervention in the politics of other countries, a view that the American party system is unique and makes a poor fit with party developments elsewhere.

Some transnational party movements are more than a century old; others have become significant since the end of World War II. The Communist internationals, the first of which was founded in 1848, have evolved in several phases: the Second International founded in 1889 and discontinued in 1914; the Third International (Comintern) established by the Bolsheviks in 1919 and dissolved in 1943 during World War II, the Communist Information Bureau (Cominform) created in 1947 and dissolved in 1956; the Comintern reestablished in 1957. In the 1970s, some eighty-nine Communist parties throughout the world, including fourteen controlling their national governments, claim a world party membership of 60 million, not including 40 million supporting voters in capitalist states. Communist unity has been marred, however, by the rise of national communism (Titoism), Maoism, and Eurocommunism. Transnational communism, as is the case in most party movements, has thus developed factions and intense leadership competition.

In 1945 the British Labor party convened the remnants of the Second, or Socialist, International. The movement has grown until, in the last decade, the Socialist International has reported a membership of nearly 20 million among its fifty-seven party affiliates (Socialist, Labor, and Social Democratic) in fifty countries, with nearly 80 million voters supporting Socialist tickets in their respective home countries.

Christian Democracy had its partisan beginning in the nineteenth century. Following World War II, European Christian Democratic parties softened their strong Catholic orientation, broadened their programs and appeals, created regional organizations in Eastern Europe and Latin America, and by the mid-1970s claimed affiliated parties in sixty nations.

Liberal parties followed a similar postwar development, creating the World Liberal Union, or Liberal International. Liberals have been somewhat less successful as electoral parties, their most important affiliate in this respect being the Liberal party of Canada.

There have also been numerous "minor" transnational parties in this century: the Fascists, the International Peasant Union or "Green International," the Aprista (Alianza Popular Revolucionara Americana) parties in Latin America, and the pan-Arab Ba'th parties.

Relevant to transnational party development has been the growth in numbers of transnational organized interest groups, or nongovernmental organizations (NGOs). Some 2,500 of these transnational pressure groups currently operate in world affairs.

Transnational party activity may be found in regional political institutions, most notably in the European Parliament, less overtly at the United Nations, in the domestic politics of emerging and developing nations, and in the revolutionary or pre-governmental politics of nationalist movements.

As Americans become more aware and more involved in the emerging transnational party system, there are likely to be consequences for the future development of party politics within the United States. The use of the Central Intelligence Agency as the vehicle for cooperation with foreign parties is likely to give way to more open and traditional types of partisan collaboration across national boundaries. Global party political activity is likely to supplement military and economic techniques of foreign policy implementation. Parochial national political issues are likely to be restated as global issues. The doctrine of nonintervention is certain to be subjected to reexamination as the concept of national sovereignty becomes recognizedly more myth than reality. Factional developments within the Democratic party are likely to become more closely keyed to transnational collaborations. As a consequence, world-minded political activists among the young may become more interested in the major United States parties and less so in the Marxist parties. Above all, American political leaders will undoubtedly come to realize that a transnational party system may well provide the essential alternative institution to war as the principal means of elite competition in the world political community.

Epilogue

Is it the whim of a numerologist, the figment of a mystic's mind, or historical coincidence that 1776, 1876, and 1976 appear to be years of fundamental redirection in the politics of the American community? The case is easily made for 1776, the year of the Declaration of Independence, and 1876, the year of the Hayes-Tilden crisis and the beginning of an end to the bitter Reconstruction era. But what of 1976?

The Bicentennial year indeed did have all the earmarks of fundamental national redirection. For the first time in over two generations the United States was not engaged in a hot or cold war, not suffering a depression or a recession, and not tearing itself apart with ghetto riots at the base or Watergates at the pinnacle. In 1976 the nation elected a president from the Old South, the first since the days of the Virginia Dynasty. Social change and political crosscurrents pressed upon the president, the world, and the nation and were evidence of a transition in progress.

Dilemmas of a Transitional Era

But absent from the push-and-pull of the opening year of the nation's third century was the civic cohesiveness generated by some overriding crisis of war or economic depression or the unifying magnetism of a charismatic leader. President Carter personified the times and, often bravely, articulated its dilemmas. Carter was himself a bundle of anomalies, a Wilsonian moralist who was at the same time a seasoned political tactician and propagandist. His approach to the Democratic party was similarly anomalous.

As a Georgia Democrat, Carter had little concern for party organization, having spent most of his political life campaigning in primaries against other Democrats. In one-party Georgia, it was the primary elections that counted. Thus, Gerald Ford was Carter's first serious Republican opponent and the 1976 presidential campaign was the first in which Carter had to rely upon the organized support of his party. Once elected, Carter again needed his party's

366

support in Congress, where Democrats held an oversized majority in both houses. Carter found congressional Democrats divided, difficult, and unresponsive, yet his own management of party affairs was routine and minimal. Both the president and the electorate seemed to agree that political parties were an archaic distraction from the business of politics. As a consequence, the Democratic party was perceived as just another claimant for presidential attention and resources rather than as a instrument of political action.

The latter impression was reinforced during the Party's second midterm Conference, conducted in Memphis from December 9 to 11, 1978. As though the Administration were something apart from the Party, the President brought with him most of his Cabinet and nearly 200 members of the White House staff. When the more than 1,600 delegates dispersed themselves among numerous policy workshops, the large Administration entourage did the same, presenting Administration viewpoints and listening to feedback from the delegates. This apparent distance between Administration Democrats and Party Democrats caused some uneasiness among the delegates. In marked contrast, Senator Edward M. Kennedy's fervent appeal for support of the Party's social programs evoked an emotional response more familiar at such Party gatherings. The President's call for cuts in government spending and a firm stand against inflation struck no such chords.

In world politics, the United States was still traumatized by its painful Vietnam experience but unable to shed its status as the world's most powerful nation. No longer willing to serve as policeman for the world, the nation was nonetheless drawn into every international and intranational crisis. Sensing the emergence of a neo-isolationism in the United States, the Soviet Union took the opportunity to seek out and aid political allies in the trouble spots of Africa, the Middle East, and Southeast Asia. Every foreign policy issue caught the Carter administration and the American people between, on the one hand, a desire to disengage from the conflicts of others and be left alone, and, on the other hand, a recognition that world interdependence was here to stay and would continue to be manifest in the undramatic as well as dramatic daily transactions of international life. Thus, the Carter administration sought arms limitation agreements at the same time that it maintained the flow of arms to friends and allies, tried to defend the cause of human rights at the same time that it conducted business-as-usual with oppressive regimes, and challenged Soviet involvement in crisis areas without itself intervening in a significant way. Such ambivalence seemed also to mark other foreign policy issues: the world's inflation rate, the emergence of new and competitive superpowers, the economic and social demands of developing nations, the promotion of international trade, etc.

Ambivalence reflected fundamental transitions in other aspects of world politics. Although the sovereignty of nations was clearly eroding each day in small increments, supranational bodies such as the United Nations, the European communities, the Organization of African Unity, and others were not yet fully competent forums of world or regional politics. Although increasingly visible, transnational political parties, organized interests, and corporate enterprises were not yet the principal nongovernmental actors in world affairs that they have been in many national and local communities. Although military techniques of international influence were plainly dangerous and increasingly ineffectual, other political and economic instruments of power were not yet honed for regular practical use. While it was everywhere obvious that the structure and process of world politics was changing with unprecedented speed, the design for a new American global strategy and a modern foreign policy was still gestating. Unwilling to pursue the policeman role, Jimmy Carter grasped opportunities to place the United States into the role of global middleman and mediator. His most dramatic exercise of this new role came during his masterful conduct of negotiations between President Anwar Sadat of Egypt and Prime Minister Menachem Begin of Israel at Camp David.

The dilemmas of a transitional period were even more evident in domestic politics. It seemed as though some Grand Ledger Keeper was calling the United States to account for decades of affluence, easy-spending, and waste. Extravagent use of energy resources would have to end. The ravenous national appetite for consumer goods and the consequent drain on national resources would have to be curbed. The citizenry's compulsion to eat, drink, and smoke itself to death would have to be discouraged. Demands for more profits and more wages and the consequent inflationary spiral would have to be restrained. The growing demands for government services and the concurrent resistance to taxes would have to be reconciled. Jimmy Carter, a rational man, lectured his countrymen on these and other communal dilemmas. But what politician can continue to say "can't" and "don't" and very long remain popular? Politics is an inflationary process. Deflationary policy postures can be dangerous to aspirants for public office, particularly incumbents.

Even the attributes of the president's countrymen were changing. With each passing year, the American electorate was getting older (20 percent would be over sixty-five years of age by the year 2000), more educated, more affluent, more suburban, employed increasingly in professions, more geographically and socially mobile, and more independent of party affiliation. Democrats, by contrast, have in the past been young, less educated, poorer, urban, in low-skill occupations, and less mobile. The president and his party will need to take notice of the changing attributes of their constituency; future programs and candidates will need to reflect the emerging composition.

The changes may prove difficult to identify and measure. The difficulties may be summarized here in the form of questions. In a postindustrial society with a diminishing work force, how shall full employment be defined and will "elective unemployment" be an acceptable concept? How will the social security system be kept solvent and older citizens kept productively employed? How will the younger citizens, reluctant to vote, be attracted into the party system? As leisure time increases, will a "leisure ethic" replace the traditional American work ethic, and with what policy consequences? How will the nation's educational resources respond to the rise of an "information society" in which information processing and knowledge production shall be major industries? Will a "politics of diet" emerge in response to future concerns about food quality, the practice of agribusiness, and the importance of food as a tool of foreign policy? How will the requirements of health services and environmental protection reinforce each other? In what ways will the nation's many institutions be restructured to serve their basic purposes better—the prisons rehabilitate criminals, the schools teach students, the mental health programs resocialize the psychotic, the welfare programs encourage employability, the medical programs prevent as well as cure illness?

The relevance of these many problems for the future of the Democratic party need not be drawn out here. However, other questions may be asked whose direct relevance is both clear and immediate. Can the party organize itself to provide old services under new conditions: as employment agent, welfare provider, protector from injustice, ombudsman, civic educator, recreation center, leadership recruiter, and so on? Will modern technology permit registration and voting procedures to make the electoral process easily available to the tens of millions of potential voters who do not now participate? Will changes in the electoral college procedure for electing presidents compel a more rapid centralization of national party agencies? Will public financing of party organization and/or candidate campaigns have salutory or detrimental effects upon party ethics and management? Will the future primary election systems be designed to reinforce or undermine party integrity and responsibility? How will interactions with transnational party movements affect future Democratic party organization and behavior?

In sum, from the present to the Democratic bicentennial in 2032, the party will be confronted with new constituencies, contexts, political problems, and policy dilemmas. The party will need to convert old coalitions into new ones, mobilize unfamiliar as well as familiar components of the party-in-the-electorate, and promote candidates and programs that best serve the nation. Democratic party leadership promises to become a more demanding pursuit than ever before.

Replenishing the Reservoir of Leadership

The history of the Democratic party thus far nourishes optimism about its future. For Democrats, institutional survival, managerial skill, and awareness of the connections among political institutions have been concerns to which the party has recurrently given its close and often contentious attention. The party has repeatedly worried vigorously and loudly about its representativeness as a political organization. Have organizational arrangements enabled the party to represent the citizenry at large, the voters who have supported it, the rank-and-file party workers who have helped it to function, and the leaders who have grappled with its management? Has the party reflected in its choice of issues and programs a fair representation of the problems and political demands emanating from its many constituencies? Has the party been judicious, when in office, in its distribution of the nation's resources—material, spiritual, and other—to those it claims to serve? Since there can be no final answers to such questions, what has been noteworthy is that the questions continue to be asked. This self-questioning may serve as a measure of the party's vitality.[1]

Between now and 2032, the nation and the world will experience profound changes in its physical and social conditions. The facilitation of these changes will continue to be a special challenge for the leaders of one of the nation's and the world's most tested instruments of change, the Democratic party. If nothing else, a political party is an organization seeking to place its leaders into public offices and to obtain for its leaders certain initiatives in public policy-making. In sum, a party is naught without skillful leaders, and, without leaders, change cannot be achieved.

Two basic tenets in the American philosophy about politics are (1) that *any* adult individual can be a politician and (2) that *every* citizen should try to be politically active, that is, a working politician. The plain facts are, however, (1) that politics is a highly specialized and demanding kind of work and (2) that most citizens are not and cannot be interested in becoming politicians. Even a candidate for dogcatcher must have specialized political knowledge: who makes up his prospective constituency, what vote it takes to win, how to campaign and win support, how to differentiate between a campaign promise and a public policy, how to get nominated, how to raise money and other resources for campaigning, how to operate the government, when to fight and when not to fight, and on and on. Of course, a citizen ought not have to become a full-time working politician in order to engage in party work. Yet, with so much going on in contemporary party processes, it is apparent that new forms of part-time participation need to be designed and implemented.[2]

If not many citizens are interested in political work and if very few have acquired the highly specialized skills needed, who is to lead the parties and fill the offices of government? As every party leader worth his or her salt knows, the general supply of personnel is small indeed—and the supply of *talented* personnel almost infinitesimal. The Democratic party cannot and should not try to train the philosopher-kings recommended by Plato. But the Democratic party can and must continue to produce the high-quality professional politicans—the skilled political managers and brokers—who have led it through a long, proud history, have elevated it to the nation's majority party today, and have guided it in its search for the national consensus.

Leaders, after all, are key persons in the collective decision-making processes of all human groups and organizations. A distinguishing characteristic of leaders is their role as decision-making specialists. They are particularly knowledgeable about the group or organization's procedures of decision. They are motivated to influence the collectivity's choice of alternatives. They tend to have an unusually large personal investment in how the choice goes. The skills and preferences of leaders are also important in determining—sometimes intentionally, sometimes not—which of the basic methods of collective choice, discussed at the beginning of this book, will prevail: the violent, the verbal, or the numerical. Some leaders are inclined to resort to war, some prefer persuasion, and others would rather take every issue to a vote. Such preferences in method and their associated skills may have profound consequences, and this is why the training and selection of party leaders may be the most influential way in which a nation may manage reform and change with a minimum of violence.

To decide by violence is primitive, "brutish," and costly; witness the consequences of the Democratic party's failure to unite upon a compromise candidate in 1860: a civil war and a devastating period of reconstruction. To decide by verbal methods, on the other hand, may be a kind of outcome achievable only by master politicians, for example, the federal Constitution, Henry Clay's Great Compromises of 1820 and 1850, and the Democratic leadership's willingness to give up the presidency in 1876 rather than launch the nation upon a second civil war. The least costly and most reliable method of collective choice for ordinary people in ordinary political circumstances is the numerical method, that is, some procedure of voting. In their reliance upon this method lies the appeal of constitutional parties in liberal democracies. The skilled party leader knows how and when to use the numerical method for a variety of political purposes: to test strength, to delay, to teach, to provide an empirically observable basis for building winning coalitions, and, finally, to decide an issue. The political party that nurtures these kinds of skills and leaders will not only keep the party system intact and strong but also win the gratitude of the nation.

Consideration of an organization's method of collective choice also illuminates the significant difference between representativeness and representation, two horns of the dilemma upon which the Democratic party has bruised itself in recent years. Representativeness refers to characteristics of a sample of a population, for example, men and women, blacks and whites, young and old, rich and poor, blue- and brown-eyed, etc. Representativeness assumes the equality of all members of the population and the sample in the distribution of these characteristics. Representation, on the other hand, refers to *a feature of the group's decision-making process:* the representative decides for and acts on behalf of the represented.

Representation, therefore, requires skill in the methods of collective choice—knowing when to fight, when to talk, and when to vote, how, by what criteria, and in which way to add up the results. This is the skill that a party's representatives and leaders *must* have if they are to be successful in their search for party or national consensus. The quality of representation should take precedence over the quantity of representativeness. To perform its essential function, a national nominating convention, for example, must have delegates who know how to choose competent and winning presidential nominees and how to build strong party coalitions. This need for skilled representation should take precedence over any quantitatively precise sample of certain population characteristics. For it is as one of the nation's most vital institutions of representation that the Democratic party best serves as an agent of consensus.

Appendix

CHARTER
OF THE DEMOCRATIC PARTY OF THE UNITED STATES

Preamble

We, the Democrats of the United States of America, united in common purpose, hereby rededicate ourselves to the principles which have historically sustained our Party. Recognizing that the vitality of the Nation's political institutions has been the foundation of its enduring strength, we acknowledge that a political party which wishes to lead must listen to those it would lead, a party which asks for the people's trust must prove that it trusts the people and a party which hopes to call forth the best the Nation can achieve must embody the best of the Nation's heritage and traditions.

What we seek for our Nation, we hope for all people: individual freedom in the framework of a just society, political freedom in the framework of meaningful participation by all citizens. Bound by the United States Constitution, aware that a party must be responsive to be worthy of responsibility, we pledge ourselves to open, honest endeavor and to the conduct of public affairs in a manner worthy of a society of free people.

Under God, and for these ends and upon these principles, we do establish and adopt this Charter of the Democratic Party of the United States of America.

Article One
The Democratic Party of the United States of America

The Democratic Party of the United States of America shall:

1. Nominate and assist in the election of Democratic candidates for the offices of President and Vice President of the United States;

2. Adopt and promote statements of policy;

3. Assist state and local Democratic Party organizations in the election of their candidates and the education of their voters;

4. Establish standards and rules of procedure to afford all members of the Democratic Party full, timely and equal opportunities to participate in decisions concerning the selection of candidates, the formulation of policy,

and the conduct of other Party affairs, without prejudice on the basis of sex, race, age (if of voting age), religion, economic status or ethnic origin, and, further, to promote fair campaign practices and the fair adjudication of disputes;

5. Raise and disburse moneys needed for the successful operation of the Democratic Party;

6. Work with Democratic public officials at all levels to achieve the objectives of the Democratic Party; and

7. Encourage and support codes of political ethics that embody substantive rules of ethical guidance for public officials and employees in federal, state and local governments, to assure that public officials shall at all times conduct themselves in a manner that reflects creditably upon the office they serve, shall not use their office to gain special privileges and benefits and shall refrain from acting in their official capacities when their independence of judgment would be adversely affected by personal interests or duties.

Article Two
National Convention

Section 1. The Democratic Party shall assemble in National Convention in each year in which an election for the office of President of the United States is held.

Section 2. The National Convention shall be the highest authority of the Democratic Party, subject to the provisions of this Charter. The National Convention shall recognize the state and other Parties entitled to participate in the conduct of the national affairs of the Democratic Party, including its conventions, conferences and committees. State Party rules or state laws relating to the election of delegates to the National Convention shall be observed unless in conflict with this Charter and other provisions adopted pursuant to authority of the Charter, including the resolutions or other actions of the National Convention. In the event of such conflict with state laws, state Parties shall be required to take provable positive steps to bring such laws into conformity and to carry out such other measures as may be required by the National Convention or the Democratic National Committee.

Section 3. The National Convention shall nominate a candidate for the office of President of the United States, nominate a candidate for the office of Vice President of the United States, adopt a platform and act upon such other matters as it deems appropriate.

Section 4. The National Convention shall be composed of delegates who are chosen through processes which (i) assure all Democratic voters full, timely and equal opportunity to participate and include affirmative action programs toward that end, (ii) assure that delegations fairly reflect the division of preferences expressed by those who participate in the Presidential nominating process, (iii) exclude the use of the unit rule at any level, (iv) do not deny participation for failure to pay a cost, fee or poll tax, (v) restrict participation to Democrats only, and (vi) begin within the calendar year of the Convention provided, however, that fairly apportioned and openly selected state Party committees, elected no earlier than January 1st of the preceding mid-term Congressional election year, from states not having state conventions authorized to elect delegates shall not be precluded from selecting not more than 25% of their respective state delegations according to the standards provided in this Charter and the By-Laws.

Section 5. The delegate vote allocable to each state shall be determined as provided in the By-Laws, consistent with a formula giving equal weight to population, which may be measured by electoral vote, and to the Democratic vote in elections for the office of President. The apportionment of delegates who are to be elected from units no larger than a Congressional district shall be determined by the state Democratic Party in accordance with the Call to the National Convention.

Article Three
Democratic National Committee

Section 1. The Democratic National Committee shall have general responsibility for the affairs of the Democratic Party between National Conventions, subject to the provisions of this Charter and to the resolutions or other actions of the National Convention. This responsibility shall include: (i) issuing the Call to the National Convention; (ii) conducting the Party's Presidential campaign; (iii) filling vacancies in the nominations for the offices of President and Vice President; (iv) formulating and disseminating statements of Party policy; (v) providing for the election or appointment of a Chairperson, an Executive Vice Chairperson of the opposite sex, a Second Executive Vice Chairperson, a Treasurer, a Secretary and other appropriate officers of the National Committee and for filling of vacancies; and (vi) all other actions necessary or appropriate in order to carry out the provisions of this Charter and the objectives of the Democratic Party.

Section 2. The Democratic National Committee shall be composed of: (i) the Chairperson and the highest ranking officer of the opposite sex of each recognized state Democratic Party; (ii) two hundred additional members apportioned to the states on the same basis as delegates to the National Convention are apportioned, provided that each state shall have at least two such additional members; (iii) the Chairperson of the Democratic Governors' Conference and two additional governors selected by the Conference; (iv) the Democratic Leader in the United States Senate and the Democratic Leader in the United States House of Representatives and one additional member of each body appointed by the respective leaders; (v) the Chairperson, two Executive Vice Chairpersons, the Chairperson of the National Finance Council, the Treasurer and the Secretary of the Democratic National Committee; (vi) the Chairperson of the Conference of Democratic Mayors and two additional mayors selected by the Conference; (vii) the President of the Young Democrats of America and two additional members selected by the organization biennially in convention assembled; (viii) the Chairperson of the Democratic County Officials Conference and two additional county officials selected by the Conference; (ix) the President of the National Federation of Democratic Women; and (x) additional members as provided in Article Eleven of this Charter. No more than twenty-five additional members of the Democratic National Committee may be added by the foregoing members.

Section 3. Members of the Democratic National Committee apportioned to the states and those provided for in Article II, who are not otherwise members by virtue of Party office, shall be selected by each state Democratic Party in accordance with standards as to participation established in the By-Laws of the Democratic Party for terms commencing on the day the National Convention adjourns and terminating on the day the next Convention adjourns. Such members shall be selected during the calendar year in which a National Convention is held, through processes which assure full, timely and equal opportunity to participate. Vacancies shall be filled by the state party as provided in the By-Laws. The members of the National Committee from each state shall be divided as equally as practicable between committeemen and committeewomen. Members of the Democratic National Committee who serve by virtue of holding public or party office shall serve on the Committee only during their terms in such office. Members of the Democratic National Committee added by the other members shall serve for the period designated at the time of their selection, but in no event beyond the day the next Convention adjourns. Members of the Democratic National Committee who serve by virtue of holding state Party office shall be selected by such Parties in accordance with standards as to participation established in the By-Laws.

Section 4. The By-Laws may provide for removal of members of the Democratic National Committee for cause by a two-thirds vote of the National Committee and may also require continued residence in the jurisdiction represented by the member and affirmative support for the Democratic Presidential and Vice Presidential nominees as a condition of continued membership thereon.

Section 5. The Democratic National Committee shall meet at least once each year. Meetings shall be called by the Chairperson, by the Executive Committee of the Democratic National Committee, or by written request of no fewer than one-fourth of the members of the Democratic National Committee.

Section 6. The Democratic National Committee shall submit to each National Convention, prior to the commencement thereof, a written report of the activities and affairs of the Democratic Party since the preceding National Convention.

Article Four
Executive Committee

Section 1. There shall be an Executive Committee of the Democratic National Committee, which shall be responsible for the conduct of the affairs of the Democratic Party subject to this Charter, the National Convention and the Democratic National Committee.

Section 2. The Executive Committee shall be elected by and serve at the pleasure of the members of the Democratic National Committee. The size, composition and term of office shall be determined by the Democratic National Committee, provided that no fewer than one-half of the members shall be elected from regional caucuses of members of the Democratic National Committee.

Section 3. The Executive Committee shall meet at least four times each year. Meetings shall be called by the Chairperson or by written request of no fewer than one-fourth of its members. The Executive Committee shall keep a record of its proceedings which shall be available to the public.

Article Five
National Chairperson

Section 1. The National Chairperson of the Democratic Party shall carry out the programs and policies of the National Convention and the Democratic National Committee.

Section 2. The National Chairperson shall be elected (i) at the first meeting of the Democratic National Committee held after the National Convention, and (ii) at a meeting of the Democratic National Committee held after the succeeding presidential election and prior to March 1 next, and (iii) whenever a vacancy occurs. The National Chairperson shall be elected and may be removed by a majority vote of the Democratic National Committee, and each term shall expire upon the election for the following term.

Section 3. The National Chairperson shall preside over meetings of the Democratic National Committee and of the Executive Committee. In the absence of the National Chairperson, the next highest ranking officer of the National Committee present at the meeting shall preside.

Section 4. The National Chairperson shall serve full time and shall receive such compensation as may be determined by agreement between the Chairperson and the Democratic National Committee.

Article Six
Party Conference

The Democratic Party may hold a National Party Conference between National Conventions. The nature, agenda, composition, time and place of the Party Conference shall be determined by the Democratic National Committee. At a meeting held during the first calendar year after each Presidential election, the Democratic National Committee shall vote upon the question of whether such Party Conference shall be held.

Article Seven
Judicial Council

Section 1. There shall be a Judicial Council of the Democratic Party appointed by the Democratic National Committee, the function of which shall be to adjudicate disputes arising out of the interpretation or application of national Party law, provided, however, that the right of the Democratic National Convention and Democratic National Committee to settle credentials disputes concerning their respective bodies shall not be abridged.

Section 2. The Democratic National Committee shall determine and provide necessary support for the Judicial Council.

Article Eight
National Finance Council

Section 1. The Democratic National Committee shall establish a National Finance Council, which shall have general responsibility for the finances of the Democratic Party. The National Finance Council shall raise funds to support the Democratic Party and shall advise and assist state Democratic Parties and candidates in securing funds for their purposes.

Section 2. Members of the Finance Council shall be selected and approved as provided in the By-Laws, and the Chairman of the Finance Council shall be elected or approved by the Democratic National Committee.

Article Nine
National Education and Training Council

Section 1. There shall be a National Education and Training Council of the Democratic Party, which shall be responsible for the creation and implementation of education and training programs for the Democratic Party in furtherance of its objectives. The allocation of funds to the National Education and Training Council shall be provided by the Democratic National Committee and shall be budgeted at least one year in advance of anticipated expenditures. In order to encourage a lifetime of meaningful political participation for every Democrat, the National Education and Training Council shall attempt to reach every young citizen as they enter the electorate at eighteen years of age.

Section 2. The National Education and Training Council shall be composed of (i) eight members elected by the Executive Committee and (ii) the National Chairperson.

Section 3. The National Education and Training Council shall operate under the guidance of the Executive Committee.

Article Ten
Full Participation

Section 1. The Democratic Party of the United States shall be open to all who desire to support the Party and who wish to be known as Democrats.

Section 2. Discrimination in the conduct of Democratic Party affairs on the basis of sex, race, age (if of voting age), religion, economic status or ethnic origin is prohibited, to the end that the Democratic Party at all levels be an open party.

Section 3. In order to encourage full participation by all Democrats, with particular concern for minority groups, native Americans, women and youth, in the delegate selection process and in all Party affairs, as defined in the By-Laws, the national and state Democratic Parties shall adopt and implement affirmative action programs with specific goals and time tables for achieving results.

Section 4. The goal of such affirmative action shall be to encourage representation in delegate selection processes and in Party organizations at all levels, as defined in the By-Laws, of the aforementioned groups as indicated by their presence in the Democratic electorate.

Section 5. This goal shall not be accomplished either directly or indirectly by the national or state Democratic Parties' imposition of mandatory quotas at any level of the delegate selection process or in any other Party affairs, as defined in the By-Laws.

Section 6. Performance under an approved affirmative action program and composition of the Convention delegation shall be considered relevant evidence in the challenge of any state delegation. If a state Party has adopted and implemented an approved and monitored affirmative action program, the Party shall not be subject to challenge based solely on delegate composition or solely on primary results.

Section 7. Notwithstanding Section 5 above, equal division at any level of delegate or committee positions between delegate men and delegate women or committeemen and committeewomen shall not constitute a violation of any provision thereof.

Article Eleven
General Provisions

Section 1. Democratic Party means the Democratic Party of the United States of America.

Section 2. The By-Laws shall provide for states in which the Democratic nominee for President or electors committed to the nominee did not appear on the ballot in elections used for apportionment formulae.

Section 3. For the purpose of this Charter, the District of Columbia shall be treated as a state containing the appropriate number of Congressional Districts.

Section 4. For the purposes this Charter, Puerto Rico shall be treated as a state containing the appropriate number of Congressional Districts.

Section 5. Recognized Democratic party organizations in areas not entitled to vote in Presidential elections may elect such voting delegates to National Conventions as the Democratic National Committee provides in the Call to the Convention.

Section 6. The Canal Zone, Guam, the Virgin Islands and Democrats Abroad shall each have one vote on the Democratic National Committee, which vote shall be shared by the Chairperson, highest ranking officer of the opposite sex, the National Committeeman and the National Committeewoman, except as may otherwise be provided by the By-Laws.

Section 7. The By-Laws shall provide for regional organizations of the Party.

Section 8. To assure that the Democratic nominee for the office of President of the United States is selected by a fair and equitable process, the Democratic National Committee may adopt such statements of policy as it deems appropriate with respect to the timing of Presidential primaries and shall work with state Parties to accomplish the objectives of such statements, provided, however, that such statements of policy shall not be deemed to be binding upon any states in which the state laws are in conflict with such statements.

Section 9. The Democratic National Committee shall adopt and publish a code of fair campaign practices, which shall be recommended for observance by all candidates campaigning as Democrats.

Section 10. The Democratic Party shall not require a delegate to a Party convention or caucus to cast a vote contrary to his or her expressed preference.

Section 11. Voting by proxy shall not be permitted at the National Convention. Voting by proxy shall otherwise be permitted in Democratic Party affairs only as provided in the By-Laws of the Democratic Party.

Section 12. All meetings of the Democratic National Committee, the Executive Committee, and all other official Party committees, commissions and bodies shall be open to the public, and votes shall not be taken by secret ballot.

Section 13. The Democratic National Committee shall prepare and make available to the public an annual report concerning the financial affairs of the Democratic Party.

Section 14. In the absence of other provisions, Robert's Rules of Order (as most recently revised) shall govern the conduct of all Democratic Party meetings.

Section 15. There shall be authentic texts of this Charter published in all of the official languages of these United States, which include French and Spanish, as well as English. Authentic French and Spanish texts shall be approved by the Democratic National Committee during calendar year 1975.

Article Twelve
Amendments, By-Laws and Rules

Section 1. This Charter may be amended by a vote of a majority of all of the delegates to the National Convention. This Charter may also be amended by a vote of two-thirds of the entire membership of the Democratic National Committee provided that at least thirty days' written notice of the meeting and any proposed amendment has been given to all members of the National Committee and has been released to the national news media. This Charter may also be amended by a vote of two-thirds of the entire membership of any Democratic Party Conference called under the authority of this Charter for such purpose.

Section 2. By-Laws of the Democratic Party shall be adopted to provide for the governance of the affairs of the Democratic Party in matters not provided for in this Charter. By-Laws may be adopted or amended by majority vote of (i) the National Convention or (ii) the Democratic National Committee provided that thirty days' written notice of any proposed By-Law or amendment has been given to all members of the National Committee. Unless adopted in the form of an amendment to this Charter or otherwise designated, any resolution adopted by the National Convention relating to the governance of the Party shall be considered a By-Law.

Section 3. Each official body of the Democratic Party created under the authority of this Charter shall adopt and conduct its affairs in accordance with written rules, which rules shall be consistent with this Charter, the By-Laws and other provisions adopted pursuant to authority of the Charter, including resolutions or other actions of the National Convention. The Democratic National Committee shall maintain copies of all such rules and shall make them available upon request.

Section 4. Each recognized state Democratic Party shall adopt and conduct its affairs in accordance with written rules. Copies of such rules and of any changes or amendments thereto shall be filed with the Democratic National Committee within thirty days following adoption.

Resolution of Adoption

Section 1. The Democratic Party of the United States of America, assembled in a Conference on Democratic Party Organization and Policy pursuant to resolution adopted by the 1972 Democratic National Convention and the Call to the Conference hereby adopts for the governance of the Party the Charter attached hereto.

Adopted December 7, 1974.
Amended as of June 9, 1978.

Notes

Chapter 1

1. Political parties have a significant developmental role in the achievement of intranation arms control, that is, the domestic monopoly of the principal instruments of violence by the central government. Ralph M. Goldman, "A Transactional Theory of Political Integration and Arms Control," *American Political Science Review* 63 (September 1969) 3: 719–33; also, "The World Is Our Precinct; World Parties and the Arms Control Process" (paper presented at Stanford Arms Control Conference, August 1974).

2. Ernest Barker, *Reflections on Government* (London: Oxford University Press, 1942), p. 19.

3. Georg Simmel, *Conflict,* trans. Kurt Wolff (Glencoe, Ill.: Free Press, 1955), p. 15.

4. H. McD. Clokie, "The Modern Party State," *Canadian Journal of Economic and Political Science* 15 (May 1949) 2: 143–55.

5. Harold F. Gosnell, *Democracy: The Threshold of Freedom* (New York: Ronald Press, 1948), pp. 156–57.

6. Edmund Burke, *Speech on the Conciliation of the Colonies,* ed. Robert Anderson (Boston: Houghton, Mifflin, 1896), pp. 67–68.

7. Sir Henry Maine, *Popular Government* (3d ed.; London: Murray, 1886), p. 30.

8. The estimate of English turnout is from Gwendolyn Carter et al., *Major Foreign Powers* (New York: Harcourt, Brace, 1957), p. 25. The population of England, Wales, and Scotland in 1831 was 16,261,000, according to University of Cambridge, *Second Abstract of British Historical Statistics* (Cambridge: 1971), p. 3 The notion that American parties predate British ones is developed in William Nisbet Chambers, "Party Development and Party Action: The American Origins," *History and Theory* 3 (1963) 1: 91–120.

9. Jeane J. Kirkpatrick, "Representation in National Political Conventions: The Case of 1972," *British Journal of Political Science* 5 (July 1975) 3: 265–322. The conclusions were based upon three sets of opinion survey data: (a) a December 1971 national survey of 2,014 probable voters; (b) a mail questionnaire of 2,449 convention delegates, with face-to-face interviews of 1,336; and (c) a national survey of voters carried out during the post-convention period in 1972.

10. Henry Saint-John Bolingbroke, *A Collection of Political Tracts* (London: Francklin, 1748), pp. 376–77.

11. Charles Seymour, *Electoral Reform in England and Wales* (New Haven: Yale University Press, 1915), p. 281 n.

12. Cortlandt F. Bishop, *History of Elections in the American Colonies* (New York: Columbia College, 1893).

13. Floy S. Wise, "The Growth of Political Democracy in the States, 1776–1828" (Ph.D. dissertation, University of Texas, 1945).

14. John C. Miller, *Sam Adams, Pioneer in Propaganda* (Boston: Little, Brown, 1936). p. 8.
15. M. C. Tyler, "The Loyalists in the American Revolution," *American Historical Review* 1 (October 1895) 1: 28.
16. Charles A. Beard, *An Economic Interpretation of the Constitution of the United States* (New York: Macmillan, 1936), p. 250.
17. Manning J. Dauer, *The Adams Federalists* (Baltimore: The Johns Hopkins University Press, 1953), Appendix III.
18. Some historians, notably Binkley and Agar, have reported that the Democratic-Republicans were essentially a loose federation of well-established local parties brought together through the coordinating activities of Jefferson. Others, Cunningham and Link, have concluded that local organizations were weak or nonexistent prior to Jefferson's efforts. Wilfred E. Binkley, *American Political Parties* (New York: Knopf, 1947); Herbert Agar, *The Price of Union* (Boston: Houghton, Mifflin, 1950); Noble E. Cunningham, Jr., *The Jeffersonian Republicans* (Chapel Hill: University of North Carolina Press, 1957); Eugene P. Link, *Democratic-Republican Societies, 1790–1800* (New York: Columbia University Press, 1942).
19. Cunningham, *The Jeffersonian Republicans*, p. 167 n.
20. Link, *Democratic-Republican Societies, 1790–1800*, p. 6.
21. Ibid., pp. 20–24.
22. Irving Brant, *James Madison, Father of the Constitution, 1787–1800* (Indianapolis: Bobbs-Merrill, 1950), pp. 415–19.
23. Letter to William Plumer, December 5, 1805, in William Plumer Papers, *Repository* Volume III, Library of Congress.
24. Theodore Segwick to William L. Smith, March 24, 1800, cited by Cunningham, *The Jeffersonian Republicans*, p. 176.
25. Edward Stanwood, *History of the Presidency* (Boston: Houghton, Mifflin, 1928), vol. I, p. 48.
26. Edward Channing, *A History of the United States* (New York: Macmillan, 1917), vol. IV., p. 232.
27. Richard Hofstadter, *The Idea of a Party System* (Berkeley: University of California Press, 1969), p. 1.

Chapter 2

1. Saul K. Padover, "The World of the Founding Fathers," *Social Research* 25 (Summer 1958) 2: 191–214.
2. Jefferson to Madison, December 28, 1794, in Andrew A. Lipscomb (ed.), *The Writings of Thomas Jefferson* (Washington, D.C.: Thomas Jefferson Memorial Association, 1903–1904), vol. IX, pp. 293–97; Madison to Jefferson, March 23, 1795, in *Letters and Other Writings of James Madison* (Philadelphia: J. B. Lippincott, 1865), vol. II, p. 38.
3. William Smith to Ralph Izard, May 18, 1796, in *American Historical Review* 14 (July 1909) 4: 780.
4. George Dangerfield, *The Era of Good Feeling* (New York: Harcourt, Brace, 1952).
5. Robert V. Remini, *Martin Van Buren and the Making of the Democratic Party* (New York: Columbia University Press, 1959), pp. 46–49. Van Buren tried to develop a Crawford-Clay ticket.
6. Ibid., pp. 130–31; Florence Weston, *The Presidential Election of 1828* (Philadelphia: Porcupine Press, 1974), p. 99.

7. Letter to Thomas Ritchie, January 13, 1827, quoted by Remini, *Martin Van Buren* p. 133.

8. Letter of February 12, 1832, quoted in John Spencer Bassett, *The Life of Jackson* (New York: Macmillan, 1916), p. 543.

9. Robert A. Dahl, *A Preface to Democratic Theory* (Chicago: The University of Chicago Press, 1956), p. 144.

Chapter 3

1. E. Malcolm Carroll, *Origins of the Whig Party* (Durham, N.C.: Duke University Press, 1925), pp. 128–29.

2. *Autobiography of Martin Van Buren*, ed. John C. Fitzpatrick (1920; reprinted, New York: Da Capo Press, 1973), p. 125.

3. *Niles' Weekly Register* (Baltimore), May 23, 1835.

4. Leon W. Cone, Jr., "Martin Van Buren: The Architect of the Democratic Party, 1837–1840" (Ph.D. dissertation in history, Univesity of Chicago, 1950), pp. 85–86.

5. *Autobiography of Van Buren*, pp. 193–94.

6. *Baltimore Sun*, May 28–31, 1844; *Niles' National Register* (Baltimore), June 1, 1844. Cf. *Richmond Enquirer*, June 4, 1844, which reported that "Mr. Walker moved the appointment of a Central Committee of sixteen—which was agreed to. The Committee will be announced hereafter."

7. Laughlin to Polk, May 30, 1844, Polk Papers, Library of Congress.

8. Walker to his constituents, August 28, 1844. Letter published in *Daily Madisonian* (Washington), September 26, 1844. Also, Johnson to Polk, June 21, 1844, Polk Papers, Library of Congress; Walker letter dated July 30, 1844, in *Globe* (Washington), August 26, 1844.

9. Eugene I. McCormac, *James K. Polk* (Berkeley: University of California Press, 1922), p. 285; Dorothy C. Fowler, *The Cabinet Politician; The Postmasters General* (New York: Columbia University Press, 1943), p. 54; Lyon G. Tyler, *Parties and Patronage in the United States* (New York: G. P. Putnam's Sons, 1891), pp. 83–84.

10. Walker to Polk, June 18, 1844, Polk Papers, Library of Congress.

11. Walker to Polk, July 11, 1844; Jackson to Polk, July 26, 1844; Polk Papers, Library of Congress.

12. Dodd, "Robert J. Walker, Imperialist," *National Intelligencer* (Washington), October 3 and 29, 1844; *Globe* (Washington), October 3, 1844; William E. Cramer to Polk, October 4, 1844, Polk Papers, Library of Congress.

13. Roy Franklin Nichols, "The Democratic Machine, 1850–54" (Ph.D. dissertation in political science, Columbia University, 1923), p. 2.

14. Fowler, *The Cabinet Politican*, Appendix III.

15. M. M. Quaife, *The Diary of James Polk* (Chicago: McClurg and Co., 1910), vol. I, p. 265.

16. "Selection of Candidate for President in 1848," Memorandum in Gideon Welles Papers, Library of Congress.

Chapter 4

1. Elbert J. Benton, *The Movement for Peace without a Victory during the Civil War* (Western Reserve Historical Society Collections, December 1918).

2. August Belmont, *Letters, Speeches, and Addresses* (New York: Privately printed, 1890), p. 24.

3. Perry Belmont, *An American Democrat* (2d ed.; New York: Columbia University Press, 1941), p. 76.

4. Burton J. Hendrick, *Lincoln's War Cabinet* (Garden City, N.Y.: Dolphin Books, 1946, 1961), pp. 268–277.

5. Ibid.., pp. 113–23; for Seward's views on presidential-cabinet relations, see pp. 80–81.

6. Ibid, pp. 331–47.

7. William A. Dunning, "The Second Birth of the Republican Party," *American Historical Review* 16 (October 1910), 1: 56–63. The names of the major parties at the national level remained objects of uncertain loyalty up to the time of the Hayes-Tilden election. Such men as Edwin M. Stanton, Benjamin R. Butler, John A. Logan, Ulysses S. Grant, and Andrew Johnson were "Democrats" in 1860 but "Republicans" in 1868. On the other hand, Seward, Chase, Welles, Blair, and Bates—all of Lincoln's "Republican" cabinet—were wholly out of sympathy with the political party that nominated Grant; Chase came close to getting the Democratic nomination to oppose Grant. The Blairs were the most notorious of the "party-hoppers," moving through Democratic, Free Soil, Republican parties, and back to Democratic party within a period of twenty years. The name "Union" first came into prominence in the 1850s when men in both the Democratic and Whig parties thought of uniting behind the Compromise of 1850.

8. Glyndon G. Van Deusen, *Thurlow Weed, Wizard of the Lobby* (Boston: Little, Brown, 1947), p. 320.

9. Frederick C. Meyer to Lincoln, June 7, 1864, Lincoln Papers, Library of Congress. *Proceedings of the First Three Republican National Conventions of 1856, 1860, and 1864.*

10. Van Deusen, *Thurlow Weed*, pp. 307–8: Ward Lamon to Lincoln, June 7, 1864, Lincoln Papers; George B. Lincoln to Johnson, June 11, 1864, Andrew Johnson Papers, Library of Congress.

11. William Starr Myers, *General George Brinton McClellan* (New York: D. Appleton-Century, 1934), pp. 425, 444.

12. Belmont, *Letters*, p. 116.

13. *New York Times*, November 1, 2, 1864.

14. Raymond to Simon Cameron, August 19 and 21, 1864, Cameron Papers, Library of Congress.

15. The election of 1864 is examined in detail by William F. Zornow, *Lincoln and the Party Divided* (Norman: University of Oklahoma Press, 1954).

16. James G. Blaine, *Twenty Years of Congress* (1886), vol. II, pp. 118–21. Blaine, for example, lists New York Senator Edwin D. Morgan as a "Republican" and Union National Chairman Henry J. Raymond as an "Administration Republican."

17. Harriet A. Weed and Thurlow Weed Barnes (eds.), *Autobiography of Thurlow Weed* (Boston: Houghton, Mifflin, 1884), vol. II, pp. 450–52.

18. "Driven from the Republican party by the Radicals, the Blairs were left adrift to cast about in the political waters of a troublous era. They were forced to reorganize a party or retire from public life. They had no intention of retiring." William E. Smith, *The Francis Preston Blair Family in Politics* (New York: Macmillan, 1933), vol. II, p. 329.

19. Weed, *Autobiography*, vol. II, pp. 450–52.

20. H. W. Raymond, "Extracts from the Journal of Henry J. Raymond," *Scribner's Monthly Magazine* (June 1880), pp. 275ff.
21. Simon Cameron to C. A. Dana, August 12, 1866, Cameron Papers, Library of Congress; Samuel Purviance to Ward, August 20, 1866, Marcus L. Ward Papers, New Jersey Historical Society.
22. Purviance to Ward, August 20, 1866, Ward Papers, New Jersey Historical Society.
23. *New York Times*, August 25, 1866. Ward to Defrees, August 25, 1866; Raymond to Ward, August 29, 1866; Ward Papers, New Jersey Historical Society.
24. *New York Tribune*, September 3, 4, 1866. Greeley to Ward, September 13, 1866; Ward to Defrees, September 14, 1866; Ward Papers, New Jersey Historical Society.
25. Forney to Chandler, November 3, 1866, Zachariah Chandler Papers, Library of Congress.
26. Walter Bagehot, *The English Constitution* (2d ed.; New York: D. Appleton, 1905), pp. 1x–1xi.
27. Allan Nevins (ed.), *Selected Writings of Abram S. Hewitt* (New York: Kennikot Press, 1937, 1965), pp. 159ff.
28. Letter of December 12, 1876, cited in Hodding Carter, *The Angry Scar* (Garden City, N.Y.: Doubleday, 1959), pp. 330ff.
29. C. Vann Woodward, *Reunion and Reaction* (Boston: Little, Brown, 1951).

Chapter 5

1. *New York Times*, September 25, 1879; May 10, 1880.
2. *New York Times*, September 14, 15, 16, 1879; Mark D. Hirsch, *William C. Whitney, Modern Warwick* (New York: Dddd, Mead, 1948), pp. 149–54.
3. Herbert J. Clancy, "The Presidential Election of 1880" (Ph.D. dissertation in history, Georgetown University, 1949), pp. 220ff.
4. Manton Marble Papers, vol. 53, no. 248, Library of Congress.
5. Quoted by Clancy, "The Presidential Election of 1880."
6. For one observer's interpretation of Tilden's intent, William C. Hudson, *Random Recollections of an Old Political Reporter* (New York: Copples and Leon, 1911), p. 110.
7. Smith M. Weed to Tilden, June 25, 1880, Tilden Manuscripts, New York Public Library.
8. *New York Times*, June 30; July 1, 5, 12, 13, 14, 1880.
9. John Hunter to Bayard, July 13 and 17, 1880, Thomas F. Bayard Manuscripts, Library of Congress.
10. Almira Russell Hancock, *Reminiscences of Winfield Scott Hancock* (New York: C. L. Webster and Co., 1887), p. 175.
11. Hirsch, *William C. Whitney*, pp. 160–73, 180–86.
12. *New York Times*, July 19, 22, 24, 1884; Marvin H. Bovee to Vilas, July 19, 1884, quoted in Dorothy G. Fowler, *The Cabinet Politician* (New York: Columbia University Press, 1943), p. 189.
13. Gorman to Manning, January 5, 1885, Cleveland Papers, Library of Congress.
14. Whitney to Cleveland, December 11, 1887, Cleveland Papers, Library of Congress.
15. *Official Proceedings of the National Democratic Convention, held in St. Louis, June 5–7, 1888 (1888)*. *New York Times*, February 23, 24; May 16, 1888.

16. Robert M. McElroy, *Grover Cleveland: The Man and the Statesman* (New York: Harper, 1923), vol. I., pp. 290–91.

17. Sheerin to Lamont, July 18, 1888; Brice to Lamont, Aug. 4, 16, 1888; Chairman of New Canaan, Connecticut, Democratic Club to Lamont, August 8, 1888; Cleveland Papers, Library of Congress. *New York Times*, August 19, 1888. Albert Small to Harrison, July 20, 1888, Harrison Papers, Library of Congress.

18. Fowler, *The Cabinet Politican*, chap. XI and p. 307.

19. Whitney to Cleveland, July 10, 1892, Cleveland Papers, Library of Congress.

20. *New York Times*, May 6, 1895.

21. William Jennings Bryan, *Memoirs* (Philadelphia: John C. Winston, 1925), pp. 109–10.

22. Wayne C. Williams, *William Jennings Bryan* (New York: G. P. Putnam's Sons, 1936), p. 137.

23. Stone to Bryan, July 14, 1896, Bryan Papers, Library of Congress.

24. Teller to Bryan, July 18, 1896, Bryan Papers, Library of Congress.

25. C. Vann Woodward, *Tom Watson: Agrarian Rebel* (New York: Macmillan, 1938), pp. 289, 294–301, 315; James K. Jones to Bryan, July 21, 1896, Bryan Papers, Library of Congress.

26. *New York Tribune*, July 27, 1896.

27. W. D. Bynum to M. L. Crawford, November 18, 1896, W. D. Bynum Manuscripts, Library of Congress.

28. Allan Nevins, *Letters of Grover Cleveland, 1850–1908* (New York: Da Capo Press, 1970), p. 457; Cleveland to Judson Harmon, September 13, 1896, Grover Cleveland Manuscripts, Library of Congress.

29. For example, Herbert Croly, *Marcus Alonzo Hanna* (New York: Macmillan, 1912) and Thomas Beer, *Hanna, Crane, and the Mauve Decade* (New York: A. A. Knopf, 1941).

30. *New York Times*, July 21, 1896; William M. Osborne to McKinley, August 11, 1896, McKinley Papers, Library of Congress.

31. Joseph B. Foraker, *Notes on a Busy Life* (Cincinnati: Steward and Kidd, 1916), vol. I, p. 498.

Chapter 6

1. V. O. Key, Jr., "A Theory of Critical Elections," *Journal of Politics* 17 (February 1955) 1: 3–18.

2. Bynum letters to L. C. Krauthoff, December 21, 1896; to Peabody, December 12, 1896 and April 30, 1897; to John P. Frenzel, June 30, and July 29, 1897; to W. R. Shelby, July 3, 1898; to Whitney, August 24, 26, 1898; to Canada, August 25, 1898, Bynum Papers, Library of Congress. *New York Tribune*, July 15, 26, 27; October 6, 1900.

3. Mack to Bryan, July 19, 1900, Bryan Papers, Library of Congress.

4. Thomas M. Patterson to Bryan, June 9, 1899; W. H. Thompson to Bryan, November 23, 1899; James Creelman to Bryan, April 22, 1900; John H. Girdner to Bryan, April 21, 28; May 29; June 16, 1900; Bryan Papers, Library of Congress. *New York Times*, July 4, 6, 7, 1900.

5. Letter to Bryan, February 1, 1898, Bryan Papers, Library of Congress.

6. Jones to Bryan, January 17, 24, 30, 1899, Bryan Papers, Library of Congress.

7. Girdner to Bryan, April 21, 1900; Jones to Bryan, April 26, 1900, Bryan Papers, Library of Congress. *New York Tribune*, May 11, July 2, 1900.

8. *New York Times,* September 1, October 9, 1900; Willis J. Abbot, "The Management of the Democratic Campaign," *American Review of Reviews* 22 (November 1900) 5: 556–62. C. E. Jones to Bryan, January 10, 1900; Hearst to Bryan, May 19 and July 4, 1900; Creelman to Bryan, May 24 and June 6, 1900, Bryan Papers, Library of Congress.

9. Homer S. Cummings to Bryan, November 8, 1900, Bryan Papers, Library of Congress; *New York Times,* February 14, 1901.

10. *New York Journal,* November 8, 1900.

11. *New York Tribune,* July 31, 1901.

12. William Jennings Bryan (ed.), *The Commoner Condensed* (New York: Abbey Press, 1902), vol. 1, pp. 21–23; vol. 2, p. 25; vol. 3, pp. 283–84.

13. *Review of Reviews* 30 (September 1904) 3: 260; *Proceedings of the Democratic National Convention, 1904.*

14. J. P. Hornaday, "Taggart and the Democratic Campaign," *Review of Reviews* 30 (September 1904) 3: 289–93; *New York Times,* October 9, 1904.

15. *New York Times,* July 15 and 22, 1905.

16. *New York Times,* August 7, September 15, 1906.

17. Paxton Hibben, *The Peerless Leader* (New York: Farrar and Rinehart, 1929), pp. 274, 279.

18. The manner in which this occurred is described in Arthur S. Link, *Wilson: The Road to the White House* (Princeton: Princeton University Press, 1947), chap. VI on "The First Campaign." Wilson's dramatic and hard-hitting campaign style, his personality, and his break with the New Jersey Democratic bosses who had nominated him captured the attention of the New York press, which in turn made Wilson's progressivism known to the rest of the country.

19. Hibben, *The Peerless Leader,* p. 296.

Chapter 7

1. The particularly relevant writings of Woodrow Wilson are his *Congressional Government* (New York: Macmillan, 1885 and 1898) and *Constitutional Government in the United States* (New York: Columbia University Press, 1908 and 1911). The summary discussion and quotations that follow are based upon A. L. and J. L. George, *Woodrow Wilson and Colonel House* (New York: John Day, 1956), pp. 144–54 and Chap. VIII. Other perceptive evaluations of Wilsonian theories about political parties include: Austin Ranney, *The Doctrine of Responsible Party Government* (Urbana: University of Illinois Press, 1954); Earl Latham (ed.), *The Philosophy and Policies of Woodrow Wilson* (Chicago: The University of Chicago Press, 1958); the biographical volumes of Arthur S. Link (Princeton, N.J.: Princeton University Press, 1947–   ); Laurin L. Henry, *Presidential Transitions* (Washington, D.C.: Brookings Institution, 1960), passim.; A. L. and J. L. George, *Woodrow Wilson and Colonel House* (New York: John Day, 1956), pp. 144–54.

2. George and George, *Woodrow Wilson and Colonel House,* p. 318.

3. Cited by Henry, *Presidential Transitions,* p. 47.

4. William F. McCombs, *Making Woodrow Wilson President* (New York: Fairview, 1921), pp. 208–9.

5. Henry, *Presidential Transitions,* pp. 52–53.

6. Ibid., pp. 80–83; A. S. Link, "Woodrow Wilson and the Democratic Party," *Review of Politics* 18 (April 1956) 2: 146–56.

7. McCombs, *Making Woodrow Wilson President*, pp. 222–23.

8. *New York Times*, March 6, May 18, 1913.

9. Ray S. Baker, *Woodrow Wilson, Life and Letters* (New York: Charles Scribner's Sons, 1946), vol. 6, pp. 252 and 258.

10. Herbert Hoover, *The Ordeal of Woodrow Wilson* (New York: McGraw-Hill, 1958), pp. 14–17. Wilson quotation is drawn from Hoover.

11. George and George, *Woodrow Wilson and Colonel house*, p. 322.

12. *New York Times*, December 15, 1919; January 5, 9, 1920.

13. According to Josephus Daniels, President Wilson considered McAdoo unfit for the office. *The Wilson Era: Years of War and After* (Chapel Hill: University of North Carolina Press, 1946), p. 553.

14. Ibid., pp. 555–57.

15. T. William Goodman, "The Presidential Campaign of 1920" (Ph.D. dissertation in political science, Ohio State University, 1950), p. 191, n. 26; letter to Goodman, August 11, 1949, cited p. 208.

16. James M. Cox, *Journey through My Years* (New York: Simon & Schuster, 1946), p. 243; *New York Times*, July 19, 1920.

17. *World's Work* 40 (September 1920), pp. 425–26.

18. David Chalmers, "The Ku Klux Klan in Politics in the 1920's," *Mississippi Quarterly* 18 (Fall 1965) 4:234–47.

19. Edgar E. Robinson, *The Presidential Vote* (Stanford: Stanford University Press, 1934), p. 21.

20. Cordell Hull, *Memoirs* (New York: Macmillan, 1948), vol. I., p. 115.

21. Ibid., vol. I, pp. 117, 118, 120, 121. The proposal for a midterm national party conference was made by the Woodrow Wilson Democracy of New York. The midterm conference, whose membership was not indicated, was intended to "formulate a program and platform to serve as the basis for an appeal to the voters of the country." All candidates for the Senate and the House of Representatives would be invited to subscribe to this program. *New York Times*, May 4, 1922.

22. Cox, *Journey through My Years*, p. 324.

23. *Herald Tribune*, July 1, 1924; *Evening World*, July 7, 1924. For a full treatment of this fascinating convention, Robert K. Murray, *The 103rd Ballot* (New York: Harper & Row, 1976).

24. *New York Times*, March 9, 1925.

25. Elliott Roosevelt (ed.), *F.D.R., His Personal Letters: 1905–1928* (vol. II; New York: Duell, Sloan, and Pearce, 1948), p. 566.

26. *New York Times*, March 9, 1925.

27. *New York Times*, March 22, 1925. A detailed proposal for a midterm conference was offered by Allen Sinclair Will in *North American Review* of March 1925, in which he suggests that the number of delegates should be equal to the number of senators and representatives in Congress from each state, plus a limited group of special members including the candidates on the last two national tickets, the national chairmen in the last two campaigns, and a group of Democratic leaders from both houses of Congress. He also suggested that the call for the conference come from the members of both houses assembled in caucus.

28. Cf. the resistance of congressional Democrats to the Raskob Conference in 1931 and to the establishment of a Democratic Advisory Council under the auspices of the national committee in 1957. Even a plan to have a Democratic congressional

conference called under the authority of the party steering committees in each house, a caucus procedure much like that of the pre-Jacksonian era, was given little support. *New York Times,* November 19, 1924.

29. Elliott Roosevelt, *F.D.R.,* vol. II, p. 640, Letter of July 14, 1928.
30. Walter Lippman, "The Reconstruction of the Democratic Party," *Yale Review* 18 (September 1928) 1:18–27.
31. Paul T. David, Ralph M. Goldman, and Richard C. Bain. *The Politics of National Party Conventions* (Washington, D.C.: Brookings Institution, 1960), p. 460.
32. *New York Times,* November 8, 1928.
33. Telegram of November 12, 1928, and Elliott Roosevelt, *F.D.R.: His Personal Letters, 1928–1945* (vol. III, pt. 1; New York: Duell, Sloan, and Pearce, 1950), p. 7.
34. *New York Times,* November 8, 9, 11, 1928.
35. *New York Times,* December 4, 5, 7, 12, 13, 18, 1928.
36. *New York Times,* December 10, 1928; January 14, 1929.
37. *New York Times,* December 6, 1928; January 17, 1929.
38. *New York Times,* January 17, 1929.
39. *New York Times,* June 15, 16, 19, 30; July 12; September 18, 1929.
40. *New York Times,* April 8, 9; May 29, 1930.
41. Hull, *Memoirs,* vol. I, p. 141.
42. Elliott Roosevelt, *F.D.R.,* vol. III, pt. 1, p. 179.
43. Hull, *Memoirs,* vol. I, pp. 142–45; *New York Times,* March 6 and 7, 1931.
44. Samuel I. Rosenman, *Working with Roosevelt* (New York: Harper, 1952), pp. 48–49.

Chapter 8

1. Robert E. Sherwood, *Roosevelt and Hopkins* (New York: Harper, 1948), p. 51; Jonathan Daniels, *The Man of Independence* (Philadelphia: Lippincott, 1950), p. 166.
2. Sherwood, *Roosevelt and Hopkins,* p. 51.
3. James A. Farley, *Jim Farley's Story* (New York: Whittlesey House, 1948), p. 62.
4. Ibid., p. 68.
5. Samuel I. Rosenman, *Working with Roosevelt* (New York: Harper, 1952), p. 147.
6. Cited by Rosenman, ibid., p. 178.
7. Farley, *Jim Farley's Story,* pp. 153–54; Elliott Roosevelt, *F.D.R.: His Personal Letters* (4 vols.; New York: Duell, Sloan, and Pearce, 1947–1950), vol. III, pt. 2, pp. 835–36.
8. Rosenman, *Working with Roosevelt,* p. 205; Cordell Hull, *Memoirs* (New York: Macmillan, 1948), vol. I, p. 860; James F. Byrnes, *All in One Lifetime* (New York: Harper, 1958), p. 119.
9. Rosenman, *Working with Roosevelt,* pp. 213–21.
10. Ibid., chap. 24.
11. Harry S. Truman, *Memoirs* (2 vols.; Garden City, N.Y.: Doubleday, 1955–1956), vol. II, p. 186.
12. Samuel Lubell, *The Future of American Politics* (New York: Harper, 1952), pp. 9–10, 12.
13. For an evaluation of the implications, Arthur Krock in *New York Times,* October 9, 1949.
14. The story of the 1952 nominating process is thoroughly reported in Paul T.

David, Malcolm Moos, and Ralph M. Goldman, *Presidential Nominating Politics in 1952* (5 vols.; Baltimore: The Johns Hopkins University Press, 1954).

15. Kenneth S. Davis, *A Prophet in His Own Country* (Garden City, N.Y.: Doubleday, 1957), p. 434.
16. Adlai E. Stevenson, *What I Think* (New York: Harper, 1956), pp. ix–x.
17. Letter to author, August 30, 1955.
18. Stevenson, *What I Think*, x–xvi.
19. John B. Oakes in *New York Times Magazine*, December 22, 1957, p. 8.
20. Thomas B. Morgan, "The People-Machine," *Harper's Magazine* (January, 1961), pp. 53–57. On the campaign, Stanley Kelley, Jr., and on the net effect of the television debates, Charles A. H. Thomson, in *The Presidential Election and Transition, 1960–1961*, ed. Paul T. David (Washington: Brookings Institution, 1961).

Chapter 9

1. *Newsweek*, August 26, 1963, pp. 25ff.
2. National Advisory Commission on Civil Disorders, *Report* (New York: E. P. Dutton, 1968).
3. Lyndon B. Johnson, *The Vantage Point* (New York: Holt, Rinehart and Winston, 1971), p. 232.
4. David S. Broder, *The Party's Over: The Failure of Politics in America* (New York: Harper & Row, 1971), p. 68.
5. Ibid., p. 89.
6. Analysis in *Washington Post*, by Ross K. Baker and Michael A. Rappeport, reported in *San Francisco Examiner & Chronicle*, January 17, 1971.
7. See chap. 11.
8. Jeane Kirkpatrick, "Representation in National Political Conventions: The Case of 1972," *British Journal of Political Science* 5 (July 1975) 3: 265–322.
9. Denis G. Sullivan, Jeffrey L. Pressman, Benjamin I. Page, and John J. Lyons, *The Politics of Representation; The Democratic Convention 1972* (New York: St. Martin's Press, 1974), p. 23.
10. Seymour Martin Lipset and Earl Raab, "The Election and the National Mood," *Commentary* 55 (January 1973) 1:44–45.
11. M. Kent Jennings and Richard G. Niemi, *The Political Character of Adolescence* (Princeton: Princeton University Press, 1974). Between 1965 and 1973 (before Watergate), the percentage of young persons who believed public officials were dishonest rose from 16 to 31 percent. In an interview, Jennings predicted that the figure would go higher as a consequence of Watergate. *Chicago Tribune*, September 2, 1974.
12. William R. Keech and Donald R. Matthews, *The Party's Choice* (Washington, D.C.: Brookings INstitution, 1976), pp. 24–27.
13. *San Francisco Chronicle*, September 25, 1974.
14. Herbert S. Parmet, *The Democrats: The Years after FDR* (New York: Macmillan, 1976), p. 313.
15. Kirkpatrick, "Representation in National Political Conventions."
16. *Democratic Review* (June/July 1975). The reference is to James David Barber's *The Presidential Character: Predicting Performance in the White House* (New York: Prentice-Hall, 1972). Among the nineteen candidates were, in alphabetical order: Birch Bayh, Lloyd Bentsen, Jimmy Carter, Frank Church, Gerald Ford (R), Fred

Harris, Hubert Humphrey, Henry Jackson, Edward Kennedy, Eugene McCarthy, George McGovern, Edmund Muskie, Charles Percy (R), Ronald Reagan (R), Nelson Rockefeller (R), Terry Sanford, Sargent Shriver, Morris Udall, and George Wallace. Republicans are indicated by (R).

17. *Washington Post*, November 5, 1976.

Chapter 10

1. Samuel Lubell, *The Future of American Politics* (New York: Harper & Brothers, 1952), p. 200.
2. Ibid., pp. 203–5.
3. Wilfred E. Binkley, *American Political Parties: Their Natural History* (2d ed., New York: A. A. Knopf, 1947), p. 260. Many of the insights of this survey of the Democratic party-in-the-electorate are drawn from Binkley.
4. The Democratic commitment to policies that respond to problems of employment, poverty, education, civil rights, health care for the aged, and conservation, particularly during the years 1953–1966, is analyzed in James L. Sundquist, *Politics and Policy: The Eisenhower, Kennedy, and Johnson Years* (Washington, D.C.: Brookings Institution, 1968).
5. Ibid. Binkley, *American Political Parties*, pp. 380ff.
6. Robert Axelrod, "Where the Votes Come from: An Analysis of Electoral Coalitions, 1952–1968," *American Political Science Review* 66 (March 1972) 1:17.
7. Everett C. Ladd, Jr., and Charles D. Hadley, "Political Parties and Political Issues: Patterns in Differentiation Since the New Deal," *Sage Professional Papers in American Politics* (1973), p. 44.
8. Theodore Lowi, "The Public Philosophy: Interest-Group Liberalism," *American Political Science Review* 61 (March 1967) 1:5–24.
9. Fred I. Greenstein, "The Changing Pattern of Urban Party Politics" in *Annals of the American Academy of Political and Social Science* 353 (May 1964), pp. 2–3.
10. Eugene P. Link, *Democratic-Republican Societies, 1790–1800* (New York: Columbia University Press, 1942), p. 6.
11. Ibid., pp. 20–24.
12. December 5, 1805, *Repository*, vol. III, William Plumer Papers, Library of Congress.
13. A recent evaluation of Tweed is more accepting of the Tweed Ring's activities as typical of machine politics and functional in that period and considers them not so costly as the dollar figures imply. Leo Hershkowitz, *Tweed's New York: Another Look* (New York: Doubleday, 1977). Cf. Alexander B. Callow, Jr. *The Tweed Ring* (New York: Oxford University Press, 1966).
14. Alfred Henry Lewis, *Richard Croker* (New York: Life Publishing Co., 1901), p. 156.
15. Ibid., pp. 156ff. Roy V. Peel's *The Political Clubs of New York City* (Port Washington, N.Y.: Friedman, 1935; reissued, 1968) provides a more objective and systematic picture of Tammany's operations.
16. Lewis, *Richard Croker*, pp. 149–50. For an excellent collection of articles about bosses and machines, Alexander B. Callow, Jr., *The City Boss in America* (New York: Oxford University Press, 1976), which also contains a comprehensive bibliography. Harold Zink's *City Bosses in the United States* (Durham, N.C.: Duke University Press, 1930) was the first to study bosses as a group, twenty case studies in all. Harold F. Gosnell's *Machine Politics: Chicago Model* (New York:

AMS Press, 1937; reissued, 1969) was the first to examine in a scientific fashion the machine as an organization.

17. For a contemporary study of the Daley organization, Milton L. Rakove, *Don't Make No Waves–Don't Back No Losers* (Bloomington: Indiana University Press, 1975).

18. For a survey of these strategies, see Fay Calkins, *The CIO and the Democratic Party* (Chicago: The University of Chicago Press, 1952).

19. Stephen A. Mitchell, *Elm Street Politics* (New York: Oceana, 1959).

20. Ibid., p. 28.

21. *Report of the National Advisory Commission on Civil Disorders* (New York: Bantam Books, 1968), p. 287.

22. On March 22, 1977, President Carter asked Congress to enact a Universal Voter Registration Act (H.R. 5400) which would enable voters to register on election day at the polling place in federal general elections by simply signing a sworn affidavit attesting to his or her identity and qualifications.

23. The experience with nonpartisan local elections is thoroughly surveyed by Willis D. Hawley, *Nonpartisan Elections and the Case for Party Politics* (New York: Wiley, 1973). On page 98, Hawley concludes from his data that "the electability of Republicans to local offices generally is greater if elections are nonpartisan than if they are partisan," although the magnitude of this bias is not so great as usually estimated by many textbook writers.

24. For a critical view of this and other antipoverty programs, see Charles R. Adrian and Charles Press, *American Politics Reappraised* (New York: McGraw-Hill, 1974), pp. 253–61.

25. The Boston experience is described by that city's Mayor Kevin White in *Democratic Review* (November 1974), pp. 48–52.

26. Ibid., p. 52.

27. Dennis Farney, "Machine Politics, 1975," *Smithsonian Magazine* (October 1974), p. 63.

28. Giuseppe Di Palma, *Apathy and Participation* (New York: Free Press, 1970), pp. 179ff.

29. See discussion in William H. Flanigan and Nancy H. Zingale, *Political Behavior of the American Electorate* (3d ed.; Boston: Allyn and Bacon, 1975), pp. 58ff, chart at p. 72. Also, Walter Dean Burnham, "The End of American Party Politics," *Trans-Action* 7 (December 1969) 2:12–22.

30. Richard S. Childs attributes the decline in party loyalty to the inability of party rank-and-file workers to influence the internal leadership selection and management of each party. "Our Ailing Parties," *National Civic Review* 59 (1970) 6:298–302 and 7:365–70.

31. For evidence and evaluation, Walter Dean Burnham, "The End of American Party Politics," p. 18, and the same author's "American Politics in the 1970s: Beyond Party?" in Louis Maisel and Paul M. Sacks, *The Future of Political Parties* (Beverly Hills: Sage Publications, 1975), pp. 248ff. Also, Walter DeVries and V. Lance Tarrance, Jr., *The Ticket-Splitter* (Grand Rapids: Eerdmans, 1971); Richard W. Boyd, "Electoral Trends in Postwar Politics," in James David Barber (ed.), *Choosing the President* (Englewood Cliffs, N.J.: Prentice-Hall, 1974), p. 185.

32. Louis Harris, *The Anguish of Change* (New York: Norton, 1973), p. 274.

33. Alan D. Monroe, *Public Opinion in America* (New York: Dodd, Mead, 1975), pp. 228–30. Also, see Boyd, "Electoral Trends in Postwar Politics"; Ladd and Hadley, "Political Parties and Political Issues"; Norman H. Nie with Kristi Ander-

sen, "Mass Belief Systems Revisited: Political Change and Attitude Structure," *Journal of Politics* 36 (August 1974) 3:540–91. Other articles on issue voting, Gerald M. Pomper, Richard W. Boyd, Richard A. Brody, Benjamin I. Page, and John H. Kessel in *American Political Science Review* 66 (June 1972) 2:415–70. Early research on the subject established that only a relatively small number of American voters rely on ideological considerations in viewing political phenomena and that there is little ideological difference in the electorates of the two major parties. A later investigation, using 1956–1964 evidence, revealed that a growing proportion of the voters have ideological orientations, that Republicans (at least for that period) tend to be stronger ideologues than are Democrats, and that Independents also tend to have a more substantial number of ideologues than do Democrats. Even more important than these proportions is the candidacy of an ideologue such as Barry Goldwater, which increases the salience of ideological concerns among the entire electorate. In this way, the influence of ideological factors on the election outcomes may be compounded. John C. Pierce, "Party Identification and the Changing Role of Ideology in American Politics," *Midwest Journal of Political Science* 14 (February 1970) 2:25–42.

34. James L. Sundquist, *Dynamics of the Party System* (Washington, D.C.: Brookings Institution, 1973).

35. For example, Angus Campbell et al., *Elections and the Political Order* (New York: Wiley, 1966), pp. 142 and 182–84. On page 142, Philip E. Converse observes that "the congressional vote in a presidential year is more nearly a party vote in large measure because the flow of information about the congressional candidates is a good deal weaker than that for the two presidential candidates. . . . The same conditions of low information mark the off-year congressional voting as well."

Chapter 11

1. Arthur N. Holcombe, *The Political Parties of To-day* (New York: Harper & Brothers, 1924), p. 109. Holcombe's later works further develop this mode of analysis: *The New Party Politics* (New York: W. W. Norton, 1933); *The Middle Classes in American Politics* (Cambridge, Mass.; Harvard University Press, 1940).

2. Holcombe, *Political Parties of To-day*, chap. IV.

3. Richard L. Rubin, *Party Dynamics: The Democratic Coalition and the Politics of Change* (New York: Oxford University Press, 1976), pp. 17ff, pp. 56ff.

4. Harriet A. Weed and Thurlow Weed Barnes (eds.), *Autobiography of Thurlow Weed* (Boston: Houghton Mifflin, 1884), p. 103.

5. Herbert Jacob, "Dimensions of State Politics," in Alexander Heard (ed.), *State Legislatures in American Politics* (Englewood Cliffs, N.J.: Prentice-Hall, 1966), pp. 21ff. Also, V. O. Key's *American State Politics* (New York: A. A. Knopf, 1956) and *Southern Politics* (New York: A. A. Knopf, 1949). The latter is a classic field study of the many forms of rural politics and political organization in the Solid South of the New Deal period. For a thorough contemporary survey of party politics at the state level, Malcolm E. Jewell and David M. Olson, *American State Political Parties and Elections* (Homewood, Ill.: Dorsey Press, 1978).

6. Advisory Commission on Intergovernmental Relations, *Fiscal Balance in the American System* (Washington, D.C.: Government Printing Office, 1967), vol. I, pp. 233–34.

7. Leroy N. Rieselbach, *Congressional Reform in the Seventies* (Morristown, N.J.: General Learning Press, 1977), pp. 58–59.

8. M. Ostrogorski, *Democracy and the Organization of Political Parties,* trans. Frederick Clarke (New York: Macmillan, 1902), vol. III, pp. 283–85.

9. John G. Stewart, *One Last Chance: The Democratic Party, 1974–76* (New York: Praeger, 1974), p. 176.

10. Paul T. David, Ralph M. Goldman, and Richard C. Bain, *The Politics of National Party Conventions* (Washington, D.C.: Brookings Institution, 1960).

11. Ibid., p. 160.

12. Ralph M. Goldman, "Titular Leadership of the Presidential Parties," in Aaron Wildavsky (ed.), *The Presidency* (Boston: LIttle, Brown, 1969), pp. 384–410.

13. For a full account of the fascinating parliamentary and factional maneuvers in the 1952 loyalty pledge fight, see Paul T. David, Malcolm Moos, and Ralph M. Goldman, *Presidential Nominating in Politics in 1952* (Baltimore: The Johns Hopkins University Press, 1954), vol. I, chap. 4.

14. Described in detail in Charles A. H. Thomson and Frances M. Shattuck, *The 1956 Presidential Campaign* (Washington, D.C.: Brookings Institution, 1960), chap. 5.

15. Jeane J. Kirkpatrick, "Representation in National Political Conventions: The Case of 1972," *British Journal of Political Science* 5 (July 1975) 3: 265–322.

16. See *Democratic Review,* February–March 1975, for detailed report of the convention.

17. James MacGregor Burns, *The Deadlock of Democracy* (Englewood Cliffs, N.J.: Prentice-Hall, 1963).

18. Henry Jones Ford, *The Rise and Growth of American Politics* (New York: Macmillan, 1898), pp. 128–29, 215.

19. Frank P. Belloni and Dennis C. Beller, "The Study of Party Factions as Competitive Political Organizations," *Western Political Quarterly* 29 (December 1976) 4:548. Another brief but perceptive analysis of factionalism is Mark N. Hagopian, *Regimes, Movements, and Ideologies* (New York: Longman, 1978), pp. 323–26.

20. Observations of Robert J. Huckshorn cited by John S. Saloma III and Frederick H. Sontag, *Parties: The Real Opportunity for Citizen Politics* (New York: Vintage Books, 1973), p. 169.

21. Ralph M. Goldman, "The Emerging Transnational Party System and the Future of American Parties," in Louis Maisel and Joseph Cooper (eds.), *Political Parties: Development and Decay* (Beverly Hills, Calif.: Sage Publications, 1978).

Epilogue

1. Questions such as these and the reforms they inspire may be a measure of the vitality of the party system as well. Austin Ranney. *Curing the Mischiefs of Faction* (Berkeley, Calif.: University of California Press, 1975), offers a comprehensive survey of party reform in the United States. Ranney points out that the principal technique of party reform has been to change party rules and procedures. Why this technique? "Of all the many factors that affect the fate of candidates, factions, policies, and programs, party rules are the most easily manipulated" (p. 209). Another approach, as suggested in this section, may lie in the training and selection of the party's future leaders as principal vehicles of change and reform.

2. For suggestions along these lines, John S. Saloma III and Frederick H. Sontag, *Parties: The Real Opportunity for Effective Citizen Politics* (New York: Vintage Books, 1973), passim.

Name Index

399

Subject Index

409

JK
2316
.G62

Goldman, Ralph Morris, 1920-
    Search for consensus : the story
of the Democratic Party / Ralph M.
Goldman. -- Philadelphia : Temple
University Press, 1979.
    xi, 417 p. ; 24 cm.

    Includes bibliographical refer-
ences and indexes.
    ISBN 0-87722-152-9

    1. Democratic Party--History.   I.
Title.

JK2316.G62   329.3'009

                                          79-1207
                                          MARC

Library of Congress
14360   892892   B   © THE BAKER & TAYLOR CO.   0327